HINDU
JAVANESE

HINDU
JAVANESE

. . .

*Tengger Tradition
and Islam*

ROBERT W. HEFNER

*Princeton University Press
Princeton, New Jersey*

Copyright © 1985 by Princeton University Press

Published by Princeton University Press, 41 William Street,
Princeton, New Jersey 08540
In the United Kingdom: Princeton University Press, Oxford

Library of Congress Cataloging in Publication Data will be
found on the last printed page of this book

ISBN 0-691-09413-6
ISBN 0-691-02856-7, pbk.

First Princeton Paperback printing, 1989

Publication of this book has been aided by a grant from the
Paul Mellon Fund of Princeton University Press

This book has been composed in Linotron Aldus

Princeton University Press books are printed on acid-free paper,
and meet the guidelines for permanence and durability of the
Committee on Production Guidelines for Book Longevity of the
Council of Library Resources.

10 9 8 7 6 5 4 3 2 1
10 9 8 7 6 5 4 3 2 1 , pbk.

Printed in the United States of America by Princeton University
Press, Princeton, New Jersey

For Nancy of Karo truth

CONTENTS

LIST OF TABLES

PREFACE

Ethnography is an exercise in learning to listen and speak, so as to share something of the effort with others. Throughout my professional life I have been fortunate to have had the guidance of fine teachers, colleagues, and friends, several of whom I would like to thank here. First thanks go to Aram Yengoyan and Alton Becker, who, more than anyone else, together introduced me to the cultural mosaic of Southeast Asia. My hope would be that both men might see in this work something of what they taught me. I also wish to thank Sherry Ortner and Raymond Kelly for their patient and painstaking help in refocusing earlier drafts of this manuscript, and Clifford Geertz and Hildred Geertz for their encouragement and intellectual inspiration. Clifford Geertz provided me with the opportunity to begin revision of this manuscript at the Institute for Advanced Study during 1981-1982. In very different ways, Dan Sperber and Marshall Cohen, visitors at the Institute, challenged me to rethink the interpretive premises of this earlier work, and I thank them for their ardor in discussion. In Boston, finally, I want to thank Dennis Tedlock for helping me to think more clearly about ethnography, and several Boston-area Indonesianists who encouraged me to conceptualize the Tengger experience in somewhat wider terms: John Bowen, Toby Volkman, and Charles Zerner.

Soepomo Poedjosoedarmo was my Javanese teacher prior to field research. Y. Padmapuspita of Yogyakarta provided linguistic instruction without which the older Tengger prayers would have remained inaccessible. I thank both men for their patience in instruction and their knowledge of things Javanese. Also in Indonesia, I wish to thank R. M. Koentjaraningrat for his support of this and other anthropological research through the Indonesian Council of Sciences. Special thanks also go to Masri Singarimbun, who acted as personal sponsor to this project, and who gave me the much-needed opportunity to interact with scholars in Yogyakarta's Population Institute. In Yogya, I should also thank Hans Daeng and Kodiran in the Department of Anthropology at Gajah Mada University. They and their fine students helped me to realize that Indonesian anthropology has a bright future. In East Java, I thank S. Soetrisno W.G., who worked with me as assistant, mountain guide, and friend. His familiarity with the terrain and people of the Tengger mountains was vital for this study.

I first visited the Tengger region with a series of short weekend visits during the summer of 1977, and I returned to do field work from December 1978 to July 1980. The field project was supported by a Fulbright-Hays Fellowship and a grant from the National Science Foundation, and I am very grateful to both of these excellent programs. The nineteen-month study began with eleven months of residence in a southern Tengger village, and ended with eight more in the northwest. In the interim, I also carried out research on household economy in a third community, also located in the south, and made several one-week visits to two Islamic communities below the Tengger northwest and two more to the southwest. In the interest of villagers' privacy, I have not used their real names at any point in the present book. In addition, where it seemed proper, I have referred to whole villages with pseudonyms, indicating in the text when I am doing so. In expressing my thanks to the people of these communities, I am thus left in the awkward position of referring to them collectively and anonymously. They were in fact neither. From beginning to end this research depended upon the kindness of the many people in my villages who took a sympathetic interest in this foreigner living among them. For them and other Tengger, I hope this work helps to correct the entirely erroneous myth that Tengger are backward and closed to the modern world, or somehow less than Javanese. While their tradition has its roots deep in Javanese civilization, Tengger are very actively participating in the development of a modern Indonesia.

Two small points of detail. The Javanese-language transcriptions presented in this book use a standard Indonesian orthography, rather than the more phonetically precise variant used in many Javanese texts. Second, I should note that this is the first of two monographs that I hope to publish on Tengger and Java. The second will more directly address aspects of political and economic change in the region, comparing Tengger with other areas of Indonesia. In the present work, therefore, I have often not pursued economic issues beyond their relevance for understanding the problem of Tengger identity and tradition in Java. I hope that readers more interested in my brief comments on moral economy and social change will understand that the present monograph is a necessary preliminary for the latter.

Finally, I wish to thank my wife, Nancy Smith-Hefner, who carried out ethnolinguistic research in a Tengger community far too distant (or so it felt) from my own villages, but who managed nonetheless to provide the intellectual and emotional support necessary for a long-term project like this one. I relied extensively on her linguistic work in analyzing the Tengger prayer tradition. In her own publications she has dealt more systematically with Tengger as a language community, and later works will explore in greater detail the ritual texts which I briefly examine here.

Boston, July 1984

HINDU
JAVANESE

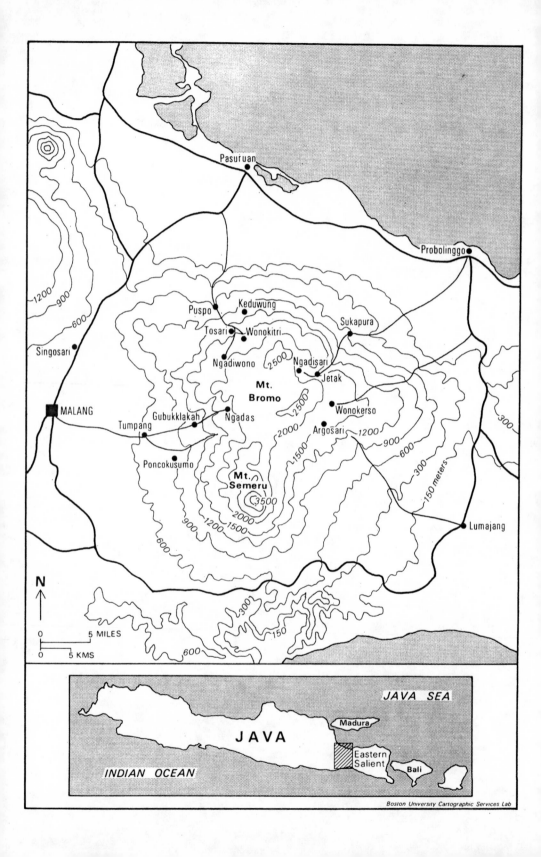

· 1 ·

INTRODUCTION

Identity in an Islamizing Java

In the summer of 1977 I traveled to the island of Java to participate in
an Indonesian language program in the East Javanese city of Malang.
Malang is a city of about one million people, situated in a wide, densely
populated wet-rice valley about 60 kilometers from Java's north coast,
and just to the west of a rugged mountain region known as the Tengger
highlands. During the three months of the language program, I took
advantage of weekends and holidays to make short jaunts into the mountains, in hope of learning more about the region's inhabitants and to
help choose a village for ethnographic research the following year. The
mountain Javanese whom I hoped to study are known as *wong Tengger*
("Tengger people"), and number just 40 thousand on this island of
almost 100 million people. Tengger have long been of interest to students
of Southeast Asian civilization. They alone in modern Java are reputed
to have preserved a non-Islamic priestly tradition over the five centuries
since the fall of Java's last major Hindu-Buddhist kingdom. Ethnographic
information on Tengger culture, however, has sometimes left unclear
the question as to whether Tengger are in fact Hindu, Buddhist, animist,
or *kejawen* "Javanists."[1] Indeed, some reports have indicated that in
modern times Tengger have converted to Islam.

[1] An estimated 90 percent of all ethnic Javanese are Muslim. Religious styles within
the Muslim community, however, vary significantly, and at times have been a source of
communal tensions (see Jay 1963; C. Geertz 1960; Ricklefs 1979). Postwar American
scholarship on Java distinguished two different categories of Javanese Muslim. The first,
known as *santri*, included those Muslims who carry out the ritual and ethical prescriptions
of Islam in a strict manner. The second, known as *abangan*, referred to those in Java's
Muslim community who are less rigorous in their performance of orthodox duties, and
are influenced by aesthetic and ritual styles to some degree related to Java's pre-Islamic
past (C. Geertz 1960; H. Geertz 1963; Jay 1963, 1969). In his *Religion of Java*, Clifford
Geertz suggested that these religious styles (and a third associated with Java's *priyayi*
aristocracy) were loosely correlated with social and economic class. More recently, a
number of scholars have taken issue with this correlation, pointing out that variation in
religious orthodoxy cuts across class lines (Koentjaraningrat 1963; Ricklefs 1979; Dhofier
1978). Some of these same critics have qualified the *santri-abangan* distinction further.
They note that within both the orthodox and *abangan* communities, there is another line
of differentiation between people of conservative and those of modernist tendency. Critics
have also noted that the terms *santri* and *abangan* are not used in a uniform fashion

3

Friends in Malang provided me with conflicting reports as to what I should expect to see in Tengger. Several university acquaintances commented that Tengger were backward, suspicious of outsiders, and, from the perspective of Java's cultural history, insignificant, since they had no courts, distinctive art, or literature. Other people in the Malang area simply said that Tengger were "still primitive." They worship rocks, trees, and evil spirits, one university student noted, and are barely able to speak Javanese. Another friend warned me that the spirits of the Tengger region are dangerous, and advised me to wear a Christian religious medallion. "The spirits are helpless if they see you are a Muslim or Christian," he added. Youths in my Malang neighborhood who claimed to have attended the annual Tengger festival at the base of the Mt. Bromo volcano provided even stranger information. Tengger, they insisted, throw live animals into the volcano's smoldering crater. Years ago they used to sacrifice human beings.

Other lowlanders with whom I spoke, however, adopted a rather different attitude toward Tengger. In a market town just below the Tengger highlands, a woman rice trader explained that Tengger are "good people, honest, upright, and straightforward, as all Javanese once were, but are no longer." On hearing that I was traveling to the highlands, an urban fellow in a bus station in the north coast city of Probolinggo took me aside to make a similar evaluation. "Their religion," he confided, "is the original religion (*agama asli*) of Java. It is like that in which I secretly believe. But I live here among the Muslims and can do nothing."

Braced, then, for an excursion into the exotic, I left Malang one clear June morning headed for the village of Gubukklakah, a non-Tengger

throughout Java, and the cultural distinction itself is often not supercharged with the political significance noted in a few regional studies (Dhofier 1978; Nakamura 1976). In light of the latter argument, it is interesting to note that the term *abangan* is rarely used either in or around the Tengger highlands. Orthodox Muslims may on occasion use the term as a derogatory epithet, but even this usage is rare. As I discuss later, non-Muslims in the Tengger region traditionally referred to themselves as "Buda people," that is, believers in the religion of Java before Islam. Nominal Muslims sometimes used the same term to qualify their identification with Islam, referring to themselves as "Buda Muslims" (*Islam Buda, Islam cara Buda*). Since Indonesian independence, however, the term *Buda* has come to be identified by many people as a sign of *kolot* old-fashionedness, except in those few remaining Tengger communities of Buda persuasion. People of nominal Muslim faith in the region today tend to speak of themselves as *Jawa tulen, Jawa asli, kejawen,* or any number of other terms that express one's identification with "Javanese-ness." In deference to this usage, I have avoided the term *abangan* in the present work, in favor of the terms *kejawen* or "Javanist Muslim." The terms are intended to refer to people who qualify their identification with Islam by insisting on the importance of Javanese customs not explicitly sanctioned by more orthodox Muslims.

hill community from which I would begin my thirteen-kilometer hike through mountain forests to the southern Tengger community of Ngadas. I had deliberately selected a southern route to the highlands, having been told that villages in this region (to the south of Mt. Bromo) were the most isolated of some twenty-eight upland communities identified as "Tengger." No sooner had I left the village of Gubukklakah, however, than I encountered the first of two surprises. A road crew was working just above the village, cutting the dense mountain forest, and laying the stone foundation for what would eventually be an unpaved vehicle road linking the lowlands with this remote corner of the Tengger highlands. Road workers commented that in one more year this rugged mountain terrain would be accessible from Malang with only a half-day's ride.

My second surprise occurred several hours later, as I neared the end of my ascent. Climbing above a dense mountain fog, I could see neat vegetable plots on steep hillsides just ahead. Beyond them sat the whitewashed houses of Ngadas, clustered tightly at the top of a ridge overlooking a narrow mountain valley cultivated with onions, cabbage, potatoes, and maize. Contrary to what I had expected, the village looked much like the Javanese community from which I had set out several hours earlier. Admittedly, the village was laid out in a more compact fashion. Houses were more uniform in style and more solidly constructed than those in lower-lying communities, mountain pine having replaced bamboo as the primary construction material. The streets had the odor of horse manure rather than truck exhaust. And there was no mosque. Nonetheless, the village for the most part looked quite similar to those in non-Tengger regions of mountain East Java.

My arrival in the village attracted a small group of friendly children, peering shyly from behind doors and corners, and gleefully whispering "londo!" (Dutchman!). Before announcing myself at the village chief's house, I decided to take advantage of the evening sun and walk briefly around the settlement, in hope of spotting a temple or religious shrine. Stories of exotic religious practices, my own recent trip to the nearby Hindu island of Bali, and lowlanders' disagreement as to the nature of Tengger religion had all made me curious as to what type of religious building the community might have. All I managed to find, however, was a small shrine set on a hillside above the village, its trees uncut and its borders neatly fenced, with a small offering table at its center. The shrine looked no different, in other words, from any number of similar *danyang* village shrines found in many East Javanese communities. Once again, my expectation of the exotic was frustrated in recognition of the familiar. I was left wondering why these people called "Tengger" excite such diverse opinion among Muslim Javanese, and why they should be considered so culturally distinct.

Other excursions that summer and nineteen months of ethnographic research (December 1978 to July 1980) helped me to understand better who Tengger are, why their identity is so problematic, and what their tradition reveals about Javanese religious history and culture. By their own account, Tengger are neither a primitive tribe nor an ethnic group distinct from other Javanese. Like other Javanese, they call themselves "Javanese people" (*wong Jawa*). Only on certain occasions do they qualify that identification by also referring to themselves as "Tengger people" (*wong Tengger*). According to their folk traditions, Tengger are descendants of non-Islamic Javanese who fled to the mountains above Majapahit, the last major Hindu-Buddhist kingdom in Java, when that court fell to Islamic forces from neighboring principalities at the beginning of the sixteenth century. They fled, it is said, so as to preserve a religion called *agama Buda* (Buda religion). More recently, many Tengger have identified this religious tradition as *agama Hindu* (Hindu religion).

Majapahit's collapse marked a turning point in Javanese cultural history. The kingdom was the island's last influential Hindu-Buddhist state, and was thus the last in a long line of Indic principalities which, over a thousand-year period, had propagated peculiarly Southeast Asian variants of Sivaism and Buddhism on the island. After Majapahit's fall, several small Hindu-Buddhist courts in the extreme east of the island (across the straits from Bali) survived into the eighteenth century (Pigeaud 1967:I:137; Ricklefs 1981:96). These had little influence, however, on developments in Java's cultural heartland. There Majapahit's successors preserved much of the political pomp and ceremony of the pre-Islamic courts, and cultivated an aesthetic and mystical tradition strongly influenced by the earlier civilization (Pigeaud 1967:I:78; Ricklefs 1979:110). Whatever the Indic trappings of these later courts, the fact remains that Majapahit's demise ultimately resulted in the dismantling of the island's once extensive network of Hindu-Buddhist ecclesiastical communities. A portion of that community's elite fled with Hindu Javanese nobility to the neighboring island of Bali, which has preserved a Hindu tradition to the present day (Covarrubias 1937; Hooykaas 1973; Ramseyer 1977). On Java itself, however, all such conspicuously non-Islamic clerical organization disappeared.

It is difficult to say what immediate impact Majapahit's fall had on popular religious organization in Java. The countryside had probably always been unevenly influenced by the Indic fashions of the courts. Even at the height of Majapahit's glory, for example, rural social or-

6

ganization does not appear to have been greatly influenced by caste concepts. Even in courtly literature, the notion of caste was not used in a fashion consistent with Indian usage (Pigeaud 1962:IV:468). Literature from the fourteenth century suggests that the countryside had a variegated pattern of social organization, with communities of freeholding peasants standing adjacent to villages of indentured bondmen, monastic communities of Buddhist and Sivaite clerics, and perhaps even several regions of semi-autonomous tribesmen (Pigeaud 1962:IV:472). Some of the more isolated non-Islamic religious communities may have survived into the eighteenth century (Pigeaud 1967:I:54; Schrieke 1955:II:336). Dutch colonialism, regional migration, and the rise of a revitalized Islam, however, would eventually combine to sweep these aside. The *resi, baru, biku*, and other priestly specialists of popular Javanese Hindu-Buddhism thus disappeared in a progressively Islamizing countryside.

This historical background helps to underscore the peculiarity of Tengger tradition in modern Java. Five centuries after Majapahit's fall, Tengger are the only Javanese population to have preserved a regionally based, explicitly non-Islamic priestly tradition.[2] Each year people from the region gather at the base of a volcano located at the center of the highlands to take part in a ceremony said to have been instituted by the ancestors who fled Majapahit's collapse (see Chapter 3). During the second month each year, Tengger villages in addition celebrate an all-souls' festival intended to bless such sacred dualities as land and water, earth and sky, male and female, and, according to some opinion, Buda and Islam (Chapters 5, 6). Rites of life passage in Tengger are also celebrated in a non-Islamic fashion, and show strong resemblance to popular ritual in Hindu Bali (Chapters 7, 8).

What distinguishes these rites from those celebrated by *kejawen* Muslims is the fact that Tengger ceremony is always built around a formal

---

[2] There is also a small non-Islamic population in a corner of the western third of the island, popularly known as Badui (Wessing 1978). Badui are ethnically non-Javanese, more closely related to the Sundanese population inhabiting the western area of the island of Java. Ethnic Javanese for the most part live in the central and eastern portions of the island. In portions of the Eastern Salient (see Chapter 2), however, Javanese are outnumbered by ethnic Madurese. For several centuries Madurese have migrated to the region from the island of Madura, off the Eastern Salient's north coast. On the topic of Hinduism in Java, it is important to note that although no Javanese population other than Tengger preserves a priestly tradition descendant from the Hindu-Buddhist period, areas of Central and East Java have in recent years seen some Hindu conversion (Ricklefs 1979). Much of this appears to have occurred in the aftermath of the violent destruction of Indonesia's Communist Party (PKI) in 1965-1966. There appears to have been an even more spectacular increase in Christian conversion.

liturgy celebrated by a type of village priest found nowhere else in modern Java. In his oldest and most secret prayers, this priest is identified as a *resi pujangga*. The liturgy he celebrates shows strong similarities with that of modern Bali's *resi bujangga* (Chapter 9, Appendix). Ordinary villagers, however, know nothing of the priest's old ritual name or the similarity of his liturgy with that found in Bali. They instead refer to the priest as a *dukun*, the same term as is used throughout Java in referring to specialists of traditional spiritual knowledge (see C. Geertz 1960:86). Despite the common title, however, Tengger distinguish their *dukun* from the "little *dukuns*" found in areas of Muslim Java, insisting that he has nothing to do with Islam but is the guardian of a faith once professed by other Javanese. According to their own notions, in other words, Tengger are not an ethnic enclave of non-Javanese ways, but heirs to a tradition with deep roots in Javanese history. The Islamization of Java, however, has made interpretation of that tradition, and the identity linked to it, extremely problematic. Whatever their earlier ties to other centers of Hindu-Buddhist civilization (see Chapter 2), Tengger have for several centuries been unable to look to Hindu Javanese courts or ecclesiastical communities. Moreover, Tengger are a mountain people, with none of the courts, castes, or literati of Hindu Bali. These facts make all the more unusual the survival of the Tengger priesthood— some twenty-eight celebrants in a like number of mountain communities—and raise important questions concerning the meaning of the tradition for modern Tengger.

What explains this tradition's cultural resilience? The answer to this question has long fascinated students of Javanese culture, who hoped to find in Tengger clues as to the nature of Old Javanese religion and keys for understanding the island's Islamization. For the most part, however, earlier investigations of Tengger have come to disappointing conclusions. Hampered by the varying quality of prayer texts, lacking recently reported materials on popular Balinese religion, and, in general, unaware of this tradition's complex history, most scholars have concluded that Tengger as a people were always an isolated ethnic enclave, as irrelevant to an understanding of classical Javanese religion as they are to an appreciation of modern Java's Islamization.[3]

[3] Pigeaud relies on Jasper's earlier (1926) account to come to what is a fairly typical conclusion of this sort: "Old manuscripts dealing with pre-Islamic religious speculation have sporadically been found in Java, and village priests in the Tengger highlands, where Islam did not penetrate, have preserved Old Javanese treatises. These remnants of pre-Islamic culture are disappointing to scholars seeking information on Old Javanese religion. The people who preserved the old manuscripts did not belong to the class of cultured ecclesiastics. In fact, even in the pre-Islamic period the Tengger highlanders seem to have formed a separate community" (Pigeaud 1967:I:49).

The "ethnic isolation" explanation of Tengger tradition, however, fails to take seriously Tengger claims that their tradition is Javanese, and ignores historical evidence that clearly indicates that Tengger have long been affected by developments in larger Java. Under closer scrutiny, the ritual tradition can provide insight into the social organization of at least one popular tradition in pre-Islamic Java. In particular, the Tengger example clearly indicates that by Majapahit times popular forms of Sivaism had sunk their roots deep into at least certain areas of the Javanese countryside. Investigation of the same tradition, however, reveals how profoundly it has been affected by the challenge of Javanese Islam. Although the ritual tradition Tengger preserve is now restricted to this mountain region, the cultural conditions to which it has responded are similar to those in many areas of rural Java, particularly those in the extreme eastern portion of the island (Chapter 2). From this perspective, the Tengger story is not that of an isolated ethnic group unaffected by developments in larger Java. It speaks to developments that have transformed all of Javanese society, and are reworking it still today.

My point of departure in the chapters that follow is the world of contemporary Tengger. Where there is historical analysis, it begins through investigation of the cultural present. While attempting to avoid the speculative errors that have plagued many analyses of Tengger tradition, I have nonetheless relied heavily on historical information throughout this work, and regard it as a vital element in any effort to understand the ethnographic present. This method is related in part to the "genetic" theoretical approach I have found useful in organizing my investigation, which I discuss below. The method is also inspired by my sense that Tengger are themselves intensely preoccupied with the image of their past, and draw heavily on it in formulating their present definition of self. In the most general sense, I should note, I have written this work as an anthropologist speaking to them and others who share an interest in Java's rich cultural heritage, and the processes shaping its redefinition today.

Cultural Reproduction

The problems involved in understanding Tengger tradition and identity begin as soon as we attempt to define the social character of this population. The Tengger region is not a self-contained political entity, and probably has not been for most of its history. According to the conventional categories of social anthropology (Nadel 1951:187; Leach 1954:5), therefore, Tengger should not be regarded as a distinct "society." Similarly, if we take as our primary criterion the categories of ascription and identification used by actors themselves (Barth 1969:10), Tengger are not an ethnic group distinct from other Javanese since, again, they themselves insist they are Javanese. Despite some differences of speech, etiquette, and, most importantly, religion, social interaction between Tengger and their Javanese neighbors displays none of the "boundary maintenance mechanisms" (Barth 1969:19) associated with genuine interethnic relations. The distinctive qualities of Tengger society reveal themselves not in interaction with outsiders, but in the less visible world of the village.

In a certain sense, in fact, the Tengger situation resembles that discussed by Leach (1954) in his classic analysis of highlands Burma, in that here too it is difficult to assume a neat correspondence between the borders of "society" and those of "culture." Tengger share most of their technology, agricultural skills, and even everyday lore with their mountain neighbors. Political and social processes are discussed throughout the region in much the same vocabulary. Even many aspects of ritual social organization (Chapter 10)—the invitation of guests, the mobilization of festival labor, the exchange of food gifts—have counterparts in neighboring Javanese communities. If it is easy to distinguish Tengger religious rutual from Muslim Javanese rites, therefore, it is less easy to talk about an integral and autonomous Tengger culture separate from that of larger Java. A similar problem arises in trying to define the borders of Tengger society. The boundaries of social action differ for the various activities in which Tengger engage, and much of that social action involves Tengger interaction with non-Tengger. Formal economic and political ties, for example, extend beyond the region, and in most respects are stronger than those found among Tengger communities. There is no distinct politico-economic infrastructure, in other words, neatly distinguishing Tengger from their non-Tengger mountain neighbors.

In speaking of Tengger society, then, we must recognize a variety of partially overlapping social fields, only some of which are concentrated within this mountain region. Similarly, in speaking of Tengger culture, we must remember that only a portion of the knowledge shared and transmitted in social life is in fact peculiar to Tengger. What is distinctive, and what I am primarily concerned with in the present work, is the configuration of social practices and cultural knowledge associated with Tengger ritual tradition. It is this configuration to which both Tengger and non-Tengger most commonly refer when commenting on Tengger identity; it is this same configuration that is of greatest comparative interest for an appreciation of Tengger culture in Javanese civilization. My primary concern in the following chapters is thus ritual meaning

10

and practice, as well as the wider social organization that helps to explain why, here alone in Java, this non-Islamic priestly tradition has survived.

From this perspective, the present work could be considered an essay in the sociology of religious knowledge, concerned with the processes by which a particular "body of 'knowledge' comes to be socially established as 'reality' " (Berger and Luckmann 1966:3), and thus to play an important role in the formation of a people's identity. Given the vicissitudes of Tengger cultural history, however, I have found it important to ask not only what the ritual tradition means, but what it means for different social actors and how, in a historical or genetic sense, it has come to acquire those meanings. Thus I have not refrained from "causal or genetic hypotheses" (Berger and Luckmann 1966:20), as a more singularly phenomenological approach to cultural meaning might recommend. Even while Tengger experience remains at center stage, the ethnographic problem obliges us to explore the larger history and social environment which situate meaningful action, but which are at the same time subject to contingencies that often escape "from the scope and purpose of the actor" (Giddens 1979:59). The interpretation of cultural meaning ultimately obliges us to attend to more than meaning alone.

The approach used here requires us to go beyond the well-worn opposition between "materialism" and "idealism" (or phenomenology), or, similarly, between organizational and interpretive approaches to history and social experience. While rightfully rejecting the idea that society is an organism in which each part can be best understoood in terms of its functional contribution to the whole, interpretive methodologies have sometimes neglected a very legitimate concern in the functional program: "What has to happen for given features of a social system to come about/persist/be altered?" (Giddens 1979:113). Systems of social action—such as the priestly liturgy at the heart of Tengger tradition—are not self-cloning realities, conceived immaculate of society and history. Their preservation presumes certain practical contingencies, and the maintenance of a social order larger than any given instance of meaningful action. These same issues of reproduction and change apply to the beliefs and knowledge borne by members of a society. Cultural knowledge does not merely "exist" independently of history and social organization. Attitudes are socialized. Knowledge is constructed, utilized, and transformed in the course of activity, always subject to some degree of historical and political accountability. To understand the reproduction and change of the people's culture, therefore, "culture" cannot be regarded as a self-enclosed and self-perpetuating ideational whole. The knowledge to which the concept of culture refers must be broken down into its respective domains—the flawless integration of which can

11

never be automatically assumed—and situated in relation to the actors who bear it, and the activities in which they engage.[4]

Expressed at such a level of generality, this observation is little more than a truism of contemporary social theory. Theorists have shown relatively little consensus, however, on the question of how to link the problem of cultural knowledge to the macro-institutional concerns of history, politics, and social structure. Studies of cultural transmission, for example, have for the most part focused on small-scale "inter-psychic process" (Tindall 1976:204), "cognitive transaction" (Gearing 1973:1229), and "face-to-face conduct" (Goody and Watt 1968:31). These studies have helped us to understand better how cultural knowledge and cognitive styles are linked to socialization and interaction. Their emphasis on person-to-person interaction, however, has sometimes made it difficult to determine their relevance for the larger problems of institutional organization and change long at the heart of much social inquiry. Goody's (1968) discussion of oral and literate religious culture proposed a partial solution to this problem, raising issues relevant for the present study. He postulated a general relationship between a culture's "intellectual technology" and the fixity of cultural knowledge itself. Oral traditions, he suggested, are more susceptible to revision and social feedback, because their transmisison is more directly dependent upon the interactional rhythms of society. By contrast, he suggested that literate traditions are more immutable, and thus less likely to show the same degree of fit between religion and society since, as in the case of world religions, "the reference point is not some locally derived myth subject to the homeostatic processes of oral tradition, but a virtually

---

[4] This is not to deny that, for certain interpretive tasks, it may be useful to "study culture on its own, apart from all other aspects of behavior" (Schneider 1976:197). However this analytic exercise should not be confused with an ontological characterization of culture as an entity which "does not have loose ends and unintegrated pieces and parts that do not articulate with other parts" (Schneider 1976:219). In speaking of culture, it is important to remember that ultimately what we are seeking to understand is human knowledge—its principles of organization, its emphases and themes, and its social distribution within a community. There is no need, and certainly no credible reason, to assume that knowledge of either individuals or groups is flawlessly articulate. In the present work, I have on occasion found it useful to look at people's cultural knowledge as if it were a single system of meanings (but not flawlessly integrated): for example, when comparing priestly liturgy with popular understanding of the same liturgy. The exercise is useful precisely for what it reveals concerning the quality of thematic consistency or inconsistency between different cultural domains. The lack of continuity between priestly liturgy and popular belief here in Tengger, for example, obliges us to return to the social world, to examine the social and historical processes that have brought about this dual economy of meaning, and that insure that actors at the same cultural event often experience quite different cultural truths.

indestructible document belonging to one of the great (i.e. literate) religions" (Goody 1968:5).

Eickelman addresses a similar problem, but challenges approaches to cultural knowledge that anywhere assume its automatic correspodence to social structure. The "forms of transmission of knowledge available in a society shape and accommodate social and cultural change" (1978:487). The implication here is that, above all for an understanding of cultural change, we must take apart our concept of culture by examining the way in which different forms of knowledge are sustained in, and dependent upon, different forms of social organization. Cultural change is often uneven because the social arrangements that sustain different types of knowledge respond quite differently to pressures from within or outside a society.

I have attempted to explore some of the general implications of this point in the present work. They suggest, among other things, that the distinction between "oral" and "literate" culture is too grossly technological. No tradition is purely "oral"; in even the simplest societies people use a variety of artifacts, mnemonics, and activities to shape attitudes and transmit knowledge. Hence not all "oral" culture is equally "homeostatic." Moreover, the cultural survival of a tradition is always determined by more than intellectual technology. The sacred scriptures of world religions have achieved their historical preeminence not by virtue of literate technology alone, but because social and political groups committed to their truth have succeeded in maintaining a role in the societies of which they are part. Similarly, here in Tengger, the system of restricted literacy that traditionally underlay the priests' learning and transmission of the liturgy (Chapter 9) was, by itself, unable to insure the survival of the liturgy in the society as a whole, which instead depended on the reproduction of a whole variety of ritual, political, and economic arrangements. Whether it involves oral or literate technology, in other words, the face-to-face process of cultural transmission must always be situated in a larger historical and political context that insures the continuing social relevance of some knowledge, and the restricted relevance of other.

This raises a second and more important point. When speaking of cultural knowledge, it is important to remember that there exist diverse spheres of knowledge in all societies, some of which may be generalized and common-sensical, whereas others are restricted according to gender, class, occupation, or role. Some knowledge is learned by almost everyone in the course of everyday existence; other knowledge may be restricted to a privileged few, and learned only through strict discipline and formal training. Although some anthropologists have been inclined to define culture as an all-encompassing system of shared "symbols and mean-ings," those working in the sociology of knowledge have more generally recognized that in all societies there is a "social distribution of knowl-edge" (Berger and Luckmann 1966:77). From this perspective, the image of culture as a "text" (Ricoeur 1979) is not very helpful, since, by leaving the question of culture's social distribution unspecified, it risks obscuring the fact that much knowledge relevant for action in the world is anything but uniform and shared. For some traditions, like this one in Tengger, the social organization of knowledge may play a direct role in the re-production and change of tradition.

All of these issues are relevant for understanding the peculiar resilience of Tengger tradition in an Islamizing Java. Priestly liturgy and popular religious culture have been affected in different ways by the challenge of a changing countryside, in part because each is sustained in a different social sphere. The liturgy is performed and transmitted by priests, and access to the priesthood is restricted by formal social rules. Only indi-viduals born into a priestly line, chosen by an acting priest, and initiated before priests of the entire region (Chapter 3) are recognized as legitimate priests and allowed to study the mysterious language of the liturgy. In the past, moreover, mastery of the liturgy was achieved in the course of studying a script that only priests were privileged to learn. These and other aspects of liturgical culture have insured it a greater degree of cultural conservatism than is the case for public commentary (mythic and otherwise) on the same liturgy. Popular knowledge of the tradition is subject to a much less rigorous social control. The priest rarely com-ments on the meaning of the liturgy, and, in general, there is in Tengger little of what one might call a formal exegetical tradition. There are a number of popular narratives on ritual and Tengger identity, but these have often changed in recent times, and been subject to considerable dispute. Popular religious opinion has, in addition, been dramatically influenced by the rise of a revitalized Islam over the past century, and the demise of Buda traditions in communities below the Tengger high-lands. As a result of all of these factors, popular religious commentary has been much less conservative than the priestly tradition itself, pro-viding changing accounts of the religious tradition and its significance for Tengger in an Islamizing Java.

The fact that only priests may study and recite the prayers of the liturgy is consistent with a ritual "hierarchy of languages" (Tambiah 1968:177) seen in many other Asian Indic traditions, and here as in those traditions it is related to a perceived hierarchy of the spiritual world. The most powerful of the liturgy's deities are known to ordinary villagers simply as "guardian spirits" (*roh bau rekso*), and can be invoked only by the priest during formal liturgy. Spirits of recently deceased relatives (*roh leluhur*), by contrast, are less powerful than the guardian deities, and can on occasion be addressed by ordinary villagers, since these spirits are, after all, but familiar kin. The system of ritual speech levels implicit in this arrangement is subject to one further restriction. Family spirits can be invoked only *after* a priest has paid homage to the guardian deities. Hence even the most elementary appeal to ancestral spirits must first proceed through the formal liturgy of the priest.

Villagers are well aware of the "logic of construction" (Tambiah 1968:178) implicit in this arrangement, and recognize that it is related to the hierarchy of the spiritual world. They have little opportunity to examine the rich linguistic detail of the liturgy, however, and they know, or say they know, little of its mysterious pantheon. Popular notions as to the nature of the spirit world are thus not generated by the liturgy alone, but are informed by concepts borrowed from the religious culture of larger Java. The above-mentioned distinction between guardian and family spirits, for example, is itself basic to *kejawen* spiritual tradition. Comparison of reports from nineteenth-century Tengger with modern commentary, however, suggests that in an earlier period the liturgy's deities may have played a more prominent public role. Over the past century—a century of widespread Islamic revival (Kartodirdjo 1972; Ricklefs 1979)—popular tradition appears to have been purged of spiritual references at variance with greater Javanese tradition. The evidence of the priest's prayers themselves indicates, however, that the liturgy has been less directly influenced by these changes, no doubt in part because of the secrecy and restrictions regulating its transmission. Although these arrangements served to insulate the liturgy from public challenge, they also guaranteed its progressive alienation from popular experience. Priestly liturgy and popular commentary, no doubt distinct in some respects from earliest times, came to express increasingly divergent cultural perspectives, the one (to oversimplify somewhat) Indic and hierarchical, the other ancestral, communitarian, and Javanist.

Such a discontinuity makes it difficult to portray ritual knowledge as a single system of meanings or "the undivided property of the whole society" (Bourdieu 1977:73). I attempt to outline this tension in the following chapters, and explain its social genesis. Discussion begins with a historical and cultural overview of Tengger in Java (Chapter 2). From there it turns to examine ritual and society, beginning with the region as a whole (Chapter 3), and then moving to less inclusive levels of social organization: village and household traditions (Chapters 4 to 8). At each level of social and ritual organization, we see evidence of the same cultural tension between the spiritual vision of the liturgy and popular

15

interpretation of that same liturgy. The myth associated with the regional festival of Kasada, for example, explains that the rite remembers
a first-founding ancestor (*cikal-bakal*) who helped to establish Tengger
society and religion by giving his life for their protection. The liturgy
for the same rite, however, makes no mention of ancestors or any act
of self-sacrifice. It speaks instead of a mysterious world deity, who
descends to earth to possess the priest and thereby create life-giving
holy water.

A similar problem of cultural interpretation arises in comparing popular accounts of the annual all-souls' festival (Karo) with the liturgy for
the same rite (Chapters 5 and 6). The liturgy addresses such Indic deities
as Siva, Brahma, Visnu, Mahadewa, and Iswara. Mythic accounts of the
same rite, however, speak not of these deities, but of the Prophet Mohammad and Ajisaka, a pan-Javanese culture hero. According to this
account, the Karo festival remembers an ancient pact between Ajisaka
and Mohammad whereby each respects the tradition of the other.

Liturgy and popular commentary show a similar lack of integration,
finally, in the most elaborate of household rites, the *entas-entas* purification of the family dead (Chapter 8). Villagers explain that the rite is
intended to remove impurities from the souls of the dead, so that those
spirits may rise (*mentas*) to the heavens. Villagers make no mention,
however, of what is, from the perspective of the liturgy, the most remarkable moment of this rite, when the priest invokes Siva in his demonic incarnation as Kala, and, in the course of a long ritual contest,
transforms Kala into his true deific form. This same liturgy identifies
the priest as a *resi pujangga*, and includes a prayer known as the *purwabumi* ("prayer of world origins"), identical in parts to a prayer of the
same name recited in modern Bali by a ritual specialist known as the
resi bujangga (Hooykaas 1974). The ritual parallel clearly indicates that
the priestly tradition in Tengger was once linked to a form of popular
Sivaism found in large areas of Java and Bali (Appendix).

These facts make all the more remarkable the almost total lack of
reference to Indic deities in myth and public commentary. From a popular
perspective, Tengger tradition sounds strikingly similar to those found
in *kejawen* areas of rural Java, purged of their more conspicuous Islamic
references. But it would be too simplistic to characterize recent developments in terms of a convergence with *kejawen* idioms alone. We see
here in Tengger something far more profound and problematic: an effort
to reshape a folk heritage so as to make it capable of meeting the challenge
of the surrounding plural society. The development resembles that associated throughout the world with the passage from more local traditions to "world" religion. Admittedly, religion here is still "thoroughly

16

intertwined with the concrete details of ordinary life," and its public doctrines may fall short of the "inclusive formulations" and "comprehensive attitudes" associated with the doctrines of world religions C. Geertz 1973d:171-72). Myth and public commentary, however, show little of the aggressive self-confidence of smaller, more autonomous folk heritages. There is a tone of doubt in Tengger folklore, an almost anxious awareness of other ways. This sensibility has affected popular attitudes toward the folk tradition. Few villagers today take seriously the old tales on the origins of red and white onions, the creation of Mt. Bromo, or any number of other myths once associated with the people of the Tengger mountains (Soepanto 1962). These are tales of a more naive era. Modern villagers have heard of science and technology, and they look to authorities other than folk tales or local elders to explain the movement of the sun, the growth of healthy plants, or the flight of modern men to the moon.

Several traditional narratives, however, continue to be told. Almost all of these, moreover, are preoccupied with the same problem: Tengger identity and the legitimacy of their tradtion. As with other peoples at the margins of modern Indonesian society, these issues have been made important by the tenuous position of Tengger in the modern nation state. The integrative revolution in politics and economy has shattered barriers between traditionally autonomous ethnic, linguistic, and political communities. It has posed questions concerning who Tengger are, the meaning of their tradition, and the role of that tradition in a plural society. In many areas of Java and Indonesia, of course, Islam has played a great role in the redefinition of local and national identity. For the non-Islamic peoples drawn into this same nation, the challenge has been to move into the larger society without sacrificing traditions integral to earlier identity. In Tengger, this effort to come to terms with the surrounding society has often moved uncertainly and with heated debate. Like many smaller populations in developing societies, Tengger have not had the scholars, archives, or time to recover their history. In communities adjacent to Tengger, by contrast, Muslim leaders concerned with the revitalization of local religion have been able to rely on Islamic organizations and ideas developed in other areas of the country. Until the emergence of the Hindu reform movement (Chapter 11), Tengger efforts to redefine their heritage in relation to the larger society could rely only on local cultural resources. As a result, the discourse developed was often defensive in tone, and addressed issues raised by the challenge of Islam rather than those implicit in Tengger religion itself. With the turn to Bali and the development of the Hindu reform movement, however, all this is changing, in a fashion that illustrates clearly a development familiar in the modern world: the transition from a locally based religious community to a "world" religion spanning diverse social communities (Chapter 11).

Symbolism and the Work of Interpretation

The expressive power of ritual symbolism has been a popular theme in anthropological study of religion. Clifford Geertz, for example, writes that ritual symbols "sum up . . . what is known about the way the world is, the quality of the emotional life it supports, and the way one ought to behave while in it" (C. Geertz 1973b:127). He characterizes the religious perspective in terms of commitment and faith, arguing that "the acceptance of authority that underlies the religious perspective that the ritual embodies flows from the enactment of ritual itself" (C. Geertz 1973a:113). Other anthropologists have similarly suggested that ritual performances "dramatize basic assumptions of fact and value in the culture . . . shaping actors in such a way that they wind up appropriating cultural meaning as personally held orientations" (Ortner 1978:2, 5).

In the chapters that follow, I too have found it useful to examine rituals as cultural performance, and to investigate their cultural status as objects of knowledge. The fact that the same ritual symbols here in Tengger appear to mean different things to different people, however, raises serious questions as to how ritual symbolism acquires the expressive force attributed to it, and in what way it is, in fact, meaningful. At issue here are fundamental questions as to the nature of what we sometimes all too casually refer to as "cultural knowledge."

The lack of integration between liturgy and popular commentary is, in fact, more complicated than it appears at first sight. Although public commentaries (especially myth) sound generally consistent with the religious idioms of *kejawen* Java, in private discussion many villagers are considerably more circumspect. They readily acknowledge that more occurs in ritual performances than is explained in myth or popular comment. The liturgy, they note, contains truths too powerful to be apprehended by any but the most spiritually adept. In private conversation, some villagers also reveal a far better understanding of the liturgy than is ever expressed in mythic text. More is seen and heard in rite than is ever acknowledged in public discourse.

This fact raises serious questions for the analysis of such cultural media as myth, ideology, and folklore. For example, to identify myth directly with a person's or people's thought—as is done when anthropologists speak of myth as "objectified" thought—risks oversimplifying the psychological depth of people. Actors may know more and at the

18

same time less than is expressed in myth or ideological statement. An individual may know less because, as some psychologists have noted, not everyone in a society need have thought through the conceptual implications of a myth, doctrine, or even kinship system (Harris and Heelas 1979:222; Piaget 1970:117). Even if it is assumed that cultural media at some point originate in the minds of real people, "they need not reflect the thought processes of individuals currently utilising the beliefs under consideration" (Harris and Heelas 1979:223). Tradition is not rethought by everyone in each generation. Indeed, for many people it need not even be the object of much intellectual concern.

Identifying myth and other public idioms with thought also risks neglecting what is, from a historical and sociological perspective, their most curious quality: their status as objects of public knowledge. Not all the attitudes and beliefs of a people are elevated to such cultural prominence. There may be good social and historical reasons for those that are. Hence the analysis of myth, ideology, and folk belief cannot concentrate on the formal or internal properties of the discourse alone, but must look to see if that discourse plays a role in a larger social dialogue, constrained by realities other than those internal to the text or mind. Here in Tengger, for example, the rise of a revitalized Islam in neighboring communities has helped determine what in Tengger tradition has been elevated to the status of mythic truth, and what has become inutterable priestly mystery.

People also always know more than is expressed in myth, ideology, or public ritual. Culture media of this sort are, to borrow a phrase from Sperber, "explicit and expressly imparted." Such explicit cultural knowledge, however, "makes sense only in as much as it is the object of an underlying tacit knowledge" (Sperber 1975:x, xi). To comprehend a people's understanding of a myth or ritual, therefore, it is not enough to look at the symbolism neatly formalized within the medium itself, as if its significance were something it carried in a prepackaged fashion. The "vehicular" image of symbolism employed in some interpretive definitions of culture oversimplifies the role of real actors in making sense of their world. From an interpretive perspective, the cultural symbolism of a myth or rite is always deficient. It yields a knowledge only inasmuch as it is the object of interpretive work performed by actors with minds, feelings, and biographies that are never as stereotyped as our analytic ideal types might suggest. To assume that everyone present to a ritual performance appropriates the same cultural truths is to deny one of the most fundamental aspects of cultural performance and, for that matter, social existence itself. "Socialization is never completely successful" (Berger and Luckmann 1966:106), hence different actors

19

bring different attitudes, feelings, and knowledge to the same social dramas. Once there, moreover, they frequently occupy different positions in the performance, and position influences who has access to, and a likely interest in, the symbolism.

Recognition of these contingencies makes the work of an interpretive anthropology more complex than is sometimes thought. The analysis of "core symbols" or "symbolic structures" alone can never tell us the real significance of a tradition for a people. We can posit no simple correspondence between social action-in-the-world, the public idioms that claim to define its significance, and the interpretive sense actors make of both. Native understanding of a ritual or myth is not a matter of "internalizing" ready-made truths. Inasmuch as such cultural media are the object of interpretive attention at all, their knowledge is constructed by actors relying upon intuitions developed in a socialization larger than the cultural performance itself. In our effort to understand the significance of a tradition, therefore, there can be no detour around society or history. Differences of social position, biography, and cognition all affect people's experience. Rather than ignoring these things by collapsing them under a single concept of stereotyped meaning, our task is to disentangle them, and learn more of their complexity by attending to the contingencies of their social genesis. We need not despair in the face of such a task, or throw our hands up at the impossibility of penetrating other minds. Thought may not be public, but much of the experience in which it is socialized and many of the domains in which it is exercised are. It is on these that ethnographers train their attention, seeking to reconstruct the tacit background to explicit cultural truth, and then, in a second-order exercise (which to some degree occurs simultaneously with the first), translating and reorganizing this experience to the interpretive schemes of their own discipline.

These are important points for understanding Tengger interpretation of their tradition. With its long prayers, abundant incense, holy water, and offerings, Tengger ritual presents a symbolic richness akin to that Turner describes among the Ndembu, where "almost every gesture employed, every song or prayer, every unit of space and time, by convention stands for something other than itself" (Turner 1969:15). In Tengger, however, the conventions that might explain such detail are not always clear. No sermon accompanies ceremony, and no one comes forth to provide "item-by-item exegesis" (ibid.:20) of ritual symbolism. Often the priest celebrates communal rites alone, acting in the name of villagers. The efficacy of ritual rarely depends upon the presence of an active congregation. The faithful performance of received ritual forms takes precedence over evangelical exhortation or collective effervescence.

In all this, Tengger resemble their Hindu counterparts in neighboring Bali. There too, we know, ordinary villagers are "not expected to pray," since the "priest serves as their spokesman"; villagers' role in worship "consists of deeds rather than words" (Belo 1953:8).

This emphasis in Tengger has been complicated by the tradition's isolation in an Islamizing countryside. Even early nineteenth-century reports note that Tengger are "cautious" and "cryptic" (van Lerwerden 1844:67) in discussing religious matters, quickly referring inquiries to the village priest (Domis 1832:329). The emphasis on proper ritual form rather than extended exegesis, however, is not solely a matter of social nervousness. There is a widespread sense among villagers that religion is by its very nature a matter whose mystery is inexhaustible. This Tengger attitude resembles that of many *kejawen* Muslims, who sometimes distinguish themselves from their more orthodox brethren by noting that religion's mystery cannot be reduced to prayer exercises repeated several times each day. It is important to note, however, that, whatever the attitudes of *kejawen* Muslims, Tengger display a healthy scepticism toward forms of Javanese mysticism known as *kebatinan*. Although their myths speak of meditating ancestors and fasting priests, Tengger show little interest in mystical endeavors conducted outside the framework of formal ritual. "I would rather spend my time planting potatoes," was one priest's answer to my question as to the spiritual merit of *kebatinan* exercises. Tengger are ritualists, with ritualists' faith in the efficacy of tried and true ritual forms. They show little interest in the witchcraft and black magic for which some Muslim regions of East Java are famous. When a baby is born, when someone falls ill, or when crops are ready for harvest, people inevitably turn to the village priest, who then performs much the same rite of burning incense, anointing offerings, and giving homage to the deities as is used in all priestly liturgy.

The faith that underlies this attitude toward ritual is not generated in ritual performance alone. Religious faith always has a longer history and wider socialization, and the power of ritual symbolism depends upon its ability to tap this experience and focus its compelling quality. It is this dialectic between ritual faith and social experience that I have attempted to explore here. Ritual organization helped to reproduce the conditions in which the liturgy's truth as a symbol of Tengger ancestry and identity remained compellingly real. The same organization proved less capable, however, of isolating Tengger from greater Java. Hence, although the role of ritual in community life managed to keep priestly liturgy at the center of Tengger society, it could neither prevent the changes that transformed the surrounding society nor render inalterable the cultural intuitions through which Tengger interpreted their tradition. The *resi pujangga* survived in a Java that elsewhere knew no such priest. As one villager explained, ritual for Tengger "is the book in which we, a people without books, have written of our history and heritage." Like all cultural objects, however, the meaning of this one depended upon a larger learning. The resulting reflection on religion and identity bears the curious imprint of an earlier Indic heritage and the shadow of an Islamizing Java.

· 2 ·

THE SETTING: HISTORY AND IDENTITY

The Region in Java

Java forms an island mass 1,000 kilometers east to west and 90 to 200 kilometers north to south. The east-west spine of the island is defined by a chain of thirty volcanic mountains and limestone plateaus, between which lie fertile lowland basins. The valleys provide the natural setting for some of the world's finest wet-rice lands, and in an earlier era provided Java's inland principalities with agricultural bounty unrivaled throughout the Indonesian archipelago (C. Geertz 1963:39; Ricklefs 1981:15).

Java's Eastern Salient (the Oosthoek or East Hook) forms the narrow eastern extremity of the island. Beginning just to the east of what is today the Malang-Surabaya highway, the region extends eastward 180 kilometers to the Bali straits, across which the smaller island of Bali is visible. Drier, more rugged, and without the major rivers of central and east-central Java, the Eastern Salient resembles the more mountainous island terrain typical of the small islands to the east of Java. A tight series of mountains dominate the landscape, creating the impression of lowland terrains always craning their neck to gaze upward at towering mountains. The valley basins in this eastern corner of Java are narrower than those to the west; river courses twist and turn, bearing the waters that sustain wet-rice communities below. The more rugged terrain, a longer dry season, and less abundant water resources make wet-rice agriculture less extensive here than in regions of Central Java.

The Tengger massif lies in the western section of the Eastern Salient, about 40 kilometers to the east of Malang, and 50 kilometers to the south of the north coast ports of Probolinggo and Pasuruan. The mountain terrain in the Tengger highlands is among Java's most rugged. Its southern flank is guarded by Mt. Semeru, an active volcano and Java's highest mountain (3,670 meters). Its northern boundary overlooks the fertile and densely populated lands of Java's north coast plain. The eastern slopes of the highlands are drier and less fertile than the luxuriant slopes of the west and southwest; the southern slopes are still thickly forested and largely unpopulated, due to Mt. Semeru's periodic activity. In all but this southern region and protected forest lands, the thick woodlands that used to cover the region's mountain ridges (Domis

23

1832:326) have disappeared, victims of the axes of land-hungry immigrants to this once sparsely populated mountain territory.

The center of the Tengger massif is dominated by a vast but now inactive volcanic crater, some 9 kilometers in diameter, with grass-covered walls climbing 400 meters from a desertlike central basin known as the "sand sea" (segara wedi). At the center of this enormous chasm there stands a cluster of five small mountain peaks, each of which also rises about 400 meters above the crater floor. Four of these five peaks are covered with a thick growth of elephant grass and bush. The fifth, known as Mt. Bromo, stands at the northern corner of this mountain cluster, and is without any grass cover. An active volcano, Mt. Bromo's peak has been torn away, replaced by a steaming and bubbling crater hole. One inspired Western visitor to the area described Bromo as an "awesome and awful" image of "nothingness and destruction . . . a monstrous mound of sterile cinders" (Leclerq 1897:214). Judging by the etymology of the terms still used to designate the Mt. Bromo terrain, early Hindu visitors to the region must have been similarly awed by the landscape. They gave it names that link it to the famous "sand sea" of Indian literature, a place of purgatorial passage to the Mt. Meru heavens.[1]

Today Tengger communities lie scattered in a narrow band below the rim of the volcanic crater, at altitudes ranging from 1,400 to 2,400 meters and at distances of 5 to 10 kilometers from the center of the sand sea itself. The altitude is high enough to keep daily temperatures in the 70s (Fahrenheit) and to drop nightly temperatures into the 40s, with two or three nights of frost each year. There are twenty-eight official village units (kalurahan) in this region, consisting of more than twice that number of nucleated settlement sites. A century ago the number of Tengger communities was greater, and included several more distant

---

[1] Gonda (1952) notes several Old Javanese texts that speak of a "sand sea" in relation to a larger spiritual terrain. "The Middle Javanese Bhimaswarga," he writes, "regards this sand sea as a locality to be crossed by those who are on the way towards hell, and in the likewise Middle Javanese Tantri Kamandaka it is a place in the infernal regions underneath the seven hells" (1952:148-49). The Old Javanese Prastha Nikaparwa identifies the sand sea "as a region north of the Himalaya, to be crossed by the Pandavas, when they have decided to renounce the world" (1952:148). According to this same text, Mt. Meru lies visible beyond the desert. In the real-world terrain of the Tengger mountains, of course, Mt. Semeru does lie to the south of the Bromo region, and is visible from the mountain cliffs above the sand sea. Gonda also notes that Old Javanese texts frequently identify hell as a volcanic caldron (kawah). The same caldron imagery is employed in the prayers for the Tengger entas-entas (Chapter 8), and is visible in graphic form among the bas reliefs of the thirteenth-century Jago temple in the town of Tumpang, several kilometers to the southwest of present-day Tengger territory (Smith-Hefner 1983:286).

from the sand sea.[2] Throughout the nineteenth century, however, Muslim immigrants moved into these lower-lying terrains, opening hillside "waste lands" to coffee cultivation, and ultimately changing the religious orientation of native populations in the region.

Early History

In Old Javanese the term *tengger* means "highlands," and thus the phrase *wong tengger* in an earlier period would have meant "highland person(s)." The term *tengger* is no longer used in this way in modern Javanese, but is partially preserved in the Indonesian language as a verb, *tengger*, "to perch or sit above." In the modern Javanese language, the term is used only as a proper noun to refer to the region and people of the Tengger highlands.[3]

The earliest known references to the Mt. Bromo region date from the first quarter of the tenth century. A stone charter dated 851 Saka (A.D. 929) granted the village of Linggasuntan autonomy in matters of taxation as a holy place for the worship of a deity at a location called Walandit.[4] Charters from neighboring communities during this same period also suggest the presence of cult activity related to Mt. Bromo. One such charter identifies the deity as Sang Hyang Swayambuwa, or the Indic god Brahma. The association of Brahma with Mt. Bromo is also evident in the mountain's name itself, *Bromo* or *Brama* being a Javanese variant of the name Brahma. In Indonesian Hinduism, Brahma was frequently identified as the god of fire. In the fourteenth-century *Tantu Panggelaran*, moreover, Brahma is referred to as "a blacksmith, and the very spot where he forged iron is the volcano Brama" (Gonda 1952:132).

Other works from this period refer to the presence of religious orders in the Mt. Bromo region. In the fourteenth-century *Nagarakertagama*, for example, the poet Prapanca identifies Walandit as the site of both

[2] Jasper's (1926) map of the Tengger region lists about forty-eight Tengger communities, but includes several villages that, according to ethnohistorical information I was able to collect, were already partially or largely Islamized. The map nonetheless can be used to assess the progress of Islam in the Tengger region. It suggests, most interestingly, that the areas of most extensive Islamization over the past century were those located in the hills of Malang and Lumajang—coffee-growing regions that attracted large numbers of immigrants (Chapter 11).

[3] In the Tengger dialect of Javanese, *tengger* contrasts with *ngare*, "lowlands," as in *wong ngare* or "lowlands people." The contrast of upland and lowland is of course a common one in Southeast Asian cosmology.

[4] These and other Tengger charters are found in Brandes (1913), especially charters XXIX, XLIII, and XXXVIII. I am grateful to Dr. Jan Wisseman for pointing out these charters.

25

Sivaite and Buddhist religious communities (Pigeaud 1962:IV:228). In 1880, a Tengger woman found a bronze charter and phallus-shaped betel holder in a field to the north of Mt. Bromo's sand sea. Dated 1327 Saka (A.D. 1407), the charter again speaks of a district called Walandit, identifying it as sacred (hila-hila), and referring to its residents as "spirit servants" (hulun hyang) of holy Mt. Bromo (Pigeaud 1962:III:171).[5] The charter's existence suggests that the Mt. Bromo region was regarded by the Majapahit court as an important spiritual territory. The region was well situated to be accorded such recognition. The wet-rice valleys just to the west of the Tengger highlands were, from the thirteenth to fifteenth centuries, the site of pre-Islamic Java's most important political centers. In the tenth and eleventh centuries, political hegemony on the island had shifted from Central Java to the Brantas River valley near the border of what is now Central and East Java. Following the defeat of the rival kingdom of Kediri at the beginning of the thirteenth century (Slametmuljana 1976:39), the state of Singasari established itself as the preeminent kingdom on the island. Its court center lay at the western foot of the Tengger mountains, and two of its most impressive religious monuments—the royal funerary temples of Candi Kidal and Jago (Holt 1967:68; Slametmuljana 1976:117)—were erected in the Tumpang valley 20 kilometers to the southwest of modern Tengger settlement. Kediri forces later returned to avenge their defeat at the hands of Singasari's forces, but Singasari's rout was itself quickly reversed when brethren forces from nearby Majapahit returned to expel their Kediri rivals. Envisaged as a continuation of the Singasari dynasty, the Majapahit court was established about 100 kilometers to the northwest of the old court, in a valley strategically situated so as to command access to both coastal and inland wet-rice territory (Robson 1981:262).

The Singasari-Majapahit dynasty became an expansionist power whose influence would be unrivaled by later Javanese kingdoms. The authority of the later Majapahit court, in particular, extended throughout large areas of the Indonesian archipelago. The state played a major role in an international trade in rice, spice, metals, and cloth, linking Majapahit to

---

[5] Although no "Walandit" can be found in this mountain region today, Jasper (1926) reports that a Javanese official once identified Walandit as the former name of a hamlet today associated with the village of Wonorejo, 15 to 20 kilometers to the west of modern Tengger settlement, at an altitude of about 600 meters. The villages of Manggis and Jengkol, also mentioned in the Walandit charters, lie nearby. All are in areas opened for coffee cultivation by Madurese and Javanese immigrants in the nineteenth century, and all are today Islamic. Jasper (1926) uses this and other geographic data to conclude that Tengger were always ethnically distinct from their neighbors and were only superficially involved in genuinely Hindu-Javanese cult activities. This assumption of ethnic isolation seems wholly unwarranted in light of contemporary historical and ethnographic data.

both India and China. Through its political and economic influence, Majapahit also played a role in the diffusion of Indic religious traditions throughout the archipelago. Both Hindu-Sivaism and Buddhism were accorded court patronage (Pigeaud 1962:IV:480; Rassers 1959; Ensink 1978), a syncretic balance that no doubt accorded well with traditional Javanese notions of dualistic harmony. Royalty were sometimes incarnated as Siva, other times as Buddha, and still others as both. The fourteenth century appears to have been a time of particularly intense religious activity, with extensive court patronage of ecclesiastical communities; some 242 recognized religious domains lay scattered about the Javanese countryside (Pigeaud 1962:IV:479). It was during this century that the Walandit cult was accorded royal recognition.

Ritual paraphernalia in modern Tengger also suggest a link between this region and other religious centers on the island. Each Tengger priest owns a small bronze holy water beaker (the *prasen*), referred to in ethnographic literature as a "zodiacbeaker" because it is decorated with carved images of animals and other objects associated with the Indic zodiac or *rasi* (see Jasper 1926; Rouffaer 1921:299; Kohlbrugge 1897). Most Tengger *prasen* are inscribed with a date, ranging from 1243 to 1352 Saka, or A.D. 1321 to 1430 (Juynbull 1921). The most common dates are those from the middle of the fourteenth century, the height of Majapahit's religious renaissance. Similar zodiacbeakers have been found in many areas of East Java, but none besides those in Tengger are still used in ritual. The distribution of such a standardized ritual implement suggests that religious activity in the Mt. Bromo region was probably once coordinated with that in other areas of Old Java and even Bali (see Appendix).

The developments that brought Majapahit to the height of its glory in the fourteenth century also paved the way for its destabilization a century later. In the course of its expansion, Majapahit had come to exercise political authority over areas of North Sumatra converted to Islam early in the fourteenth century. Whether related to these Sumatran Muslims or not, there appears to have been a Muslim presence at the Majapahit court (Ricklefs 1981:5; Robson 1981:268). By the beginning of the fifteenth century, moreover, many coastal areas throughout the western half of the archipelago (perhaps including Java's north coast ports) were in transition to Islam, at a time when political rivalries within the Majapahit court were causing severe internal stress. Sometime around 1478, the Majapahit court was overrun by a rival Javanese power, still apparently of Hindu persuasion (Noorduyn 1978; Robson 1981:279). Developments in the aftermath of this calamity are unclear, but it appears that the Majapahit court was quickly reestablished at a new location farther inland and away from the north coast, perhaps so as to put it at a greater distance from the increasingly powerful Muslim potentates on the coast (Robson 1981:279; Ricklefs 1981:34). Several years later (about 1527) the Muslim coastal principality of Demak conquered the much weakened Hindu court. With the exception of several minor principalities in the east adjacent to Bali, Majapahit's collapse eliminated the last major Hindu-Javanese court. In West Java, the Sundanese court of Pajajaran would fall to advancing Muslim power in 1579 (Ricklefs 1981:35).

There is no record of events in the Mt. Bromo region throughout this tumultuous period, but literary and mythic traditions suggest that the impact of court changes was severe. The eighteenth-century *Serat Kanda* reports that a Tengger religious teacher with forty of his followers rushed to the aid of Majapahit in its final hours, capturing two cannons in the process, one of which, legend recounts, eventually made its way to the Central Javanese court of Mataram (Rouffaer 1921:300). Mataram court histories speak of a similar event. An even stranger account of developments in the Mt. Bromo region comes from Central Javanese court documents (dated 1814). These suggest that modern Tengger may be related to the "Gajah Mada people" reported in earlier court chronicles. The Gajah Mada people were residents of a mountain apanage awarded in the fourteenth century to the famous Majapahit court minister Gajah Mada. At periods in its history, this domain is reported to have included territory to the south of Pasuruan and the east of Malang, a region that includes present-day Tengger settlement. These same court chronicles indicate that in the century following Majapahit's downfall the Gajah Mada people suffered military subjugation at the hands of Central Java's Sultan Agung. Returning in 1640 from his successful campaign against Balinese-supported Hindu principalities in the extreme east of Java, Sultan Agung swept through the mountain regions near Malang, taking a large number of "Gajah people" as slaves back to Mataram (Rouffaer 1921:300).[6]

The period from the late sixteenth to the seventeenth centuries was one of extensive bloodshed throughout much of the Eastern Salient. The small principalities in Blambangan, adjacent to Bali, were squeezed be-

---

[6] Rouffaer (1921:300) sees confirmation of this hypothesis in the now forgotten myth of an old Tengger kingdom of Masangan. First reported in La Chapelle (1899), the myth speaks of war, captives, elephants (*gajah*, the same word as is used in the term "Gajah people"), and the gods' vengeance on a Tengger village whose men refuse to extricate an elephant caught in a stream. The violence of the myth's imagery is surely suggestive of some kind of historical trauma, but any definite link with the "Gajah people" must of course remain speculative.

tween the forces of Balinese invaders and those of Central Java's Mataram. Mataram's armies attacked the area repeatedly throughout the
last half of the sixteenth century. Under Sultan Agung's aggressive
leadership from 1613-1646, the Central Javanese kingdom consolidated
its power throughout the island, with some of the most extensive warfare
occurring in East Java. Mataram's foes in Malang and Pasuruan fell in
1614, the island of Madura in 1624. Mataram's most serious East Javanese rival, Surabaya, finally collapsed in 1625 (Ricklefs 1981:41). The
Sultan's effort to oust the Dutch from their newly established foothold
in the west of the island met with miserable failure in 1628. Agung
then refocused his military campaigns on still unpacified areas of the
Eastern Salient, most of which he subdued by 1640. Given official authorization by Mecca, Agung adopted the title of sultan in 1641 (Schrieke
1955:II:250), having established his kingdom as the preeminent power
on the island of Java.

Sultan Agung's empire-building success was short-lived. His successor
failed to consolidate power in the Eastern Salient, trying unsuccessfully
in 1647 to bring the territory under direct control again (Ricklefs 1981:67).
The failure marked a turning point in the history of the Eastern Salient.
From this point on, no Central Javanese court would ever exercise effective political control over the extreme eastern area of the island. As
a result, Tengger and most of the Eastern Salient would remain outside
the sphere of Mataram influence during the culturally formative period
from the seventeenth to the nineteenth centuries, a time during which
many of the features of etiquette, language, art, and social hierarchy
associated with Central Javanese tradition (and sometimes wrongfully
assumed to characterize all of Java) would crystallize into their modern
form.

The Eastern Salient was not yet to be spared the turmoil of Javanese
power politics, however. In the 1680s, Madurese and Makassar rebels
associated with the Trunajaya rebellion against the Mataram court (Ricklefs 1981:70) were pursued by Dutch forces into the Tengger mountains,
shortly after the Dutch had committed their forces to the side of the
imperiled Mataram ruler (Jasper 1926). The incident marked the beginning of almost a century of political violence around the Tengger region,
as rebels used the mountain area as a staging ground for attacks on
Mataram and their Dutch allies. The most important of these rebels was
none other than the famous Surapati, whose effort inspired seventy-five
years of anti-Dutch resistance in Tengger and much of the Eastern Salient
(Kumar 1976). Surapati was an ex-Balinese slave who in 1684 turned
on his superiors and led an attack on Dutch forces near Batavia, after
having worked for the Dutch in military campaigns in West Java (Kumar

29

1976:18; Ricklefs 1981:79). After a second attack on Dutch forces in Central Java, Surapati fled to East Java, where he established a semi-independent court at Pasuruan that ultimately controlled much of the Eastern Salient. Combined Dutch, Madurese, and Mataram forces managed to kill Surapati near Pasuruan in 1706, but Surapati's descendants continued to put up stiff resistance in several towns for seventeen more years (Ricklefs 1981:84). Even after their ouster from the region's major towns, Surapati's followers fought the Dutch for decades, operating from rural strongholds throughout the Eastern Salient, including the area of the Tengger mountains.

The Dutch only slowly subdued Surapati's followers in the Tengger region. A year after Surapati's death, a Dutch force returned to take Pasuruan. A military fort was built near the city, and used as a staging ground for assaults on rebel strongholds in the mountains and areas to the east (Rouffaer 1921:301). As early as 1707 the Dutch commander of the Pasuruan expedition reported destroying several Tengger villages in the Pasuruan region; a major campaign against Surapati's followers in 1723 was similarly said to have destroyed a number of Tengger settlements in the Malang region (Jasper 1926:10). Anxious to demonstrate its suzerainty over the region, the Mataram court in the 1730s dispatched an envoy to the Malang area in an effort to work out a political accord suitable to Mataram interests. The failure of that effort was to play an important role in Mataram's final concession of the entire Eastern Salient to the Dutch in 1743 (Ricklefs 1981:89). Acquiring portions of Madura and Java's north coast at the same time, the Dutch East Indies Company thus acquired its most extensive prize yet in its century-long encroachment on Javanese sovereignty.

In that same year, the Dutch commander who took control of the Company's forces in the Eastern Salient reported to his superiors that the region was for the most part calm, with the notable exception of territories near Malang and Pasuruan in the Tengger mountains. There the Dutch continued to encounter resistance from people calling themselves "descendants of Surapati." In the 1760s, the Dutch launched their final mop-up campaign (Ricklefs 1981:95). The effort involved two separate attacks on rebel strongholds in the Tengger mountains, but it was only in 1764 that the last self-proclaimed "leader of the Tengger" was driven from the region (Jasper 1926:11). Further to the east, the last pocket of Surapati's descendants in Blambangan was vanquished in 1771 (Ricklefs 1981:96). The Eastern Salient was thus finally under full Dutch control. Surapati's memory no doubt lived on, but in modern Tengger there is no longer any folk memory of his glory. In the Tengger Pasuruan region, however, priests still begin their services with a prayer of incense invocation that among other things, identifies residents of the region as "descendants of Surapati."

In the final years of the eighteenth century, Dutch officials made several visits to the now pacified Tengger highlands, surveying the region, noting its curious customs, and assessing its economic potential. In 1785, a small rest hostel was established in the northwest Tengger village of Tosari, and cultivation of European vegetables was introduced (Rouffaer 1921:301). Reports on the region applauded the lack of crime, adultery, and opium, and described the people as simple and trustworthy. Dutch visitors also noted the fertility of the area's rich volcanic soil— and the disturbing lack of local population to make good commercial use of it (Jasper 1926:11). Almost a century of warfare throughout the Eastern Salient had radically depopulated the region. With rich soil but little population, the Tengger region was booty not yet ready to yield its reward. Coffee cultivation apparently was not yet known in the region (Rouffaer 1921:301). The crop's introduction into the area at the end of the eighteenth century would eventually allow the colonial government to make good use of this fertile mountain land while at the same time solving the problem of the area's depopulation.

Tengger in the Nineteenth and Twentieth Centuries

At the beginning of the nineteenth century, Java's population probably stood at around 5 million people. By 1850, it had increased to 10 million; by 1900, 28 million; by 1930 42 million, and onward to today's population approaching 100 million.[7] By comparison with today's population, therefore, Java at the beginning of the nineteenth century was still rather sparsely populated, with vast forest and wetland areas.

Estimates of Tengger population at this time vary significantly, but they all present a picture of a very underpopulated territory. In the second decade of the nineteenth century, Raffles placed the total Tengger population at 1,200 people scattered about in forty villages (Raffles 1965:I:332). An 1830 estimate put Tengger population at 3,000 in forty-

[7] I have relied here on Clifford Geertz's (1963:69) figures, themselves based on earlier Dutch estimates. The problem of Java's spectacular population growth has become something of a theoretical specialization in itself, and has been the subject of considerable controversy in recent years. Peper's (1970) analysis questions the reliability of the figures I quote here, and suggests that Java's population at the beginning of its demographic take-off was greater than commonly thought, and thus the subsequent rate of population growth was less dramatic. Peper suggests a figure of about 8 to 10 million for Java's population in 1800 (1970:84). Whatever the final verdict in this controversy, Java in 1800 was far less densely populated than today, and the Eastern Salient appears to have been grossly underpopulated.

31

eight villages; an 1848 figure, 7,000 in fifty-eight villages; and a 1920 estimate 31,000 in forty-eight villages.[8]

Dutch enterprise would soon change the demographic character of early nineteenth-century Tengger. In the fertile lowlands to the north, east, and west of the highlands, the Dutch established some of the most extensive sugar estates in all Java. Some of the estate lands were "borrowed" from and cultivated by local villagers, but others were operated as plantations employing landless laborers, many of whom were ethnic Madurese. Although Madurese had long been immigrating to the Eastern Salient, during the nineteenth century they became the dominant ethnic group in large areas of the wet lowlands around Probolinggo, Jember, Lumajang, and (to a somewhat lesser degree) Pasuruan. Railroads were built throughout this lowland area in the latter half of the nineteenth century.

Sugar could not be cultivated in the cool and dry Tengger highlands, and thus the initial impact on Tengger of the sugar estates was indirect. The most important development was the steady expansion of Madurese and Javanese into the lower-lying hill terrain below the major centers of Tengger population. Many came to cultivate coffee. Although coffee had been introduced into the area at the end of the eighteenth century, the political repercussions of the Napoleonic wars in Java (1811-1816) and political strife in Central Java had prevented extensive commercial exploitation prior to the 1830s. The inception of the Culture System at that time resulted in an astronomical expansion of coffee cultivation; between 1833 and 1850, the number of coffee trees on the island is estimated to have tripled from the earlier figure of 100 million (C. Geertz 1963:66). The most common method of cultivation was the so-called "labor-tax system," under which each family was assigned responsibility for a certain number of trees, the harvest of which was then rendered

---

[8] Jasper (1926:13) discusses the sources for these population estimates. His own figure of 31,000 Tengger in 1919 is probably too high, since it includes village populations in communities by that time swollen by immigrant Muslims. Citing an 1871 study, he notes the presence of six fully Tengger communities in Pasuruan, nine in Probolinggo, twelve in Malang, and twelve in Lumajang. The Lumajang communities, he points out, were tiny hamlets with a total population of no more than 152 people. In the Pasuruan region, in addition, there were several mixed communities of Muslims and Tengger. Pasuruan today remains the center of Tengger settlement; all six earlier communities are still Tengger and non-Islamic. Perhaps three or four of the Probolinggo communities have converted to Islam, and several more have small Muslim populations. Buda tradition has fared most poorly in Malang, where only two of the earlier non-Islamic communities remain. The Lumajang hamlets also appear to have disappeared. Jasper further notes that there were thirty-six Tengger priests in 1919; today there are twenty-seven or twenty-eight, with several of these servicing what are now largely Islamic communities.

to Dutch authorities or their native representatives (C. Geertz 1963:56). The system had first been applied in the Priangan highlands of West Java, but its extraordinary success there encouraged its "later spread to the mountainside areas of the still sparsely settled East Hook" (C. Geertz 1963:58). Coffee quickly became Indonesia's most profitable export.

From the colonial government's perspective, the coffee crop was enormously attractive. It could be grown in Java's extensive mountain highlands, where water was often insufficient for irrigation agriculture and population still sparse. In theory, then, its cultivation did not interfere with food crops, and it made accessible a previously underexploited ecological niche. Other hill crops such as tea, pepper, and indigo were also introduced into highland areas like Tengger, but none achieved the spectacular success of coffee. Suddenly, what the Dutch once regarded as Java's mountain "waste lands" offered almost unlimited commerical opportunities—as long as sufficient numbers of workers could be induced to move into thinly populated mountain terrains.

The government had Java's demographic situation on its side in providing such an inducement. Warfare and famine plagued Central Java during the first half of the nineteenth century, and poverty and landlessness were rampant on the island of Madura. Hence much of the labor required for coffee agriculture in the Tengger highlands and other areas of the Eastern Salient was provided by a steady stream of Central Javanese and Madurese immigrants. By the mid-nineteenth century, most lower-lying Tengger villages had been swamped by new immigrants. Migration into higher terrains in the Mt. Bromo region was restricted by two facts. First, the territory above 1,400 meters was more densely populated than lower-lying terrains. Second and equally important, coffee in this area of Java does not thrive above 1,200 meters altitude. This "coffee line" still provides an approximate line of demarcation between Tengger and Islamic settlement in the Tengger highlands. Lower-lying Tengger communities were eventually Islamized (Chapter 11).[9]

Economic penetration of the Tengger highlands was paralleled by the extension of colonial administration into the region. In the late eighteenth century, an assistant regional chief, appointed by native officials in the colonial administration, took up residence in the village of Ngadiwono in the Tengger northwest. From 1817 to 1840 a regional chief

[9] I discuss additional aspects of immigration to the region in Chapters 4 and 11. It is important to note here that not all immigrants to Tengger were even nominal Muslims. Bodemeijer (1901) mentions a Probolinggo Muslim's conversion to Tengger faith (1901:304), and village histories throughout Tengger still indicate that in several cases village founders were lowlanders coming to live in "Buda land."

33

(*demang*) resided in the nearby community of Tosari. This lowland-appointed official had the authority to appoint the Tengger head priest (*lurah dukun*) (see La Chapelle 1899:35), which suggests that native administrators in the colonial government sought to bring Tengger priests under their control in a fashion similar to their authority over Islamic *penghulu*. In 1840, the administrative headquarters for Tengger was moved out of the region into the lower-lying Islamic communities of Puspo (in the Pasuruan area) and Sukapura (in the Probolinggo region) (Rouffaer 1921:307). These villages were closer to the coffee and commercial enterprises that were the primary concern of the colonial administration. One cultural consequence of this change, however, was that from this point on the government's regional bureau for Tengger would include in its service an Islamic *penghulu*, charged with supervising local religious affairs. There was no corresponding office for non-Muslims.

It is not clear from historical evidence what posture Tengger adopted toward these Islamic officials. As early as 1785, a Dutch report had noted that Tengger males were sometimes circumcised (Rouffaer 1921:306). Throughout Java, circumcision is usually associated with Islam. A later Dutch visitor to the region also noted the practice, and added that Tengger also visited a Muslim *penghulu* in lower-lying villages for marriage ceremonies (Domis 1832). Both practices, the official insisted, were merely the "outward appearance" of Islam, adopted "out of fear" of native government authorities (Domis 1832:338). In actuality, he observed, Tengger worship a variety of deities, the most important of whom are Brahma, Visnu, and Siva. Several years later, another Dutch official came to a similar conclusion, noting that circumcision and marriage were performed in an Islamic fashion because of "pressure" from Muslim government officials (van Lerwerden 1844:62). Proof of the rituals' insignificance, he added, could be seen in the fact that no religious ceremony (*slametan*) accompanied the Tengger circumcision (unlike the custom in the lowlands), and the Islamic marriage ceremony, performed in non-Tengger villages by the *penghulu*, was always followed by much more extensive priestly ritual back in the Tengger community.

It was only during the "liberal period" at the end of the nineteenth century, however, that the Dutch administration began to take a more active interest in Tengger religion and the advance of Islam. Some of this interest was no doubt strategically motivated. The incorporation of Java's *priyayi* elite into the colonial government and increasing Western economic penetration into Java's countryside had contributed to a growing anti-Western and anti-*priyayi* sentiment in many areas. Throughout the nineteenth century, Java's countryside was shaken by a series of rebellions, many of which adopted Islamic symbols and the idea of a

34

holy war as mobilizing cries against the Dutch infidels and their native lackeys (Kartodirdjo 1972; 1966:Chapter 5). From 1873 to 1903, moreover, the Dutch were embroiled in the brutal subjugation of North Sumatra, where native resistance was once again spearheaded by an Islamic leadership (Siegel 1969). It was during this period that the famed Islamologist Snouck Hurgronje was appointed to an advisory post in the colonial government. Under his guidance, the government devised a strategy of coopting "secular" leaders while suppressing Islamic opponents.

Contrary to our sometimes excessively Indic images of precolonial Java, Islam had always played an important role in Javanese resistance to Western colonialism. Sultan Agung himself had used Islam as a rallying cry against the Dutch in Batavia in the 1620s. At the end of the same century, Trunajaya used Islamic appeals in justifying his rebellion against Mataram and its Dutch allies (Schrieke 1957:II:239; Ricklefs 1981:71). Conditions in late nineteenth-century Java, however, conspired to give greater orthodoxy to Javanese Islam, and to make its appeal more widespread than in earlier periods. The incorporation of Java's native gentry (*priyayi*) into the colonial bureaucracy served to estrange the rural population from traditional elites at the same time that colonial penetration was provoking severe discontent among the rural masses (Kartodirdjo 1972:89; Carey 1979). The legitimacy of the traditional elite was increasingly challenged, creating a political vacuum in which alternative leaders—like those associated with rural Islam— began to play an increasingly active political role. Islam was not the only organized political force in the nineteenth-century Javanese countryside, but Islamic ideology was perhaps the most successful of all in responding to the "felt need for a more complex ideological framework capable of linking together and subsuming localized centers of discontent" (Kartodirdjo 1972:112). The nineteenth century saw a spectacular increase in pilgrimage from Java to Mecca (Ricklefs 1979), and the growing community of returned pilgrims contributed to the development of a more self-conscious orthodoxy among at least a portion of Java's Muslim community (C. Geertz 1969:68). Muslim revitalization was not without its ambiguities. There was considerable tension, for example, between traditional Muslim teachers more willing to accommodate Islam to Javanese ways, and more fundamentalist *hajis* (Ricklefs 1979:115). Among Java's *priyayi* elite and at least a segment of its peasantry, there was also a growing awareness of the incompatibility of some "Javanese" tradition with Muslim orthodoxy. As a result, tensions between fundamentalists and *kejawen* Muslims may also have increased at this time (Jay 1963; Ricklefs 1979:117). For large numbers of Javanese, however, Islam became a key term in the articulation of a new Javanese identity, self-consciously opposed to the Dutch and their native allies (Carey 1979; Kartodirdjo 1972).

This, then, was the period during which Dutch administrators began to give more attention to Tengger cultural traditions. Sometime during the last decade of the nineteenth century, the Dutch residents of Pasuruan and Probolinggo informed lower-level native administrators that those Tengger not desiring to be married by an Islamic *penghulu* would be allowed to have the marriage ceremony performed by a Tengger priest. The consequence of this ruling was that almost no Tengger underwent the Islamic service (La Chapelle 1899:52). Several Dutch observers went futher, however, suggesting that Tengger should be cultivated as a "counterinfluence" to Islamic organizations in the Eastern Salient (La Chapelle 1899:36). Interestingly, however, the strategy was denounced by a number of Dutch officials responsible for the administration of Tengger territory (von Freijburg 1901; Bodemeijer 1901). The logic of their comments was consistent with the ideology of progressive evolutionism common among nineteenth-century Western thinkers. Tengger religion, they suggested, was doomed to extinction, since it was "less civilized" than Islam. In addition, these observers suggested that the social habits of Java's Muslims were more refined than the "tattered and unmannered" habits of non-Muslim Tengger. Dutch need not fear Islamization in Tengger, it was suggested, because Islam itself is a better mode of transition to Christianity (von Freijburg 1901:334).

Tengger leaders never endorsed this strategy that pitted them against their Muslim neighbors. As the folk narratives discussed in later chapters make clear, Tengger continued to approach religious issues in terms of tolerance and dualistic complementarity. Moreover, they continued to see themselves as but one among a variety of related "Javanese" religious traditions. However accommodating their own notions, however, the world of late nineteenth-century Tengger was rapidly changing. In the first decade of the twentieth century, a vehicle road was extended into northwest Tengger; eventually four large hotels operated in two communities in the area. The hotels brought with them a supporting community of Muslim merchants and workers, and soon the Tengger community of Tosari had a large and economically powerful Muslim population. During this same period, road construction into hill regions below Tengger settlements resulted in a massive influx of outsiders and a steady dispersion of settlements (von Freijburg 1901:332). Road construction into the southern and eastern areas of Tengger settlement began in the 1920s, but was aborted with the Great Depression of the 1930s.[10] In 1910, elementary schools were established in two Tengger communities, Tosari in the northwest and Jetak in the northeast. Both were staffed exclusively by lowland Javanese. During these same decades, lower-lying Tengger settlements at the periphery of Tengger territory, areas that had been swamped by non-Tengger immigrants, were shaken by the first in a series of Islamic reforms promoted by the politically dominant Muslim community (Chapter 11). These developments posed a serious challenge to people who had long seen themselves as linked to a larger Buda community in other areas of Java, and who believed that Buda and Islam were kindred traditions (Chapter 6).

Concepts of Tradition

Throughout Java and Islamic areas of the Indonesian archipelago, the most common term for referring to a region's manners, tastes, customs, and beliefs is the Arabic-derived term *adat*. *Adat* is often posed in opposition to *agama*, a Sanskrit-derived term that means "religion or divine precept." *Adat* is similarly distinguished from *hukum*, an Arabic loan word for divine judgment, command, or law. Whatever the terms with which it is contrasted, the distinctive characteristic of *adat*, at least for orthodox Muslims, is that the beliefs and practices to which it refers are not divinely inspired. *Adat* is a social fact, a matter of humanly contrived beliefs, etiquette, and life ways. Given the historical and social distinctiveness of different peoples, it is inevitable that *adat* customs will vary from region to region. Precisely because of this variation, however, *adat* is quite different from religion. Religion is a matter of divine commandment. It is God-given, not man-made, hence it must stand above the vagaries of regional custom and diverse local ways. Where the two conflict, reform Muslims insist, custom must be reformed in a fashion that does not violate religious imperatives. The man-made cannot stand above the divinely enjoined.

Not everyone in Indonesia, least of all in Java, agrees with this es-

[10] The Dutch initiated other roadbuilding projects into the highlands in the 1920s, beginning construction on three new access routes to complement the already existing Tosari route. The Depression and later Japanese occupation halted the program, and road construction into the region began again only in the 1970s, through the joint effort of government work teams and village crews. About one-half of the villages in the region had at least dry-season access to vehicle roads when I first visited the area in 1977; four-fifths had road access when I left in 1980. The transport infrastructure has accelerated changes in commercial agriculture, a process which has in turn profoundly affected household consumption, savings, and investment (Hefner 1983b).

37

sentially Islamic characterization of *adat*. Having been borrowed into many of the languages of even non- and nominally-Islamic peoples in the region, the term has itself acquired a variety of regional usages. Even many Indonesian Muslims would take issue with reformist notions that insist on the necessity of purging *adat* of anything inconsistent with orthodox principles. Equally importantly, throughout the history of Southeast Asian Islam there has also been considerable disagreement among Muslims as to just what those orthodox strictures are. Beliefs and practices long considered properly "religious" by some Muslims have come to be criticized by others as inconsistent with the teachings of true Islam. This interpretive dialectic has gone on since the very beginning of Southeast Asian Islam, but is has been particularly influenced over the past two centuries by the spectacular ascendance of reformist schools of Islam in certain areas of the Muslim world. This complex history makes it very difficult to hypostatize the cultural content of *adat* throughout Indonesia. In Muslim Indonesia, the substance of *adat* has not been a historyless assortment of traditional "customs" transmitted independently of Islam. *Adat* has itself everywhere changed with ongoing developments in the religious attitudes and political influence of Muslim orthodoxy.

Tengger concepts of tradition resist such a systematic distinction between divine principle and customary ways. They speak not of *adat* (a rarely used term), but, at least prior to the Hindu reform movement, *ngaluri* and *cara*. *Ngaluri* (naluri, luri-luri) is a term also commonly used in nominally Islamic areas of rural Java. It refers to ancestral traditions, or—perhaps too neatly—all that which is maintained as tradition by virtue of its origins with one's ancestors. Because of its implicit reliance on ancestral precedent, the concept is unpopular among modern Tengger leaders sensitive to the need to develop a vocabulary of cultural legitimation premised on something other than local heritage or historical precedent. In an earlier era, however, the attraction of the term lay in just this ancestral appeal. In a world of diverse rural communities, the term provided a ready-made explanation and justification for regional cultural differences. Every community, after all, has its own founding ancestors, and they, like people today, had different beliefs, customs, and ritual habits. From such an ancestral perspective, it is difficult to argue that any one set of traditions is inherently superior to another, except when one is talking about what is best for one's own community. There there is a cultural precedent, made compelling not by the detail of doctrinal sophistry, but by the debt of the living to their progenitors.

Like many other Javanese, Tengger also speak of local customs as *cara*, "manner" or "way," as in *cara Tengger* (the Tengger way) or *cara ngare*

38

(the manner of lowlanders). Unlike *ngaluri, cara* does not directly imply any ancestral or spiritual sanction for customary tradition. Here as in other areas of Java, the concept is more commonly linked to statements about the diversity of customs from region to region, and the need for tolerance in the face of such diversity. *Nagara mawa tata, desa mawa cara*—"the city (or court) has its order, and villages their ways," affirms a well-known Javanese aphorism. The implicit suggestion is that those social differences are an inevitable consequence of human existence, and as such they should simply be tolerated—or so suggests one current in Javanese commentary on tradition. Tengger add a sort of populist twist to this general Javanese attitude. Unlike, for example, many Central Javanese, they do not look to the social manners of courtly *priyayi* to find the prototype for what is most excellently "Javanese." Each region has its own *cara*; there is no necessary ladder of distinction. Here the concept of *cara* rejoins that of *ngaluri*: all *cara* are ultimately based on the ties of the living to their first-founding ancestors, and the world of those ancestors, like that of today, was itself already culturally diverse. Hence no *cara* can claim moral precedence over another.

Islamic notions of tradition and religion provide an alternative vision of cultural things for many Javanese, one which, at least in its reformist form, puts in question traditions justified by ancestry or regionalism alone. As will become clear in later chapters, this form of Islamic cultural discourse has had a profound impact on modern Tengger concepts of tradition and identity. It is important to recognize, however, that Tengger themselves have always insisted that their religion is not merely a regional or ancestral cult. Like other Javanese, Tengger use the word *agama* to refer to religion. Tengger never speak, however, of a distinct "Tengger religion" (*agama Tengger*) in the same way as they speak of Tengger *ngaluri* or *cara*. Theirs, they insist (or did, prior to the Hindu reform movement), is Buda religion (*agama Buda*), which is to say the religion of Majapahit and pre-Islamic Java. The same term has been popularly used throughout post-Majapahit Java to refer to the religion of the pre-Islamic period, even in classical Javanese literature (Pigeaud 1962:IV:48). For reasons not entirely apparent to modern historians, Hindu names were (until modern times) almost never used to refer to pre-Islamic religion, even though the Majapahit court supported both Hindu and Buddhist ecclesiastics. The implication of this label for Tengger cultural discourse is important, however. By calling their religion "Buda" rather than simply "Tengger," Tengger underscore their belief that their religion was always part of a wider Javanese heritage.

Before the advent of modern education and Hindu reform, Tengger spoke of three variants of Buda religion: *Buda Tengger, Buda Jawa*

(Javanese Buda), and *Buda Bali*. *Buda Tengger* is the term they use when referring specifically to the priestly tradition of the Mt. Bromo region. This *Buda Tengger*, however, was always considered a regional variant of a Buda Javanese heritage that reigned supreme in the time of Majapahit, and, so it was thought until quite recently, was also preserved in modern times in at least several other corners of Java besides Tengger. Elder villagers often pointed out to me that large areas of the lowlands surrounding Tengger were once also Buda, and many continued to express the faith that there must surely still be Buda people in other areas of Java today. Whatever the historical or sociological accuracy of their views, it is quite true that until quite recently many communities below Tengger preserved religious traditions related to those more elaborately performed in Tengger (Chapter 11). Ethnohistories from the highlands also reveal that many nineteenth- and even twentieth-century immigrants to Tengger identified themselves as Buda and readily adopted local religious customs. Although the cultural history of Java's Eastern Salient remains to be written, ethnographic evidence from Tengger and nearby lowland communities indicates that the term "Buda" enjoyed until quite recently a wider usage than is the case in areas of Central Java from which we have ethnographic information. The usage may very well have been related to the relatively retarded development of Islamic institutions in more remote areas of the region prior to the present century (Chapter 11).

Tengger also speak of "Balinese Buda" (*Buda Bali*), and have long insisted that Balinese religion is in some sense kindred with their own. It is impossible to say just what, if any, contact Tengger may have had since Majapahit times with Balinese active in the Blambangan region of East Java. Tengger folklore itself provides no clues on this issue. It simply acknowledges that both Tengger and Balinese tradition were Buda, and, as such, both had originated in the kingdom of Majapahit. Since Indonesian independence, modern media, education, and the Hindu reform movement (Chapter 11) have expanded Tengger awareness of their Hindu Balinese neighbors, and it is to Bali that many modern Tengger have turned to develop the most revitalized understanding of their tradition and religious heritage. The movement for Tengger affiliation with Balinese Hinduism began in the 1950s. The newly independent Republic of Indonesia technically required all of its citizens to profess a recognized world religion, at first including only Islam, Christianity, and Buddhism. Only after years of vigorous campaigning did the Balinese in 1962 succeed in getting formal recognition of their faith as a legitimate national religion (Boon 1977:214; C. Geertz 1973d:189). Prior to that time, they—like Tengger Javanese—were in the politically awkward position of professing a faith not recognized as legitimate by the national government. It was in this context that a handful of Tengger at first explored the possibility of joining forces with Balinese Hindus. Many Tengger traditionalists, however, fiercely opposed the move, and still do so today. Although by 1980 more than half of all Tengger communities had officially changed their religious designation from Buda to Hindu, the debate between Buda traditionalists and Hindu reformists continues to polarize Tengger society. The issue is at the heart of Tengger efforts to forge a new discourse on tradition and identity in a modern Indonesia.

Identity and Social Interaction

Throughout Java, people of one region as opposed to another are called "people (*tiyang, wong*) of so and so"—*wong* Yogya, *wong* Banten, *wong* Malang, *wong* Tengger. With each such designation there is the suggestion that regional variation also entails sociocultural difference, much as in other areas of the world. Yogya people, for instance, live in the area around the most important of Central Java's courts. Yogya's people, it is thought, are higher mannered, their talk is softer, their food sweeter, and their young women shyer and more alluring than, say, people from the East Javanese city of Malang, *wong* Malang. Regionalism always hints at real social difference. From this same perspective, Tengger can be seen simply as occupying an extreme position on this same continuum of regionalism. Contrary to the tourist brochures sometimes published on the area, Tengger are not an ethnic or tribal group (*suku*) apart from other Javanese. There are no real boundary maintenance mechanisms (Barth 1969) used in Tengger interaction with outsiders to signal allegiance to a separate ethnic identity. In interaction with outsiders, in fact, Tengger appear eager to adopt general Javanese styles, and show a remarkable lack of conservatism in dress, economic aspirations, and educational attitudes. There are distinctly Tengger linguistic and interactional styles, but these are shared in the intimacy of the village sphere, not in interaction with non-Tengger. This inconspicuous affirmation of a Tengger identity is no more clearly illustrated than in Tengger speech.

The Tengger dialect of Javanese is characterized by several marked variations on the standard dialect, none of which are radical enough to make Tengger speech unintelligible to outsiders.[11] In language-conscious Java, however, small linguistic variations carry enormous social signif-

[11] A richly detailed linguistic description of the Tengger dialect can be found in Smith-Hefner 1983. The general features of the dialect include differences in pronouns, pronunciation of -*a* in open syllables, transitive verb markers, some lexical items, and the restricted use of formal *kromo* Javanese.

icance, and their combined effect here in Tengger is sufficient to convince many speakers of standard Javanese that the Tengger dialect is at best folksy and at worst downright uncivilized. From the perspective of social relations, the most distinctive aspect of the Tengger dialect is its restricted use of Javanese speech levels. In standard Javanese, the skillful mastery of speech levels is one of the most important of social graces—a delicately tuned linguistic index of status and intimacy in every social interaction. Although the lexical content of the language levels varies from Central to East Java (and varies more extremely the lower the speech level), their interactional assumptions remain remarkably consistent. A speaker must utilize different lexical items, etiquette, and (to a lesser degree) syntax when talking to equals, intimates, or inferiors as opposed to strangers or social superiors. Language levels internalize perceptions of social distance and hierarchy, as if (the comparison is technically only partially accurate) the *tu-vous* distincton of French were extended to include hundreds of lexical items, some involving more than two lexical alternatives. Not all words have different forms in other language levels, and not all lexical items from one level are the same from region to region. But the principle of address the system presumes, and the perception of the social world it helps mold, remain relatively consistent throughout large areas of Java.

What is most interesting about Tengger speech is that, in the face of a linguistic system that constantly demands social differentiation, Tengger tend to be—again, by the standards of Javanese speech—undifferentiating. At least traditionally, Tengger used the same language level in speaking with everyone in the community. A few honorifics might be dropped into speech directed toward one's elders, and in addressing deities the priest on occasion might fall into a full-blown formal Javanese (*kromo*), but otherwise most people most of the time spoke a Tengger variant of *ngoko* "low Javanese." Today, in fact, many older people and women in more remote villages know but a few greetings and expressions in *kromo* high Javanese (Smith-Hefner 1983). All of this is changing in modern Tengger, however, with education and increasing interaction with outsiders. Most village men, in particular, now display a competence in high Javanese easily equal to that of non-Tengger farmers in this same area of East Java.[12]

---

[12] I have two distinctive memories of incidents involving use of the Tengger dialect. The first is general—my experience of the ease and familiarity of interaction my own use of Tengger *ngoko* allowed with villagers, once they recognized that I was, in some small way, local. I have a less pleasant memory of the embarrassment I caused a group of Tengger friends early in my fieldwork. Meeting them once in a non-Tengger community below the highlands, I addressed them with a Tengger *ngoko* greeting. Several local children

The restricted use of high Javanese in Tengger is consistent with the cultural history of Tengger in the Eastern Salient. Although some kind of linguistic register long appears to have been common throughout the region (Smith-Hefner 1983), other areas of the Eastern Salient were probably also latecomers to the use of *kromo*, since they too lay outside of the Central Javanese courtly domains from which the modern system of language levels appears to have diffused in the late seventeenth or eighteenth century. This political fact, combined with the force of local solidarity, insured that regional dialects remain strong not just in Tengger but in large areas of this eastern territory. Even as Tengger speech changes, moreover, it is doing so in a way that testifies to the strength of a regional "Tengger" identity. In particular, even as Tengger begin to learn *kromo* Javanese for formal interactions and encounters with non-Tengger, they retain their own dialect of low Javanese *ngoko* for use in interaction with fellow Tengger. In other words, although they are now beginning to learn a standard form of Javanese *kromo*, they continue to speak a form of *ngoko* clearly marked as Tengger-Javanese. Although many villagers are quite capable of speaking more standard variants of *ngoko*, and indeed may do so with lowland friends, they consistently use a Tengger *ngoko* in addressing fellow Tengger.

The speech example is revealing, and indeed works in a way analogous to more general aspects of Tengger identity. Tengger "speak Javanese," but know a dialect which is marked as nonstandard or regional. The dialect is not used in interaction with outsiders, however, and thus does not provide a visible social boundary between Tengger and non-Tengger. In the village world, the dialect works as an index of solidarity between people who know how to speak "the Tengger way" (*cara Tengger*), and who respect the assumptions such speech implies for those who do. A Tengger identity is thus consistently, if inconspicuously, distinguished from that of non-Tengger Javanese. With outsiders, the identity is unseen and unheard, or at least minimized to a degree that avoids any suggestion of ethnic distinction. A claim to local ways is made nonetheless, and made a continuing reality in interactions that recall a sense of shared ways, a *cara Tengger*.

---

heard the exchange, and proceeded to follow us until we had left the village, mimicking our speech, and taunting us with cries as to how "ugly" Tengger speech was.

REGION AND RITUAL

From the perspective of political and economic organization, it is difficult to find reasons for identifying the villages of the Tengger highlands as a distinct social region. Formal organization exists not between villages, but between individual villages and political and economic centers located outside Tengger territory. Government administration of the region underscores clearly this lack of lateral integration between Tengger communities. The higher levels of that administration are at no point organized so as to coincide with a distinctly Tengger region. For example, Tengger communities are today scattered in four separate regencies or administrative districts (*kabupaten*): Pasuruan, Probolinggo, Malang, and Lumajang. Only a small corner of each district actually extends up into the mountain territory where Tengger settlement is located. Each district includes a larger number of non-Tengger than Tengger villages within its overall borders, and none of the districts has ever been directed by an administrator of Tengger background.

Much the same situation exists at the next lower level of national administration. The subdistricts (*kecamatan*) in which Tengger communities are located include both Tengger and non-Tengger villages. No subdistrict chief has ever come from Tengger. It is only at the last and lowest level of government administration, the village itself, that one finds Tengger playing an administrative role. Their superiors in government are always non-Tengger. The organization of which they are part at no point links Tengger communities in a distinctively Tengger administration.

The administrative organization of the Tengger highlands is thus segmentary and vertical, linking each village to a higher level of political administration, but providing no formal bonds between Tengger communities. Like so many potatoes in a sack, each Tengger village (*kalurahan*) has its own officials and is responsible for its own programs, always looking outside the Tengger region for directives and coordination; no indigenous "Tengger" polity exists to counteract the administrative fragmentation of the region. In terms of formal political structure, in other words, Tengger is no more a "region" than any other group of randomly selected villages in the East Javanese countryside.

Regional economy is characterized by a similar lack of lateral organization. There is no regional division of labor that might link villages in the exchange of specialized goods and services. Almost all Tengger make their living from farming, producing much the same assortment of crops as neighboring communities. Hence they trade not with fellow Tengger (except in cases of Tengger middlemen), but with non-Tengger merchants located outside of Tengger territory. Prior to the twentieth century, in fact, there were no market sites in the Tengger region itself. All were located in lower-lying non-Tengger communities, from which urban markets were more easily accessible. Few Tengger devoted their full-time energies to trade, even though the region as a whole has long been dependent upon lowland merchants for metal goods, clothing, and basketry; there was (and still is) almost no manufacturing, handicrafts, or weaving in Tengger. Some things have changed since Indonesian independence. There is now a bustling market in the northwest Tengger community of Tosari, complete with stores, restaurants, and tailor shops (few of which are Tengger-owned). Snack shops and dry-good stores suddenly appeared in communities throughout the highlands beginning in the 1970s, signaling a new phase in the increasing socioeconomic differentiation of Tengger communities. For the most part, however, these developments have not created stronger economic ties among Tengger communities themselves. They have merely brought an economic net-work based in the lowlands one step further into this mountain hinter-land.

It is much the same in other aspects of regional economy and polity. Although recent road construction has facilitated movement between highlands and lowlands, it has not had as great an effect on travel between Tengger communities. Roads run vertically, from mountain to valley, and generally bypass all but the closest neighboring villages. There are no irrigation networks in Tengger that might require villages to coor-dinate resource management. No cooperatives exist that might recruit their membership from different communities. There are no clans, castes, or other kin groups to provide intraregional corporate organization. Although marriage between individuals from different communities does occur, even rather frequently in northern Tengger, it creates no formal ties between villages or even between the parents of spouses. In the years since Indonesian independence, finally, the political parties that organized masses of rural Javanese in the 1950s achieved little success in Tengger. Almost all communities (except those with a substantial Muslim population) voted *en bloc* for the ruling Nationalist Party. Today they vote Golkar, contemporary Indonesia's ruling government party.

In short, one sees in Tengger almost none of the intervillage organ-ization characteristic of much of the rural lowlands or, to an even more spectacular degree, rural Bali (H. Geertz 1959). At least as the terms

are conventionally understood, there is no distinctively Tengger politico-
economic infrastructure to which we might point as the real key to this
Tengger identity. What infrastructure there is by no means neatly segregates Tengger from non-Tengger. There is one important exception
to this generalization, although it is more a field of activity than it is a
formal organization or political structure. The exception is regional ritual. More than any other activity, ritual provides a motive and an
organization for social interaction among people from diverse Tengger
communities. It is of central importance in the maintenance of a sense
of shared identity among people from those communities. Its cultural
role challenges many of our assumptions as to the nature of ritual. We
are used to thinking of ritual as a reflection of a more primary social
reality, rather than as an active social force itself. Even within the
anthropology of religion, we often speak as if ritual were a symbol of
something really occurring elsewhere. Such an assumption may be helpful, inasmuch as it encourages us to explore the relationship between
religion and the larger social world, or inasmuch as it reminds us that
the sentiments and knowledge ritual symbolism evokes are not created
from nothing in the ritual moment alone. To be aware of these issues,
however, is quite different from perceiving ritual as a reflection of a
somehow more objective world. Religious ritual itself is a mode of social
practice. As a social practice, it involves not only intentions and meaning
but the movement of resources and people. It is thus an active force for
social experience, and a creative medium for cultural communication.

It plays such a role on a regional level here in Tengger. Each year,
one festival mobilizes villagers from throughout the region in a fashion
unrivaled by other social activities. The popular or "mythic" narrative
associated with the rite, moreover, does what regional polity and economy do not. It explains that the residents of this rugged mountain terrain
are not a random group of unrelated villagers, but a people with a shared
identity, a common religious heritage, and a vital interest in the preservation of both.

The Kasada Festival at Mt. Bromo

Each year, just after midnight on the fifteenth day of the last month of
the Tengger calendar year, thousands of villagers gather in the sand flats
at the base of Mt. Bromo to celebrate a religious festival called by the
name of the month, Kasada. Seated side-by-side on a cement platform
at the base of the volcano, the twenty-eight priests of the region invoke
the spirit of the mountain, and present it with the offerings of food,
crops, money, and small livestock brought to the site by the people of

46

the region. In theory, every Tengger household sends a representative (*wakil*) to the sacrifice bearing fruits of the past year's labors. After the priests have completed their anointing and offering of the sacrificial goods, villagers begin the ascent up the north slope of Mt. Bromo to the crater (*kawah*) where they throw (*nglabuh*) their offerings into the gently steaming depths below. By the time the sun rises several hours later, most of the ritual participants have disappeared, having completed the most important of their annual ritual duties.

Kasada's date is fixed in tradition so as to coincide with the full moon of the last month of the Tengger calendar year. The full sequence of events, however, begins the day prior, back in the village. The priest at that time begins the ritual progress toward Mt. Bromo by burning incense and uttering a prayer of ritual announcement (*semeninga*) which informs the gods of the impending departure for Mt. Bromo. The ceremony is performed privately in the priest's house, usually in the presence of his rutual assistants; as in so many Tengger services, ritual efficacy does not depend upon popular ritual participation. The next day there is a similar ritual announcement to the gods, this one performed on the cliffs above the sand sea, just prior to the priest's descent into the sacred Mt. Bromo terrain. This ceremony similarly does not usually involve collective worship. In recent years, however, seven Hindu reform villages in the Tengger northwest have begun coordinating what was previously a ritual service performed by individual priests, so that now the predescent incense announcement has been elaborated into a large ceremony witnessed by thousands of villagers from seven villages. This participatory elaboration of a traditional ritual scheme is consistent with other efforts by the Hindu reform movement to develop a more congregational mode of worship (Chapter 11). Thus far, however, the innovation has not spread to other corners of Tengger.

The Kasada ceremonies culminate with the invocation of the Mt. Bromo deity and the presentation of offerings. Although extended over two days and celebrated by people in all Tengger communities, the sequence of events that leads up to and includes the meeting at Mt. Bromo is really just an elaborated variation on ritual themes common to most Tengger ceremony. The means and ends of most rituals respect the same general pattern: through priestly prayer, the deities are brought into this world and given homage with offerings brought by ritual participants and purified with holy water by the priest. The ritual sequence always begins with the priest's utterance of the prayer of incense announcement, recited by the priest as he holds an unlit piece of frankincense before his mouth. Only at the completion of the prayer does he place the incense rock on the hot coals of his incense brazier (the *prapen*), thereby creating the smoke which, in theory, conveys the prayer message to the gods. This ritual of announcement is the minimal ritual act. No liturgy can occur without it, and, in large rites, it must be performed again before each new phase of worship. Where it stands by itself—announcement alone, without the invocation of the deities and the presentation of offerings—this prayer of incense announcement is given a special name, the *semeninga*, or "announcement," "informing." The announcement may inform the gods of an impending ritual service, an important recent event (such as the birth of a child), or the intention of an individual to carry out some major ritual obligation.

By itself, then, an incense announcement does not invoke the gods but merely informs them of some fact. Where the deities are also invited to descend to a ritual service and receive the homage of the living, the priest extends the prayer of announcement to include an appended prayer of invocation. To invite deities in this fashion, however, is to take responsibility for their reception once present. It is absolutely improper to invite the deities without food offerings. Specially arranged offering trays (*sajenan*) of cooked meat, rice, and sweets must be prepared by one of the priest's assistants (Chapter 9), and these must then be purified by the priest with holy water prior to their presentation to the gods. Only after a prayer of purification, therefore, does the priest invite the gods to consume the invisible "essence" (*sari*) of the foods thus presented. The offerings' material remains are not destroyed, and may be redistributed to ritual participants after the service. Having invited the gods to enjoy the offerings, the priest concludes this basic ritual sequence with a formal ritual obeisance (*sembah bati*); his hands in prayer position and reciting a prayer, the priest draws his hands to his waist three times. This completes the minimal ritual sequence that must greet the gods whenever and wherever they are invoked. If there is additional ritual work to be done (marriage, the blessing of the dead, and so on), it always takes place after this initial and invariant ceremony of spiritual invocation, reception, and worship. The general goal of all Tengger ritual is to bring about some kind of blessing. Blessing comes only through the deities' presence, and the deities can be made present only through the neatly prescribed patterns of priestly liturgy.

This, then, is the basic pattern of spiritual interaction which in theory underlies all Tengger liturgy. A service can be condensed into a single five-minute ceremony, or, as here in Kasada, extended over several days with repeated appeals to the deities. *Sajenan* offerings may be presented just once, or they may be repeatedly offered over the course of three, four, or even five days. The core liturgical service, finally, can stand alone (as in small rites), or it can be complemented by gay social festivity including dancing, drinking, and dining. From this perspective of ritual elaboration, Kasada is a large ritual in terms of social scale but it is extremely simple in terms of liturgical detail. Its prayers are short and simple, and there is no dancing or feasting. (Back in the village the day after the Mt. Bromo ceremony, however, villagers exchange food gifts [ater-ater] of sticky-rice cakes with neighbors and relatives.) No other rite, however, mobilizes people from the entire mountain territory in common ritual service. It does so, moreover, for an especially important purpose. Mt. Bromo, Tengger believe, is the center of their world. According to popular opinion, the deity worshiped there is no ordinary spirit, but an ancestor turned god who gave his life so that his descendants could live in peace and harmony.

Popular belief thus assumes that it is this ancestral guardian who is invoked Kasada night at the base of Mt. Bromo's northern slope. At midnight on the evening of the ceremony, villagers come by the thousands to the ritual site, bearing small offerings for the services about to begin. Merchants from the lowlands ring the site, selling food, drink, and household goods at small stands illuminated by gas lanterns. Youths from the urban lowlands also saunter about the crowd's perimeter, enjoying what is for them a carefree escape from the city. Interspersed among the crowd of Tengger worshipers, however, are small groups of Chinese and lowland Javanese, some from far-away corners of Java. Many of them bear offerings for presentation to the spirit of Mt. Bromo. Their presence indicates that Kasada's ritual symbolism has a wider appeal than to Tengger alone.

Tengger priests are at the center of attention. They sit cross-legged in a long line atop a concrete stage located in the sand flats at Mt. Bromo's base (called the *poten*). Before them stand their ritual implements: a metal incense brazier (*prapen*), a bronze holy water beaker (*prasen*), a bowl of betel and bananas, and an assortment of offerings brought by villagers seeking individual priests' direct appeal to the spirit of the mountain prior to the Kasada services proper.[1] Above the *poten* stage stand tall bamboo poles decorated with long streamers of red and

---

[1] These personalized appeals to spirits are known as *ujar* in Tengger, *nadar* or *nazar* in Muslim areas of Java. For Tengger, an *ujar* is a spiritual contract made by an individual with the spirit of a particular territory, sanctioned by the priest. The supplicant usually requests some favor of the spirit, such as success in agricultural enterprise, and promises to return with offerings at some later time if the request is granted. Muslim Javanese who undertake *nadar* sometimes deny flatly that such vows have anything to do with a spirit; they prefer to identify *nadar* with the magical power of words (see Keeler 1982). Typically, however, Tengger are much less reluctant to identify the source of an *ujar's* efficacy with a spirit agent.

white cloth. Mid-point on the stage, there is an even larger arch of flowers, palm leaves, bamboo, and colored paper. The whole scene is illuminated by electric lights (introduced in the 1970s), creating a bright bubble of color in the desolate wastes of the midnight sand sea.

The services begin with a welcoming address from the chief priest (*lurah dukun*). Speaking through a microphone he greets the assembled crowd, and asks forgiveness for any inadequacies or inconveniences which may arise in the course of the night. Shifting from *kromo* Javanese to Tengger *ngoko*, he then recites a short tale which explains the origins and purpose of the Kasada ceremony (see below). Concluding his address quickly, he takes his seat at the center of the line of priests. At his signal, the priests turn away from the crowd to face Mt. Bromo, and begin. Each priest takes a piece of frankincense into his right hand, moves it to this lips, spits gently three times, and begins to pray. The priests' eyes are closed in concentration, and their voices barely audible even at a close distance. Completing his prayer, each priest places the incense on the coals of the incense brazier, and, as the smoke wafts up to the heavens, touches its edges with the tips of his fingers on his outstretched hands. As the incense crackles and smokes, he takes his holy water beaker with his left hand, moves it through the smoke of the incense, and, with his right hand, takes his leaf-and-flower anointer and sprinkles holy water to his left, center, and right, purifying the offerings to be presented to the spirit of Mt. Bromo. Hands held in prayer position, he then draws his hands to his waist three times in obeisance to the now assembled gods. With this, the liturgy is done, and the people may begin their ascent to the volcano, to throw their offerings into its crater.

Those years when there is a new candidate for the priesthood, villagers delay their departure so as to observe his initiation. The ceremony is brief, without additional offerings. The initiate comes to the center of the *poten* stage, under the archway of palm-leaf and flowers. As the other priests watch, he kneels facing in the direction of Mt. Bromo, his arms outstretched and his palms turned heavenward in a gesture of supplication. He wears no special dress. He is supported from behind, however, by an elder priest. This man places his chest to the back of the youth, and extends his arms around the initiate's body in such a way that he supports the young man's own extended arms. The ritual scarf of the priesthood (the *sampet*) is in turn wrapped around the shoulders and arms of the elder priest in such a way that it extends around his back out front to the initiate's hands, from which its ends dangle. At a sign from the chief priest, the initiate begins his slow and deliberate recitation of the Kasada prayer of invocation, in a voice which, unlike that of the elder priests moments earlier, is clear and audible. It is the same prayer as recited by the priests themselves. A collective *inggih* (yes!) from the elder priests acknowledges the initiate's successful completion of the prayer and, with it, his admission into the priesthood. From this point on he may begin study of the full corpus of priestly prayer (Chapter 9).

The priests need not accompany villagers to the lip of the Mt. Bromo crater. Villagers complete the night's ceremonies themselves, throwing their offerings into the crater's depths. (Although most priests are now unfamiliar with the term, elder priests sometimes refer to these offerings as *pahoman*, probably from the Old Javanese *homa*, "fire offerings," cf. Pigeaud 1962:II:22.) Unlike village-sponsored rituals, all offerings are prepared by individual households; there are no collectively prepared objects from whole villages or nonhousehold organizations. Just inside the lip of the crater, a small number of men vie to catch food, animals, or money before such offerings fall too far into the crater below. Tengger insist that all such scavengers are non-Tengger. The spirit of the mountain, however, consumes only the invisible essence of the offerings, hence the scavenging, while resented, is tolerated. Having presented their offerings to the mountain, villagers set off immediately for home; by the time the sun is clearly visible in the sky, most Tengger are gone, leaving the sand sea to bands of lowland youths and petty merchants packing up their portable stalls for the return trip to the lowlands.[2]

---

[2] Until the 1950s, when large crowds made the full service impossible, the ceremony at Mt. Bromo's base was complemented with another at the lip of the crater. I should also note that there are other activities that occur during the course of Kasada night which involve non-Tengger. The most interesting of these occurs at the famous Widodaren Cave, on the slopes of the mountain of the same name adjacent to Mt. Bromo at the center of the sand sea. A small stream flows from inside the cave to the sand sea floor below, where it disappears. Tengger and non-Tengger folklore alike identifies this stream as the source for water that flows to communities below the highlands. During the main night of Kasada celebration, dozens of people gather in the cave to make *ujar* vows to its guardian spirit. The *ujar* here is similar to that undertaken by Tengger at the base of Mt. Bromo, with the important difference that the men who act as ritual intermediaries for such vows are not Tengger priests, but *juru kunci* ("caretakers") from Muslim communities in the hill regions just below Tengger settlement. These ritual specialists recite prayers that address the Prophet Mohammad, Allah, and Islamic saints alongside more Tenggerlike spirits of the Mt. Bromo region. Not all of these celebrants, it is important to note, are entirely removed from Tengger tradition. Many whom I met come from communities which, three or four generations ago, were Tengger, and at least some ritual specialists are descendants of Tengger priests who converted to Islam. Although they now identify themselves as Muslims, these men frequently use fragments of Tengger prayer in the *ujar* ceremonies, and some utilize Tengger-style ritual implements. Tengger priests tend to look suspiciously at such men, referring to them derisively as "little dukuns" (*dukun cilik*). One Tengger priest once explained to me that his father used to visit the Widodaren cave regularly,

51

Myth and Ritual Meaning

The effort to interpret any religious ritual immediately encounters two problems: what things to emphasize in what is an almost infinitely detailed stream of social behavior, and whose perspective to adopt when we speak of an actor's experience. The first problem can be resolved at least in part in the course of confronting the second, since an interpretive account of ritual action takes as one of its central concerns the exploration of those things the actors in a ritual performance regard as being of central importance. This actor-oriented approach to the problem of meaning does not exclude investigation of things that may not figure directly in actors' experience of a cultural event. In analyzing the Kasada rite, for example, it is helpful to note that its imagery of a sacred mountain at the center of the world is a familiar theme in Southeast Asian Indic tradition (von Heine Geldern 1942; C. Geertz 1980:227; Hall 1981:247). Here in Tengger, however, the association of such an axis-of-the-world with royalty or political hierarchy—an association common in Old Java and other areas of Southeast Asia—is entirely absent. This sacred mountain has an ancestral face. Such an observation sheds comparative light on Tengger tradition, although it does not directly contribute to our understanding of the ritual's meaning for contemporary Tengger.

From a more sociological perspective, one can examine the segregation of roles and responsibilities in a ritual to find clues as to whether the social organization of the event affects actors' perspective on the rite and its symbolism. The core Kasada ceremony, for example, vividly illustrates the profoundly different roles of priests and people in Tengger religious ceremony. The priests alone perform the initial incense announcement to the gods back in the village. At Mt. Bromo, they alone occupy center ritual stage. It is their chief who acts as master of ceremonies, and they as a group who burn incense, anoint the offerings, and recite the prayers that invoke deity. Throughout all of this activity, there is no point-for-point activity on the part of ordinary villagers. Their role is primarily to bear offerings. They recite no prayers, and, sitting quietly in small groups, most are at too great a distance to hear or see clearly the priests' ritual invocation. Although there is in the Kasada rite the kind of "central situational focus" (Irvine 1979:779) commonly associated with formal social events, the focus is not socially organized in such a manner as to draw ordinary villagers into the specific detail of the liturgy.

---

but he himself no longer bothered, since the place was always crowded with "Muslims and Madurese." Many ordinary Tengger, however, continue to visit the cave, both during the month of Kasada and every thirty-five days on *jumat legi*, "auspicious Friday."

The social organization of ritual performance thus makes it difficult to give special status to the verbal and gestural symbolism internal to the liturgy as if it were the primary source for popular understanding of the rite. As will become clear shortly, to do so would risk neglecting the interpretive diversity of Kasada. The separation of priestly and popular roles, however, does not mean that villagers receive no instruction concerning what priestly ritual involves. Having observed much the same patterned activity in smaller rites back in the village, they are familiar with the general form of priestly invocation and worship. Moreover, whatever the obscure detail of the liturgy itself, most villagers are familiar with the Kasada tale that the chief priest recites prior to the religious service. The Kasada tale is popularly regarded as the most authoritive account of the origins and meaning of the festival. As we shall see, however, its commentary does not resolve the problem of ritual interpretation as much as it displaces it to another level of interpretation and debate. I recorded the following version of the Kasada tale in the Tengger northwest:

In late Majapahit times there lived a priest named Kyai Dadap Putih who came from nearby Majapahit to meditate in the Tengger mountains. There he met a young woman, also from Majapahit, named Rara. Rara had left the lowlands in search of her lost father. At first startled to encounter Dadap Putih, she was happy when she learned that he too was from Majapahit. He adopted her as his daughter, and she him as her father, and together they meditated in the Grinting forest (in northwest Tengger).

Around this same time a young man from a village in the Tengger mountains set out in search of his long-lost uncle, who had disappeared while meditating in the mountains. The youth was named Joko Seger, and he searched the forests of southern Tengger and the mountains around Mt. Bromo. Finding no sign of his uncle, he began to meditate (*tapa*). On the thirtieth day of meditation, he encountered Rara, and fell deeply in love with her. They meditated together on the mountain known as Ragaulan, she so quietly that Joko Seger gave her a second name, Rara Anteng, Rara the tranquil.

The youths returned to Rara's home to meet Kyai Dadap Putih. They informed him of their desire to marry, and he approved. They were thus married, and lived happily in the mountains. Yet after many years they were still not blessed with children. They thus set out for Mt. Penanjakan, above the Mt. Bromo sea, where they meditated for six years: one year facing east, another to the south, another to the west, one to the north, one to the earth, and another to the sky. In their meditation they made a vow to the spirit of Mt. Bromo: if blessed with twenty-five children, they would return to give the youngest to the mountain. At this moment Mt. Bromo exploded into a bright flame, an auspicious sign.

Soon thereafter Rara gave birth to her first child, quickly followed by another, then another, and another, until there were twenty-five children. Parents and children lived happily in villages around Mt. Bromo. One night, however, the spirit of Mt. Bromo appeared to Rara in a dream. He requested that she make good on her promise to give him the youngest of her children. Rara awoke at this point and told Joko of her dream. Frightened, they fled with all twenty-five children to the forests around Ngadas, in southern Tengger. En route, however, the earth shook and the mountain burst into a flame so enormous that it stretched out and stole the youngest child from the family's midst. The child taken was the boy known as Dewa Kusuma. With this the mountain suddenly became still, and there was heard a voice: "Hey, gather together father, mother, sisters, brothers. I leave you today so that you may live together forever in peace and blessed harmony. I, Dewa Kusuma, become your representative (*wakil*) before He Who Is All Great (Sang Moho Agung). I ask but one thing of you: each year, may you return to this place and remember this day, the fifteenth night in the month of Kasada. Bring with you a portion of the fruits of the earth and water, and give this as offering to the mountain. Through this your crops will be abundant and your children many. This alone I ask of you, to remember me each year this way."

Having heard Dewa Kusuma's request, Rara Anteng, Joko Seger, and their twenty-four children left to open the forest around Mt. Bromo and its sand sea. Cultivating the land, they built homes and founded villages throughout the region. From that day too they have remembered the words of Dewa Kusuma.[3]

---

[3] There are several versions of the Kasada tale, the major difference among them being the names given to the key ancestral figures. Kyai Dadap Putih is also sometimes accorded a much larger historical role. Elder villagers in one southern Tengger community once told me that Dadap Putih would one day return to reestablish Buda religion throughout Java. The messianic implication is clear. Typically, friends in the more cosmopolitan villages of the Tengger north denied ever having heard such an account, and were a bit shocked by it. Another version of the Kasada myth explains the creation of the sand sea (see Raffles 1965:I:333). In this tale, Dadap Putih's daughter is requested in marriage by the demon king Bima. Unable to refuse his request directly, Dadap Putih devises a plan by which to frustrate Bima's proposal. Bima can marry Dadap Putih's daughter, the father explains, only if he can construct a sea in the Tengger mountains in a single night. Bima sets out

At first sight, one of the most striking things about this myth is that, although it purports to explain the origin and meaning of the Kasada festival, it seems to pay remarkably little attention to many of the most conspicuous features of the rite itself. The myth makes no mention of the priests, the detail of the liturgy, or the initiation ceremony that sometimes accompanies the Mt. Bromo rite. Rather than myth "expressing" the same themes as seem to preoccupy the rite (as some theories of myth and ritual might suggest), the Kasada tale appears preoccupied with sociological issues in no direct way evident in ritual performance. In particular, it tells a story of social relationships, relationships that themselves speak to the question of Tengger identity and its relation to Islam. The Kasada story is a moral tale that legitimates tradition by linking it to founding ancestors, and insisting on the importance of both for the living.

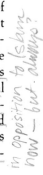

in opposition to Islam — but always? now?

These larger themes are developed almost inconspicuously, through the arrangement and rearrangement of family ties between characters in the tale. The first such rearrangement of social relationships is that between Dadap Putih, a Majapahit priest, and Rara, a daughter in search of her father (also a priest). Both actors are from Majapahit, and both are from non-Muslim priestly families, facts that ease the actors' transition into a new relationship, that of adopted father to daughter. We hear few other details of their relationship, but the social message is clear. A non-Islamic identity is being constructed.

Rearrangement of family ties is also the thematic device by which Rara meets her future husband, Joko Seger. Interestingly, Joko is presented as a mountain boy, not a Majapahit priest. (Some versions of the Kasada tale are more explicit on this detail.) He too is in search of a kinsman who has disappeared while meditating in the forest, and in his search Joko encounters and falls in love with Rara. Although so far dramatic action is lacking, the story has already made several important points, from a sociological point of view. Joko and Rara, we know, will become the ancestors of modern-day Tengger. They are non-Muslims and, equally importantly, their relationship is in some sense a happy

---

on the task, and almost succeeds. Seeing the demon's progress, Dadap Putih and daughter begin pounding rice so as to awaken livestock who, thinking it is morning, begin to cackle and crow. Bima is fooled by the ruse and thinks that he has failed. In disgust, he throws away the coconut with which he has scooped the land to make the sand sea, and the implement becomes Mt. Batok (adjacent to Mt. Bromo). Variants of this same myth, interestingly, are used in Central Java to explain the construction of the Lara Jonggrang temple at Prambanan, and in West Java to explain the origins of Mt. Takubang Prahu. Consistent with their posttraditional scepticism toward most of their mythic heritage, contemporary Tengger reject this portion of the Kasada tale as entirely fantastic.

marriage of Majapahit priestliness and mountain culture. The characters move about, moreover, in a territory familiar as that of contemporary Tengger, a fact which underscores all the more their appropriateness as ancestors. No word has yet been heard, however, of one important figure, the spirit of Mt. Bromo.

Mt. Bromo is introduced in the course of the resolution of a problem internal to Rara and Joko's relationship: infecundity. Childless, Rara and Joko set out to meditate for six years, in the process orienting their meditation in a directional fashion consistent with a classification scheme found throughout Java and Bali (von Ossenbruggen 1977; Pigeaud 1977). The introduction of the spirit of Mt. Bromo into the story, however, is remarkable for how little is said as to who or what the mountain spirit is. No name is given to the mountain spirit. He is referred to simply as a *dewa* (spirit or deity), and he remains faceless, at least at this early point in the tale.

The bargain struck with the mountain spirit resolves Rara and Joko's problem of infecundity, but does so only by introducing the equally serious problem of how to make payment on the promised child. The last of the twenty-five children must be sacrificed, but its parents are now unwilling. The repayment problem clearly reveals that the benevolence of the mountain spirit is tinged with an element of malevolence. The life-giver now threatens to become life-taker. Some versions of the Kasada tale make this point clearer by recounting that the mountain sent plagues and droughts to press its point. In the present tale, parents and children simply attempt to take flight, but the mountain is too powerful, and an arm of flame reaches out to steal the youngest child from their midst.

At this point in the story we realize that a remarkable transformation has occurred. The voice heard emanating from the mountain is now no longer that of the faceless mountain spirit, but of Dewa Kusuma, the child himself, and it is he who instructs his family and their descendants to preserve his memory and respect the Kasada tradition. The previously menacing spirit of the mountain has, in effect, been humanized. In his place there stands a benevolent relative or, for modern Tengger, an ancestor-guardian. Whoever or whatever the earlier spirit was is now conveniently neglected, repressed by this humanistic inversion. The new relationship of Tengger to the mountain spirit is one of kinship and spiritual debt; this ancestor gave his life for his descendants. The genealogical relationship affirmed in the myth is, of course, secondary to the spiritual reciprocity underscored. The myth defines modern Tengger not only as kin, but as members of a larger moral community, defined by this act of ancestral self-sacrifice. The myth thus seeks to create a moral imperative for the Kasada ritual's cultural reproduction. The rite must not be forgotten; it is the very basis of Tengger welfare.

The Kasada Myth in Javanese Tradition

As with all cultural products, the visible text here assumes a less visible corpus of knowledge and an assortment of axioms as to the nature of the world. The Kasada myth does not create its cultural images from nothing, nor does it establish its moral authority in the simple act of its enunciation. The text assumes a larger cultural universe and a shared body of experience. It then attempts to take and rework these in the service of a more distinctive cultural message.

At its most general level, for example, the Kasada myth employs an assortment of cultural ideas that Tengger share with their non-Tengger neighbors. The symbolism of mountains, gods, and ancestors, for example, is a powerful one in Javanese tradition.[4] In ancient Java, mountains appear to have been identified as the celestial abode of the ancestors; in Hindu-Buddhist times, this symbolism was accommodated to Indian cosmology by identifying the mountains as the home of Hindu deities (Pigeaud 1962:IV:8). Even in contemporary Islamic Java, one occasionally hears that the Hindu gods did not die with the coming of Islam, they simply retired to mountaintop abodes.

This same linkage of mountains and supernatural power takes a somewhat more diffuse form today in the lowland villages below the Tengger highlands. Throughout the region, Mt. Bromo and Mt. Semeru are often referred to as the domains of especially powerful territorial spirits. These are the spirits, for example, who are thought by syncretic lowlanders to control the flow of life-giving waters from the mountains to the village below. The identification of mountains with water and fertility is a

---

[4] It is not just in Java, moreover, that this symbolic configuration is important. In Balinese cosmology, mountains play a similarly pivotal role in world cosmology. Mt. Agung at the center of the island is identified as the abode of the gods (Belo 1949:9) and the "navel of the world" (Covarrubias 1937:6). Wind directions also take this mountain as the axis, mountainward being north no matter where one stands on the island (Swellengrebel 1960:39). As is also the case in Tengger, Balinese priests always face toward the central mountain when performing religious services. Similar mountain imagery is prominent in many areas of Indonesia. The Kedang of East Indonesia, for example, trace their origins back to ancestors who emerged from the crown of a mountain near the center of the island (Barnes 1974:34). Historically, too, mountains played an important role in Old Javanese cosmology. Preeminent among Hindu Javanese deities, Siva was identified as "Lord of the Mountains" (Pigeaud 1962:IV:8), an association which may have been related to the earlier identification of mountains as the abode of ancestral gods. It is also, of course, a common epithet of Siva in India.

common one in Old Javanese literature (Pigeaud 1962:IV:45), and, as we shall see, it reappears in the prayers that accompany the Tengger priests' liturgy for Kasada. In Islamic villages below Tengger, however, more syncretic communities still celebrate annual village ritual festivals (*slametan desa, slametan tuyo*) designed to give homage to the spirits of the mountains and insure the flow of their waters. The cult of the *danyang banyu* (water spirit) is one of the most resilient in syncretic Islamic communities throughout the region. In what is perhaps the most common element in the annual ritual at the water spirit's spring, a female dancer is accompanied by village leaders to the site, where the woman and the men dance after presentation of offerings to the water spirit. The sensuality of dance is supposed to appeal to the water spirit and insure the abundance of its waters. This same diffuse symbolism of mountains, water, and supernatural force informs the still extensive participation of lowland villagers in the Tengger Kasada festival, the only such Tengger ritual event in which non-Tengger remain an important presence.

There is a consonance of cultural imagery between the Kasada myth and syncretic Javanese belief at a somewhat more abstract level of interpretation, as well. As noted above, the myth humanizes Mt. Bromo's countenance by shifting attention away from the earlier (and somewhat menacing) spirit of the mountain to an ancestral guardian, Dewa Kusuma. The myth in effect identifies the Mt. Bromo worship as a cult of guardian ancestors. In doing so, the myth brings the ritual's meaning in line with a general body of cult activity throughout syncretic Java, the so-called *punden* cult of first-founding ancestors. This is one of the most widespread of cults found throughout rural Java. Almost every village in Java has a *punden* ancestral shrine identified as the burial place of a person or couple thought to have been the village's founder(s). These first-founding ancestors are referred to as *cikal-bakal* or *akal-bakal*. In all but the most modernist reform Muslim villages, there is usually also some kind of village ritual festival held each year to remember these ancestors and request their blessing (see C. Geertz 1960:26-28). In more orthodox Muslim communities, the ancestors may simply be identified as saintly predecessors thought to have had special powers (*keramat*), who are perhaps still capable of interceding with Allah for the community. In more syncretic Javanese communities, by contrast, these same ancestors may very well take on the attributes of full-blown guardian spirits with strange powers and equally strange appetites. In at least some Javanese villages, such ancestors may be difficult to distinguish from territorial spirits known as *danyang*, spirits not specifically identified as ever having been human. The cultural idiom in both types of traditions is much the same, but the specific beliefs derived from the idiom vary significantly.

Whatever the precise nature of the spirit beliefs, the *punden* ancestral shrine is usually the site of an annual village festival intended to cleanse the village of all ill influences and insure its welfare in the year to come. Here again particular beliefs vary according to religious orthodoxy: *kejawen* Javanese tend to identify the source of ill influence as evil spirits who must therefore be ritually banished from the community; more orthodox Muslims insist that the ritual is simply intended to secure God's blessing. The social activity involved in the cult is at any rate much the same, and it shows a striking resemblance to Tengger cult activity at Mt. Bromo:

> Every village family is expected to send a representative with a tray of appropriately prepared food to the ceremony. . . . All residents are equally blessed by the founding spirit, and equally obligated to participate in the yearly village ritual by which the whole community collectively honors him. (Jay 1963:33)

From the perspective of Javanese *punden* cults, in short, the Kasada festival looks like a *punden* ceremony writ large, operating at a regional level rather than just a village one. The form of offering is much the same, its obligation similarly incumbent upon all, and the ancestral idiom through which it is explained uses similar terms of ancestry and territory. Indeed, Tengger often refer to Dewa Kusuma as a "first-founding ancestor" (*cikal-bakal*) and to Mt. Bromo itself as a *punden* shrine.

All of this suggests that the main body of imagery used in the Kasada myth strays very little from that common throughout rural Java. The ancestral idiom is reworked, however, to convey a message that is more distinctively Tengger: that this acephalous assortment of mountain villages is in fact a people, one that shares a common ancestry, territory, and religion. By linking its ancestors to Majapahit, moreover, the myth uses this Javanese ancestral idiom to affirm an identity at variance with that of larger Java. Tengger are non-Muslims, linked, the myth suggests, to the religious traditions of Majapahit.

There remains a problematic air about the Kasada tale nonetheless. It is remarkably tight-lipped about the details of priestly worship. There can thus be no question here that "myth regarded as a statement in words 'says' the same thing as ritual regarded as a statement in action." (Leach 1954:13-14). There is nothing in the tale to explain why this cult of a first-founding ancestor, if that is what it is, requires the presence of priests wielding a complex liturgy. The relationship between myth and rite is problematic because it is informed by a more pressing cultural

59

preoccupation. Hence the myth conveniently overlooks those aspects of the ritual tradition which are glaringly inconsistent with Javanese notions of *punden* and ancestry. The tension between what is said in the myth and the detail of the rite becomes all the more apparent when one examines that portion of the ritual service least accessible to ordinary villagers, the priests' prayers at the base of Mt. Bromo.

The Prayer to the Mt. Bromo Spirit

When, during the Mt. Bromo ceremonies, the chief priest finishes his welcoming address and turns to join his fellow priests in prayer to Mt. Bromo, he recites an invocation similar to this one given to me by a priest in the Tengger northwest:

> Hong mandara mountain your servants together we offer homage to you Lord (*Tuhan*) in this place we sit with the people of the region to bless the earth in this month Kasada. (We do) this so that the spirit Lord of the Body will enter the nine openings of the body and diminish the cravings of our spirits and add to the heavenly waters, flow so that they may flow over those made beautiful, anoint so that all may be anointed. Those from the greater region and the four directions to the center (have come). All come as one, seated together your children from the four directions to center in this the *poten* place we are as one all together your servants.

> Hong mandara mountain your servants together we offer homage to you Lord in this place. We sit with the people of the region side by side in ceremony. We present the essence of the offerings. In our souls there is but one thought and one attitude. (If what is offered be) deficient let that deficiency be corrected. (If what is offered be) excessive let that excess disappear. Those from afar approach, those close join in closer yet. Here is the Spirit Lord of the Body, enter the nine openings of the body, diminish the cravings of the soul so that the heavenly waters may be increased flow anoint together all as one together in one seat from the greater region here together as your servants.[5],

As with most of the Tengger priests' prayers, this one begins with the Javanized form (*hong*) of the Indian sacred syllable *om*. The prayer addresses itself to the spirit of the "mandara mountain" (*mandara giri*), a sacred mountain image common in Indic religious literature throughout

---

[5] There is considerable variation in the form of this prayer among priests.

Southeast Asia (cf. Pigeaud 1962:IV:45; Hall 1981:42). More relevant to our immediate concerns, however, is the fact that the prayer emphasize a distinction unmentioned in the Kasada myth: priestly "servants" (*pulun*) of the mountain are distinguished from the people for whom they perform the ritual service. Why the priests are recognized as playing a special ritual role becomes clearer later in the prayer: it is they who will become vehicles for a spirit known as "Lord of the Body" (*Sang Hyang Dewa Raga*). The spirit enters the body of the priests through their nine orifices (eyes, ears, nostrils, mouth, penis, anus). The numeral symbolism of this image is suggestive of a parallelism between the body and the nine wind directions so commonly referred to in Javo-Balinese tradition (cf. Covarrubias 1937:296). The most astounding fact here, however, is the deity's possession of the priest. There was no hint of this event in the Kasada tale. From the perspective of the prayers, however, the priest is no mere descendant among a similar mass of descendants. He becomes a vehicle for the deity's work. The product of that spiritual labor will be a most critical resource, holy water. The image of spirit possession as a means for the creation of holy water is also found in the Hindu tradition of Bali, where, to take but one example, the high caste *pedanda* priest is possessed by none other than Siva (Hooykaas 1973:10; 1977:51).

Reversing the movement of people to the world center, here at Mt. Bromo the holy water created by this ritual act is enjoined to flow out from the center over the land and its people, making "beautiful" or holy all those who have assembled for the worship. Here again the Javanese symbolism of mountains, water, and supernatural power appears in yet another context, although knowledge of this imagery is restricted to Tengger priests. Curiously, here in the prayer one hears absolutely no mention of the spiritual personae so important in the popular Kasada myth. Indeed, little of the detail of the prayer finds direct counterpart in the myth. Both speak of world renewal, but the spiritual means of that renewal are described quite differently in each: ancestral guardianship in one, spirit possession and the flow of holy water in the other.

Although the detail of the prayer may seem strangely removed from that of the Kasada myth, the prayer for the most part seems far more richly consistent with other aspects of the priests' ritual performance. The pivotal role of the priests, for example—unmentioned in the public myth—is entirely intelligible from the perspective of the prayers. The priests are central figures in the ritual drama because it is they who are possessed by the deity. The prayers also make better sense of the gestural symbolism involved in the initiation of new priests. The candidate, recall, kneels facing Mt. Bromo, his arms extended in a gesture of supplication, and his back supported by an older priest. The young man is making explicit with his body the action described in the prayers: he is receiving the spirit of the mountain. For this powerful encounter the young initiate needs the support of an elder priest. And it is this act—possession by the world deity—which makes a man a priest. Nothing is heard of this in myth or public comment.

The paradox of Tengger tradition is that so little of this richly textured and "integrated" liturgical symbolism is appropriated in popular accounts of what ritual involves. The problem is not simply that priests know more than lay people. It is a qualitative problem as well: the tone, idioms, and personalities of priestly prayer are fundamentally distinct from those heard in popular myth. All the more curiously, the priests by at least one action appear to endorse the truths of public myth. It was the chief priest, after all, who recited the Kasada tale to the people at Mt. Bromo just prior to his recitation of the liturgical prayer.

Judging by the more candid comments of several priests, however, the chief priest's apparent endorsement of the Kasada myth is not without its ambiguities. In private discussion, for example, one priest confided to me that he had "never quite understood" the Dewa Kusuma tale. His prayers, he noted, make no mention of such a spiritual figure. Another priest confessed to me once that Kasada was "not really" intended to honor Dewa Kusuma, at least not "first of all." It is directed he said to God All-Mighty (*Sang Hyang Widi*). Like most priests, however, this man was extremely reluctant to point out such doctrinal discrepancies in public. More important than any public comment on the meaning of the rite, he said, was the need for people to continue "coming together" and to support the performance of the rite itself. The power and mystery of the liturgy remained, whatever people's interpretations.

Conclusion

The discontinuity between myth and priestly liturgy should not be overplayed. Both, after all, speak of blessing and renewal, and both give spiritual urgency to annual celebration of Kasada. In addition, whatever myth's claim to doctrinal authority, it is clear that on a less elevated level of commentary, villagers understand more of the ritual tradition than myth bothers to mention. They are familiar, for example, with the general Javanese symbolism of mountains, spirits, and water. They understand the logic of priestly prayer, with its pattern of announcement, invocation, offering, and worship. They appreciate that these ritual acts require a specialist capable of mastering the method and power of the liturgy. Even at a distance, therefore, ordinary villagers understand more of ritual than public myth bothers to account for, and they are sensitive to the fact that, as they themselves say, the liturgy contains truths too powerful for apprehension by the spiritually untutored.

It would be a serious error, then, to assume that myth is here an accurate reflection of what people really know. We risk impoverishing our understanding of people if we directly equate the truths of a myth or ideology with their thought, or the actual content of their knowledge. Clearly all of these things are related, but the relation is far more complex than some analyses of myth might suggest. One important reason for this is that the constraints to which myth responds are quite different, and more sociohistorical, than those that directly impinge on the less formalized, and less conspicuous, thought processes of a person. Accounts like the Kasada tale are intended to be public documents. They serve a practical function in public culture as landmarks for public discussion and as guides for collective self-definition. They are thus subject to a rigorous process of evaluation and social control. Inevitably, people understand much more than is elevated to prominence in this fashion. Why should the Kasada tale have emphasized the themes of ancestry and territory while ignoring much of the even publicly perceived detail of priestly rite? The answer to this question requires that we investigate more than the internal structure of a cultural discourse. The discourse is informed by a history and social dialogue subject to cultural politics. It thus must be understood as situated speech, *parole*, not as a timeless system of rules, a *langue*.

Much of the appeal of the Kasada tale, for example, can only be understood in light of an ongoing dialogue, even a cultural contest, between Tengger and an Islamizing Java. There is another version of the Kasada myth that underscores this point clearly. This version is sometimes heard in villages on the periphery of the Tengger highlands, in communities once Buda but now Islamic. The story centers again around Rara Anteng and Joko Seger, Tengger ancestors. We learn that they are married and, as before, living in the Tengger mountains. In this version of the tale, however, Rara and Joko already have twenty-five children. The difficulty plaguing their relationship is thus not infecundity but poverty. They have so many children that they are miserably poor. Here again, however, Rara and Joko devise a plan: if given riches by the spirit of Mt. Bromo, they will sacrifice all twenty-five of their children to that same spirit. Unlike the earlier version of the Kasada tale, in other words, the spiritual contract here is to be put to the service of selfishness, not parenthood. Rara and Joko go through with their scheme, throwing all of their children into Mt. Bromo's fiery depths. The parents are then rewarded with wealth. It is at this point that the new moral to the story becomes most apparent: the sacrificed children, we learn, are miraculously spared Mt. Bromo's fiery waste. They enter the mountain's depth only to reemerge from the earth at a spring located just below the Tengger territory. The children then immediately set out for Mecca, where they study with the Prophet Mohammad. They later return to Java to become missionaries of Islam. Rara and Joko, by contrast, remain non-Islamic, the evil ancestors of modern Tengger.

Like the earlier version of the Kasada myth, this one is a moral tale, preoccupied with questions of ancestry, identity, and religion. The message of the earlier version of the tale, however, has been clearly inverted. Tengger ancestors were evil, Islam was their children's salvation. Together these two versions of the Kasada myth present two sides of an intense argument concerning cultural legitimacy. It is this argument which helps to explain the topic and focus of public comment on the meaning of Kasada. The question of cultural self-definition has taken precedent over a more sustained excursion into the detail and doctrine of priestly liturgy. A people's tradition and identity are at stake.

Variants of the "Tengger" version of the Kasada tale are reported in Dutch sources as early as 1785 (Rouffaer 1921:304). This same anxious preoccupation with the legitimacy of their tradition and the identity it supports appears again and again, however, in other areas of popular Tengger tradition. This concern often explains what is backgrounded and what highlighted in popular commentary on ritual. We see in all of this an interesting example of an important kind of symbolic process: one body of cultural symbolism, priestly liturgy, has become a symbol for meanings larger and other than those formalized in its liturgical depths. The liturgy has in effect been drawn into a social dialogue on identity, and imbued with meanings it does not, in any formal sense, carry within. In the meantime, the canons encoded in the interior of the liturgy have been backgrounded from public dialogue. There is a more pressing cultural problem at hand. The meanings repeatedly affirmed in public accounts of tradition address this problem, in part by appealing to a wider sense borne by villagers to ritual performance. Although evoked and reworked in the ritual process, this more general experience of self and others is not created in ritual alone, but in the more diffuse interactions of Tengger social life.

· 4 ·

VILLAGE WORLD AND VILLAGE CONCEPTS

Village organization in Tengger is not rent with the ambiguity of social forces that characterizes the region as a whole. Social activity within each Tengger community is characterized by a much greater overlap of political, economic, and ritual bonds than is found elsewhere. Although, as in other modern Javanese communities, local government has been formally integrated into a national political administration, villages still exercise corporate control over a variety of resources and activities, including land, water rights, cooperative labor, and ritual. Government-sponsored programs are usually also implemented at a local level by the officials of each community. With the exception of the priesthood, there exists no formal system of kinship, polity, caste, or status between individuals or groups in different villages. In short, the village is the locus of a number of primary social activities. Thus ritual does not have to swim against the organizational current of local life; it reinforces it.

In addition, at the community level many of the distinctive ideas on the popular meaning of the ritual tradition are forged and made compelling. In particular, the ancestral idioms so important in popular commentary on the ritual tradition are here given an experiential depth. On a practical level, there are important functional linkages between ritual and other social practices that serve to recreate a social environment in which such elevated idioms appear consonant with the general order of social life. It is above all in the village, in other words, that Tengger come to regard the priestly tradition as a popular heritage. The imprint of ritual ideas reveals other lessons as well, however, lessons which suggest that in preserving its popular role, the ritual tradition may have acquired new meanings and neglected earlier ones.

Settlement as Adaptation and Symbol

The political instability that plagued the Tengger region through the end of the eighteenth century (Chapter 2) played an important role in the location of old settlement sites. Villages founded prior to the territory's pacification still tend to be situated on hillsides and valley walls, high above the fields villagers cultivate, and often uncomfortably distant from the springs to which they go for water. Older settlements are also densely nucleated. Houses are separated by only a few feet, with no

65

yard or garden land between buildings, and no trees to obscure vision of the surrounding countryside. Houses are built on terraces (*gampengan*), the defensive functions of which appear to have consisted of the good view they gave of the countryside and the fact that they made passage through the village difficult except by way of the main road.

The extension of colonial administration into the highlands beginning in the late eighteenth century facilitated a gradual relaxation of regional tensions, a relocation of some villages, and a dispersion of later settlements. Occasional violence still plagued some communities, however. Even in the 1830s, Dutch reports indicate that some southern Tengger villages were attacked by bandits (Jasper 1926); village histories in one southern village still recount that in the mid-nineteenth century the entire village was temporarily deserted after a particularly vicious brigand raid left the village chief and several other men dead. Shortly after this period, however, the population began to increase throughout the area, largely as a consequence of lowlanders' immigration. Mountain "waste lands" were opened to the cultivation of coffee, tea, and other cash crops. Lower-lying Tengger settlements were surrounded by more dispersed communities of Madurese and Javanese.

For the most part, Tengger villages today differ little in appearance from neighboring non-Tengger mountain communities. The earlier style of Tengger house with its narrow front, veranda, and a single long back room (Raffles 1965:I:330; Domis 1832:331) has in this century given way to a dizzying variety of house styles, ranging from simple wooden shacks to large plaster and plate-glass homes built by carpenters from the urban lowlands. The distinctive wooden carvings once seen in Tengger (Jasper 1926:6) have also all but disappeared in favor of a more finished, lowland-style home. As in dress and other decorative fashions, Tengger here display little social conservatism, eagerly imitating styles first developed in the lowlands.

More remarkable perhaps is the fact that Tengger villages have no temples, statues, shrines, or other structures that might announce to an outsider the non-Islamic faith of the community. When visiting my village of residence, one lowland professor lamented what he called the absence of indigenous art. Tengger villages, he complained, looked "just like a Javanese village." The ubiquitous aestheticism of Hindu Bali finds no counterpart in these villages. Elder villagers report that in earlier decades old statues and religious implements had been found in fields and forests, but none remain today. The exceptions are the priest's ritual implements, brought out only during ritual performance (Chapter 9), and a small whitewashed building found in some but not all Tengger communities, called the "shrine of worship" (*sanggar pamujan*). This building is built on an axis determined by the village's relation to Mt. Bromo, and its four-cornered roof is supposed to face in each of the four wind directions. The structure is not really a temple—it has no altar, statues, or interior decoration, and it is only large enough to accommodate the village priest, his assistants, and a ritual witness or two. During village rites (in those communities that use the building at all), the priest performs his services inside the structure, while the women who bear offerings to the ceremony stand outside, out of sight and sound of the priest's celebration. Religious architecture thus replicates ritual social hierarchy. Since men do not carry ritual offerings in Tengger, they usually do not attend these village ceremonies at all, except in communities influenced by Hindu reform.

There is thus little in the layout of the village that might provide a clue to its religious tradition. At a less visible level, however, clues exist, particularly in a variety of things that repeatedly seem to turn the attention of the community toward Mt. Bromo. Such an orientation is evident, for example, in the open-skied ancestral shrine known as the *sanggar* ("place of worship," not to be confused with the *sanggar pamujan*). The primary purpose of this simple shrine is to serve as a touchdown point for guardian spirits invoked to the village. From this perspective, the shrine functions much like a Balinese village temple (*pura*) (see Belo 1953:2). In appearance, however, there is little visible similarity between the two. The Tengger shrine is a natural setting, little reworked, with none of the *pura*'s sculpture, columns, archways, walls, or pavilions. It is just a small, open-air yard located at the base of several large trees, with a small offering stand made of wood at its center. The Tengger shrine is thus virtually indistinguishable from similar village shrines (*danyang, sanggar*) found throughout rural Java, usually dedicated to village ancestors or territorial spirits (C. Geertz 1960:26).

In one point of detail, however, the Tengger shrine is distinctive. It never lies within the village, as is common in the lowlands, but always outside of it on a hillside located on a direct line leading from the village to Mt. Bromo. In a few Tengger villages, this Bromo orientation is replaced by a southern skewing, that is, the shrine lies on a hill to the south. The directional orientation is in both cases remarkable, because a number of other activities show a similar directional skewing. This was the orientation, for example, in the Kasada ritual, which moves from village to Mt. Bromo. More interestingly perhaps, priests in ritual always pray facing in the direction of Mt. Bromo—except in that handful of villages where they face to the south. A southern orientation reappears in burial: the body of the deceased is always placed in the ground with its head to the south. According to some nineteenth-century accounts,

67

finally, houses in old Tengger communities were built with their front door facing toward Mt. Bromo (Domis 1832:351; van Lerwerden 1844:82). Houses are no longer built with this orientation.

Contemporary Tengger have no consistent explanation for this directional skewing toward Mt. Bromo and/or south. When I pointed it out to them, villagers were as curious about the directional system as I was, but they confessed that they could see no unifying scheme to the whole thing. Instead they explained each instance of directional symbolism differently. Burial with head to the south, for example, was simply said to be the inverse of the Muslim practice of burying the dead with their head to the north; Buda people do the opposite of Muslims. Priests face Mt. Bromo, I was told, to honor the Mt. Bromo spirit. No one could come up with any deeper reason than village tradition to explain why in other villages the priest usually faces south while praying.

An additional clue was forthcoming several months into my research. In one or two Tengger communities still (and many more forty years ago), there is a different directional system from that used elsewhere in Java, although the words for the compass points are the same. In these Tengger communities, the direction of Mt. Bromo from a village is or was always referred to as "south." All other compass points adjusted themselves accordingly, so that, while all communities agreed that Mt. Bromo was "south," the other directions varied according to where one stood in relation to the volcano. The fact that Tengger used to identify the direction of Mt. Bromo as south, helps to resolve the problem of why some priests today pray toward Mt. Bromo and others pray to the south. In the old days, priests everywhere prayed toward Mt. Bromo and thereby toward the "south." When communities began to adopt the general system of directions used in Java, some priests continued to pray toward Mt. Bromo, but a few prayed toward the more widely accepted "south." This explained the confusion over southern skewing as opposed to Mt. Bromo directionalism, but it left unexplained why Mt. Bromo would have been identified as south in the first place.

Such a link between mountains and a directional system is not without precedent in Indonesian tradition. In Bali, particularly, the four cardinal directions are similarly defined in relation to the mountain lying at the center of the island. Whereas in Tengger to move mountainward is to go south, however, in Bali movement toward the mountain is identified as "north." In both cases, all the other cardinal directions then adjust themselves to this mountain anchor. The parallelism between the two systems is thus restricted at best. And it still leaves unexplained the basic question as to why Mt. Bromo would be identified with south.

Anthropologists are used to seeing in such symbolic parallelism evidence of an underlying meaning. Was this Tengger system only a coincidence?

There is an answer to the question, but its key term lies hidden from public view in the depths of priestly prayer. In the most important of the priests's prayers, the deity Brahma (Bromo, Brama) is identified as the god of south and of fire. The identification is made in the course of a longer classificational scheme that identifies Iswara, Brama, Mahadewa, Visnu, and Siva as the deities of east, south, west, north, and center, respectively. A similar parallel classification of deities and directions is common in Balinese liturgy (see Belo 1953:27; Covarrubias 1937:296) and in pre-Islamic Javanese literature where, as noted earlier, the god Brahma is also identified with Mt. Bromo (Gonda 1952:132).

From the perspective of prayer, all of the directional symbolism seen in Tengger—*sanggar* location, burial position, orientation in worship, the location of the house door, the cardinal directions—looks like a complex spatial mnemonic designed to remind a people of their spiritual orientation to a mountain and a god. The fact that modern Tengger do not recognize this common weave of meanings, however, indicates once again the depth of the interpretive dilemmas Tengger have faced in maintaining their religion in a changing Java. The directional symbolism seems as if it should be integrated around a common theme. Such structural parallelism is the kind of thing that anthropologists are trained to seize upon as a key to the organization of public meaning. In the face of this Tengger data, we might be tempted to bypass native experience and proclaim the complex structure of the system as integrated, unified around an underlying meaning. The Tengger example shows clearly, however, that if our goal is not just an archaeology of knowledge but an ethnography of experience we can take no such shortcut around real people's reports and experience. To confuse our "unified" account of Tengger spatial symbolism with the meanings experienced by Tengger today would be to lose sight of the history and pathos of Tengger religious tradition. Whatever the meanings earlier attributed this system of directional symbolism, modern Tengger interpret it, as they must, against the background of more pressing, proximate concerns, informed by the realities of a Java far removed from fifteenth-century Hindu Majapahit.

Settlement and Spirits

One cannot discuss concepts of space and society among Tengger without at some point considering their understanding of the spirit world. The Kasada myth indicated how intimately concepts of space, society, and spirits are related: Dewa Kusuma and family are eldest of the Tengger ancestors and, because of that status, guardians of the region and its people. One finds similar linkages between society, space, and guardian spirits at lower levels of social organization. Like the region, for example, each village has its own assortment of guardian spirits, consisting (at least according to the most common view) of those human ancestors who first cleared the forests for cultivation and established a human settlement. As far as most villagers are concerned, it is these first-founding guardian ancestors (*cikal bakal*) to whom most priestly ritual is directed.

The terms villagers use to refer to different types of spirits underscore this ancestral bias in popular perception of the spirit world. Lay villagers generally distinguish two categories of spirits, "guardian spirits" (*roh bau rekso*) and "family spirits" (*roh leluhur*). As far as the average villager is concerned, both categories of spirits consist of ancestors. Guardian spirits, however, are more powerful and distant than family spirits. Although it is assumed that each guardian deity is an individual with a particular identity and life-history, in actual practice villagers almost always refer to guardian spirits collectively and anonymously. With the important exception of the Dewa Kusuma myth, there are virtually no myths concerning guardian spirits of territory and society. Guardian spirits form a faceless group, more powerful than and spiritually superior to ordinary family spirits, but faceless nonetheless. In what way these higher spirits are more powerful is not an issue about which there is widely agreed upon or neatly formulated explanation.

Unlike the more distant guardian spirits, family spirits (*roh leluhur*) are clearly recognizable, close, and familiar. Family spirits consist of the souls of recently deceased relatives, with whom one is thought to retain an active social relationship. Each family has its own set of family spirits, and the list is clearly demarcated in village tradition. It includes one's grandparents, parents, siblings, children, and grandchildren, when and if any of these relatives are deceased. Other people will, of course, have a different set of "family spirits," defined by the same limited set of kin relatives; *roh leluhur*, in short, form a kind of spiritual kindred around the nuclear family. It is these spirits toward whom a family has an active ritual responsibility. During village and household rites, one brings out a piece of clothing from each such spirit, wraps it around a small flower-and-leaf figurine, and has the priest invoke the souls of these relatives to tables where they are presented with food and drink. Relatives beyond the grandparental generation are presumed to have found their "place" (*panggon*) in heaven and thus to have joined the assembly of more august guardian spirits of the village, and hence are no longer accorded such simple homage.

The spirit world is thus thought to have a clear hierarchy, even though both categories of spirits are "ancestors." That hierarchy is defined in proportion to social distance from the living, or in proportion to the breadth of social group over which a spirit is guardian (spirits of region are more powerful than village guardian spirits). These are the principles underlying Dewa Kusuma's role: as eldest ancestors, he and his family are the most august guardian spirits. Village guardian spirits are thought in turn to be "descendants" (turunan) of this first ancestral family, although there are no myths to establish such relationships between regional spirits and their village descendants. The living residents of each Tengger village, finally, are said to be "descendants" of the first-founding ancestors of the community. Here, however, the potentially metaphoric quality of the descent idiom reveals itself. Recent immigrants to Tengger villages are said to be "descendants" of village ancestors just as much as anyone else. The descent relationship is more a social or spiritual fact than it is a genealogical one.

At the base of this spiritual pyramid are the souls of the family dead (roh leluhur). The least august of the ancestral spirits, these family spirits are nonetheless the most familiar and beloved; in fact, these spirits provide the cultural image for popular perception of the more remote and powerful guardian ancestors. The Dewa Kusuma myth weaves its tale not in terms of distant world deities wielding incredible powers, but in terms of family ties and devotion. A similar familial quality is projected onto all guardian spirits. An interesting consequence is that Tengger tend to show much less ambivalence toward guardian and territorial spirits than do most lowland Javanese of kejawen sympathy. Lowland Javanese more readily tend to identify territorial spirits as nonhuman or semi-human, and thus potentially malevolent; guardian spirits quickly become predatory if not placated (cf. Jay 1969:326; C. Geertz 1960:26). Tengger tend in the first instance to speak as if guardian spirits are in fact benign ancestors. At lower or less ideological levels of generalizations, however, villagers' views on the spirit world become more complex, we shall see.

This two-tiered vision of spiritual hierarchy is the most commonly acknowledged scheme among Tengger, and many villagers speak as if these were the only categories of spirits. More doctrinally sophisticated villagers, however, are quick to point out that Tengger also recognize a monotheistic God above and beyond ancestral and territorial spirits. They speak of this God with a variety of terms, most of them consistent with terms used by other Javanese. Like Javanese Christians, for example,

71

Tengger will on occasion refer to God as Allah, particularly when speaking with Muslims. More commonly, however, Tengger refer to God with the more neutral terms *Tuhan* (Lord God) or *Sang Hyang Widi* (God All-Mighty). Most modern Tengger prefer the latter term, because it has a distinctive Javanese ring to it, and because it has long been used in priestly liturgy. Hindu reformists in Tengger have thus been able to claim, quite rightly, that Tengger have long recognized a single Godhead, as is required under the Indonesian constitution. Hindu Balinese reformists similarly emphasize the importance of such a belief, and, coincidentally, also generally refer to their God as *Sang Hyang Widi*. The fact that the expression is the same in Tengger and Bali is a happy historical coincidence, though the term seems to have had a longer popular usage here in Tengger.

Sang Hyang Widi is conceptualized in terms quite different from those applied to other spirits. He is a kind of God above gods, the ultimate and unmoving source of spiritual power. Unlike family or guardian spirits, this deity cannot be invoked in priestly worship. He is never presented with offerings. He is associated with no single territory or social group. His identity, in short, is of a much more general and elevated sort. For precisely this reason, however, many villagers find modernist leaders' exhortations concerning the importance of *Sang Hyang Widi* ethereal or abstract. Popular conceptions of the spirit world (*donia alus*), after all, are built up from relations in the visible world (*donia kasar*), and are thereby infused with the warmth of family ties and community allegiances. *Sang Hyang Widi*, by contrast, is a Supreme Deity of all humans. For Tengger who increasingly define themselves in less local terms, *Sang Hyang Widi* seems destined to play an ever more critical cultural role.

Sang Hyang Widi's reformist role aside, most villagers explain priestly ritual with reference to the simple categories of family and guardian spirits. The purpose and meaning of the liturgy are never linked to the various demons, witches, devils, or spooks so common in *kejawen* discussion of the spirit world (see C. Geertz 1960:16-29). Tengger spiritual commentary has a much more familiar and even familial bias. Indeed, many villagers speak as if there were a point-for-point parallelism between levels of social organization and the hierarchy of the spirit world. The highest deities are the oldest ancestors, and it is they who are guardians of Tengger territory. In cultural fact, however, Tengger spiritual thought is not so neat. In particular, there is a problem of public idiom and personal knowledge. Although the dualistic model of family and guardian spirits is the one most popularly used in discussion, it fails to make sense of everything Tengger know or believe concerning ritual and the spirit world. The problem becomes particularly apparent when one moves from more formulaic discussion of religious doctrine to an examination of ritual detail.

In talking about different types of ritual offerings, for example, Tengger recognize not two but three different categories, and most people insist that each category corresponds to a different class of spirit. The first and most important type of offering is the *sajenan*, or offerings that can be presented only to guardian deities by the priest in formal liturgy. Each type of *sajenan* has a name and is distinguished from others by the color, shape, and number of its component food items. Each *sajenan* is also, at least in theory, supposed to serve a different spiritual function. The *tumpeng walagara* or "wedding rice cone," for example, is supposed to bless bride and groom in marriage, and also bless the village in which they reside. In any single rite, there may be several *sajenan*, each with its own spiritual function, and each contributing to the assortment of spiritual interests served in religious ceremony. In practice, of course, many villagers do not know the particular purpose of different *sajenan* offerings, but in general they understand this more general principle that each type of offering serves different spiritual purposes. Villagers also understand that only the priest can present *sajenan* offerings to spirits, since he alone has mastered the sacred language and gestures with which guardian deities are invoked and worshiped. Equally importantly, no other type of offering can be presented to any other type of spirit before the priest has invoked and worshiped the intended spirit recipients of *sajenan*. Ritual protocol clearly signals spiritual hierarchy.

The second category of food offerings are those given to the more familiar category of family spirits (*roh leluhur*), foods called *suguhan* or, literally, "foods for guests." As the name indicates, this category of offerings is identical in shape and form to foods given to ordinary living guests at a ritual festival. There are thus no specially named subcategories of *suguhan*, nor recognized spiritual functions served by the offerings other than feeding family spirits. These offerings can be presented by nonpriests, since no special ritual language or gestures need to be used when presenting them. A household simply set these foods out next to the clothes of deceased relatives during ritual festivals. In more elaborate rites, the priest may then burn incense and present the foods, but in smaller ceremonies an ordinary person may do so. The restriction on offerings holds whatever the case: offerings to lesser spirits can be presented only after the priest has given worship to higher guardian deities.

The third category of ritual offering, called *tamping*, presents even greater difficulties for the ancestral orientation of popular belief. Visually as well as ritually, *tamping* look like leftover offerings for a low-class category of spirits. *Tamping* are bite-size offerings prepared from portions of the *sajenan* offerings after the latter foods have been presented to the gods by the priest. A pinch of meat, a spoonful of white and yellow rice, a rice-cake sweet, a slice of banana, all wrapped rather rapidly in a small shred of banana leaf—some ten to fifty (as one wishes) of these small offerings are quickly prepared in the moments after the priest completes his worship of higher spirits. An ordinary villager prepares the *tamping* from foods that he tears from a larger *sajenan*. Once readied, the *tamping* are then carried by a household youth to the village spring, road intersections, the cemetery, bridges, old trees, underpasses, and any other spooky spots where, as villagers say, a person is likely to be "bothered" (*diganggu*). The bearer of these low-status offerings throws them casually to the ground at each destination, without the slightest ritual gesture or word, usually to the delight of a village dog or two, well accustomed to local ways. The spirit recipients of these offerings benefit from none of the familial warmth of other spirits; one priest neatly summarized the *tamping*'s intent as, "eat this, and don't bother me."

Whatever the apparent evidence of ritual practice, there is no consensus among villagers as to who the intended recipients of the *tamping* are. Villagers do not speak of spirits of the "lower world" as in Bali (Swellengrebel 1960:40), although the ritual practice here looks very similar. Indeed, some Tengger flatly deny that the *tamping* have anything at all to do with spirits. A good friend—who also happened to be an assistant to the village priest—once vigorously denied my suggestion that *tamping* must be intended for some kind of earth or underworld spirit. The purpose of these offerings, he insisted, is simply to "spread the blessing" of ritual by redistributing food sanctified by the presence of higher deities. In his view, in other words, the *tamping* are not offerings for spirit agents, but vehicles for the contagious conveyance of spirit force. This informant went on to deny outright the existence of any spirits other than family spirits, guardian deities, and Lord God (*Tuhan*).

Although the priest for whom this ritual assistant worked later apologized to me for his assistant's "lack of understanding"—the *tamping*, the priest assured me, are definitely intended for bothersome spirits of the fields, forests, water, and earth—the incident illustrates well the tendency among Tengger villagers to play down or deny the importance of nonanthropomorphic or nonancestral spirits. In almost all discussion, Tengger speak first and most confidently about family and guardian spirits, both of which are conceptualized in ancestral terms. Besides the example of *tamping*, however, there are other instances in which this ancestral orientation fails to take account of the true complexity of Tengger religious tradition. Whereas the Kasada myth of Dewa Kusuma clearly exemplifies this Tengger tendency to "ancestralize" even territorial spirits, the myth implicitly recognized a more complex spiritual reality. Mt. Bromo itself was first identified not with Dewa Kusuma the ancestor, but with a less-than-human mountain spirit who had a distinctly ambivalent relationship with humans. Only after this mountain spirit had threatened Tengger with fiery destruction was he, in effect, "replaced" by Dewa Kusuma, a benignly self-sacrificing ancestor. Another instance in which ritual practice seems to acknowledge a less than benign spirit is that related to what Tengger call the "water offering" (*tumpeng banyu*). This offering is in effect a low-status *tamping*, but it is the only *tamping* prepared more elaborately than the normal bite-size *tamping* laid out around the village: it includes a full cone of cooked rice (*tumpeng*) and, more significantly, a cooked breast of chicken, its chest cavity ripped open to expose the animal's heart and liver. The offering also includes a small flower-and-leaf figure that looks abstractly human. The whole water offering, in other words, looks like an offering intended to substitute for what the water spirit may really desire, a human. The form of the offering is consistent with villagers' views that the village spring is a potentially dangerous place. It is less consistent, however, with the ancestral and benevolent bias of most Tengger accounts of the spirit world.

When presented with such specific examples of ritual activity, the majority of villagers acknowledge that, indeed, not all spirits are either benign or ancestral. Malevolent earth spirits abound—at the spring, cemetery, road intersections, livestock huts, and a variety of other spots around the village. Despite the evidence of ritual practice, however, other villagers, a minority, deny the existence of such earth spirits, keeping their beliefs in line with the ancestral view of spirits repeatedly affirmed in most popular narrative. This same resistance to the idea of malevolent or nonhuman spirits influences Tengger attitudes on the ghosts, ghouls, and witches of lowland *kejawen* tradition (C. Geertz 1960:16-29). As Javanese speakers, Tengger are familiar with the terms for these beings, and some villagers privately express belief in their existence. Most villagers, however, either deny the existence of these spirits, or minimize their importance for Tengger by insisting that they do not live in the cool mountains of the highlands.

There is, in short, a dual emphasis to Tengger spiritual belief. On the one hand, the central role of priestly ritual focuses popular attention on those spirits said to be worshiped in the liturgy. In those domains where there is no explicit ritual precedent—possession, witchcraft, divination—villagers are hesitant to express beliefs, and often minimize or dismiss certain spiritual beliefs by asserting that they are not part of Tengger tradition. Lay villagers thus tend to mold their image of the spirit world around what they have heard are the spirits involved in priestly liturgy. A few exceptional individuals aside, the Tengger priest never plays the role of a shaman, medium, or diviner. Confronted with any kind of spiritual problem—an eclipse of the sun, a birth, illness, or death—the priest does much the same thing that he does in other ritual performances: burns incense, anoints offerings, and gives worship to assembled deities. Whatever the mysteries of lowland *kebatinan* sects, or the strange powers of Blambangan's famous experts in black magic, priestly rite is the anchor for popular belief in Tengger. It does not so much generate a fixed body of spiritual dogma as provide a field and focus for beliefs deemed "Tengger."

As we have seen, however, there are limits to this ritual focusing of belief. Some ritual practices consistently point to a third category of spirits with less familial characteristics. Tengger mythology consistently ignores the evidence of such practice. In private discussion, meanwhile, most villagers acknowledge the existence of earth spirits and others prone to pestering and predation. But this belief is never accorded ideological legitimacy in statements of public doctrine. The latter show instead an ancestral bias, stronger in fact than is generally the case among Java's *kejawen* Muslims. The bias is no doubt related to the way in which Tengger talk about identity and religion with much the same set of concepts: those of ancestry, guardianship, and the continuity of the world of the living with that of the dead. "Javanist" Muslims, by contrast, are at least to some degree influenced by Islamic doctrines that regard as devils spirits not explicitly acknowledged in Islam, a view that has become more prominent with the popular advance of reform Islam. Tengger experience little such ambivalence. Ancestral spirits are at the center of popular cosmology as well as of folk sociology. Popular understanding of these spirits is in turn influenced not just by religious tales or popular doctrinal comments, but by patterns of interaction in the village world.

Formal Roles and Organization

Like other Javanese, Tengger refer to the territory and population of a rural community as a *desa*. Prior to the end of the nineteenth century, most Tengger *desa* consisted of a single nucleated settlement sharing certain resources and social obligations: agricultural lands, a group of *pamong* village officials, a village priest, a spirit shrine, a cemetery, a spring or stream, a system of cooperative labor (*kerja bakti*) for village maintenance, and an assortment of religious festivals financed by the community. The social integrity of the traditional *desa* was disrupted at the end of the nineteenth century. At that time, the colonial government attempted to simplify rural administration throughout Java by consolidating smaller *desa* into larger administrative villages, called *kalurahan*. In Tengger, most of the new administrative villages incorporated two or three of the earlier nucleated villages. The latter still retain their old names, as well as most of their earlier corporate resources. The larger administrative village, however, has its own chief (*petinggi* in Javanese, *lurah* in Indonesian) and secondary officials, identical to those associated with village administration in other areas of Java (except that there is no Islamic religious official). The modern administrative village is also responsible for such things as public buildings, schools, and the public lands provided as compensation for village officials. Government-sponsored programs such as boy scouts and family planning are also coordinated by officials of the administrative village, not of each old *desa*.

For many activities, the traditional nucleated *desa* remains the primary locus of social organization. Kin ties, task groups, and ritual exchange relations (Chapter 10) are most commonly organized within its borders. Until recently, people from outside the *desa* were barred from renting or buying village land, a restriction that has been abolished in most communities since independence. Road construction, increasing social stratification, and educational mobility are likely to continue to reduce the integrity of Tengger communities. By Javanese standards, however, Tengger villages remain remarkably vital, and are characterized by a greater overlap of economic, kinship, and ritual ties than is typical of many lowland communities. It is important to note, however, that the internal organization of Tengger communities has never made them impermeable to change from the outside. Since the early nineteenth century, all Tengger communities have absorbed large numbers of non-Tengger immigrants. The modern Tengger community was thus probably never "closed corporate" (Wolf 1967) as such. Its social organization has not effectively excluded outsiders as much as it has influenced their manner of assimilation, once arrived.

The distinctive nature of Tengger village organization is seen, first of all, in the poverty of formal groups, titles, status distinctions, honorary names, and other social markers that might formally define the status of one person or group against another. This social "poverty" is a relative fact, of course, in this case relative to the surrounding Javanese society. In the traditional Tengger village, one found no corporate organization other than that of the family and the village itself. Nor were there, or are there today, castes, status groups, social clubs, or religious societies. Contrary to the pattern in some rural Javanese communities (see Koentjaraningrat 1967:267; Jay 1969:313), Tengger do not distinguish actual descendants of the village's founders from recent immigrants to the community; everyone is equally descendant from those guardian ancestors, irrespective of actual genealogy. Tengger also do not distinguish named classes of villagers according to their rights to own village land, another common feature of lowland village organization. With the exception of the priest, village officials, and such nontraditional roles as the local school teacher, there are in the Tengger village no groups or formal statuses that might visibly contradict ideological affirmations of the village as an assembly of independent and equal (*pada-pada*) households.

There is a second ideological aspect to village organization that serves to link these social values to key concepts of Tengger religion. Social relations within the Tengger community are consistently differentiated from those entertained with non-Tengger Javanese. In social interaction as in speech (Chapter 2), Tengger abide by interactional styles that consistently signal their allegiance to certain Tengger values, values which, while by no means egalitarian, are nonetheless less differentiating than those seen in lowland society.

Tengger kinship neatly reveals this pattern of an almost silent Tengger inflection of Javanese social values. Tengger kinship terminology is much the same as is used throughout Java. Kinship is organized cognatically and generationally, with a largely symmetrical distribution of rights and duties between maternal and paternal relatives (H. Geertz 1961; Koentjaraningrat 1960). Here, as throughout most of Java, there is no corporate kin group larger than the family. Although task groups are frequently recruited from among close relatives, there is no term or concept as such for the kindred, and the social boundaries of occasional task groups are flexible, varying according to the task at hand and the relatives available.

Marriage patterns reveal one distinctively Tengger variation on Javanese kinship. As throughout Java, marriage occurs outside the third collateral line, and does not create formal bonds between parents-in-law (*besan*). Tengger, however, take the "depoliticized" pattern of marriage even further. Bride and groom, for example, often first initiate their engagement privately, only later announcing the agreement to their parents, a pattern of youth initiative that is uncommon in lowland society (H. Geertz 1961:57). If, after engagement, premarital and nuptial gifts are exchanged, the Tengger groom gives them directly to the bride, without the formal aid of a procession of relatives, as is common in the lowlands.

In address between kin the ideological emphasis of Tengger kinship is clearest, however. In standard dialects of Javanese, it is considered important that a child address his parents' siblings with qualifying adjectives that define that sibling's relationship as elder to or younger than the parent. Father's elder brother is thus called "big father" (*pak de*), or, similarly, mother's younger sister is called "little mother" (*bu lik*). Such distinctions serve to distinguish close aunts and uncles from the more distant generational superiors uniformly addressed as "father" (*pak*) or "mother" (*mbok, mak, bu*). Tengger address ignores this differentiating emphasis entirely. Parental siblings are uniformly referred to as "father" or "mother," just like one's true parents, as are all of one's parents' generational cohorts. True parental siblings thus receive no greater terminological distinction than anyone else in the village.

A parallel deemphasis of intragenerational seniority and genealogical precision occurs among people of the same generation. Cousins, for example, are all called by personal name rather than by a kin term. To do so elsewhere in Java would be considered a sign of extreme familiarity or disrespect (H. Geertz 1961:24), since cousins are addressed with terms that indicate whether they are an elder or younger "sibling." Not surprisingly, the same pattern obtains between siblings in the Tengger family: Tengger siblings address each other by personal name, whereas polite usage in the lowlands requires that age distinctions be recognized with an appropriate kin term. Husbands and wives in Tengger also avoid the lowland pattern of addressing each other as "elder brother" and "younger sister," relying instead on the personal name. Thus all the relationships which in the lowlands are terminologically modeled on the elder-younger sibling relationship are in Tengger address identified in much less hierarchical terms, as personal-name relationships.

The system of address in Tengger, in short, is simpler than that common in lowland society, and tends to reinforce a kin-based, generational vision of the village world. An individual addresses people of his parents' generation uniformly as "father" or "mother." In practice, of course, kin and nonkin can be distinguished, but there is no emphasis on doing so in public address. The same principle applies to people of one's grandparents' generation, or one's great grandparents. Close kin are not differentiated from others. Personal identity is also less consistently marked for fine discrimination of status. Personal names may be used in public address, and, in general, they play a much more prominent role here than in many other areas of Java. The Central Javanese pattern of changing to a mature, less individuated name at marriage (Keeler

1982) does not occur here. With the birth of a child, parents optionally acquire a teknonym—"father of so-and-so," or "mother of so-and-so"— but even this index of adult status is not considered mandatory. Many people continue to be called by the name given them at birth.

One irony of these less differentiated styles of address and status is that, in modern Tengger, they continue in the face of a general awareness that they violate the more consistently hierarchical styles of standard Javanese usage. In speaking of these things, Tengger would often apologize to me, saying they knew they "should" use the "more polite" forms of lowland address even though they did not. As always, Tengger are all too Javanese in their sensibilities. All these small twists of address and name, however, are important because they influence villagers' sense of the community—and of the "Tengger way"—as nonexclusive, familial, and less formal than the non-Tengger world. The inattention to age differentiation and genealogical precision divests kinship of its potentially disruptive exclusivity. In place of a world of close and distant kin, Tengger speak of the village in terms of simple generational differences, each generation identifying its cohorts for the most part by personal name. Hollowed in public speech of any strict genealogical referent, kinship terminology is thus all the better suited for another task: providing an idiom for all social relations within the village.

The kinship model is, of course, an idealized image of social relations, but it is ideologically and practically important, nonetheless. In myth and other cultural narrative, villagers are consistently identified as "relatives" (*dulor*), defined by their common descent (*turunan*) from the community's founding ancestors. The idiom is more a social fact than a genealogical one, since recent immigrants to the community are just as much "descendants" of the founding ancestors as anyone else. Related to this perspective is the fact that, when they do speak of status differences within the community, villagers tend to speak as if status were simply a matter of seniority and generation. Village leaders, for example, are chosen for their role in local government according to their wealth, generosity, and ties with other members of the village's social elite. People refer to them, however, as "village elders" (*sesepuh desa*), and their relationship to other villagers is frequently compared to that of parents to children. Age is one of the least important of considerations in choosing village leaders, in fact; one regularly encounters village chiefs in their thirties. Such a way of talking about social hierarchy, however, allows one to recognize differences of status without sounding offensive or contradicting more ideological characterizations of the community. And although villagers prefer to speak as if status differences were primarily a matter of age, wisdom, and inner power, they know better, at least when it comes to privately evaluating the performance of any particular village official.

To refer to a fellow villager in terms of his or her wealth, by contrast, carries no such neutral moral tone. To call someone a "rich person" (*wong sugih*) is a highly charged statement, rarely made in public. Most villagers reject any suggestion that the village is internally divided between wealthy and poor. Yet in private, when talking about particular people, villagers readily speak of "haves" (*wong duwe*) and "have nots" (*wong ora duwe*). On several occasions people even pointed out to me that differences between the two have increased in recent years. Few of these villagers, however, would then go on to say that wealthy people are more powerful or even more highly respected. Their reluctance to identify wealth with status is not entirely a product of ideological obfuscation. Wealth *does* have an extremely ambiguous social status. It is only when it is channeled into appropriate domains, such as ritual festivity, that it conveys unambiguous prestige. As I discuss later, however, such moral restrictions on the use of wealth appear to be changing in the face of agricultural intensification and increasing socioeconomic differentiation (Hefner 1983b).

Status as seniority or generation involves the recognition of several distinct phases in the life process. Children are children, loved and indulged, but for those very reasons rather irrelevant to the scheme of status. Children's roles begin to change when they join their parents in the fields. Marriage continues this slow transition to adulthood, an achievement complete only when the married couple establishes an independent hearth and income. Newlyweds most commonly go to live with the parents of the bride, staying for an average of two to three years. Long before the end of that period, however, the young couple begins cultivation of land given to them by both sets of parents. Not long after their first harvest, the young couple boards off a corner of the maternal parents' home and sets up a separate kitchen. From this point on they are considered adult, and liable for ritual contributions, labor taxes, and other adult responsibilities.

It is parenthood, however, that completes one's coming out as an adult. Shortly after the birth of their first child, parents become sponsors of rituals for their children. They thus begin to participate actively in the ritual exchange system so important in the determination of a person's standing in the village (Chapter 10). This pattern of parental sponsorship of ritual festivals comes to a close when one's children have married and begun to sponsor their own rites. Grandparents then withdraw from the circuit of ritual exchange in which they have participated for most of their adult life, and they sometimes stop attending ritual

81

festivals entirely. Ritual festivals are an important social arena for people still actively establishing their standing in the village, but it is considered inappropriate for elderly men and women to take too active a role in such things. The elderly are respected, but they are also expected to be socially retiring. Even before death, grandparents are supposed to have transmitted the greater portion of their land and household wealth to their children and, in some cases, grandchildren. Some grandparents resist doing so for fear of becoming dependent or losing the attention of their children. Nonetheless, it is not uncommon in Tengger villages to see grandparents who live at the edge of extreme poverty, even while their now married children are sufficiently well off. Although most Tengger show little practical concern for mysticism or asceticism, there is a distinctly renunciatory quality to the role of the very old—a sense that a person should refrain from the pleasures of food, fine furnishings, and festivity.

It is, then, this generational vision of the village world that informs the relatively idealized notions Tengger have of status and village hierarchy. In actual life judgments of status are made in terms of far less abstract considerations. At high levels of generalization, however, villagers prefer to speak as if the village were an assembly of generational cohorts, ceaselessly marching as equals through the world, preceded by earlier generations and followed by later ones. This is the reality to which kinship terminology is so finely tuned, and this is the cultural vision that is reinforced by the absence of formally recognized groups, statuses, or titles. The two important exceptions to this undifferentiated scheme—village priest and chief (with, to a lesser extent, the officials he appoints)—are of special interest for an understanding of Tengger cultural history because both have been defined in part by their role in the stewardship of the ritual tradition itself.

Priests and Chiefs

To be eligible for office, priests (*dukun*) and chiefs (*petinggi*) must be able to demonstrate *tis* or *titisan*, a relationship of descent through maternal or paternal relatives back to some prior holder of the office. The term *tis* is etymologically related to the Javanese word for reincarnation (*nitis*), but, whatever speculation such a derivation might inspire, modern Tengger deny that *tis* has anything to do with reincarnation. Villagers are familiar with the religious concept, but few believe in it as a spiritual reality. *Tis* is instead said to be a relationship of descent that legitimizes one's eligibility for an office by virtue of the possibility of having the particular kind of spiritual power that runs in only some

families. In recent years, government supervision of elections and occasional direct appointment of officials have made the question of *tis*
irrelevant for candidates to most offices. However, people still speak as
if *tis* is important for becoming a priest.

The position of village chief is the most powerful of traditional statuses
in the Tengger village. The chief's responsibilities include a variety of
things identical to those associated with the role throughout Java: tax
collection; approval of land sale and rental; registration of births, deaths,
marriages, and divorces, as well as immigration and emigration; and
appointment of the various village officials who help in the performance
of these tasks (see Jay 1969:353). The chief presides with his fellow
officials over village meetings held each month to discuss government
programs, village projects, security, and other issues. Until quite recently
these meetings were open to all adult males; over the past several years,
however, government directives have required villages to replace the
earlier open meeting with a more restricted forum, consisting of village
officials and neighborhood representatives appointed by the village chief.

The Tengger *petinggi*'s role is more culturally distinctive, however,
in that it is also linked to a variety of important religious activities.[1] For
example, whenever the guardian deities are invited to descend to the
village for ritual festivals, the chief must be at the side of the priest
acting as a "witness" (*saksi*) to the deities' invocation. During the annual
all souls' festival, it is the village chief who first dances with the gods
invoked to the village shrine; the priest dances afterward. All household
festivals can be scheduled only with the prior approval of the chief and
priest. When such household rites include a formal invocation of high
guardian deities, the chief must once again be in attendance. Whenever
a cow is slaughtered for ritual offerings and feasting, the chief and the
priest are always given several choice cuts of meat as a "witnessing fee"
(*keretan, titi*). In the course of ritual feasts, the chief, priest, and village
officials are often invited to eat at a table specially prepared for village
dignitaries. The same men enjoy the exclusive privilege of dancing during the first of three nights of *tayuban* when such dancing accompanies
household or village festivities. At the end of such events, the village
chief and priest are always the first two people to receive food gifts (*ater-
ater*) sent out from the household sponsoring the festival. The list of
such ritual privileges goes on and on, extending into virtually all major
ritual domains. The village chief, priest, and village officials are all freed

---

[1] The responsibilities described here are less characteristic of the chief's role in communities of the Tengger northwest where, due in part to Dutch influence, village leaders
take a somewhat less direct role in ritual performance.

from payment of the annual religious tax (*torun*) used to support festivities during the annual all-souls celebration (Chapter 5), the most
important village festival of the year. At the birth of a child, the village
chief or his wife is supposed to be among the first to visit the mother
and child. At weddings, the chief and priest are often included in the
circle of "elders" to whom bride and groom come to pay their formal
respects. When the village chief first assumes office, he is blessed in a
special ceremony (the *mayu desa*) designed to "reinvigorate" the village
as a whole. These and other aspects of the village chief's role clearly
suggest that he is responsible not only for the secular welfare of the
village, but for its spiritual interests as well.

The village chief, however, never plays the role of ritual specialist.
He is witness to all important rituals, but is not qualified to be their
celebrant. The latter role is the exclusive responsibility of the Tengger
priest. Other villagers may be capable of muttering a prayer or two, and
some may claim special skills in lowland-style spiritual knowledge (Chapter
9), but only the priest can perform rituals specifically designated "Tengger." The division of ritual responsibilities implicit in all Tengger liturgy
is, in fact, neatly summarized in the relationship of priest and chief. The
priest alone invokes and addresses guardian deities, but, for all important
ceremonies, his labor is incomplete without the witnessing presence of
the village chief. Villagers themselves take note of this relationship,
identifying the chief's role as "witness" (*saksi*) to the invocation of
guardian deities with the relationship of a household head to his guests.
Guests would, of course, be dishonored were they not greeted and attended to by the head of a household.

Whatever their social prominence, however, chiefs and priests do not
constitute a distinct caste or social class. Priests are not brahmans whose
purity is posed in contrast with the secular authority of a princely caste.
Nor, to cite the Balinese example rather than the Indian, is the priest a
celebrant whose primary role is "to stage mysteries and raise incantations
around which the cult of royal divinity could gather" (C. Geertz 1980:125).
According to popular belief, after all, the guardian deities to whom
villagers direct their attention are, in some elevated way, ancestors,
equally ancestral to everyone in the village. At this rather idealized level
of cultural commentary, therefore, the social hierarchy evident in ritual
practice is subordinate to a theme of ancestral equality. In day-to-day
life, of course, the prestige and authority of any individual chief depend
upon a far more complex assortment of variables than prominence in
ritual. Chiefs are expected to be wealthy, and to be generous with their
wealth. They are supposed to distribute their favors widely, and avoid
anything that suggests an exclusive relation of patronage. Villagers take

all of these things into consideration when evaluating the performance of a particular chief, but make little mention of them in their more ideological statements on his role.

There is a practical logic to the relationship of priest and chief, one that creates an alliance important for the ritual tradition itself. There are social and economic rewards to the chief's ritual role, although they do not extend to ritual outside the village. During the Kasada festival, priests sit alone atop the *poten* ceremonial stage. No village chief is invited to speak, and none shares the limelight of the ritual performance. The priests' social distinction is here unqualified. When we turn to the village world, however, the positioning of roles in ritual performance changes. The chief always sits next to the priest, in effect basking in the glow of ritual performance. Priests and chiefs are thus allies in village rituals that implicitly affirm their social distinction. Thus ritual organization rewards the village chief for his support of the ritual tradition, so providing an important social incentive for that support.

Informal Social Interaction

Informal interaction is often a blurred domain in the sociologist's world of status and role, but it is nevertheless one in which the ideas and ethos of a people are shaped. This point is particularly important in Tengger, since it is in situational interaction, rather than formal organization as such, that much of what is distinctively "Tengger" is evident. It is in these interactions, too, that Tengger find experiential confirmation of the formal idioms so often used to describe the village world—idioms that identify villagers as "all the same" (*pada-pada*) or all "relatives" (*dulor*). Whatever the practical inequalities of political and economic life (some of which I discuss below), day-to-day interaction in Tengger is consistently skewed toward nonexclusive styles and aggressively informal tones. As with kinship address, these serve to give substance and compellingness to the relatively idealized idioms by which Tengger talk about themselves.

Something of this experience is evident in casual interaction on the streets of the village. There are in Tengger no mosques to serve as centers for social gathering, and the food shops that have recently sprung up around the highlands have not yet come to play the role of meeting centers common in many lowland communities. Every Tengger village, however, has its street corner where men regularly gather to stand and converse, their bodies shrouded against the mountain cold by *sarong* wrapped around their shoulders. Randomness and nonexclusiveness are the norm in all such informal gatherings. Although one man may take

85

the lead in telling a story, men converse as a group, other people laughing and interjecting comments throughout the discussion. It is considered impolite for two individuals to break off into a separate conversation. Individuals come and go, joining the group without greeting, and departing with a simple *ayo wis* ("OK that's it"). As in many other areas of rural Java (see Jay 1969:238), men tend to avoid close friendships, cliques, or other forms of exclusive interaction that might conflict with the open informality of public interaction. Hence the conversation is casual and open to all. Like other Javanese, Tengger refer to this aimless, collective conversation as *jagongan*, literally "to sit about," or "to sit about in casual conversation." Although it emphasizes qualities of informality and nonexclusivity widely stressed in village interactions, *jagongan* is for the most part a masculine prerogative. Women are free to come and go about the village as they wish, but they tend to find their social pleasures while working with other women—fetching water, washing clothes, pounding maize, or, the most prized of activities, helping in the kitchen during a ritual festival. Many married women literally work the entire day, pausing only during the last hour or two of the night, when all guests have departed, the fire has dimmed, and husband and wife may share a rice-cake or a drink of sweet coffee.

A similarly nonexclusive tone characterizes the Tengger manner of exchanging greetings, to which Tengger always point when asked about differences between themselves and lowland Javanese. To exchange greetings is to *takon*, literally, "to question," but in this context "to exchange a question as greeting when meeting." Such a greeting usually involves an inquiry as to the interlocutor's destination, typically expressed with the question, "where are you going?" (*sira kate nendi?*). As with so much social interaction in Java, however, the inquiry is not so much concerned with eliciting the factual information it requests, as it is with simply greeting the other person and, while doing so, commenting on the quality of social relationship entertained by the two people. The pronoun (*sira*) and the language level (Tengger *ngoko*) immediately mark the question as "Tengger," and the tone of the inquiry as aggressively intimate. It is the tone and style of one's response which are more important than the information one conveys as to one's destination. To respond in any fashion other than that of the Tengger dialect would, of course, be a humiliating betrayal of the little social pact just offered. To be too vaguely neutral in one's response—saying, for example, "I'm going west" (a common style of response in the lowlands)—risks appearing condescending. To *takon* is, in effect, to engage another person in an interactional nod, and the addressee is supposed to respond with the sort of easygoing straightforwardness which shows that the nod, Tengger style, was appreciated. Indeed, one of the most devastating criticisms one can make of a fellow villager is simply to comment that he or she "doesn't *takon*." No more succinct comment on a person's arrogance and ill will can be made. To *takon*, in short, is to acknowledge that both persons in the interaction know who they are and—with the kind of omnipresent awareness of non-Tengger ways that informs all Tengger social life—that they are both sufficiently familiar, equal, and "Tengger" to address each other in this informal style.

The reception of guests is another sphere in which Tengger consistently distinguish themselves from their non-Tengger neighbors. Tengger refer to such interhousehold visitation as *sanja sinanja*, and proudly point to it as proof of how they treat all guests as members of the family. Upon entering a house, for example, guests in Tengger proceed directly to the kitchen, where they sit on short-legged benches (*dingklik*) next to the kitchen hearth. Such a custom strikes lowlanders, with their stricter sense of the kitchen as private "family" space distinct from the "public" space in the front room, as audaciously forward and impolite. Guests warm themselves around the fire as the hostess sets water on the fire for coffee or tea. Even in extremely poor households, the male host usually sets out cigarettes for the visitor, or, if cigarettes are lacking, he apologizes directly for his inability to receive his guest properly. If the guest then stays longer than several minutes, he is treated in addition to a meal. Here, as throughout Java, the giving of food is an extremely important social act directly identified with family ties, a fact to which Tengger themselves point in underscoring their "familial" reception of guests. It is far less common in lowland society, however, that an ordinary guest is ever given more than tea and some sweets.

The actual linguistic etiquette that accompanies presentation of the food is startlingly straightforward, to a degree that vividly underscores the lesser emphasis among Tengger on elaborate linguistic politesse. If, for example, a guest attempts to leave before the hostess has had time to prepare his drink, he is inevitably reproached with a loud chorus from host and hostess, "drink first" (*ngombea digik*). If the guest nonetheless insists on leaving (which he may prefer to do, for fear of looking as if he came to get food and drink), he responds flatly, "I already have" (*wis mari ngombe*). When the food is finally ready, and the hostess sets it on a short table next to the guest, the guest studiously ignores its presence, until the host points to it with his finger (rarely the thumb, as in Central Java), and with a pleasantly assertive tone says, "quick, to the food. Eat!" The guest maintains his unconcerned attitude nonetheless, looking uninterestedly at the food set before him. To thank the hosts for the food, or to comment on the fine quality of the cooking, would appear socially inept, or risk suggesting that one had really come with the intention of getting a free meal. Villagers take a sociologist's perspective on the matter, pointing out that it is the host and not the guest, after all, who is honored in the exchange. For this reason, guests are under obligation to eat something, but never too much. The happy medium—whereby one honors the hosts for their efforts, without shaming oneself through excess—is to consume a few handfuls of rice or corn meal, and then sit back relaxedly, with the neutral expression of a job well done. On seeing that the guest has eaten so little, the host and hostess inevitably protest, saying, "why so quick! And so little eaten!" The guest now more firmly reassures his hosts that he has eaten "sufficiently," sometimes announcing the fact earlier with a simple burp. The hostess thus removes the food, with a sigh that announces that she is disappointed that so little was eaten. The whole style of the interaction is remarkably ritualized around Tengger, although it is fast changing in a few areas where lowland influences are becoming stronger. Everybody knows that there is a good deal of bluffing and acting in the interaction, and indeed—rather uncharacteristically by Tengger standards—people will readily point out and discuss the social logic of the exchange. None of this, however, seems to diminish the genuine pleasure that villagers take in such relatively ritualized interactions, nor alter their conviction that, in this sphere of social behavior, Tengger genuinely demonstrate the familial and nonexclusive character of village social life.

All of these informal social activities—street interaction, *takon* greeting, and *sanja-sinanja* visitation—are casual examples, but they play a big part in Tengger commentary on the distinctive qualities of village life. Surely social interaction elsewhere in Java shares many of these same features. Robert Jay's classic description of a lowland Javanese community, for example, notes that villagers stress the fact that the village is "one great nuclear family" (Jay 1969:292). Hildred Geertz has similarly noted the tendency among Javanese villagers to identify all close acquaintances as kin, and, among "true" kin, to avoid consistent differentiation of close kin from those distant (H. Geertz 1961:18). Jay fills out our picture, noting that villagers in his community put great stress on randomness in social relations, disapproving of cliques and exclusive social relationships (1969:238). Young boys, he adds, are "aggressively egalitarian" (1969:261), and indeed, despite significant differences of income within the village, villagers in general "are unwilling to accept, even at low levels of conception, the picture of their community as divided into socially unequal parts" (1969:266).

Tengger are Javanese, of course, and it is therefore not surprising that they share many social values with their rural lowland counterparts.

Two social facts, however, make the Tengger situation distinctive. The first is that these ideas of equality and nonexclusivity within the village are key themes of Tengger ritual tradition, at least as it is popularly understood. Lowland cults of guardian ancestors and territorial spirits provide a very similar consonance of spiritual and social idioms, but, particularly over the past century, the role of such cults has been seriously qualified with the rise of a revitalized Islam. In Tengger, the parallelism seen between popular conceptions of social order and the spiritual world provides the ritual heritage with a compelling element of social depth. Here, as everywhere, religious idioms are powerfully compelling not simply by virtue of their internal logic, but because they are capable of tapping and articulating more general sentiments as to the moral nature of social existence.

The second distinctive aspect of these themes of Tengger social interaction is that, in this area of Java, informal and nonexclusive styles have a special identity: they are "Tengger." There is a parallel here with the Tengger dialect of Javanese. Like the dialect, social idioms in Tengger tend to emphasize nondifferentiating and nonexclusive patterns of interaction. Contrary to our sometimes rarefied stereotypes of Javanese society, many of these same patterns are found in the rural lowlands, as Jay's (1969) work shows so well. The status of such values is quite different in the two regions however, by virtue of the fact that less differentiating styles in lowland society are in effect "marginalized" through their identification as less formal, less polite, and less powerful than more elaborate social styles. Tengger culture resists this hierarchical displacement by taking the same values and identifying them as "Tengger"—thereby giving them an integral, self-referential quality that the same values in the lowlands lack. To speak Tengger *ngoko*, to be aggressively undifferentiating in interaction, is not therefore to be coarse and rural, but to be "Tengger." Local customs are not mere shadows of forms projected more brilliantly in the city, at the court, or in more refined circles, but are complete and valuable in themselves—the way of the ancestors, *ngaluri*.

One suspects that this pattern of aggressive parochialism may have once characterized many other areas of rural Java, particularly those far from Central Java's courts. Political developments over the past two centuries, however, have insured that such self-validating regionalism would fare poorly in the face of more hierarchical social styles promoted first in Central Java and later in urban centers across the island. Tengger have better resisted such hierarchical trends in large part because their religious tradition forced them to see themselves as a people in some sense apart from their neighbors. To fail to do so would risk reducing the whole body of Tengger custom to the status of one more regional *adat*, inevitably inferior to social styles more brilliantly elaborated elsewhere.

From a historical perspective, there is an irony to all this. Scholars have long noted that Hindu-Buddhist tradition first moved into Java and Bali's hinterlands through a process of interaction between what Clifford Geertz has called courtly "exemplary centers" (1980:13) and rural dependencies. After the fall of Hindu Majapahit, the preservation of Tengger tradition in effect required that this cultural dynamic be severed, or at least severely restricted. One need not postulate some functional teleology or hidden cunning of history to understand how this occurred in Tengger. There was simply a complex convergence of circumstances, leading to the preservation of a more aggressively regionalist cultural tradition and religious idiom. Road building, education, television, and agricultural commercialization are all part of an integrative revolution that is now well on its way to transforming the social conditions underlying Tengger self-perception. As will be later evident, however, religion continues to play an important role in the reforging of a collective self-definition in the face of changing social conditions.

A Moral Economy

Economic variables have played both a direct and an indirect role in the reproduction and change of Tengger ritual tradition. For example, the problem of land control, which I discuss below, has directly affected Tengger interaction with their non-Tengger neighbors. In particular, movement of land-hungry Muslim immigrants into the lower-lying hill regions around the Tengger highlands played an important part in the Islamization of the native population already inhabiting these terrains. The links between economic and ritual organization, however, are also seen directly within the Tengger village. Traditional forms of labor organization, for example, have been influenced by values drawn from the ritual domain. Certain forms of labor organization thus show a pattern of organization determined by standards other than those of univalent utilitarian efficiency. There are also important practical linkages between ritual festivals and patterns of economic investment, consumption and exchange. The remainder of the present chapter discusses the first two major variables—land and labor organization. The larger problem of ritual investment, consumption, and exchange, however, is addressed in Chapter 10, after examination of the village ritual tradition itself. The analysis of both economic domains reveals a linkage between economic, social, and ritual organization that has served not only to provide a social impetus for reproduction of the ritual tradition, but that has also influenced popular perception of that tradition's meaning.

The Problem of Land in History   The recent history of land control in Tengger can be roughly divided into three periods, each of which corresponds to a different stage in the development of rural economy in Tengger, and to problems of cultural identity related to that development. Although detailed accounts of agriculture in nineteenth-century Tengger society are lacking, it appears that prior to the middle of the last century the region's population was sparse, land relatively abundant, and agricultural technique extensive (Chapter 2). As in many other areas of mountain Java, swidden cultivation was the dominant form of agriculture, and maize was the primary staple. Reports from early nineteenth-century Tengger indicate that residents of the region traded extensively with lowlanders for the textiles, metal goods, and manufactured items that, even at this time, Tengger did not themselves produce. As is still the case, maize—although the most extensive cultigen—was by local custom not allowed to be sold. Hence villagers cultivated small plots of vegetable crops (onions, potatoes, cabbage, carrots) as cash crops for sale in lowland markets.

The mid-nineteenth century marked the beginning of the end of the swidden system throughout Tengger. Warfare and administrative policies in colonial Java had pushed large numbers of people from Central Java and Madura to the sparsely populated terrains of the Eastern Salient (Chapter 2), a process that continued under the Culture System with the introduction of coffee cultivation into Java's mountain "waste lands" (C. Geertz 1963:53; Carey 1979). Land scarcity in the more densely populated terrains of northern Tengger (and, by the end of the century, in all of Tengger) resulted in the development of a dual cultivation system, combining fixed-field cultivation of nearby fields with swidden cultivation of distant fields and forest lands. The development of a more intensive form of dry-field agriculture was reinforced at the end of the nineteenth century, when the colonial government closed off large sections of forest land in an effort to diminish what was by that time already a serious problem of flooding and water control in lowland areas. A stricter cultivation policy was further implemented with the surveying of village lands and the deeding of land titles to individual households in the first and second decades of the twentieth century. From this point on, swidden cultivation was restricted to a few public forest lands, periodically opened by the forestry department for cultivation by local farmers in exchange for land reforestation.

Population growth and the closing off of forest lands forced farmers

91

to cultivate existing terrains ever more intensively, and to open even the most marginal plots to cultivation. Previously forested hillcrests were cultivated, resulting in serious problems of erosion and landslide, the effects of which are visible throughout Tengger today. Beginning in the 1920s, farmers began to compensate for shrinking landholdings by devoting ever-larger portions of their arable land to the cultivation of vegetable cash crops, more remunerative than maize, and more amenable to intensification (allowing double- or triple-cropping rather than the single crop of maize). In soils cultivated in such an intensive fashion, however, fungi and insect pests quickly become a problem. In the 1930s a potato and vegetable blight swept through the highlands, making continuous vegetable cultivation impossible. It was only with the introduction of fungicides and pesticides in the 1970s that intensive vegetable cultivation would again become possible. The switch back to intensive vegetable cultivation was occurring throughout the highlands at the time of my research (1978-1980), and with it have come important changes in labor relations, investment, and exchange (Chapter 10; Hefner 1983b).

In the early nineteenth century, swidden lands were controlled by village communities and distributed on a usufruct basis, with individual families owning titular rights over terrains earlier cultivated. There does not appear ever to have been a system of communal landholding like that once seen in areas of lowland Java (see Jay 1969:309). Today almost all agricultural land is privately owned, although until recently villages reserved the right to restrict cultivation of such land to residents of the village. Besides this private land, most villages have a small amount of land allocated as compensation for village officials. Known as *ganjaran* or *bengkok*, this land was first set aside by the Dutch, but is not found in villages of the Tengger northwest, where village officials are compensated for their services through an annual household tax. Although exact amounts vary from village to village, village chiefs on average receive about three hectares of land, whereas other officials are entitled to one or two hectares. By the standards of modern Java, these are substantial amounts of land, especially given the fact that they tend to be located in some of the choicest terrain in the village. Since village officials tend to come from the more affluent sector of the community, control of these additional properties frequently reinforces already existing lines of economic differentiation within the village.

By world standards, population densities relative to agricultural lands are extremely high in Tengger, ranging from 300-500 persons per square kilometer of agricultural land. Figures from the three villages in which I performed economic research are fairly typical (Table 1). The severity of these figures is underscored by the fact that an average of 92 percent

Table 1. Population Density on Agri-Land

Village	Population Density per Square Km. Agri-Land	Mean Agri-Land Controlled per Household
South village #1	433	1.5 ha.
South village #2	314	1.2 ha.
North village	371	1.5 ha.

Note: Figures are based on a larger survey of household economy conducted among 342 households in three Tengger communities. Two of the three were my field residences, one in the north and the other in the south, and the third village was several kilometers from my southern field residence. Both of the southern communities were opened to vehicle traffic with the completion of a road project toward the end of my year of residence there. Both are Buda, and have steadfastly resisted the Hindu reform movement (Chapter 11). By contrast, the northern village is Hindu, and the wealthiest and most commercially successful of all communities in the Tengger northwest. Survey figures are based on a random sample of households according to the following percentages in each community: 60% (142 households) in southern village #1; 87% (58 households) in southern village #2; 49% (142) in the northern village.

Figures in the second column include land rented, borrowed, or currently used by the household but owned by the Department of Forestry. In contrast to the pattern seen in wet-rice regions of Java, the actual incidence of renting, borrowing, and sharecropping is low in Tengger, although it has increased somewhat over the last generation. Forestry lands borrowed by villagers swell mean landholdings in each village by about .2 ha.

of all land in these villages is under cultivation (the remainder being used for roads, cemeteries, house sites, and so on), and a significant portion of this cultivated land is thus terrain which, from the perspective of soil erosion and water control, should never have been cultivated at all.

A more accurate indication of the social distribution of land can be seen in Table 2. Despite small variations in the overall patterns of land control, figures from all villages are remarkably consistent. In all three villages, approximately 2-3 percent of all households are effectively landless, while an additional 1-5 percent own less than a quarter hectare of agricultural land. An additional 20-25 percent of village households own between one-quarter and one-half hectare of agricultural land. Landholding figures from the upper end of the economic spectrum, by contrast, reveal a consistent pattern of landholding concentration, although its scale is modest by comparison with many areas of lowland Java. About 10 percent of all households in these three villages control approximately 30 percent of the community's agricultural lands. Approximately 25 percent of households in a given community, moreover,

Table 2. Distribution of Land by Class and Village

				Land Size				
	0 ha.	.001-.249	.250-.500	.501-1.00	1.01-2.00	2.01-3.00	3.01-4.00	4 ha. +
South vil. #1	3(0)	1(.5)	23(6)	25(13)	21(21)	14(25)	7(17)	5(19)
South vil. #2	2(0)	5(1)	25(8)	30(22)	23(29)	9(16)	5(16)	2(8)
North vil.	2(0)	3(.5)	20(6)	30(17)	24(25)	11(18)	4(11)	6(23)

Note: The first figure in each column refers to the percentage of village families controlling the amount of land specified at the top of the column; the figure in parenthesis refers to the total percentage of all village agricultural land controlled by this group of families.

control 50-60 percent of the land. The remaining 75 percent of the village thus gains its livelihood from some 40-50 percent of village land, It is interesting to note that this pattern of land concentration is weakest in southern village #2, which, of the three communities, was the least commercially developed.[2]

By comparison with areas of lowland Java, these figures reveal a very modest tendency toward land concentration. In wet-rice areas of Central Java, it is not uncommon to find figures of 27 percent landless (Hull and Hull 1976:6), and frequently higher, whereas the upper 5-10 percent of the village population often controls some 50 percent of village agricultural lands. Figures from Tengger are generally consistent with those seen in other areas of mountain Java (see Collier et al. 1979:21), most of which reveal a similar pattern of land concentration. Even viewed superficially, however, the social impact of such economic inequality in Tengger seems to be real enough. Figures from the 342 households surveyed in the three communities revealed that people owning more than 2 hectares of agricultural land ("land wealthy," by local standards) tend to have more births and a higher proportion of surviving children than do villagers of the same age owning less than 1 hectare of land. Fertility tends to be about 50 percent higher among the former group. The land poor also tend to be more prone to marital instability, with a divorce rate some 50 percent higher than that found among the land wealthy. It is, in addition, the land wealthy who have been innovators in agriculture in recent years, using more fertilizer, pesticides, and wage labor than the land poor. The wealthy also sponsor more expensive ritual events, providing the main driving force behind the inflation in ritual expense that has recently transformed the ritual festival system (Chapter 10). In addition, the wealthy tend to be more fluent in high Javanese and Indonesian, tend to travel more to the lowlands, and, in recent years,

---

[2] These figures do not take into account variation in land ownership due to changes in the domestic cycle. In all three villages, for example, several of the landless households were elderly widows who had given their agricultural land to their children and turned to food-shop operation for their livelihood. An additional point of interest here is that in more subsistence-oriented communities actual purchase of land is not common. In the one southern community in which I was able to examine land records for a thirty-year period, only 17.5 percent of all households had ever purchased land, and amounts purchased represented only 16 percent of these households' landholdings. The low incidence of both land sale and rental in this community was traditionally reinforced by a taboo on the sale or rental of land to people from outside the community. The abolition of this restriction was one of the first major changes to take place in the aftermath of the village's opening to vehicle transport, a development that brought hordes of entrepreneurs to the community almost immediately.

have introduced new styles of conspicuous consumption into the village world.

These and other figures indicate that there are real socioeconomic inequalities in Tengger communities, and that these inequalities have a noticeable impact on patterns of welfare and social life. Political and economic developments that transform the social character of the Tengger community could, at some point, undermine the communitarian appeal of this popular tradition. Radical social inequality could make the kinship idiom of village social life an empty slogan. The question here is not simply economic; it is cultural and moral as well, having to do with the way in which economic realities are popularly perceived and constrained by generalized notions of propriety and the public good.

For modern Tengger this is an important but difficult issue, because much evidence indicates that Tengger society today is in the midst of profound economic, social, and moral readjustments. I discuss some of the more general changes in Chapters 10 and 11. For the moment, I focus on the more traditional economic scheme since, at the time of my research, it was still operative in much of Tengger, and even where it is not, it forms the background to present-day developments. What I am particularly concerned with here is the "moral economy" (Scott 1976) of Tengger economic life, the way in which economic production, consumption, and distribution are influenced by local social arrangements, and cultural notions as to the proper uses of wealth. The cultural contours of this moral economy, I should note, differ from those sometimes postulated for other areas of Southeast Asia, including lowland Java. In particular, the moral constraints on economic activity here are not concerned with the provision of "subsistence guarantees" (Scott 1976) as such, but with the movement of wealth into socially sanctioned ritual spheres. In the remainder of this chapter I will focus on this problem in relation to labor relations of production; in Chapter 10 I will return to the problem of consumption. In both domains one sees a complex of economic, ritual, and social activity that is at the heart of the priestly tradition's practical role, and resilience, in the life of these mountain communities.

The Division and Ritualization of Labor   Compared with the "occupational multiplicity" (White 1976) found in lowland Javanese communities, Tengger villages tend to be characterized by occupational unanimity. The overwhelming majority of villages are farmers, working their own land, and deriving the largest portion of their income from its produce. Wage labor in agriculture has become an important source of income for the land poor only since Indonesian independence. There

96

have always been a handful of men in each village, in addition, who work part time as carpenters or brick layers. And over the past ten years in many communities a small nonagricultural sector has emerged, centered primarily on trade, transportation, and small stores. Virtually none of the poorly remunerative household industries pursued by lowland poor—mat making, basket weaving, sugar processing, and brick making—are found in Tengger, and more specialized professions such as sewing, furniture making, and food processing are also relatively rare.

Agriculture is thus the main activity. From the perspective of its labor input, agriculture is primarily a household affair. At least under the subsistence system that dominated Tengger agriculture until recently, farm labor involves little large-scale mobilization. The traditional subsistence crop of maize and market vegetables could in theory be well cared for by household labor, only occasionally supplemented by a few relatives or neighbors. In this respect, upland dry-field agriculture differs significantly from lowland wet-rice cultivation. Maize can be planted, weeded, and harvested in a piecemeal fashion. There is a general need to coordinate planting and harvesting with the wet and dry seasons of the Eastern Salient (which in this area are pronounced), but there are few of the strict constraints of precision timing required by wet-rice agriculture. Harvesting can be accomplished over several days by a small group of workers. At least on the small scale of cultivation characteristic of subsistence agriculture, vegetable crops can be planted and harvested in a similarly piecemeal fashion. Indeed, this was the traditionally preferred practice, since the staggering of planting allowed a farmer to harvest small quantities of vegetable crops for day-to-day cash needs throughout the year. Recently developed patterns of intensive vegetable cultivation have, of course, changed all this considerably: crops must be sprayed and dusted regularly, and planting and harvesting is usually done much more systematically. But for the agricultural regimen once practiced throughout Tengger—a primary crop of maize, with a few small plots of vegetable crops for market—most labor needs could be met with small groups of laborers.

These, at any rate, are the objective requirements of subsistence cultivation in Tengger agriculture. Customary restrictions on agricultural production, however, tended at times to stand these requirements on their head. Whatever the objective constraints, for example, harvest (and to a less consistent degree, planting) of the maize crop was until quite recently supposed to be performed by large, festive labor parties of dozens or sometimes even more than one hundred workers. This stipulation applied only to maize cultivation; vegetables—always a cash-crop, and in areas of commercial development today the primary cultigen—have never been subject to such social restriction. The restriction on labor organization in maize harvests is all the more curious because, according to customary notions, the number of laborers mobilized was not supposed to vary according to the size of the field to be worked but according to the social and economic status of its owner. Higher-status villagers were supposed to sponsor larger and more festive labor parties, with an abundance of fine food. Middle-income villagers could sponsor much more modest events. At issue in such economic events, of course, is more than the efficient satisfaction of a singular economic end; production has been socialized according to a very status-sensitive plan.

Tengger distinguished two types of cooperative labor, different from each other in terms of social style, tone, and terms of reciprocation. The festive cooperative labor utilized in maize harvest is known as *sayan*. *Sayan* projects usually involve large number of laborers—more, ideally, than required for the concrete productive task at hand—and the labor is not subject to any strict rule of later reciprocation. The host to the *sayan* labor is always supposed to provide food for the workers, and the food is supposed to be of a quantity and quality superior to that of everyday fare, much as in a ritual festival. The second form of cooperative labor is known as *gentenan*, or, literally, "turn taking," and as its name suggests this form of labor organization is rigorously reciprocal. Far fewer laborers are mobilized for *gentenan* projects; the tone and intensity of work are more serious; each worker brings his or her own meal; and returns on services are made soon after. Often a single *gentenan* team of seven or eight individuals will go from field to field, performing the same task on each more or less similarly sized plot of land, and not stopping until everyone's fields have been worked. The task group is always disbanded after the return on labor is complete. *Gentenan* is still used quite often for the slash-and-burn preparation of swidden fields in those villages where forestry lands are occasionally made available for swidden cultivation. According to the reports of elder villagers, *gentenan* was the dominant form of labor organization used in the preparation of swidden lands when these were once extensive. With the shrinking of landholdings, the effective elimination of most swidden cultivation, and the introduction of wage labor into Tengger agriculture in the early decades of this century, *gentenan* has become rare.

Sayan or festive cooperative labor is entirely different, although it too has been subject to restrictive pressures over the past generation. Besides its role in maize cultivation, *sayan* is still used in the erection of house frames and roofs. For both types of activities, *sayan* parties can involve dozens of laborers; much as during ritual festivals, some workers stand around idly chatting while others toil, and the event as a whole is supposed to be relaxed and jovial. As with ritual festivals, each *sayan* worker is personally invited to the event by its sponsors. These same sponsors (husband and wife) in turn play a relatively minor role in the direct coordination of the labor task itself. The sponsors' role is to act as hosts, supervising most importantly the preparation of the three meals—morning, midday, and evening—that *sayan* workers usually enjoy.

The social atmosphere of a large *sayan* meal resembles that of ritual festivals. Laborers are invited in shifts into the dining area specially prepared in the front room of the sponsors' house, and take their place at tables piled high with foods prepared by women *sayan* workers throughout the day. Each meal has three distinct courses: a first course of sweet cakes and coffee, after which the plates are removed, rice bowls are brought in, and the meat course is served; the third course then repeats the earlier one of coffee and sweets, finished off with a cigarette and casual conversation. Outside of ritual festivals, these *sayan* meals are the only occasions on which meat is served.

The form of these meals is quite different from that typical of lowland festival meals. Preportioned servings—standard in the lowlands—are never used in Tengger. Each man is given his own plate, and serves himself of rice and meat. Throughout the meal, the male and female heads of household walk about, moving from the back kitchen, where they supervise food preparation, to the dining room, where they urge diners to "move quickly" to the food and to "eat abundantly." The serving of the central meat course is always a serious moment: conversation stops as diners focus on the meat and rice before them. Each guest occasionally glances to his side, eyeing other people's plates so as to insure that he is not left in the embarrassing position of still having food on his plate when, without the least word, all eating stops, and conversation begins again. Upon entering the dining area and seeing that his guests have finished, the host protests, complaining that everyone has eaten too quickly and too scantily. The guests politely refuse any further food, insisting that the fare was "already sufficient." Seeing that his urgings fall on deaf ears, the host finally relents, and directs his servers to remove the meat plates of the guests and bring in the second serving of sweets and coffee. Unlike the meat course, this final course is casual, each diner making sure to eat only one or, very rarely, two of the sweet cakes piled high on a plate before him. Conversation is friendly. After a few minutes, however, one of the older men among the guests inevitably requests leave of the host, noting that he has "finished eating" and that which he was served was "sufficient." The host again protests, urging the guest to stay, but suddenly the guests are all on their feet, taking leave of the host and filing out of the room. Minutes later, the next wave of worker-diners shuffles in.

Wages are never paid for *sayan* tasks, but the foods prepared for prestigious *sayan* events, and the large number of laborers mobilized, insure that the total cost of at least the most prestigious *sayan* projects is greater than would be required for the hiring of wage laborers to do the same task, were this allowed. The economic means mobilized for the occasion, in other words, far exceed the more limited economic task at hand. If efficiency were the point of the whole thing, it would be better served by reducing the number of laborers and cutting back somewhat on the lavishness of the food fare. This is, of course, an option that has always been open to poor villagers, whose *sayan* events tend to look like rather drab facsimiles of the far more illustrious parties thrown by the wealthy. Over the past generation, in addition, this same option has been legislated by village chiefs in the field of agricultural *sayan*. (Housebuilding *sayan* was left intact, and still functions much as before.) In village after village in the first years of independence, local village chiefs, getting wind of new ways, took action to restrict the incidence of agricultural *sayan* by forbidding the use of meat during such events. *Sayan* without meat is, of course, not very distinctive, and this restriction quickly knocked the wind out of the sails of agricultural *sayan*. Today agricultural *sayan* thus tends to be a small-scale affair, with simple vegetable dishes, and a good deal less social bustle. *Sayan* is still the norm during maize harvests, but today such events rarely attract more than a dozen people. Only housebuilding *sayan* remains intact as a testimony to glories once greater.

Most of the village officials who moved to restrict agricultural *sayan* were, of course, wealthy, the same group of people upon whom the obligation to sponsor expensive *sayan* parties was greatest. In the modern period, it is this same group of villagers who have felt most acutely the attraction of new forms of conspicuous consumption. Brick-and-mortar homes, factory-assembled furniture, kitchen ware, cassette players, and motorcycles have all begun to compete with *sayan* parties and, as we shall see, religious festivals as indices of status in the modern Tengger village. The social lessons of the old *sayan* system are nonetheless of great interest, for they show an important parallel with the ritual festival system itself. Prior to the introduction of wage labor into the region in the 1900s, Tengger farmers had three options for mobilizing labor groups: household labor, supplemented occasionally with a few close kin and neighbors; *gentenan* rotating reciprocal labor; and *sayan* festival labor, to varying degrees of lavishness. Of these options, the first two were fine for most agricultural tasks. The third option, *sayan* labor, was concerned with more than the practical satisfaction of a specific technical end. At its elaborate extreme, *sayan* is a hybrid of productive exigencies and conspicuous display: "conspicuous production." The *sayan* hosts are not simply concerned with getting a single job done, they are making a claim to status in the village. The abundance of food, its quality and expense, the deliberate inflation of the number of workers relative to the limited labor task at hand—all of these deviations from the single-minded logic of harvesting or housebuilding show that *sayan*, at its affluent extreme, is not really single-minded. It is social, and borrows its ideas from the ritual festivals that traditionally have been the very substance of good social standing in the self-absorbed world of these small mountain communities.

There is an interesting contrast in all this with traditional forms of harvest labor in the wet-rice lowlands. Tengger themselves note that *sayan* for them takes the place of *bawon* "harvest shares" given to those who participate in the rice harvest in lowland Java (Stoler 1977; Collier et al. 1973). Traditionally women perform the rice harvest, and each woman is compensated for her labor by receiving a portion of the total rice crop that she herself has cut. Well aware of the lowland *bawon* system, Tengger give no harvest shares to those who participate in the maize harvest, and in fact speak as if the very idea of such a thing is distasteful. Given the much-discussed redistributive merits of the *bawon* system, and its importance for the lowland poor (Stoler 1977), the Tengger attitude seems at first perplexing. It is less so once one has participated in *sayan* festivals, even in their present-day restricted form. The *sayan* host is not a patron to so many clients—which, rightly or wrongly, is the manner in which Tengger view the *bawon* patron—but a sponsor of village festivity and entertainment. His generosity enlivens the village, counteracts the anomie of everyday agriculture, and, according to local notions, makes the village guardian spirits happy. *Sayan*, in short, pretends to want nothing of the self-conscious allocation of favors seen in the *bawon* system. At its extreme, *sayan* is supposed to display a conspicuous disconcern for calculation and expense. The more excessive its economic expenditures, the more successful it is socially.

That the village elite has in the postwar period sought to reduce the incidence of agricultural *sayan* is no doubt an important index of social changes now shaking the region. The symbols of social status are increasingly drawn from outside the village domain. We see in the remnants of the old system, nonetheless, a larger cultural logic, a sociocultural system linking notions of prestige, propriety, and economy. Village society asserts a moral right to the production and consumption of wealth, recognizing economic rights other than those of individual pro-

101

ducers with independent responsibility for their labor and wealth. *Homo economicus* is thus socialized, and according to a quite particular cultural plan.

The traditional taboo on the sale of maize in Tengger once gave additional force to these social and moral restrictions on economic activity. Its sale forbidden, whatever surplus maize was produced in the village had to be consumed there. Prior to the shrinking of landholdings and the shift to commercial crops, such surpluses were not uncommon. The one domain in which they could be strategically utilized, of course, was that of festival meals. This practical linkage of production restrictions and conspicuous consumption insured, in short, that surplus production was channeled into status-enhancing social festivities rather than more financially profitable market sale. Production and consumption were thereby linked to the creation of social distinction, and the reproduction of a moral order consistent with the social contours of these mountain communities.

Conclusion

Tengger villages present an interesting variation on Javanese themes. What at first looks like structural anomie, a poverty of formal roles and statuses, under closer inspection turns out to be a neatly meshed world of persons at once familiar and, through a variety of practical arrangements, committed to a tradition called "Tengger." The absence of formal groups and statuses, the lack of precision in kinship address, the emphasis on personal names, the relative unimportance of marriage as a mechanism of social alliance, the identification of the village as one body of relatives, the stewarding roles of priest and *petinggi*, and the peculiar restrictions on economic activity—all of these things help to give the formal idioms of ritual life an air of experiential realism and interpretive depth. This is the background against which an interpretation of popular Tengger tradition must be set, for it is through this more diffuse and ongoing social experience that Tengger themselves come to witness and appreciate their ritual heritage. This, of course, makes the task of ritual interpretation all the more complex. One cannot speak here of a privileged "deep structure" or "core symbolism" embodied in ritual performance and forever generating the same prefigured meanings. In cultural interpretation there can be no shortcut around history and social experience. To grasp Tengger understanding, one has to look outside and around ritual forms to the larger experience that informs the sensibilities actors bring to cultural performance and refine there. The ten-

102

sion peculiar to Tengger ritual tradition is that, while priestly liturgy has maintained a relatively high degree of cultural stability, the larger universe in which Tengger live has not, and thus the interpretations constructed in ritual encounters have changed, or at times have been a matter of dispute.

· 5 ·

VILLAGE RITUAL AND ISLAM

The *slametan* or ritual festival stands above all other events in the community as uniquely "Tengger." No other event attracts such attention; none consumes such wealth; and none benefits from such an elaborate system of organization and etiquette. To define it simply, a *slametan* in Tengger is a public religious ceremony involving priestly invocation and worship of deities, the witnessing of that event by lay persons, and, at least in most instances, some kind of meal communion or social festivity to celebrate the occasion. From a religious perspective, the key moment in all this is the priest's invocation of the deities. Without their presence, there is no blessing, and thus, in theory, no reason for celebration.

At first sight there is an irony in this identification of the *slametan* as a distinctive feature of Tengger identity. A ritual of the same name is found throughout Java, except in those reform Muslim communities where it has been abolished. "At the center of the whole Javanese religious system," Clifford Geertz has written (1960:11), "lies a simple, formal, undramatic, almost furtive little ritual: the *slametan* . . . the Javanese version of what is perhaps the world's most common religious ritual, the communal feast." The irony, however, is only superficial. What Tengger regard as a *slametan* differs significantly from the lowland event of the same name. The precise nature of that difference illustrates well the non-Islamic quality of Tengger ritual, and, by implication, the degree to which popular Javanese tradition elsewhere has accommodated itself to Islam.

Islam and Adat in the Javanese Slametan

To be *slamet* is to be safe, blessed, well off, and, as Javanese often say, "free from obstacles or hindrance." For both Tengger and non-Tengger Javanese, the most general function of the *slametan* is simply to maintain this state of physical and spiritual well-being. The ritual form can thus be applied to any number of village or household enterprises in which blessing is sought. In both Tengger and the lowlands, for example, there are *slametans* for pregnancy, birth, early childhood, marriage, death, and other moments of life passage. There are also a variety of what Clifford Geertz (1960:83) has appropriately called "intermittent *sla-*

metans," designed to bless a person or group during such occasional events as moving, traveling, falling ill, or coming into good fortune. Although the basic ritual form in each tradition remains the same, its application and elaboration are virtually endless.

Javanese Muslims also use the *slametan* to celebrate important dates in Islamic history—the birth of the Prophet Mohammad, the prophet's ascension into heaven, and the beginning and ending of the Muslim month of fast, to name but a few (see C. Geertz 1960: 78). The *slametan* has no explicit sanction in Koranic tradition or pan-Islamic institutions, of course, but it has long played an important role in Javanese Islam. The exact nature of that role varies somewhat with the religious orthodoxy of Muslim Javanese communities. *Kejawen* and orthodox Muslim communities alike celebrate the birth of the Prophet Mohammad and the end of the fasting month, but the celebration of many other Islamic holidays varies widely. In some of the modernist reform villages to the southwest of Tengger, for example, village leaders have recently suppressed *kejawen* ceremonies traditionally held at the village spirit shrine, and, not without considerable grumbling from some villagers, have replaced these annual celebrations with orthodox Islamic holidays held at the village mosque. In neighboring *kejawen* communities, by contrast, villagers deliberately avoid celebrating more formal Muslim holidays, preferring to devote their ritual energies to annual celebrations held at the spirit shrine, accompanied by feasting, dancing, and drinking.

Whatever the religious orientation of the community, and whatever the occasion celebrated, the lowland-style *slametan* is always centered around a prayer meal held at some point in the course of what are often larger festivities. The term *slametan* can refer to this prayer meal alone, or the prayer meal with accompanying festivities. The term *kenduren*, by contrast, refers to the prayer-meal portion of the *slametan* alone. In identifying the *kenduren* prayer meal as the "center of the whole Javanese religious system," Clifford Geertz (1960:11), correctly conveys Javanese perceptions as to what is and what is not of critical religious importance in a *slametan*. One can have a *slametan* without entertainment, customary processions, receptions, and dancing, but one cannot have a *slametan* without a *kenduren* prayer meal. There is a problem of religious perception here. All of the former activities are in some sense just "tradition" or *adat*. The prayer meal, however, is religious, the primary means whereby the *slamet* blessing desired is achieved. Although some people may believe that the accompanying customary activities in fact fulfill spiritual functions, virtually everyone would agree that, in lowland tradition, only the prayer meal benefits from unambiguous religious status, and it is, in some sense, primary. There is a tension here between Javanese tradition and Javanese notions of Islam, a tension which, as we shall see, extends into the very heart of lowland *kenduren*.[1]

With the exception of certain birth *slametans* (which sometimes include women) and an occasional children's *slametan*, the prayer portion of a *kenduren* is primarily a male affair. Women take an active role in food preparation and the exchange of food gifts that occurs at the rite's conclusion, but they do not join directly in prayer. Invited moments prior to the prayer meal, men drift in slowly, seating themselves on mats laid out on the floor; there is usually no formal status seating. Each guest enjoys a glass of sweet tea and a cigarette, joining in the friendly conversation that precedes the ritual service. When the host feels that all guests have arrived, he, or a representative selected by him, rises and welcomes the guests, addressing them in his most elegant Javanese. He explains the purpose of the prayer meal, citing, for example, the circumcision of his son, or the marriage of his daughter, and then asks the blessing of those present and their forgiveness for any inadequacy that may arise in the course of the prayer meal. This introductory speech is known as an *ujub*, and is one of the most important ritual speech acts in the lowland *slametan*. Although the speaker's opening remarks in the *ujub* are relatively consistent from rite to rite, the concluding portion of the *ujub* varies significantly according to the religious orientation of the *slametan* sponsors. If the host is a *kejawen* Muslim, he, or the speaker acting for him, concludes the *ujub* with the recitation of a prayerlike litany, composed in Javanese, which invokes the blessing of a variety of spirits, including first-founding ancestors, territorial guardians, Islamic saints, spirits of the earth and sky, and others thought to play a role in maintaining the spiritual welfare of the community.[2]

[1] In at least some communities of *kejawen* persuasion, this tension has been pushed to its sociological conclusion, with calls for a rejection of Islam and a return to the "religion of Old Java." Several such anti-Islamic organizations were active in lowland communities to the west of the Tengger highlands during the 1950s, with membership numbering in the thousands. The bloodshed of 1965-1966 appears, however, to have decimated their ranks. In the aftermath, membership in the region with which I am familiar dwindled from more than ten thousand to fewer than one hundred, and there has been no resurgence of non-Islamic organization. Elsewhere in Java, however, reports indicate that the events of 1965-1966 resulted in considerable conversion to both Christianity and Bali-style Hinduism (Ricklefs 1979; C. Geertz 1972). My own impression is that in most areas of the Eastern Salient the progress of Islamization over the past thirty years has been steady, whereas, with the exception of developments in the Tengger region, non-Islamic organizations have met with only limited popular success.

[2] I recorded a typical *ujub* in a syncretic community of Javanese and Madurese in the Pasuruan region below northwest Tengger. The prayer invoked the spirits of Mt. Semeru, Mt Bromo, the local spring, the island of Madura, the Muslim apostle of Surabaya, Father

As the litany comes to an end, those present respond with a collective *inggih* (yes), testifying to their role as witnesses to the ritual event.

More orthodox Muslims—particularly those influenced by reform Islam's call for the suppression of rites not explicitly sanctioned in Islam—tend to avoid this invocational *ujub* entirely. In their *kenduren*, the *ujub* speech concludes with a simple expression of thanks and a repeated appeal for forgiveness for any inadvert improprieties. The *ujub* here is purely a secular ritual, a matter of customary protocol, not spiritual invocation. In both *kejawen* and *santri kenduren* however, the portion of the prayer meal that follows the *ujub* is much the same. The *ujub* host surrenders the floor to an Islamic prayer leader, who leads the group in the recitation of a long, deeply intoned Islamic prayer. The prayer is always in Arabic, and is usually selected from the Koran or other religious texts to provide relevant commentary for the ritual event (marriage, circumcision, and so on) at hand. Those present punctuate the prayer leader's chants with occasional *amin*, and at other times join him directly in the chanting. Those unfamiliar with Arabic—in *kejawen* communities, sometimes the majority of those assembled—sit quietly. What is interesting about all this from a religious perspective is that even *kejawen* Javanese recognize the importance of this Islamic prayer. There can be no *kenduren* without it. "Javanist" Muslims thus quite openly acknowledge their respect for and dependence on Islamic forms of learning and worship, even where, as is so often the case, they also acknowledge their own lack of education in those same forms.[3]

Given the range of orthodoxy in Javanese Islam, it is remarkable that the *kenduren* displays the uniformity that it does. Only those at the two extremes of the lowland religious spectrum—reform Muslims who reject any ritual form not explicitly sanctioned in Islam, and those few

---

Sky and Mother Earth, and the Prophet Mohammad. Two other examples of *ujub* in English-language literature can be found in Jay 1969:209 and C. Geertz 1960:41.

[3] C. Geertz's description of an Islamic *modin's* refusal to perform burial services for the member of an anti-Islamic *kejawen* sect provides a fascinating example of the problems of this ritual dependency (Geertz 1973c:153). Both Mitsuo Nakamura (1976) and Zamakhsyari Dhofier (1978) point to the fact of this ritual dependency as proof that the contrast between orthodox and *kejawen* Muslims is not always as antagonistic as some discussions of so-called *abangan* and *santri* culture would suggest. *Santri* Muslims lead what is, from a religious perspective, the most important portion of the *slametan*, and *kejawen* Muslims often readily acknowledge the spiritual virtue of orthodox religious leaders. Whatever the nature of the contrast between *kejawen* and *santri* Muslims, it is probably important to recognize the considerable historical and regional variation characterizing their relationship. In particular, one suspects that the intensely politicized situation in Central Java during the 1950s should not be regarded as the prototype for their relation at all times and in all regions.

kejawen Javanese who avoid even the most basic Islamic practices—
refuse to use this elementary ritual form. As the variation in the *ujub*
itself demonstrates, however, there is a cultural struggle over religious
matters even at the heart of this standard religious ceremony. Evidence
of a similar dispute over the form and meaning of the *kenduren* is also
seen in other aspects of the rite. Incense, for example, is one such element
of variation: *kejawen* Javanese tend to use it, reform Muslims do not.
In traditional "Javanist" ceremony, the role of incense was similar to
that seen in Tengger and Bali. The incense acts as a messenger to the
gods, and a ladder by which they descend to offerings whose invisible
essence they consume (see, for Bali, Belo 1953:12). Reform Muslims
scrupulously avoid including incense in their *kenduren* lest its presence
be interpreted in just this fashion. Food is often subject to similar variation. *Kejawen* Javanese set it prominently at the center of the prayer
room so that, in the course of the ritual, the spirits invited may enjoy
its essence. Modernist Muslims, by contrast, often insist that food be
kept in the back kitchen until the completion of all prayers, thereby
avoiding any suggestion that the *kenduren* foods are offerings for spirits.
These simple variations on ritual form allow the same ceremony to have
quite different meanings according to the religious orientation of its
sponsors.

There is one more element of variation in the lowland prayer meal
that deserves special mention. In most *kenduren*, the man invited to
lead the guests in Islamic prayer is a local elder or Islamic leader, adept
in the recitation of Arabic-language prayers. He is not really a "ritual
specialist"—aside from leading the assembled in prayer, he performs no
special acts, and demonstrates no other religious skills. In a small number
of *kejawen* Muslim communities, however, the man who leads the prayers does a good deal more, and is indeed something of a ritual specialist.
In such communities, the same man is always invited to recite the *ujub*.
Known as the "caretaker" or, literally, "keeper of the keys" (*juru kunci*),
this man is also responsible for taking care of the village *danyang* or
spirit shrine. For each household or village *slametan*, he must prepare
offering trays for the spirits of the village shrine. The sponsors of the
slametan at some point in the festival are also supposed to visit the
shrine, but they can enter its confines only in his presence, and after
he has notified the spirits that the visit is going to take place. During
the prayer meal, it is this man who recites the *ujub*, which inevitably
includes a long prayer of invocation to village ancestors and guardian
spirits. At the end of a *slametan*, the *juru kunci* receives the offering
trays earlier offered to the spirits. Much like a Tengger priest, finally,

most *juru kunci* inherit their role from their father; the role is transmitted in only certain family lines.

There do not appear to be many *juru kunci* of this sort left in Java, although several were operative in villages below Tengger. What is so interesting about the role is that it looks very much like a cultural compromise between Islamic religion and an earlier tradition. The exclusive and hereditary nature of the role, in particular, may recall a period when rural Javanese Islam depended upon a more restricted social organization—when, in particular, Islamic knowledge was not to be inculcated in all, but mastered only by those socially and spiritually qualified to apprehend its truth and control its power. The growth of rural centers of Islamic study (*pesantren*) in nineteenth-century Java may have contributed to the demise of the role, and, equally importantly, the redefinition of Islamic learning. Religious study became a duty of all rather than the privilege of a special few. This was an important but often unnoticed aspect of Java's continuing Islamization.

Although he is the most unusual of lowland ritual specialists, the *juru kunci* is not alone in his claim to special ritual perogatives. In traditional wedding ceremonies, for example, there is a "bridal dukun" (*dukun temanten, dukun paras*) who helps prepare the bride and who also, at least in some communities, recites spells over the bride and groom when they meet. Other *adat* ceremonies have their customary specialists as well: *calak* for performing circumcisions, *dukuns* for the first cutting of a child's hair, midwives (*dukun bayi*) for pregnancy and birth, and others. On occasion many of these ritual experts burn incense, present offerings, and mutter barely audible prayers under their breath. It is a testimony to the force of Islam in even *kejawen* areas of Java that the cultural status of these ritual activities is at best ambiguous. Few would dare call such things "religion." This term is reserved for ceremonies like the *kenduren* prayer meal where recognized Islamic leaders recite Muslim prayer. From this perspective, it is interesting to note that, an occasional *juru kunci* aside, none of these ritual specialists perform their labors within the context of activities, like the *kenduren*, explicitly referred to as religious. They work outside of it, in ceremonies regarded even by staunch "Javanists" as customary *adat*. Some people might wish to insist that the *adat* ceremonies are profoundly spritual, and for those people they therefore are. Nonetheless, only the explicitly Islamic portion of a *slametan* is widely regarded as "religion."

There is thus a peculiar cultural vision to the lowland *slametan*. It expresses an interpretive tension between what people may call "customary" and what they can call "religious." The vision no doubt varies according to region and social group throughout Java. But its most

109

common expression testifies to a profound and ongoing process of Islamization. It is this tension between "custom" and "religion" that most clearly distinguishes the lowland *slametan* from its Tengger counterpart. Tengger tradition resists the secularizing categorization which, in lowland society, distinguishes the customary and Javanese from the religious and Islamic.

Core and Periphery in the Tengger Slametan

If the *slametan* in Islamic Java is built around the *kenduren* prayer meal, the Tengger *slametan* puts its spiritual focus on the ritual labor of a priest. Without his prayers of invocation and worship, no deity is present, and, without deity, there is neither blessing nor a state of *slamet*. Tengger are much more ritualistic and objectivistic in their explanations of ritual action than most Javanist Muslims. Tengger rarely speak of ritual with reference to its impact on one's inner experience. They speak of things in the world: the coming and going of spirits, the presentation of offerings, and the contagious blessing conveyed by spirit presence. For Tengger, in other words, the action implicit in the process of *nylameti*—making someone or something *slamet*—has a practical object and specific spiritual agent. Among *kejawen* Muslims, by contrast, spiritual agency is often left vague or unexplained, as if the primary force behind spiritual labor were mysterious and unknowable, and its primary consequence a wonderous inner glow or hidden power. Tengger sometimes speak of inner states and mysterious forces, but they rarely invoke such concepts when explaining what priestly ritual involves.

This more ritualistic vision of the *slametan* also influences the manner in which Tengger view the festivities that accompany priestly rite. All services, big and small, must conclude with some kind of communion meal, even if it is no more than a few plates of rice and soybean curd shared by the priest and the household sponsors of a rite. The larger festivities that accompany major village festivals or important rites of household passage (marriage, purification of the dead, and so on) may of course extend over several days, and include almost round-the-clock feasting, drinking, dancing, and theater performance. The important point is that the festivities which accompany priestly services are not identified as secular custom apart from the more properly religious labors of the priest. With each serving of meals for guests, ancestral spirits are given a new serving of fine foods. When dancing commences late at night, a small offering of sacred betel and bananas is set to the side of the dance floor, to serve as a perch from which ancestral spirits may enjoy the amusements of the living. By honoring and entertaining ancestral spirits, such festivities play an integral role in bringing blessing to the village as a whole.

There is another important practical difference between the Tengger and Islamic *slametan*. The *kenduren* prayer meal usually stands apart from *slametan* festivities, and benefits from rather pronounced situational focus. It would be considered highly improper to hold a *kenduren* in one portion of a house while elsewhere guests are drinking, feasting, or enjoying puppet theater. This is much less clearly the case in Tengger. If the priest's worship is the ritual center and, technically at least, condition for the occurrence of a *slametan*, it need not be the social focus of attention. The priest may celebrate some rites alone or off in a corner of a room while other people are eating or dancing. Other people may often be present: the priest's assistants (Chapter 9), for example; village officials; or the husband and wife sponsoring a household rite. Indeed, in a few village services, as in the Kasada festival at Mt. Bromo, large numbers of people may be in attendance. In many household and village ceremonies, however, people not required to participate directly in services need not attend, and would not be thought to derive any special benefit were they to do so. In general, there is no notion in Tengger that careful observation of or participation in priestly services necessarily brings blessing. For each ritual, certain actors are expected to be present, but those not required to participate usually do not, busying themselves instead with other work or the larger festivities of a *slametan*.

Villagers refer to this division of ritual responsibilities as "representation." The village priest, they say, "represents" (*mewakili*) them before the gods, and village officials "represent" them in witnessing the work of the priest. In the Kasada festival at Mt. Bromo, one member of a household may "represent" his family in presenting offerings. Similarly, in household rites, one member of a family may "represent" his kin during certain key moments when family participation is required. Actual physical presence to a ritual, or observation of the priest's performance, is not a condition for the receipt of spiritual benefit. The degree to which such "representation" occurs in traditional Tengger rites distinguishes the tradition from the at least nominal emphasis placed on male participation in the lowland *kenduren*. Not surprisingly, it is this very quality of ritual organization in Tengger that has recently been challenged by the Hindu reform movement, which has sought to introduce more congregational forms of worship (Chapter 11).

Despite the limited emphasis on popular participation, Tengger concepts of the *slametan* have long linked its spiritual effects to the wider social community. Even the smallest rite of life passage (birth, haircutting, and so on) includes among its offerings items intended to secure the blessing of the village as a whole. The offerings that seek to bless a newborn, for example, also remove the impurities of birth (which can destroy crops and render soils infertile) and bless village lands. The *walagara* blessing of newlyweds insures not only their fertility, it is said, but that of village land and water. These and other notions as to the purpose of ritual impress upon villagers that *slametan* performance is never simply a private duty. "More household *slametans* makes the village more *slamet*," a village chief once declared during a public meeting, urging his fellow villagers to fulfill their ritual duties. The lowland guest who happened to be sitting next to me chuckled, and whispered, "what can all this dancing and feasting have to do with religion?" This Muslim man's view of Tengger ritual imposed much the same distinction of "religion" and "custom" on Tengger *slametans* as many Muslims impose on lowland events. Tengger themselves make no such distinction, viewing the sponsorship of feasts and festivities as a key element in public morality and religion.

Village Slametans

As in the lowlands, Tengger use *slametans* to celebrate everything from individual rites of passage to calendrical village holidays. Some of the events Tengger mark in this fashion are similar to those celebrated throughout Java, but others are not. One can distinguish two different types of *slametans* within the Tengger village according to their respective sponsor. There are those of the household and those of the village. A few other organizations—recently, for example, schools—occasionally sponsor ritual festivals, but the vast majority of events are financed and organized either by individual households or the village as a whole. The remainder of this chapter will discuss village *slametans*, and household events will be viewed in later chapters.

Tengger have a greater variety of village *slametans* than do even *kejawen* Muslims. There are six more or less standard events celebrated throughout the region. Only one of these (*barikan*) is found by name in other areas of Java. Another of the six (*galungan*) is found at least by name in neighboring Bali, but the form and meaning of the Tengger event are distinctive. Together, the six Tengger *slametans* indicate that the community is defined not only by material, but corporate spiritual interests as well.

1. *Pujan.* From the Sanskrit and Old Javanese term for "worship," Tengger *pujan* are celebrated in the fourth, eighth, ninth, and twelfth months of the Tengger calendar year; several villages celebrate a fifth *pujan* in the seventh month, in addition. Once marked by feasting at

the village priest's house, *pujan* today involve a brief invocation and meal at the priest's house. Supported by food contributions from all households in the village, attendance is restricted to village officials and the priest.

2. *Barikan.* Its precise etymology unclear, the *barikan* is identified by modern Tengger as a rite of *balikan* or the "turning back" of evil from the village. In some communities *barikan* occurs every thirty-five days, but in others it takes place only after eclipses, earthquakes, and volcanic eruptions. The liturgy is celebrated at the village chief's house. Women bring baskets of cooked food to the front steps of the house. While village officials act as "witnesses," the priest blesses the food and returns half to the women. The half which remains is used to make a communion meal for the priest and village officials. The half taken home is eaten by members of each household, who thereby share in its blessing. A small portion of the home food is in addition made into *tamping* earth offerings, set out by each family around the house and fields.

3. *Galungan.* Held every 210 days to bless village land, water, and people, the ritual detail of *galungan* is almost identical to *barikan.* Unlike the Balinese festival of the same name, Tengger do not identify *galungan* as an all-souls' commemoration. In Hindu reform villages, however, the rite has recently been reworked so as to resemble more its Balinese counterpart.

4. *Karo.* A ritual blessing of "couples" or "dualities," Karo is the Tengger all-souls month, and the most important of all village *slametans* (discussed below).

5. *Unan-unan.* Literally a ritual "to fill in," the *unan-unan* is held every five years during the leap-year month that occurs because of the discrepancy between the lunar and solar calendars used by Tengger priests. Held at the village shrine, the rite requires the offering of a water buffalo, intended to serve as a vehicle to the heavens.

6. *Mayu desa.* This ritual of "village renewal" occurs whenever a village chief is inaugurated, and is designed to bless the village during his administration.

Although the *unan-unan* and *mayu desa* are also known by other names, the similarity of these rites throughout the Tengger region provides strong testimony to the historical integrity of the tradition and its regional social foundation. The complex of rites is found in no other area of modern Java. Indeed, in Islamizing Buda communities, one of the first steps taken toward Islamization is inevitably the dismantlement of this Tengger ceremonial complex and its replacement with village rites deemed more appropriately "Javanese" (Chapter 11).

113

Form and Meaning in Village Slametans

There is a certain doctrinal anonymity about village *slametans*. Each is called by a distinct name, occurs for different occasions, has its own offerings and prayers, and shows a slightly different style of organization. With the exception of Karo, however, public comments on the importance and meaning of these rites present all of them as just so many variations on a single theme. All are intended, one is told, to bless village lands, insure the abundance of its water, protect the living, and, as always, affirm the bond of the living with the dead. The emphasis in describing the rites, in other words, is on their practical consequences, not their cosmology or interior symbolic detail. In theory, it is assumed that each rite must in some sense be different from the others. But just how or why is never explained in terms of the nature of the ritual work accomplished or the specific deities for which the rites might be intended. As far as most villagers are concerned, all ritual invokes the same faceless assortment of guardian deities. Hence, despite the fact that there are four or five *pujan* during the year and that the priest's prayers consistently identify four and five deities with the wind directions (Chapter 4), neither villagers nor priests identify the *pujan* with the worship of any particular deity. Inasmuch as villagers take note of ritual detail, they focus on the way in which each ritual is celebrated in different places and that it involves different types of feasting or festivity. It is, in other words, the sociology of ritual performance to which villagers pay particular attention.

All of the village rites are organized around a common redistributive pattern: foods are collected at the house of a village dignitary (the priest or the chief), or sometimes at the village shrine, where they are blessed and presented as offerings by the priest to the gods, and then afterward a portion of the offerings is consumed by the officials who have "witnessed" the ceremony, while another portion is made into *tamping* earth offerings. The *pujan* illustrates this pattern clearly, and also shows to what degree ordinary villagers are drawn into the ceremony. The morning of a *pujan* day, village women bring a small tray of uncooked foods (usually some rice, sugar, and bananas, with a small coin as well) to the village priest's house. Helped by youths recruited for the *pujan* celebration, the priest's wife takes the foods and throughout the remainder of the day prepares them either for the *pujan* offerings or for the meal that village officials celebrate that night at the conclusion of the priest's ceremony. (In a few northern Tengger villages, the *pujan* meal is now limited to the priest and his assistants). When, in the evening of the ritual gathering, offerings are ready and the table prepared for the village officials' meal, the actual ritual service—a more or less standard invocation of the gods—lasts only about five minutes. The remainder of the evening is devoted to the meal, which involves no additional ceremony or ritual form. The *pujan* circuit is completed the following morning. Trays of cooked food (*ater-ater*) are sent from the priest's house to village officials, and small earth offerings are set out by the roadside, cemetery, bridge, and other locations around the village. The primary role of ordinary villagers in all this is to provide raw materials for the ritual offerings, a gift for which, in theory, they are later repaid with spiritual blessing. Villagers also celebrate *pujan* by taking time to cook and exchange small food gifts (also called *ater-ater*) with neighbors and kin. Similar food gifts are also exchanged during Karo. For that rite, however, the food gift consists of a sweet red rice cake (*juada*) whereas for *pujan* it is always a salty, white sticky-rice cake that is exchanged. As throughout Java, the color symbolism of red and white is associated with male and female. Here in Tengger too, villagers refer to the red-white contrast as a symbol of the larger fertility theme with which all village *slametans* are concerned.

From the perspective of their social organization, all village *slametans* display a familiar blend of communitarianism and hierarchy. On the communitarian side, the one to which villagers most consistently refer, every household is expected to contribute offerings to the performance, and everyone benefits from the resulting spiritual blessing. Villagers also emphasize the egalitarian nature of *ater-ater* exchange. Unlike the more common pattern of the lowlands, elders give food gifts to youths, and youths to elders, in no particular order of precedence. Similarly, each household is enjoined to exchange food gifts with all of its neighbors, regardless of wealth or social standing. Everyone, villagers insist, is "just the same" (*pada-pada*).

As soon as one observes who manages these ritual events, however, it becomes obvious that there is a hierarchy to ritual performance as well. For example, the priest is said to "own" the four *pujan* festivals, whereas the chief "owns" Karo, *barikan*, and *galungan*. "Ownership" obliges each individual to take responsibility for recruiting the laborers needed to prepare foods and serve during ceremonial meals. It does not necessarily imply any special spiritual privilege. In practice, however, most villagers play no direct role in these ceremonies. They are "represented" before the gods by the priest and village officials. No ordinary villagers are present, for example, during the celebration of the *pujan* at the priest's house. During *barikan* and *galungan*, women come bearing offerings to the village chief's house, and, in theory, they can watch

115

the ritual services from a distance.[4] But they are not invited to draw close to the priest and village officials so as to see or hear the services clearly. Male villagers, moreover, do not even attend these last rites, since, as in Bali, women alone are responsible for carrying offerings to rituals. As a result, many Tengger men never have an opportunity to see a *pujan*, *barikan*, or *galungan*, although each year they contribute to these celebrations. Once again, ritual practice is not organized in a fashion intended to enhance villagers' appreciation of ritual word and action.

This pattern of ritual-at-a-distance tends to reinforce villagers' caution in discussing doctrinal questions. The most common reaction of even close acquaintances to my questions concerning ritual problems was to refer me politely to the village priest. Villagers are of course familiar with the general themes of the ritual tradition—ancestry, fertility, blessing, and the like. Whereas priestly ritual is distinctive to the Tengger region, however, these more general themes differ little from those heard in *kejawen* regions of rural Java. From the perspective of ordinary villagers, therefore, it is neither the fine points of liturgical detail nor the names and identities of the deities invoked that make this priestly tradition compellingly "Tengger." Details on such matters are obscure and, whatever one's actual knowledge, best left to the priest. What is most distinctive about the ritual tradition is its more general appeal to issues and values given focus in the course of social life. It links the living to their ancestors, preserving a bond important for the welfare of the living and for their identity as Tengger Javanese.

No single village ritual summarizes these themes of social and spiritual continuity as does the annual Karo festival. Karo is an all-souls month, a time during which the souls of the family dead return to the community, reside with their living relatives, and bring blessing. Karo is also a time of special foods, new clothes, and interhousehold visitation. In fact, Tengger villagers compare Karo to the celebration and visitation that occur each year at the end of the fasting month in Muslim Java (see C. Geertz 1960:379). Asked their religion, many elder Tengger will respond *agama Karo*—"Karo religion," "the religion of two." The dualism of the terms is important, and deliberate. It refers to not only the familiar Indonesian themes of male and female, birth and death, earth and sky, but to the equally important duality of Islam and Buda. Between

---

[4] In Hindu reform villages, Karo, *barikan*, and *galungan* are no longer celebrated at the village chief's house, but at the local *sanggar* spirit shrine (in some villages now known as a *pura*, the Balinese term for temple). The reform movement has consistently sought to make the *sanggar* a kind of Hindu equivalent of an Islamic mosque, with more regular congregational worship.

the "two" referred to in the name of the festival, Tengger hear a dialogue on identity, and a difference that might deny them.

Karo and All-Souls

In Javanese the word *karo* means "second," "two," "both," or "with." In Tengger, the proper noun Karo refers in addition to the second month of the Tengger calendar year and the ritual which occupies most of that month. Karo is a ritual invocation of ancestors and guardian deities writ large—large as the village, in every village which calls itself Tengger.[5] Karo is exceptional not only because its festivities extend over a two- to three-week period, but because, more than any other village ritual, it draws ordinary villagers directly into much of the detail of the celebration. There are two levels of ritual performance: one that is sponsored by the village as a whole, and another that is the responsibility of each individual household. The village as a whole makes the initial invocational appeal to guardian deities and family spirits, but during the central days of the Karo celebration those same spirits are reinvoked to individual homes, home after home, until the priest has worked in every household, and all villagers have renewed their ties with the spirits of the family dead.

There is a small variation in the form the ceremonies take in each village. Different villages begin the Karo celebration, for example, at different dates specified by tradition. In the northeast and northwest, in addition, there are commencement ceremonies that draw together several villages in traditional dancing. In general, however, most Tengger communities begin the Karo festivities with a *semeninga* ceremony that announces to the gods the impending liminal period of ritual activity. Several days after this opening ceremony (which is usually a private affair celebrated at the priest's house), each household brings a contribution of food and money (called *torun, pupon*) to the house of the village chief, where the rice portion of the food offerings is set out in a mountainlike pile and blessed by the priest.[6] In the week that follows,

---

[5] My description here is based on observation of the festival during the Karo month in 1979 and 1980. I witnessed the ritual ceremonies from beginning to end in three villages, and saw portions of the same cycle in another seven. Nancy Smith-Hefner also kindly provided me with detailed information on the rite in the Tengger northeast. A fuller account of the rite is found in Hefner (1982).

[6] The value of the *torun* contributions varies widely between villages. The fee is set by village officials in light of the extravagance of village festivities. In my southern Tengger village, the average fee during 1979 and 1980 was about Rp 1,500 (approx. US $2.50). It was twice that amount in the more affluent villages of the northwest, which sponsored expensive *ludruk* theater. All households in the village are usually assessed the same fee,

there is a flurry of related preparatory activity. The village chief summons dignitaries of the village to his home, assigns them tasks for the festivities about to begin, and then shares with them a ceremonial meal (the *mepek*). The same men return to the chief's house the next day. They move quickly to dismantle whole walls, erect new partitions, and build a temporary extended roof, under which dancing and dining will occur during the central days of Karo.

Ritual invocation of the deities begins the next day. The village priest, officials, a gaggle of children, and several women dancers (professionals hired in the lowlands for all Tengger dance festivals) gather in the village *sanggar* shrine. Offerings are laid out, the priest burns incense, and the deities are invited to descend to the village for the beginning of the core Karo ceremonies. Once present, the spirits are treated to a special dance performance by the female dancers (*tandak, tledek*),[7] who present them with glasses of beer or wine as if they were living human dancers. The village chief then joins the dancing women for one tune (played by a small, portable *gamelan* ensemble), and is followed by the village priest. The dancing continues this way until all of the male dignitaries have had an opportunity to dance before the spirits, and enjoy the single glass of alcohol to which each dancer is entitled. The spirits present for this dance performance, it is said, are the family spirits of living villagers, not the higher guardian deities. The latter descend briefly, enjoy the invisible essence of the *sajenan* offerings, and, presumably, then do as they will. From this point on, however, the less august family spirits take up residence in the village, where they stay with relatives until redispatched to the heavens at the end of Karo.

These spirits are accorded special ritual attention during each new phase of the Karo celebration. Each time a family has a meal during these first days of Karo, it is supposed to set out a small portion of the same foods for spirit relatives. Some villagers are pious and energetic

---

with the exception of widows, who are asked to pay either nothing at all or one-half the general amount. Village officials, curiously, are spared any payment, in recognition of their role in organizing the festivities.

[7] *Tayuban* dancing is found throughout Central and East Java, but it appears to have been especially popular in earlier times throughout the Eastern Salient. *Tandak* or *tledek* are the professional female dancers who accompany the male dancers by singing, dancing, and presenting drinks. In many areas of the Eastern Salient, *tayuban* dancing has, since Indonesian independence, been severely restricted as a result of the pressures applied by orthodox Muslims and certain government administrators. It appears that in earlier times Tengger women used to dance with their men, and the professional women hired in the lowlands were not used (cf. Domis 1832:347; van Lerwerden 1844:66). The modern form of *tayuban* in Tengger, with its expensive cash payments and social differentiation, appears to be a relatively new innovation, introduced into the area from the lowlands.

in their preparation of spirit foods, others lackadaisical, but virtually everyone has some food items for the spirits. The most important ritual activity, and the most frenzied social festivity, however, begin only a week after the initial descent of the spirits to the village. His house readied, a bull slaughtered, and dozens of people helping in the kitchen, the village chief opens his home to the community for the celebration of the Karo feast. Beginning late in the afternoon, groups of women and children gather gaily around the chief's house, dressed in their finest batik *sarong* and *kebaya* blouses. They await their turn to eat at the tables set up in the dining area of the chief's now considerably expanded house. These are the foods for which the villagers' Karo contributions have paid—sweet cakes and coffee, thick morsels of beef and pig-fat gravy, steaming mounds of white rice, an abundance of rich foods that many people only rarely eat. This pattern of eating in sex-segregated shifts is the style of especially large *slametan* feasts; smaller household festivals, and smaller ritual meals in the course of larger events, can include men and women together.

Women and children finish taking their meals around 9:00 p.m. This being only the first of three nights of feasting, many women will eat the next days rather than the first. In large festivals, men usually take their turn dining later in the evening, although male and female guests from outside the village come at all hours. During the first night of large festivals like Karo, however, the men entitled to come to the festival are dignitaries only—the chief, his fellow officials, the priest, respected elders, and what is usually a sizable contingent of lower-level government administrators from the lowlands. Other men can enjoy the fare only during the second and third night of festivities. Like the women, men eat in shifts. Once they finish their meal, however, male guests have the additional option of joining in the dance performance that begins around 9:00 and continues to the first light of day.

A woman dancer (*tandak, tledek*), dressed in a man's jacket and made up to look like a cross between a pirate and a prince, announces the beginning of the night's dancing by singing a song of welcome. In all large Tengger festivals today, this song (and all the other songs sung throughout the night) is broadcast into the village by a powerful loudspeaker system. For most men this is the sign that the women's feasting has finished, and the male portion of the night begun. Local women may stay to watch their husbands dance, but they never join in the dancing or drinking of alcohol. The men sit in chairs at the edges of the dance floor, listening to the opening song, and awaiting the invitation to dance. Once the woman finishes her opening song, there is a pause as she and other women dancers (there may be from two to eight) dress themselves in the alluring finery of *tandak* dress. The dance begins with the women's reappearance, but the order of male dance is precisely regulated. For each set of three tunes, one man is invited to dance, another to dance opposite, and others may gather at the edge of the dance floor, clapping respectfully or dancing around the central dancers. The order of men invited to "assume the dance scarf" (*ketiban sampur*) is supposed to be determined by a man's status, highest status first. The task of making such sensitive status discriminations is usually given to a high village official or respected elder, whose own social preeminence in effect puts him out of range of challenge. Each man has the right to lead the dance floor in this fashion at least once during the night, playing opposite an attractive woman dancer and, at the conclusion of his performance, dashing down a glass of beer, wine, or Javanese gin. When honored in this fashion, a man is obliged to make a cash payment (*bowo*) to the house kitty, and the money is recorded in a *bowo* book and ultimately goes to the festival sponsor. Payment is made in full sight of everyone, hence it tends to be inflated according to one's social standing. Although the *bowo* is ideally supposed to be reciprocated, its amount is substantial, and its return is insured only if the donor is himself the later sponsor of a large ritual festival. Smaller payments, in addition, have to be made to the women dancers, usually by the man's inserting a bill into the woman's brassiere. Largely because of these expenses, many middle-income villagers, and the vast majority of poor village men, avoid the dance floor entirely, sometimes privately complaining of what they see as an "un-Tengger" form of entertainment.

The most important of the priest's Karo rites begins the next, or second, day of the three-day feast. The ceremony is held again at the village chief's house, where the priest's assistants erect a special two-legged offering stand (the *tuwuhan*) for a ceremony called the "great offering" (*banten gede*). A ritual of the same name is used in all of the most powerful rites of spiritual invocation (Chapter 8). The *tuwuhan* itself stands upright, a wooden beam linking its two legs. The legs consist of sugar-cane stalks, palm leaves, flowers, and small branches; the connecting beam is hung with bananas and packets of cooked rice, maize, and meat. No ordinary villager can give a name to the spirit for whom all this is intended. They do know, however, that it is designed to serve as a touch-down point for a very powerful—some say the most powerful—heavenly deity. The ceremony in which the spirit is invoked is itself short and simple. Facing the *tuwuhan*, the priest stands and recites a prayer appealing to the deity to come and assist him in the ritual about to take place (Chapter 8). He then sits down again, burns incense, anoints the offerings, and, as always, invites the gods to consume their invisible essence.

Only after the *banten* does the priest set out for individual households. For the next two, three, or four days, he will go from house to house performing exactly the same ceremony. First appealing to and giving worship to the guardian deities, he then invites the souls of the family dead to descend to the house of their living relatives. This ceremony is known by a variety of terms (*sesanti, sesanding, dederek*), all of which refer to the family spirits that are thought to stand shoulder-to-shoulder before the living at the conclusion of this rite. Each household is responsible for preparing *sajenan* offerings for the guardian deities, and *suguhan* food plates for the souls of deceased relatives. The reception of the latter spirits receives the most attention. A piece of clothing from each of one's deceased relatives (only those still remembered and in the lineal family line) is wrapped around a small leaf-and-flower figurine known as a *petra* or *puspa petra* ("flower of the ancestors"). The full group of these figurines is then placed on a long pillow above a table of offerings set out for the family spirits and guardian deities. The priest visits each house for only a few minutes. Although villagers inevitably invite him to rest and eat both before and after the service, he usually begins the ceremony immediately and leaves quickly. It is a rather standard ritual format: incense is burned, the offerings are anointed, and the spirits are invited to eat. Family spirits, it is assumed, tag alone behind the guardian deities, and after these latter have enjoyed their offerings, the former are presented with their food plates. Then, for this one brief moment each year, family members are invited to come face to face with the souls of their relatives. Some people step forward and bow respectfully; others whisper a private message to a loved one. A moment later, however, the priest brings the rite to a conclusion, singing a song of "turning back" (*tundungan*), enjoining the spirits to return to their "place in the east." A handful of flower petals launched toward the *petra* and a wave of the priest's ritual scarf (*sampet*) send the spirits on their way.

The rite now done, the head of the household unobtrusively slips some money into the priest's hand (usually Rp 400-1,000 per household), and the priest heads off. Their spiritual obligations fulfilled, family members move quickly to wrap up the food plates presented to the family spirits and send them off to neighbors and relatives. The sending of these food gifts (*ater-ater*) is a sign to people in other parts of the village that the priest's labor is done. Later in the evening, neighbors, relatives, and friends will descend upon the household to share an obligatory Karo meal. This interhousehold visitation (*sanja-sinanja*) is an important part of the Karo festivities, and continues throughout the village for the better portion of a week. That section of the village where the priest first finishes his services is the first to receive guests from other neighborhoods. The visits are later returned when the priest completes his work elsewhere. Each man and woman is obliged to visit close kin, neighbors on all sides of the house, and close acquaintances (including those in nearby villages). An average villager may thus visit from twenty to forty households, eating in each. It is quite proper for a person to fulfill his visitation obligations by sharing just a few handfuls of rice or a pinch of meat. Most individuals visit several households each night, and it is always in poor taste to eat heavily. It would be unthinkable, however, for someone—even the poorest villager—not to prepare Karo foods and receive guests.

The last Karo rite takes place at the village cemetery one week after the *banten* ceremony. The spirits have now been in the village for two to three weeks, and this final rite, known as the *nyadran*, is designed to end the liminal period and send the spirits on their way. The term *nyadran* is from the Old Javanese *shradda*, a Hindu ritual for the dead (Pigeaud 1962:IV:172). A ceremony of the same name as that in Tengger, however, is still celebrated by many Javanese at the end of the Muslim month of fast. The lowland *nyadran* usually involves a family's visiting the grave sites of parents and other close relatives. The grave is tidied up, flowers may be set out, and a prayer may be said. *Kejawen* Muslims in addition sometimes set out small offerings, the idea being that the spirits of one's relatives may descend to the site. The Tengger *nyadran* builds on a similar theme, but it is much less ambiguous about the fact that family spirits are invoked. In some Tengger communities, in fact, whole villages troupe out together—the chief, his officials, and the priest to the front of the parade, sometimes with a brightly caparisoned dancing horse for entertainment. Upon arriving at the cemetery, villagers set out mats on the grave sites of their relatives, and arrange picnic foods for themselves, people at adjacent graves, and, of course, the spirits of the dead. It is a festive, not a somber affair: everyone is dressed in holiday best; those owning cassette players bring them along, blasting out *gamelan* music; and everyone shares food. After everyone has arranged the grave site, the priest burns incense and presents offerings to the guardian deities. He then invites the family spirits to eat the food plates borne by their relatives. At this sign, individual families anoint the graves of relatives with fragrant holy water, utter a quick prayer to their relatives, and then distribute food to family members and those around. People move freely around the cemetery, exchanging greeting and food with other villagers. In the meantime, it is thought, family spirits sit happily among the living, enjoying this final hour of communion with them. Then, with no further liturgy, the ceremony is done. As a dancing horse and village officials lead the way, Karo comes to a close.

Despite variation in minor detail, the basic pattern of the Karo cycle—repeated invocation of guardian deities and the residing presence of family spirits over a two- or three-week period—is remarkably consistent around Tengger. There are two points of variation worth noting, however. In two Tengger villages each year, one in the northwest and the other in the northeast, the Karo season begins with a traditional pole dance known as the *sodoran* (from *sodor*, "spear, staff"). The dance is only performed during Karo, and only in these villages. Its style varies considerably between the northeast and northwest (Hefner 1982), but its overall movement—and exegesis—is the same in both communities. The dancers are always men. For much of the dance they carry long bamboo poles (the *sodor*). In the northwest these poles are filled with various agricultural seeds; in the northeast, they are simply adorned with red and white cloth (color symbolism associated with male and female, fertility). The dance form is relatively simple: holding the poles out straight before them, the men (first a single dancer, then whole groups of men) advance toward dancers at the other side of the room, then retreat, repeating the in-out movement three times. On the third and final approach, the dancers walk past each other, turn around, and face each other again, only to repeat the same advance-and-retreat pattern. This goes on for some time, embellished with various hand movements and formal utterances from the side of the dance floor. The dance finally culminates with a rising crescendo of *gamelan* drum and gong, at a feverish pace, during which the dancers shake the poles they carry with increasing fervor. In the northwest version of this dance, the actors bang their poles so excitedly against the ground that the bamboo poles shatter, sending their seed contents spilling out onto the ground. In the northeast, by contrast, the poles are not broken. Throughout the dance there, however, two village chiefs sit to the side of the dance floor, one dressed as a groom, the other dressed in a woman's scarf to look like a bride. In both the northwest and northeast, the male dancers themselves are referred to as "bride and groom" (*manten*), and the dance is thus said to represent the sexual interaction of male and female.

The second major point of variation in the Karo proceedings is also a pole event, this time whip fighting with rattan sticks (*ujungan*). This occurs in a few Tengger villages at the end of the *nyadran* festivities. The *ujungan* is a beautiful martial art, combining the skills of dancing, boxing, and fencing. Young men usually volunteer for the contest. They

123

fight in pairs, each man wielding a rattan stick, advancing toward the other and, in a sudden movement, attempting to reach over the back of his opponent and strike the other's bare back. The two men take turns striking each other. Fighters move with dancelike movements, trying to throw the opponent off balance. The man to be struck holds the rattan stick with two hands behind his head, attempting to raise the stick at just that moment when his opponent reaches for his back, so as to deflect the stinging blow. This martial art is found throughout East Java, where it is often used as a form of magic, to induce rain during droughts. At first sight one could hardly imagine an activity further removed from the quietistic ethos of Central Javanese performance, but the martial contest is distinctively Javanese, nonetheless. Skill in the endeavour lies in the ability to sustain hard blows without bruises, and without losing one's good humor and smile.

Most Tengger regard the *ujungan* as a form of traditional sport or entertainment. In several Tengger communities of Buda persuasion, however, the activity is subject to a more curious interpretation. The fight, one Buda priest told me, represents the contest of Islam and Buda. Its purpose, he added, is to expel all evil and ill will from the relationship of Muslims and Buda people. Some Tengger offer a similar interpretation of the *sodoran* pole dance. The dance not only represents male and female, they insist, but the complementary interaction of Islam and Buda. This, they argue, is the purpose of Karo as a whole. The "two" referred to in the festival's name includes not only male and female but an equally fertile complementarity—Islam and Buda.

Conclusion

Karo's rich detail invites comparison with traditional forms in other areas of Indonesia, with which it shows sometimes surprising parallels. Rattan fighting, for example, is found in areas of Eastern Indonesia, where it is often also associated with fertility symbolism, as here in Tengger. Pole dancing is also found in Bali, where the *baris* spear dance often plays a role in ritual (Covarrubias 1937:230). The richest comparisons with Tengger Karo, however, lie within Java of an earlier era. Prapanca's fourteenth-century description of the *rajapatni* invocation of royal family spirits at the Majapahit court, for example, shows what are—given the social and historical distance of the example—astounding parallels with Tengger Karo. In Majapahit, as in Tengger, the spirit of the dead is invoked and invited to take up temporary residence in a *puspa* flower figurine (Pigeaud 1962:IV:175). Once present, the spirit is entertained over a three-day period, with mountain-shaped rice offerings (176), flower salutations (185), fighting dances (196), and feasting and dancing. Despite six hundred years of cultural change, the details of how one celebrates the presence of family spirits are remarkably similar to those seen in modern Tengger.

Whatever their comparative interest, however, these points of similarity do not directly inform Tengger understanding of their tradition. When asked Karo's purpose, villagers inevitably respond by comparing it to the Muslim festivities of *Hari raya idul fitri* which come at the end of the annual fasting month (an event which Tengger, unlike even Christian Javanese, do not mark with social festivity). Both occasions are times for recalling the memory of deceased kin, and reaffirming social ties with family, neighbors, and associates. As mentioned above, many Muslim Javanese also use the occasion to visit the graves of their parents and grandparents, sprinkling the grave site with water, and sometimes even appealing to the family spirits. The parallels between Karo and the Muslim *nyadran* are thus real enough, although they fail to make apparent the greater complexity and religious importance of the month-long Karo celebration.

It is, at any rate, in this direction—toward modern Java and its cultural challenge—that modern Tengger look in explaining the meaning of Karo. According to some accounts of Karo's origins, moreover, the rite was instituted in ancient times, when the Islamic Prophet Mohammad and the Javanese culture hero Ajisaka established a pact. The "followers of Mohammad" and those of Ajisaka, the pact stipulated, would forever recognize the necessary complementarity of Buda and Islam, and live together with mutual respect and tolerance. As the tale of Aji and Mohammad will indicate, however, this exegesis of the Karo tradition is itself in need of exegesis, and is a matter of interpretive dispute.

· 6 ·

CULTURE CHALLENGE AND CULTURE HERO:
THE TALE OF AJISAKA AND MOHAMMAD

There are numerous versions of the Tengger Ajisaka tale. The following is a translation of an oral version recounted to me by an elderly man in a southern Tengger village of Buda persuasion.

It was still in the time of Ki Kures, who lived in poverty with his wife. They could do nothing: to eat, they gathered leaves and grasses in the forest, and with this they fed their children. While in the forest one day, Ki Kures entered a large cave. There, to his surprise, he encountered an enormous serpent (*naga*), known as the Antaboga. The serpent spoke to Ki Kures: "Ki Kures, if you wish to feed and clothe yourself well, bring me each day a portion of milk." Ki Kures left and returned the next day with a bamboo container of milk. As he poured the liquid into Antaboga's open mouth, the serpent instructed him to reach in and select a jewel or piece of gold. Ki Kures did this every day, and from this he became very wealthy.

Ki Kures also had a son, named Bambang Dursila. The youth was extremely mischievous, loving only to play and gamble. He became suspicious of his father's new wealth, wondering from where it came. Thus one day he followed his father and saw him enter the cave and give milk to the *naga*-serpent. The next day Bambang went himself to the cave, bringing milk, and hoping to trick and slay the animal. But the *naga* knew already of Bambang's plans. As the youth drew near, the Antaboga lashed at him with such force that Bambang was thrust into a tree, dead.

Ki Kures came later to the cave and saw his son. "How can this be, my lord? My son dead?" The Antaboga replied: "You must not worry, your son died trying to kill me." Ki Kures became very upset. "My lord *naga*," he said, "my son's wife is pregnant." "Tomorrow," the *naga* replied, "when the child is born, name it yourself if it is a girl. But if it is a boy, bring him here that I may see him."

The child was born a boy. Ki Kures brought him to the *naga*, who took him and raised him as his own son, teaching him many wonderful powers. He taught him how to make himself invisible, how to bend steel, how to block knives or bullets, how to control

126

his strength in many ways. Antaboga named him Aji, because he was so handsome. Ki Kures exclaimed to Antaboga: "I have never seen one so handsome as he!" Antaboga responded: "Ah, but there is one who is even more handsome, whose name is Nabi Mohammad. Your grandson must now go to study (ngaji) with him."

Aji went to Mecca, where he studied with four companions, Abu Bakar, Usman, Umar, and Ali. One day the Prophet Mohammad came to the five companions, and addressed Aji. "Aji?" "Yes my lord Gusti," responded Aji. "You must go now to investigate an epidemic. People alive in the morning are dying by evening. You must learn why this is happening. Go and check the jamjam water. If it is clear, the plague will soon pass. If it is cloudy, the plague will continue."

Aji set out immediately with his four companions. En route a devil entered Aji's bowels, making him ill. He excused himself to relieve his discomfort. His companions awaited his return, but he did not appear. Alarmed, the four companions returned to Mecca, telling Mohammad what had happened. "We come bearing bad news, our Lord prophet. Aji cannot be found." Mohammad responded: "Enough! We need not worry. Persons who disappear reappear. Don't worry." The prophet then looked at one of the pillars (saka) in the great mosque and saw Aji hiding invisible in the pillar. "Who is this hiding in the mosque pillar?" Mohammad exclaimed. He then understood what had happened. Mohammad spoke: "Henceforth you will be known as Ajisaka. You will be my equal, yes it is so Aji! When you become male, I will be female, when I become male, you will be female. When you walk the night, I walk the day; when I walk the night, you walk the day. The seven days of the week will be mine, the days of the five-day week will by yours." Mohammad then named the days of the seven-day week: Senen, Seloso, Rebo, Kemis, Jemuah, Sabtu, Minggu. And these were the days of Ajisaka's five-day week: Legi, Pahing, Pon, Wage, Kliwon. But Ajisaka still had his own ideas, and thus gave different names to the seven days of Mohammad's week: Dite, Soma, Anggara, Buda, Respati, Sukra, Tumpak. Twelve were the names of the days, the two made one.

Two other men then appeared. One came from the west, and was named Setia; he was to be Mohammad's servant. The other came from the east, and was named Setuhu; he was to become Ajisaka's servant. Mohammad turned to Ajisaka and said, "Aji, now you must go to the country of Medangkamulian, in the southeast. Take there a primbon prayer book and an almanac for determining aus-

127

picious dates. Go there, the belief in that country is still not true belief. The king among the people eats human flesh. His name is Dewotocengkar."

Ajisaka departed immediately. Mid-route he realized he had forgotten his *kris* dagger. He turned to Setuhu and said, "Go fetch my sword and make sure that you allow none other than me to have it." Meanwhile in Mecca, Mohammad found Ajisaka's *kris*. He thus commanded his servant: "Take this sword to Ajisaka and make sure that none other than he takes it from you." Each of the two servants set out on his journey, and after much travel the two men came face to face. Setuhu spoke to Setia: "I have come for my master's *kris*." Setia responded: "I can allow no one other than Ajisaka to have it." Words gave way to struggle as each servant sought to grasp the sword. First Setia pulled it to him, then Setuhu pulled it back, back and forth, back and forth, until each was pierced by the blade and fell dead. Setia fell to the north, Setuhu to the south. It is for this reason that Muslims bury their dead with the head to the north, and Buda people bury theirs with the head to the south.

When their servants failed to return, Ajisaka and Mohammad grew worried. Each finally set out to find his servant. Meeting mid-route, Ajisaka and Mohammad saw the bodies of their faithful servants lying in the road. Saddened, the two lords then agreed to honor the memory of their servants. Mohammad created the thirty letters of the Arabic alphabet; Ajisaka created the twenty letters of the Javanese alphabet. The twenty and thirty make fifty, which is five surrounded by a zero, as the four corners of the house enclose its center. Mohammad then addressed Ajisaka: "Yes it is so. You must continue your work in the east. In Medangkamulian you must build a house of prayer. There you will find your followers. I return now to Arabia."

The people of Medangkamulian were very backward. Aji taught them to build a place of worship, a *sanggar*. The people pronounced the two sentences, the profession of faith. Aji explained that the two sentences (*kalimah loro*) had the following meaning: "There are two expressions. If there is male, there is female; if west, east; and it is for this reason that we must perform the Karo worship." To worship two (*loro*) is to worship Karo. In worship we remember Setia and Setuhu, the will of Mohammad and Ajisaka, the memory of the slain servants.

In Medangkamulian all admired Ajisaka's wisdom and good looks. Aji lived with an elderly widow, who had taken him as son. One day a servant of the evil king Dewotocengkar came to the house, to tell the widow that she had been chosen as the next victim of the king's cannibal appetite. On hearing this, Ajisaka immediately volunteered to take her place. The old woman protested, saying, "But you are such a handsome person, a man like a prince. You must not die." But Ajisaka went ahead and was taken before the evil Dewotocengkar.

The king was delighted to learn that one so young as Ajisaka was to be his meal. He asked Ajisaka if he was indeed prepared to die. Ajisaka replied, "Yes, but you must grant me one final wish. For my grave, you must grant me a land area as broad as my turban. That much land I request of you." The king agreed, and instructed his servant to unravel Aji's turban. As the turban was unfurled, it stretched to the east, south, west, and north. It was so large that Dewotocengkar was himself forced to retreat before its breadth, until he was pushed to the cliffs above the south sea. Suddenly Aji snapped the cloth, pushing the evil king into the water, where he turned into an enormous white crocodile. Aji then called all the people of the country to join him in throwing stones at the evil king, so that he would never again ascend onto land. Dewotocengkar cried: "Hey Ajisaka—all your children and descendants to the smallest mouse, any who dare come near this water I will capture as my own." Aji replied: "That makes no difference, for you are now in the water and must never again return to land."

Free of their evil king, the people of Medangkamulian made Ajisaka their king. He taught them many things. The learning and prosperity of the kingdom were great.

Mythic Word and World

As with the earlier Kasada myth, the Ajisaka tale is a story of two cultural traditions told through the interaction of personnages: Ajisaka and Mohammad, Buda and Islam. The story moves the main actors through a series of episodes that provide important, if at times implicit, comment on the quality of their relationship. Personal relationship is here of course symptomatic of a larger cultural process. The myth is not merely a tale of Islam and Buda, but of the evolution of Javanese culture.

From the start we hear sounds of a new order and of the demise of the old. It is, the story begins, the time of Ki Kures. Despite the honorific Javanese title (*ki*), Kures is recognizable as a character from a less ex-

129

clusively Javanese literary tradition. In popular Javanese Muslim tradition, the Kures are the pagan enemies of Mohammad at the time of
Islam's founding in Arabia. Here in the Aji tale, however, Kures is a
simpler symbol of a precultural past, at a time when people "could do
nothing." Ki Kures is a forager; he and his family are miserably poor.
Only his name gives hint of a larger impending religious order. It is
Kures's poverty that creates the condition for the first important relationship introduced in the myth. Ki Kures will meet the great *naga*-
serpent, Antaboga, and become his servant.

Two worlds have met. Related to the *naga*-serpent found in much
Asian folklore (cf. Tambiah 1970:169), Antaboga in Javo-Balinese tradition is none other than the world serpent who lies at the foundation
of the world (Covarrubias 1937:7). In this narrative, however, his role
is less vast; whatever he may have once meant to Tengger Javanese,
Antaboga now figures in no other popular tales. In this tale, Antaboga
plays a central role in the readjustment of relationships that leads to
Ajisaka's appearance. Antobaga kills Ki Kures's son, and this act ultimately results in Antaboga's becoming teacher to Aji, the son of Bambang Dursila. Aji, the eventual culture hero, is thus of very humble
origins: the grandson of the pagan Ki Kures, he is also the son of the
good-for-nothing Bambang. Expressed formally, the movement of personnages is simple: elimination of the father facilitates a new and higher
relationship, that of teacher to student. This relationship, however, is
no more than a bridge to another. Aji's knowledge and good looks, it
is said, are only surpassed by those of the prophet Mohammad. So Aji
is off to Mecca, to *ngaji*, a term used in Java for formal Islamic study.
The change of relationship—here Aji's movement from Antaboga to
Mohammad as teacher—once again signals the inauguration of a new
cultural era. From the pagan Ki Kures, savagery personified, to the
syncretic Antaboga, we have now come to one "yet more handsome."
This cultural stage, a Muslim one, will also eventually be superseded.

In Mecca Aji studies with four companions: Abu Bakar, Usman, Umar,
and Ali. The four-plus-one balance is recognizably Javanese in its numeral classification, but Aji's four companions figure in another tradition
as well: they are the four successors to Mohammad as caliphs of the
Islamic nation. Aji's cultural quest has brought him to a curious milieu
indeed. At this early point in the tale, Aji's relationship with Mohammad
is unquestionably that of social inferior. In the Javanese-language version
of this tale, Aji addresses Mohammad in respectful high Javanese, whereas
Mohammad responds in the low Javanese of a superior addressing a
subordinate. Mohammad commands Aji—but even early in the tale,
there is a tension to their relationship that becomes more apparent as

the story progresses. Mohammad, for example, orders Aji to go to the *jamjam* spring to perform divination concerning a plague. *Jamjam* is Javanese for the Arabic *zamzam*, the name of a holy spring in Mecca, and still the site of pilgrim activity. En route to the spring Aji falls ill. According to this version of the Aji account, Aji has been possessed by a devil (*iblis*); in other versions of the same tale, however, Aji is said to encounter not a devil but an archangel (*melaikat*), an Islamic spirit being that in Javanese folk tradition often plays a spiritual role very similar to that of Indic *dewa* as a source of power, guardianship, and knowledge. According to these tales, Aji learns from the archangel things that even the Prophet Mohammad (who is, after all, still a human) does not know. Aji's wisdom thus comes to exceed that of Mohammad's, and the stage is set for the curious mosque encounter described in the present version of the Aji tale.

Aji's relationship with Mohammad has changed. He returns to Mecca and, trickster style, hides in the main pillar (*saka*) of the great mosque. The ruse is at once suggestive of Aji's new relationship with the prophet and indicative of the meaning of Aji's full name. Aji is to be Ajisaka or, according to this pop etymology, "Aji of the pillar." At this point in the text the dynamic tension between Aji and Mohammad becomes clearer; Aji and Mohammad become, literally, polar opposites, bound to each other in their difference. When one is night, the other is day; when one is the moon the other is the sun; when one is female the other is male. The two primary systems of weekdays used in Java are also explained by Aji and Mohammad's relationship. Aji is the owner of the five-day week (the terms of which are Javanese), whereas Mohammad is the owner of the seven-day week (the terms of which are derived from Arabic). Aji's trickster role appears once again, however; he has his own ideas as to what one should call the days of the seven-day week. The terms that he uses (*dite*, etc.) are in fact the Sanskrit-derived terms still used in some cultural settings in Java; Javanese popularly think of these Sanskrit terms as the Old Javanese names for the seven days of the week. In this tale however, Aji's use of the Old Javanese terms provides one more example of Aji's tricksterish ways, putting what is Javanese before orthodox Islam.

The balance between Aji and Mohammad, however, is not yet complete. Mohammad still commands Aji in low Javanese, and Aji is still the servant of the Prophet's will. The appearance of Setia and Setuhu, servants to Aji and Mohammad, will ultimately allow for a displacement of this relationship. On order from Mohammad, Aji leaves for Medangkamulian, the mythical first kingdom of Java according to popular Javanese tradition. Aji forgets his *kris* dagger, Mohammad finds it, and the servants of the two set out to return the *kris* to Aji. Setia and Setuhu meet, clash, push and shove, and fall back dead. Each is, in effect, victim of overscrupulous fidelity to a master's command. The fate of the two servants is, of course, intended to give warning to anyone inclined to be overzealous in obeying religious masters. Patience and religious tolerance are the way to avoid conflict and pain. Setia and Setuhu learned the hard way. Their position in burial, however, will serve as a reminder to others who serve Aji and Mohammad: followers of Mohammad will be buried with their head to the north, followers of Aji, to the south. Arabic and Javanese script are also invented, the myth recounts, to commemorate the servants' unfortunate clash. Here too the message of the myth is that two key, and often opposed, aspects of Javanese and Islamic culture are, in reality, not at all antagonistic. Both were invented to remember the same disaster, and to prevent its recurrence. Those inclined to see Arabic and Javanese writing as opposed ways of knowledge must remember this and never repeat the servants' mistake.[1]

Aji returns to Medangkamulian after this reencounter with Mohammad. In that country, he teaches the people to build a *sanggar*, a traditional (and not necessarily Islamic) house of worship, rather than an Islamic *langgar*. He also instructs people in the meaning of the *kalimah loro*, that is, the "two sentences," usually understood to mean the Islamic profession of faith, recognizing Allah as God and Mohammad as his prophet. Ever the trickster, however, Aji has other ideas as to the meaning of the "two sentences." His ideas have to do with the necessary unity of opposites: male and female, east and west, Islam and Buda. According to Aji, this is the true meaning of the *kalimah loro*, and it is a meaning that also underlies the Karo celebration. Islam and Buda celebrate the same truth.

While working in Medangkamulian, Aji lives as an adopted son to an elderly widow. Earlier bereft of a father, Aji became a student (to the *naga*); now adopted as an adult son, Aji becomes teacher. His new relationship to the widow, however, will serve to introduce the final conflict of the Aji tale: Aji will take the place of the widow as victim of

---

[1] In the once-Buda communities to the southwest of present-day Tengger settlement, for example, there were in the last century two different literary specialists associated with what were often regarded as two competing religious traditions. Muslim literati used Arabic script (or its simplified *pegu* form) for religious instruction and *moco* readings at *slametan* festivals. Buda people, by contrast, had literary specialists who wrote in Javanese script and recited *moco* stories—like the Ajisaka tale—which spoke of the need for complementary coexistence of Buda and Islam. Some villages had literary specialists who read both scripts and recited tales of both an Islamic and *kejawen* nature. But one additional aspect of the Islamization process described in Chapter 11 was the banning of public *moco* reading of non-Islamic literary works.

the flesh-eating king, Dewotocengkar. The evil-king's name signals a larger cultural reference: from *cengkar*, "without," and *dewoto*, "deity, spirit," Dewotocengkar is godlessness personified. Aji's task is to change all this, and introduce another cultural order into the kingdom. To do this, Aji resorts to another in his bag of tricks. His turban—an item of dress conveniently identifiable as either Muslim or Hindu—covers the island and forces the evil king into the south sea. The story here touches on a familiar theme in Javanese folklore: the dangers of the south coast and of oceans in general. To this day the cult of *Nyai Roro Kidul* in Central Java identifies that sea goddess as the being who periodically snatches unsuspecting male bathers from the shore. Here in the Aji myth, however, the sea's danger is identified with the evil king who, on entering the water, becomes a white crocodile—a fitting image for the south sea's dangerous pounding surf. Dewotocengkar's warning gives voice to a generally recognized value of inland Javanese society: Javanese should stick to land and avoid the seas, where danger and death lurk.

On land, however, a new cultural order has emerged. It is the age of Ajisaka, and the cultural evolution about which the Aji tale has spoken appears complete—if rather inconclusively. Mohammad remains unheard, but still in the background. It was he, after all, who commanded Aji to bring religion to Java. It would thus appear to have a rather fragile independence, this kingdom of Ajisaka.

Tengger and Non-Tengger in the Aji Tale

Few of the terms massed in the Ajisaka tale appear distinctively Tengger. The tale abounds with Islamic references, and makes almost no mention of specifically Tengger practices or beliefs. Indeed, comparative and historical evidence suggests that the tale is not an orthogenetic product of Tengger tradition. I recorded variants of the same tale in *kejawen* Muslim communities far to the south of the Tengger highlands. There are nineteenth-century versions of the same tale in the National Museum in Jakarta, most of which come from non-Tengger areas of Java.[2] The central narrative of the Ajisaka tale appears to have been popular in lowland areas of the Eastern Salient before it was adopted by Tengger.

An urban man from a community to the east of Malang once visited my first village of residence in southern Tengger, and heard me discussing the Aji tale with villagers during a *slametan* meal. Something of a self-taught specialist in mystical matters, Pak Dar later took me

---

[2] My thanks here go to Nancy Smith-Hefner, who worked through many of the Ajisaka texts in the National Museum in Jakarta.

aside to explain what he said was the "true" meaning of the Ajisaka tale. He said that Aji went to Mecca, yes, but not to become a Muslim. He sought to acquire Mohammad's spiritual knowledge (*ilmu*). In this respect, Pak Dar pointed out, Ajisaka was similar to him. After independence, Pak Dar had been an army administrator in the Tengger highlands, and took advantage of his frequent visits to the area to study with a local priest. He was not interested in the detail of the priestly liturgy (here he imitated in grotesque fashion the stylized gestures of priestly invocation) but the *ilmu* that lay behind it. "I was not a student of the priest, but a thief of his knowledge." The agreement between Aji and Mohammad, Pak Dar explained, stipulated that islands to the west of Java would become Islamic, whereas those to the east would remain Buda. When I pointed out to Pak Dar that the pact seems to have been ignored, since most of Java is now Islamic, Pak Dar shrugged and added that, in fact, the dividing line between Islam and Buda lay just to the west of the town in which he lived.

Pak Dar was typical of some lowland visitors to the Tengger region. He saw Tengger as "true" or "native" Javanese (*Jawa asli*). As a student of *kebatinan* mysticism, however, he had rather little patience with the detail of Tengger liturgy. He sought to get at what he thought was the metaphysical essence behind the Tengger priest's ritual hocus pocus; he wanted *ngelmu* knowledge, not religious community.

This and other evidence indicate that the Aji tale once played a role in a religious cult linking Buda Tengger to non- or nominally Islamic people in communities below the Tengger highlands. To this day, there are at least two separate burial sites (*punden*) where Setia and Setuhu are reputed to be buried. One of these lies near Turen, well over 40 kilometers from any Tengger settlement. According to this site's caretaker, pilgrims flocked to the area until the massacres of 1965-1966; since then, people come only rarely. Where did most of these pilgrims come from? According to the caretaker's report, most were from the Turen area, and communities to the south and east here in the Eastern Salient, although some came from as far away as Central Java. Tengger Javanese, the man added, were known to visit the site but were not its most frequent visitors.

The fact that Tengger joined in a spiritual cult which was in no way exclusively "Tengger" provides testimony to the changing self-perception of this people in the face of a revitalized Javanese Islam. Like the earlier Kasada myth, the Tengger version of the Ajisaka tale is concerned with cultural legitimation of a threatened tradition. But the terms the tale mobilizes for its task are profoundly different from those heard in the Kasada myth. Gone entirely is any mention of the sacred geography

134

of Tengger territory. In its place one sees a somewhat less parochial cultural terrain that includes Mecca, the *jamjam* spring, and Medang-kamulian. Gone too is any mention of Tengger ancestors and social organization. The sociological reference in this tale is much less local: it appeals to all followers of Ajisaka, all non- or nominally Islamic Javanese. The strength of the myth's appeal lies in its very generality; it speaks, evidently, to mystic townspeople as well as to mountain ritualists.

Because of the generality of its appeal, the myth speaks only sparingly of the ritual which, according to Tengger interpretation of the tale, it is supposed to explain. Coming as it does after a parade of syncretic and Islamic references, the myth's mention of the Karo celebration appears anomalous, as if it were tacked on to an already existing tale. Judging by comparison with non-Tengger variants of the Ajisaka tale, the reference to the Karo celebration does appear to have been appended to a preexisting moral tale. Several non-Tengger variants of the tale that I collected in lowland communities were similar to the above version in all major details except the reference to the Karo celebration; the lowland versions made no such mention. Historical evidence also suggests that the Ajisaka myth entered the Tengger region later than it did some of the surrounding non-Tengger communities. Based on research carried out in 1867, Meinsma reported that "Of the coming of Ajisaka (to Java), the Tengger know nothing" (Meinsma 1879:132). Meinsma was a meticulous researcher, and his report seems credible. Only a few decades later, however, Jasper reported that turn-of-the-century Tengger cited the Aji-Mohammad myth as their own, and linked it to both the Karo festival and the *sodoran* dance (Jasper 1926:41). A University of Indonesia research team, working in northeast Tengger in 1955, noted a similar association; Karo and the *sodoran* "remember the deaths of the two faithful servants" (Wibisono 1956:41).

The period between Meinsma's research and that of Jasper at the beginning of this century was, of course, a critical one in modern Tengger history. The advance of Dutch colonialism in the countryside had engendered a political crisis throughout Java, and a revitalized Islam was in the forefront of a growing anti-colonial and anti-traditional movement (Carey 1979, Kartodirdjo 1972, 1973). The agricultural lands below the Tengger highlands were major centers of Dutch enterprise, and it was in these areas that a progressive and politically self-conscious Islam began to grow as a social movement. It challenged not only the oppressive policies of Dutch colonialism, but also village traditions that were deemed parochial and out of step with the political and religious challenge of the era. A new identity had to be forged, based on a moral community greater than that specified by village traditions and first-founding ancestors. The Aji tale spoke to this same crisis. It too proposed a new identity, but one, it was hoped, that left room for the followers of Ajisaka along side the community of Mohammad.

Ajisaka Vanquished

As a tool for cultural legitimation the Aji myth was, at least for Tengger, critically flawed. In defending a non-Islamic tradition it adopts a number of Islamic references. A tension thus remains between Aji and Mohammad, one that is apparent in the Javanese dialogue in the Aji text. It is always Aji who speaks as social subordinate to Mohammad. Mohammad speaks as Gusti or Lord to a subordinate. Aji nonetheless manages to get his way most of the time through trickster artifice. But this does not so much resolve the tension between the two leaders as it defers it through deviousness. Aji is a trickster, not a victor, and from this perspective the curiously unfinished tone of the tale is appropriate. The tale in effect ends with a standoff that refuses to acknowledge itself as such. Although nominally under Mohammad's command, Aji is a unreliable messenger of the word because he is, quite simply, too committed to Javanese ways. In building a place of worship, he thus constructs a *sanggar* rather than a Islamic *langgar*. For scripture, he uses a Javanese *primbon* rather than the Koran. Yet he never proclaims his independence from Mohammad. It should come therefore as little surprise that, in communities below Tengger, there exists a final chapter on Aji's fate. I recorded this oral addendum to the tale in a recently Islamized community to the south of Tengger. My informant explained that Ajisaka was a good king, but a lousy religious teacher. One day a messenger named Subakir arrived from Mecca with a letter from Mohammad. Mohammad wished to discuss the progress of Aji's work, so Aji was ordered to return immediately to Mecca. Aji set out in a sailing vessel for Mecca, accompanied by his wife and son. They sailed and sailed for many days. But one day, in the middle of the ocean, it became dead calm. No wind, no motion, no sound—nothing. That was it, finished, the end of ole Ajisaka. Aji couldn't do anything, and no one could do anything for poor Aji. "I don't know if he died or what," my informant explained. "But no more was ever heard from him. He was finished, kaput, right there in the middle of the sea. That's Ajisaka." As in the earlier version of the Aji tale, the dangers of the sea are again brought into mythic service. This time, however, the sea simply swallows its victim in its vastness. There is a new order arising, one that knows nothing of Ajisaka, which will proclaim the glories of one "even more

136

handsome." What better metaphor for the Islamization of rural Java? There is here no conversion by the sword, but the benign if deliberate neglect of a collective memory. The culture hero does not die; he and his truth fade away.

Those Tengger who still endorse the Aji-Mohammad pact bitterly deny the truth of this mythic addendum. Most of these true believers live in southern Tengger villages, areas that have resisted the Hindu reform movement (Chapter 11). For them, Ajisaka established a pact between Buda and Islam that must be renewed each year through the celebration of Karo and the remembering of the slain servants. "The *ujung* rattan fight must be performed each year," a southern priest once told me, "so as to cast away the evil of the battle between the servants of Aji and Mohammad." Village leaders throughout most of the Tengger north, however, today reject the Aji tale, and deny that it has anything to do with the Karo celebration. The disagreement over the myth and its relation to Karo has further alienated traditionalists in southern Tengger from Hindu reformists in the north.

Myth, Ritual, and the Conflict of Interpretations

The Aji and Mohammad myth is not the only tale of Ajisaka. Long before he figured in a tale with Mohammad, Ajisaka was already a familiar figure in Javanese folklore. He is associated with the earliest of Java's Hindu kingdoms (cf. Raffles 1965:II:66), and his arrival in Java is said to have been the beginning of the Javanese *saka* era. Aji is also said to have been the creator of *gamelan* music, Javanese script, and a variety of other distinctive elements of traditional Javanese culture. He is a culture hero *par excellence*, familiar to everyone who studies Javanese script. When a child learns that alphabet for the first time, he or she usually learns a little jingle by which to remember the order of letters. Sound-similarities between the letters and Javanese words create the following tale:

Ho no co ro ko	There were two servants
Do to so wo lo	Who did not deviate from their orders
Po do jo yo nyo	Equal in victory (happiness)
Mo go bo to ngo	Stopped dead together.

The story which is told with the jingle is that of the two servants, also mentioned in the Aji and Mohammad tale. The *kris* over which the two servants struggle is, as in the Tengger tale, Aji's. In this Aji tale, however, both servants are identified as aides to Ajisaka; Mohammad

137

is not drawn into the story, and the tale is not thought to have anything to do with Islam. There is another Ajisaka tale widely known throughout Java that similarly makes no mention of Islam, elements of which have also made their way into the Aji-Mohammad story. According to this account, Ajisaka was the son of an Indian Brahmanic family. He was also a seeker of knowledge, as in the Aji-Mohammad tale, and he sailed off from India for Java to learn more of the islands to the east. He arrives in a kingdom called Medangkamulian, and there does battle (turban and all) with a man-eating king named Dewotocengkar. His victory brings an era of knowledge and great prosperity to the heretofore backward people of Java. As Poerwadhie (1957) has noted, Aji's odyssey here symbolizes cultural evolution, centered on the transition from pre-Indic to Indic culture. It is this version of the Ajisaka tale that my Central Javanese friends were most familiar with; none had ever heard of the Aji-Mohammad tale.

The Tengger version of the Aji tale uses these other Aji accounts as building blocks in a story with a different cultural message. Ajisaka's identity, above all, is much more ambiguous than in these other tales. Neither Indic nor Islamic, nor even just Javanese, Aji is all of these at once—a fitting figure for the turbulent terrain of nineteenth- and early twentieth-century East Java. What is curious about the Aji tale in Tengger, however, is its relation to the Karo festival and the *sodoran* pole dance. Even in those accounts in which Tengger reportedly identify these ritual events with the servants of Mohammad and Ajisaka, villagers are also heard to identify these ritual activities with sexual and fertility themes not mentioned in the Aji myth. Both Jasper (1926) and Wibisono (1956), for example, stress that Karo and the *sodoran* remember the slain servants of Aji and Mohammad. Not noting the inconsistency, however, both authors then go on to say that some people identify elements of these ritual activities with other meanings: the dancers in the *sodoran* are said to be bride and groom, their movement in and out is said to represent sexual intercourse, and so on.

In providing observers with these descriptive details, Tengger villagers may themselves have been unconcerned as to whether the fertility interpretation of Karo and the *sodoran* conflicted with the themes stressed in the Aji-Mohammad tale. What more appropriate image of complementarity, after all, than the fertile interaction of man and woman? Something was going on, however, in the larger cultural context. When Meinsma was in Tengger in the 1860s, after all, Karo was a regular ritual tradition, but Tengger "knew nothing" of Ajisaka. A half-century later, the dualities represented in Karo and the *sodoran* were associated in interpretive exegesis with Mohammad and Ajisaka. Yet another half-century later, when I came to Tengger to witness the Karo celebration, the majority of Tengger denied that either Karo or the *sodoran* had anything to do with Ajisaka and Mohammad, whereas a minority of Tengger (most in the southern region) insisted otherwise. To judge by Jasper's (1926) description of the *sodoran*, the basic ritual detail had not changed dramatically in the period between his study and mine. What had changed was the larger social world in which Tengger lived, and the experience they brought to their interpretation of the rite. It was this larger changing experience which underlay the interpretation and reinterpretation of Karo and the *sodoran*. The meaning of the rites, in other words, was not timelessly stored away in fixed ritual symbols or pregiven meanings. There can be no such essential center to ritual interpretation.

In practical terms this was the point illustrated in the comments of an elder, Pak Joyo, in the Tengger northwest. He had heard of my interest in the Aji tale, and took me aside to explain that the version of the tale I had collected in southern Tengger (where I was living at the time) was "mistaken." Northern Tengger, he explained, had also once believed in the Aji-Mohammad pact. Some village elders, however, always rejected the tale, saying that it was a scheme to lead Tengger bit by bit to Islam. In the 1950s, the lowlands around Tengger were tense with religious and political strife. Leaders in one northern village brought together community elders to dicusss Tengger history. These elders insisted that the true meaning of Ajisaka could be seen in the *sodoran* dance. The *sodor* poles were symbols of the "staff of life," and the dance itself represented sexual intercourse. Why else, Pak Joyo explained, would the poles have been filled with seeds? Tengger ancestors were concerned with a fundamental truth. They understood the origins of life, and recognized that this was God's plan. All Tengger rituals thus celebrate this same theme of male and female, creation and life. "It is a simple truth, one which does not try to impose itself on others." Ajisaka, Pak Joyo added, was merely a symbol of these concerns. He had nothing to do with Islam. He was a "shield to protect our tradition," and to help us remember: "Never forget the way of your ancestors."

At the time of my research, most southern Tengger were familiar with such criticisms of the Aji-Mohammad tale, but bitterly rejected them, nonetheless. When a Hindu Tengger school teacher once visited my southern village of residence, he tried to explain to the local priest and village chief the importance of the Hindu reform movement. He defended that movement's criticisms of the old Aji-Mohammad tale, and spoke of the need to build a truly modern religion, with its own scripture, commandments, and national organization. The priest and chief stood adamant in their opposition to the northerner's comments. Who came first to Java, they asked, Ajisaka or Hinduism? Which is older, the *Weda* of which Hindus speak or Ajisaka's teachings? Knowing of my interest in the Ajisaka tale, the southern village chief turned to me at one point in the conversation, visibly upset. I had visited northern Tengger recently, he said. So could I please tell him one thing: Had not Tengger ancestors in the north also once spoken of Ajisaka and Mohammad? Did they too not speak of *ngaluri* and the inviolability of Buda ways?

Conclusion: Aji and Identity

The gulf between the Kasada tale—first recorded in Dutch sources in 1785—and the Ajisaka myth clearly reveals the depths of the identity crisis shaking turn-of-the-century Tengger. The contrast is striking. Whereas Kasada looks up toward Mt. Bromo, Aji looks out on Java. Kasada's contract linking territory, people, and ancestral progenitors is replaced in the Aji tale with an almost desperate appeal for an alliance between all those faithful to Ajisaka's ways—all those, in other words, who identify with *kejawen* or Javanist culture. The ancestral legitimation of a territorial tradition thus gives way in the Aji tale to a more appropriately pan-Javanese appeal, neatly symbolized in the figure of Ajisaka. Under his banner, Java's diverse local traditions could be characterized in terms more general than those of some backwater parochialism. There is a problem with Aji, however. His appeal is formulated within such an Islamic framework that, at least for non-Muslims like Tengger, it is already fatally compromised. Perhaps sensing this, many modern Tengger have come to regard the tale as "dangerous and wrong," as one priest in north Tengger explained.

From the perspective of religious rationalization, the Ajisaka tale is a fascinating document. The religion from which it comes fits neatly into the category of neither "traditional" nor "modern" religion, as we understand these terms in a contemporary (and largely Weberian) sense. The world of Ajisaka's followers had not experienced secularization or a "disenchantment" of its territory; it preserved much of its spiritual vitality. There is nonetheless something dramatically untraditional about the tale. It displays little of the confident self-assurance one so often encounters in the narrative traditions of small-scale societies. It has caught wind of other ways, and appears anxiously aware of their challenge. Hence it talks not of local ancestors occupying a familiar terrain, but of Mohammad, Mecca, the *zamzam* spring, Abu Bakar, archangels, and a host of other beings who, at least from a philological perspective, can hardly be considered autochthonous fauna. The story is thus quite deliberately not just Tengger, but pan-Javanese. It addresses the cultural plight of a variety of non- or nominally Islamic traditions in a Java witness to a revitalizing Islam. It insists that although that Islamic heritage is itself proper and true, so too is the heritage of Ajisaka and Java. In other words, the Aji tale seeks to create a new self-definition for a threatened Javanese tradition. In the area of rural East Java around the Tengger highlands, in particular, it was intended to provide a disparate assortment of local traditions with the terms for a new and more expansive social identity, articulated in terms of a pan-Javanese identity rather than *punden* cults of first-founding ancestors. Mohammad's counterpart, Aji was the prophet of this pan-Javanese community.

Ajisaka was, however, a flawed prophet for a compromised community. The pan-Javanese community promised in the Aji tale never really came into existence. It would be swept aside by an integrative revolution that, beginning in nineteenth-century Java, slowly redefined the self-perceptions of rural populations increasingly pressed by the demands of a modern political economy and by the collapse of received self-definitions. Out of these same circumstances, Java's Islamic community managed to forge the cultural idioms and the organizational apparatus for the construction of a national movement premised on a revitalized religious identity (Kartodirdjo 1972). Events of the twentieth century would reveal, however, that the community hoped for under the terms of the Aji tale failed to materialize as planned. The alliance sought between Tengger and other "followers of Ajisaka" would, with a few isolated exceptions, be forgotten or repressed. Aji's erstwhile proponents would have to come up with other solutions to the problem of self-definition in a changing Java.

· 7 ·

LIFE PASSAGE AND RITUAL

Until recently, the household was the only corporate social group operating within the Tengger village, and *slametans* celebrating the birth, growth, and life passage of its members were the only organized ritual activities besides those of the village itself. New corporate groups have been introduced into the village since Indonesian independence—scout clubs, farmers' co-ops, and the like—and now on occasion these may sponsor ritual events. The Hindu reform movement has, in addition, sought to develop more congregational modes of worship less immediately dependent on household and village socioeconomic organization. Prior to these innovations, however, ritual activity in the Tengger community occurred only if sponsored by some social body, and only the village as a whole or individual households ever acted as ritual sponsors. Sponsorship of household rituals was, in turn, linked to the rhythms of the household and family cycle.

In terms of spiritual intent, the distinction between village and household *slametans* is only relative. They use many of the same *sajenan* offerings, and thus, in theory, fulfill many of the same spiritual ends: blessing village lands, insuring the abundant flow of water, guarding the welfare of the living. The priest begins both kinds of rites, moreover, with much the same prayer of announcement and invocation, always securing the blessing of the village as a whole before he mentions the concerns of any single household or individual sponsor. In ritual, private interest and public welfare are always linked. The reality of this ritual linkage is a key theme of Tengger commentary on the moral importance of the ritual tradition.

There are various household rites, ranging in scale from simple five-minute services involving the presentation of a single *sajenan* offering, to three-, four-, or five-day events involving dozens of offerings, hundreds of guests, elaborate feasting, and entertainment. The large events turn rural hamlets into veritable towns, attracting visitors from distant villages and peddlers hawking their goods from lowland cities. The scale ultimately depends upon the nature of the ritual and the financial means of the sponsoring household (Chapter 10). The type of ritual performed, of course, depends upon the nature of the ritual task at hand. The core life-passage rites are celebrated by most Tengger households, but beyond these there are various rarer and more specialized ritual events. There are rites, for example, that celebrate the renewal of marriage vows between husband and wife years after their original wedding, rites for the expulsion of bees from one's house rafters, and rites to turn away the evil resulting from a murder or suicide. What is important to note about all household rites is that, much more than village ceremonies, these tend to draw householders directly into ritual celebration, and thus play a greater role in informing villagers as to the nature of ritual performance. As in all Tengger rite, however, interpretation of these events shows the varied influence of a larger dialogue with Islamic Java.

The Problem of Ritual Specialists

Sole celebrant of regional and village rites, the Tengger priest is not alone in celebration of household ritual events. As is the case throughout Java, villages here have two other ritual specialists, the midwife or "baby dukun" (dukun bayi) and the "circumcision expert" (calak, dukun sunat). The status of each in the Tengger community bears testimony to the unfinished, and sometimes awkward, accommodation of the priestly tradition to more widespread Javanese customs.

Both the midwife and circumcision specialist perform services more or less similar to those performed by their lowland counterparts. The midwife, for example, is responsible for pre- and post-natal care of mother and child. She assists the mother during birth, cleans and bathes the child, and, as througout Java and much of Indonesia, sees to it that the placenta and umbilical cord are washed and given a proper burial. The latter items are considered the "younger siblings" of the newborn child, whereas the amniotic fluid and blood that precede birth are referred to as "elder siblings." Together, all four compose the "four siblings" (dulor mpat) of a child, spirits who act as guardians (but also sometimes pests) throughout one's life. Similar notions are found in lowland Java (C. Geertz 1960:46) and, with an inevitable rococo degree of additional detail, Bali (Hooykaas 1974). The ritual attention given the dulor mpat in Tengger is for the most part optional. Some people prepare red-and-white rice porridge (jenang abang jenang putih) in honor of these spirits during birthdays, weddings, and the like, but this is entirely a matter of personal preference. Tengger priests do not recognize the dulor mpat in prayer, and, in general, regard them as "things for little (that is, lowland) dukuns," as one priest informed me.

This, and the general question of by what authority she performs ritual, insure that although the practical importance of the midwife is widely recognized, her ritual role is not. In many (but not all) Tengger communities, the midwife performs various rituals, burning incense,

143

anointing a homemade offering or two, and reciting prayers of a generally syncretic Javanese cast. She blesses the pregnant mother in the seventh month of pregnancy, anoints the child at birth, blesses it again five days after birth (or when the umbilical scab falls off), and ritually "scrapes" both mother and child of impurities some forty days after the child's birth. Unlike the Tengger priest's ritual, however, the *dukun bayi*'s ceremonies are never "witnessed" by village officials. The ritual knowledge she wields, even where regarded as legitimate, is referred to as an *ilmu* or *ngelmu*, "spiritual knowledge," and distinguished as such from the spiritual expertise of the Tengger priest. Only the latter is specifically "Tengger"; the midwife's ritual knowledge benefits from no such identification with Tengger tradition. Cultural resistance to her ritual role is taken to an extreme in the most self-consciously Tengger communities of the northwest. There the midwife is barred from burning incense and anointing offerings; the priest, at least in theory, is supposed to celebrate all rituals of pregnancy and birth. The role of the midwife is thus reduced there to the status of a technical expert with no ritual expertise.

The role of the circumcision specialist (*calak, dukun sunat*) suffers from even greater cultural ambivalence in Tengger. In part this is due to the cultural associations of circumcision in Java. Whatever its precise Middle Eastern origins (where it is an Arabic and not strictly Islamic custom), Javanese strongly identify circumcision with Islam. The circumcision ceremony itself is sometimes referred to as "Islamizing" (*islaman*). It is said that in his early nineteenth-century revolt against the Dutch, Diponegoro required of his followers only that they make a profession of Islamic faith and that they be circumcised (Carey 1979:77). Tengger who practice circumcision categorically deny that it is an Islamic ceremony alone, insisting, more generally, that it is simply a Javanese custom. Buda Tengger, for example, distinguish between what they call "Buda circumcision" (*sunat Buda*) and "Muslim circumcision" (*sunat Islam*). The former involves the making of only a small incision on the end of the penis, a practice known throughout Java as *sunat belek,* and often associated with non- or nominally Muslim Javanese. According to Tengger, "Muslim circumcision" involves the removal of a far larger portion of the foreskin.

Contemporary Tengger, however, disagree as to the significance of the circumcision rite. Several Hindu reform communities in the Tengger northwest, for example, have recently banned the rite. The action was taken partially in reaction to accusations from Muslim Javanese that, since Tengger circumcise, they must really be Muslim. Formal association with Balinese Hindus reinforced criticism of the rite, since for most

Balinese circumcision is regarded as a distinctly Islamic custom (Boon 1977:210). Tengger reform leaders, however, have further justified their banning of circumcision by claiming that there were always villagers in the northwest who refused to circumcise their sons. A particularly prominent priest in the northwest, for example, had, even before Indonesian independence, spoken out against circumcision. According to this man and several other elderly informants in the Tengger northwest, many men in the late nineteenth century were not circumcised. Southern Tengger, however, reject this claim, and regard the Hindus' banning of circumcision as further evidence of their departure from Tengger tradition.

Whatever its precise religious meaning, the fact remains that in no Tengger village is circumcision performed by the Tengger priest. Like the midwife's rituals, the public role of this nonpriestly tradition has been limited in other ways, as well. Contrary to the lowland pattern, neither *kenduren* prayer meal nor elaborate festivities accompany the circumcision rite in Tengger. Although a circumcision ceremony may be held in conjunction with priestly liturgies (such as marriage) that do inspire ritual festivals, by itself the circumcision rite is never marked with elaborate festivity because it is not a priestly rite.

What all these social restrictions do, of course, is separate priestly ritual from that performed by more run-of-the-mill specialists. Only priestly rite is identified as Tengger *ngaluri* or ancestral custom. It is consistent with other aspects of Tengger tradition, of course, that in distinguishing priestly rite from that of nonpriests, ordinary villagers do not refer to the different categories of spirits invoked by each. The distinction is made in terms of sociology, not cosmology. That is to say, it is the status of the priest's liturgy as uniquely "Tengger" to which villagers point in affirming the spiritual preeminence of that liturgical corpus, not the inherent superiority of the deities invoked by that liturgy.

The Major Household Slametans

The most socially significant household rites are those directly associated with important points of passage in an individual's or family's life history. The form and festivity of these rites are more or less standardized throughout Tengger. Less common household ceremonies, by contrast, tend to be less uniform in name, style of elaboration, and frequency of performance. Tooth-filing rites (*pangur*), for example, continued to be celebrated in several southern Tengger communities as late as the 1950s. Ritual tooth filing is still an important rite of life passage in Bali. In most areas of Tengger, however, both the ritual and practice of tooth filing appear to have been discontinued as early as the end of the last century.

Other *slametans* are uncommon because they are optional and villagers tend to be unconcerned with the spiritual problems they are designed to address. Tengger are well aware, for example, of the theoretical importance of the Javanese *petungan* or numerological system (see C. Geertz 1960:30-35), an especially elaborate variant of which is mastered by the Tengger priest. The theoretical awareness, however, entails little in the way of practical concern; hence, although people may consult the priest concerning especially important dates, on a day-to-day level most people worry little about such matters. Most of the rites thus associated with calendrical numerology—the Javanese birthday (*weton* or, in Tengger, *metri*), the "exhaustion" of one's birth numbers (*neptu telas*), and so on—tend to be neglected, except in those situations where illness or misfortune prompts a person to search about for possible ritual solutions. There are other *slametans* for similarly intermittent occasions. When a rice steamer (*dang*) falls from an oven, when bees get into house rafters, or when the harvest storage structure (*sigiran*) collapses, an all-purpose rite for placating and banishing evil spirits (known by a variety of names: *ruwat* exorcism, *nyaur*, and so on) must be performed. When a couple wishes to renew their marriage vows and bless their children, they may celebrate a *slametan mayu*. There are many such occasional and optional rites, but few attract the social interest and the economic resources of the four primary rites of life passage celebrated throughout Tengger: the ritual hair cutting (*tugel kuncung, tugel gombak*), the *walagara* wedding ceremony, death and burial, and the *entas-entas* purification of the dead. Chapter 10 will discuss the economic network that supports these often expensive ritual events. For the moment, however, we will focus on the role of these rites in Tengger society. As the most prominent household rituals, these rites, like so much of Tengger tradition, have been drawn into the debate on Tengger identity and its relation to Islam.

The Tugel Haircutting Ceremony   The *tugel* ceremony of haircutting is the most technically elementary of the four core rites, but it is also subject to the most divergent interpretations. The rite itself is very simple: having announced the ritual event and invoked spirit presence, the priest cuts a few hairs from a young boy's toplock (the *kuncung*) or from a girl's forelocks (the *gombak*). The priest then invites guardian deities to bless the child, and requests evil spirits to be satisfied with the sacrifice of hair rather than the child itself. The prayers for this ceremony describe the child as having been made from the iron of man and woman, and request that the iron of both sexes be forged into one strong body, like the laminated metalwork of a Javanese dagger.

It is not the technical detail of this rite that is subject to divergent interpretation, but its cultural role as a distinctively Tengger rite of passage. In the more staunchly Tengger communities of the northwest, the rite used to be called the rite of "becoming buda" (*mbuda'en*), and was said to contrast with the Muslim rite of circumcision. Everybody in the village was thus supposed to undergo the haircutting ceremony in early childhood as a symbol of incorporation into the Buda community. (Today in these communities the same rite is still practiced, but is identified as a rite of initiation into Hinduism.) People in the Tengger south and northeast, however, reject this interpretation of the rite. Not all children, they insist, need undergo the ritual, only those who have inherited the right and duty to do so from their parents. The ceremony thus has nothing to do with incorporation into a Buda or Hindu community; an individual must experience the rite only if his or her parents have. Why some families should undergo the rite and others not is something upon which even Tengger in the south and northeast cannot agree. These are regions that accommodated a far larger number of immigrants from the lowlands than did the northwest; these are the areas where circumcision is still practiced, the midwife has an active ritual role, and, in general, one sees a greater degree of cultural syncretism. Could the haircutting ceremony, I suggested to some informants, have originally been rejected by Muslim immigrants to the Tengger highlands? Or, conversely, could it have been used as a sign of social distinction among local Tengger in the face of Muslim immigrants? Villagers vigorously denied that the rite could have ever had anything to do with Muslim vs. Buda, or old vs. new residents of the village. It was, they insisted, simply a ritual custom, practiced by those whose parents had earlier practiced it. Could the haircutting ceremony in those villages, I suggested, have had something to do with the higher ritual status of those who practice it? No one could answer this question with certainty, although sponsors of the rite liked this hypothesis better than my first.

The example illustrates the sometimes perplexing dynamics of Tengger ritual interpretation. In the Tengger northwest, the haircutting rite was put in the service of cultural differentiation, distinguishing Muslim from non-Muslim. If this was ever the meaning of the rite in the south and northeast, however, it is no more. In villages otherwise stressing common descent and collective spiritual ancestry, the haircutting rite provides a small measure of internal social differentiation; some people have the right to perform the ceremony, others do not. The social history of the Tengger region, and the rite's role in contemporary village society make any judgment on the originary meaning impossible.

The Walagara Wedding   Tengger customs of courtship and marriage express well the familiar, rather personalistic tones of village life, and present an interesting contrast with engagement and marital practices customary in many other areas of Java. Parents may, as in most of lowland Java, arrange their children's marriage, but in most cases they do not. An ill-suited partner, Tengger point out, does little good, especially since divorce can be initiated by either spouse and is quite common (terminating some 50 percent of all marriages).

Among Tengger there is no single fashion for arranging engagement and marriage, a fact that itself contrasts sharply with the rather formally prescribed pattern reported from much of lowland Java (H. Geertz 1961:57). Where the boy and girl themselves initiate engagement, the boy usually takes the initiative, sending a letter or verbal message to the girl through the help of one of his close friends. One villager recalled the contents of his proposal letter:

Tak rabi, gelem ya ora?	I'll marry you, want to or not?
Ne'e gelem, surat iki balasen.	If you want to, respond to this letter.

The girl's reply was equally direct:

Isun gelem dirabi.	I would like to be married.

After the boy and girl come to agreement, the boy must request the hand of his bride from her parents, a request that he makes (again quite contrary to the lowland manner) directly, sometimes accompanied by a friend. It may take several trips to the kitchen of a girl's family for a young man to work up the courage to make his request, and, where the young man is especially nervous, he may ask a friend to make the statement for him (in his presence). The boy's parents never accompany him on this proposal visit. (In the more familiar lowland pattern, the proposal to the bride's parents is usually made by the groom's parents, especially his mother. The matter is always a very delicate one, discussed only indirectly at first when the parents meet, with much self-abasement on the part of both family parties. A *Mak Jomblang* or spokeswoman, usually a neighbor or relative of the groom's family, may accompany the parents of the groom to help conversation along). After the boy gets up the courage to state his intentions to the bride's parents, the latter take the girl into a back room for a moment, to ask her opinion in the matter. If the girl indicates that, indeed, she wants to marry the boy,

Figure 1.   Priest on Kasada night
with assistants beneath ongkek *garland*

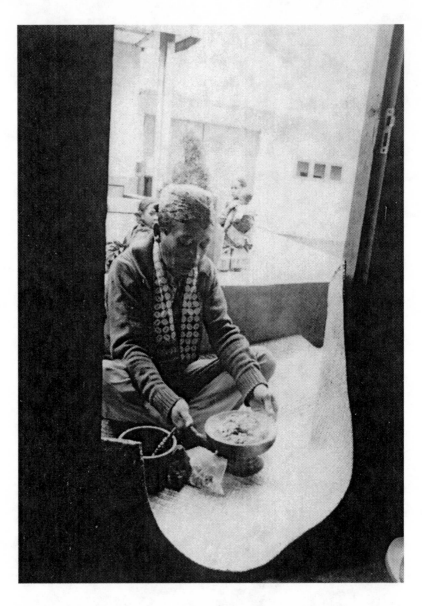

Figure 2.   Incense announcement at the doorway
requests blessing for the ceremonies about to begin

Figure 3. A holy water beaker (pra-sen), dated c. 1347, decorated with fig-ures from the Jav-anese zodiac

Figure 4. The priest's ritual imple-ments: bell, brazier, holy water beaker

Figure 5. *Village ceremony on* petinggi's *front steps; priest and* petinggi *to the front,* pamong *assembled in back*

Figure 6. *Housebuilding pauses for the priest's ceremony*

Figure 7. Food set out on graves is presented by kin with incense and obeisance

Figure 8. Slametans are for children, too

Figure 9. Entas-entas pa-lukatan, *northwest style;* the priest covers those who will serve as host bodies to the souls of those to be purified

Figure 10. Petra *flower figurines, clothed in the clothes of the recently dead*

Figure 11.   Priest

Figure 12.   Priest

Figure 13.   Schoolchildren at prayer in a new Bali-style temple

and if the parents agree, the three return to where the boy waits, and ask again if indeed he seriously wants to marry the young woman. If he says yes, the agreement is made, and only then does the boy return to his own home to announce his engagement to his own parents.

Several days later the parents of the boy must visit the bride's house to "authorize" (nggenahen) the engagement. As in any social visit, the parents proceed directly to the kitchen of the girl's parents, where they are invited to sip coffee and munch on small snacks (jajan). The conversation is relatively informal, and once it is clear that the engagement is agreeable to both families, they set a date for the wedding. After this meeting of the parents, the young man may begin to make regular visits to the house of the girl and her parents, chatting and sipping coffee in the early hours of the evening. Some time shortly after he begins these visits, he also starts to help the bride's parents in the fields, balancing his labor there with that on his own parents' land. This style of premarital interaction would be unthinkable in many other areas of Java, where the groom is supposed to avoid all members of the bridal family until the very day of the wedding. Even after the wedding, the relationship between parents of the bride and their son-in-law tends to be rather stiff and formal (H. Geertz 1961:27; Jay 1969:139). This almost awkward style of interaction is in Tengger replaced by what tends to be a slightly indulgent, asymmetrical joking relationship. The mother of the bride in particular may gently tease the young couple as to their future plans, and she takes pleasure in seeing them together in her household. The most vivid expression of this relatively relaxed parental attitude toward the fiancés is, or was, the Tengger custom of allowing the fiancés to sleep together in the home of the bride prior to the actual wedding day, a custom similar to the Balinese custom of gendak, or premarital co-habitation (Covarrubias 1937:141). Well aware of Muslim and Dutch attitudes on this matter, modern Tengger prohibit the practice, although some parents discreetly tolerate it still.

As in other areas of Java, the groom usually gives an engagement gift (peningset) to the bride. Here, too, the manner of presentation is direct and informal—the boy simply comes by one night and presents the gift (a set of clothes, some fine batik cloth) to the bride—without the long procession of female kin sometimes seen in the lowlands. The giving of gifts, however, is taken as a sign that the wedding day is approaching, and, since both the bride and groom's households sponsor some kind of marriage festivity, the parents of the fiancés busy themselves with wedding preparations. The first formal ceremony begins the day prior to the actual wedding service, when the bride and the groom visit parents, the village chief, the priest, and a few other close relatives to ask the blessing of each in marriage. This request for the blessing of one's elders occurs in other areas of Java as well, but most non-Tengger with whom I spoke commented that it would be unusual to include the village chief and priest in the circle of elders. The bride and the groom kneel before each such elder, hands in respectful *sembah* position before their faces (the same posture as is adopted when giving homage to ancestral spirits in ritual invocation), and announce their intent to marry. The elder responds with a more or less formulaic statement of support: "Yes, I give you my blessing, may you become grandparents with many children and descendants" (*Ya, tak estoni sampai dadia kaken-kaken, ninen-ninen, anak-anak berenean*).

The series of rites of which a *walagara* wedding consists begins the following day. The exact order of events varies from village to village, in large part because from the mid-eighteenth to late-nineteenth century a portion of the marriage ceremony had to be performed outside the Tengger village in lowland Muslim communities (see La Chapelle 1899; von Freijburg 1901; Bodemeijer 1901). This ceremony was known as the *pernikahan*, and was performed by an Islamic *modin*. According to at least some reports, during this rite the Tengger groom had to recite an Islamic profession of the faith, or else Javanese officials would refuse to recognize the marriage as legitimate. At the end of the last century, this practice was stopped when Dutch officials began to take a more active interest in Tengger welfare (Chapter 2). Villagers were thereby given the option to be married by either an Islamic *modin* or a Tengger priest. Today only Muslim villagers are married by an Islamic *modin*.

Adapted from the Islamic ceremony, the language and ritual of the Tengger *pernikahan* preserves obvious Islamic influences. For Tengger the rite is primarily a legal ceremony; although the priest does recite a short prayer, no incense is burned, no deities are invoked, and thus no offerings are presented. The actors in the ceremony are the priest, the groom (not usually accompanied by his parents), the bride's father or another elder male kinsman, referred to as the *wali* (as in Muslim marriages), and the bride herself. Interestingly, in most areas of Muslim Java, the bride does not attend the *pernikahan*, but is represented by her *wali*. Here in Tengger the *wali's* role is more perfunctory. He initiates the proceedings by asking the priest to marry the bride and groom. The priest then invites first the groom and then the bride to recite the marriage vows; they hold each other's hands as they do so. At the conclusion of their vows, the priest recites a short prayer, after which the groom gives the bride a small gift of money (*mas kawin*), the amount of which is usually the same for all marriages. Whereas the groom in lowland rite also gives a gift of the *mas kawin*, in at least some Tengger communities the bride's response is distinctive: receiving the groom's money gift, she immediately reciprocates with a similar cash payment to the groom.

This concludes the legal wedding ceremony. From this moment on, the bride and groom are free to live with each other, a pattern again contrary to the lowland custom. The *walagara*, or wedding ceremony before the gods, can occur immediately after the *pernikahan* or several days later. Whatever the date, it is this religious event which is made the object of festival elaboration. It begins with a *semeninga* announcement to the gods (Chapter 3), informing them of the impending union. The bride and groom are then separated for several hours, until the groom returns to the bride's house for the ritual "meeting" (*temon*) of bride and groom. A more elaborate ritual of the same name is celebrated throughout Java. The Tengger *temon*, however, is rather simple. The groom walks to the bride's house (without the procession of relatives common in many lowland rites), and meets the bride at the front door to her house. She faces out, he faces in. In the path between them sits a large stone mortar and pestle (*gandak pipisan*), identified by villagers as a symbol of male and female. Its resemblance to the Indian *yoni* and *lingga* is, of course, striking, but Tengger are not familiar with the Sanskrit terms. Atop the pestle there sit a raw egg, a handful of cooked sticky rice, and a flower. To its side on the floor are arranged a glass of perfumed water, a dish of uncooked rice, and a large plate containing several coins, betel quid, banyan leaves, and a miniature rice ladle carved from coconut.

The groom removes his shoe, and sets the big toe of his right foot atop the raw egg that sits on the stone pestle. The priest, his wife, and ritual assistant stand to the side of the bride and groom, the priest with ritual implements in hand. On a cue from the priest's wife, the bride leans down, bows to the groom's foot, and then anoints his big toe, still precariously located on top of the egg. The bride then stands and joins her right hand with the groom's. Burning incense, the priest recites an incense announcement informing the gods of the marriage, and inviting them to descend to the offerings to bless it with their presence. The priest's wife, meanwhile, leans forward and grasps the hands of the bride and groom. With her free hand, she showers their hands with rice, coins, the rice ladle, and betel quid, "so that the bride and groom may be happy and prosperous together." She then turns the couple's hands over and back three times, "to symbolize their sexual union." As the priest anoints their hands for the last time, the groom crushes the raw egg with his big toe, completing the *temon* rite.

The *temon* is the first half of a *walagara*, and it corresponds in a

151

general way with the lowland ceremony of the same name, although in the latter no priest officiates. The second portion of the Tengger *walagara*, however, has no ritual equivalent in the lowlands. It involves the ritual invocation of guardian and family spirits, much as occurs in Karo and other large rites, at which time the bride and groom pay ritualized respect to the spirits of their deceased relatives. The bond between the living and the dead is thus reaffirmed. With this invocation, the priestly services in the *walagara* come to a close, and the social festivities of dining, drinking, and dancing begin.

The Tengger wedding ceremony neatly summarizes the contrasting conceptualization of tradition and religion among Tengger and Islamic Javanese. In Tengger, the *pernikahan* or legal ceremony is little more than a technical formality. For the most part it is a secular ceremony, in the sense that it uses neither incense nor offering, and thus invokes no deities and brings about no blessing. It is the *walagara* that bears the burden of spiritual appeal and is thus the most religious of wedding ceremonies. The case is otherwise in the Islamic lowlands. Although the ceremonial meeting of bride and groom is rich in symbolism (see C. Geertz 1960:57) and social drama, it is, for most people speaking at high levels of generalization—not a religious ceremony as such, but *adat* custom. The key religious moments in the Muslim wedding are the *pernikahan* and the *kenduren* prayer meal that precedes it, rites which include Islamic prayer and little distinctly Javanese symbolism. In short— and again viewing the ceremonies from the perspective of general ideological commentary—the ceremonial meeting of bride and groom has, in the lowlands, been redefined as *adat* custom, distinct from religion as such. In Tengger, by contrast, the religiosity of the customary meeting of bride and groom has been preserved by secularizing the legal ceremony (the *pernikahan* burns no incense and invokes no spirits) and preserving an explicit spirit presence in the ritualized meeting of bride and groom. Although the symbolism mobilized in the lowland event appears richly elaborate, and although, for some syncretic Javanese, it may express deeply spiritual themes, it is almost never referred to as "religion" as such. This is not the case in the Tengger event, where the imagery of fertility, abundance, and ancestry are all easily recognized as expressive of primary religious concerns: ancestry, descent, and the continuity of the world of the living with that of the dead.

Death, Burial, and the Afterlife   With the birth of their first child, a young couple begins to sponsor the rituals of spiritual nurturance of which, up to that time, they had only been recipients. The cycle of intergenerational spiritual reciprocity is thus begun anew. This reciprocity is no simple reflection of some more primary social reality, but is itself a constituent element in the formation of social relations. Parents' ritual responsibilities toward their children are among the most important and, outside of food and shelter, financially demanding of all they must meet in providing parental care.

As children grow, marry, and receive the largest portion of their inheritance, parents begin to withdraw from the ritual exchange circuit (Chapter 10) so important in village social life. Ideally, they are supposed to live on but a small portion of their remaining farm land, so that their children may live from the larger portion. So as to avoid economic dependence, however, parents may attempt to retain a larger portion of their wealth. To do so to the detriment of one's married children is considered extremely improper, however. One is, in old age, dearly loved, but, like a child, rather irrelevant to the primary social scheme. Having withdrawn from the ritual exchange system, an old person feels too embarrassed to attend ritual festivals, since coming "empty handed" is considered impolite. By age sixty or so, men also tend to stop dancing *tayuban*, leaving the floor to those still young enough to enjoy its graces and titillation.

Death finishes an elder's social limbo. It also opens a new cycle of ritual reciprocity, as now the parent becomes the object of his child's ritual blessing. Death itself triggers a flurry of activity in the village. A family reports a death immediately to the village priest and chief. Village officials are then supposed to go quickly to the house of the deceased, to pay their respects and make sure that preparations for the burial are well under way. In at least small and mid-sized Tengger communities, everyone who hears of the death is also supposed to proceed to the house of the deceased. Neighbor women come bearing food for the ritual meal which, as in all rituals, must be shared after the priest completes his ceremony. The household of the deceased is not supposed to have to supply any food for the funeral meal. Moments after word of the death has been heard around the village, the household is bustling with food preparation, conversation, and the reception of guests.

The corpse is placed in the front room of the house, atop a short-legged sleeping platform, and is covered with a plain cloth and, above this, a finer batik cover. A white ceremonial cloth (*majang*)—always present in ceremonies involving the invocation or departure of family spirits—is hung on the wall in back of the platform. On top of the platform sit a small lamp ("to clear the way of the soul in its journey"), food plates like those prepared for all family spirits, a dish for coin gifts from visitors, and a large bundle of muslin cloth in which the corpse will eventually be wrapped for burial. Guests enter the room and proceed directly to the side of the corpse, where they stand quietly for a moment, sometimes addressing a few words to the spirit of the deceased, like this rather common statement of blessing:

> I give you all the supplies I can as you return home this day; receive them for your return. May you get a labor which is good, a place which is wide and nice. Strength and blessing to you from my family and me.

> *Eyang nyangoni sakwasane sira mulih dina iki; tampaen karo wangsul. Oleha penggawean sing enak, papan sing jembar, long-gar. Eyang wenehana kuat slamet sak anak rabine eyang.*

A small group of men prepare the wooden litter on which the body will be carried to the cemetery. Other men stand about chatting quietly in the front yard. Always more industrious, women come and quickly pay their respects, then either depart or stay to help with meal preparation.

As throughout Java, death in Tengger is something to be received calmly and stoically, without grimness or melodrama. Death is supposed to be a "calm, undemonstrative, almost languid letting go" (C. Geertz 1973c:153). But there are, of course, moments—particularly at the death of a young adult or spouse—when grief breaks through with sad wailing or even hysteria. Such display is considered unhealthy and spiritually dangerous, however, so it is strongly discouraged. When they speak of the proper attitude toward death, Tengger rarely use the rather high-flown intellectual statements heard in less populist corners of Java. They rely little on such terminology as that associated with the concept of *iklas*, the flattening of emotion and withdrawl from its disturbing force (see C. Geertz 1960:70). They speak instead of attitudes linked to activities in the world, as in the concept of *nrima*, the mute or unprotesting acceptance of things over which one has no control. The practical corollary of this attitude is, among other things, that villagers attempt to involve surviving kin in activities like food preparation and the reception of guests; busy work or routine is the best practical guide for a calm spirit. The spouse of the deceased is usually kept particularly busy. If a woman, she works elbow-to-elbow with other women in the kitchen; if a man, he is expected to stay out in the front room with guests, seeing to it that they are quickly given hot coffee, cigarettes, and sweets.

The emphasis in a funeral is thus on a quick, orderly, and undemonstrative dispatching of the soul of the dead person, coupled with as quick a return as possible to everyday routine for the living. The priest and his assistants play the most important role in this orderly dispatch. Upon arrival at the house of the deceased, the priest takes a small bamboo container of water, recites an incense announcement over it, gives half to his ritual assistant (for washing the corpse), and the remainder to a small group of men who will pour it on the ground of the grave they will dig. The actual bathing of the body is sometimes done by relatives of the deceased who—the supreme test of *nrima* resignation—hold the body on their laps. In some Tengger villages, however, the bathing of the corpse is the responsibility of the ritual elder (*wong sepuh*). This same man then dresses the corpse for its trip to the cemetery (his wife may do so for women). The burial dress is similar to that used in other areas of Java: a long cotton sheet is ripped into smaller pieces designed to serve as a shirt, *sarong*, head-cover, and waist band. After the orifices of the body are filled with cotton swabs, the corpse is wrapped in the long muslin cloth, bound at the head, waist and feet. The only distinctively Tengger feature is the inclusion of a quid of betel leaf on the face, hands, and feet of the deceased, so that he may later "perform ritual obeisance before God." Once dressed, the corpse is wrapped in a larger woven mat, covered with a batik cloth, and set on top of a wooden litter for the procession to the cemetery. Before it leaves, the children of the deceased walk three times underneath the litter, symbolizing, it is said, the cutting of ties between the living and the dead. The soul is to begin its journey to another world.

As in other areas of Java, women do not accompany the funeral procession to the cemetery, which always lies at the edge of the village. The exception to this rule is the one or two women who bear the priest's ritual offerings to the grave site; the carrying of *sajenan* here, as always, is a woman's responsibility. Other women watch from their doorways as the funeral procession passes, sometimes placing salt on hot coals so as to produce a snap-, crackle-, pop-sound, thought to ward off malevolent spirits attracted to death. For much the same reason, the funeral procession stops at all road intersections so that the men carrying the corpse litter may rotate it three times, confusing any evil spirits that may be following the corpse. Evil moves in straight lines. A similar custom, and a similar notion of spirit movement, is found in Bali (Covarrubias 1937:374). Taking the agnostic's perspective on such customs, some Tengger villagers, however, deny that the rotation has anything to do with evil spirits, insisting that it is, quite simply, a Tengger custom.

At the grave site, the corpse-bundle is unlashed and—with another triple movement, this time up and down—handed down to three men who stand ready to receive it in the grave. The head of the corpse is placed to the south, recalling the fate of Ajisaka's servant (Chapter 6); the straps on its gown are loosened "so that the soul can easily depart." The face is covered with green leaves to protect it from the earth, and the funeral litter itself is placed diagonally over the corpse to protect it in the grave. The pole to which the burial litter was lashed during transport is also interred with the corpse, the pole's "head" (that is, that portion corresponding to the upper portion of the tree from which the pole was made) placed to the south, like the head of the corpse. When asked, people say that the burial of the pole in this fashion is Tengger custom, with no larger significance. The unremarked parallelism is nonetheless suggestive: according to Tengger custom, when wood is placed in a fireplace it is also supposed to be positioned "head first." Given the (now forgotten) association of the south with Mt. Bromo and fire (Chapter 4), there seems once to have been a kind of symbolic identification between a human corpse and a log in a fire. The example, if true, provides one more instance of an apparent directional symbolism that is for the most part mute in popular culture.

In some villages, a few private possessions of the deceased (clothes, tools, some coins) may be placed in the grave, to help the soul of the dead in his afterlife labors. Workers quickly cover the grave, and mark it with a small wooden block (*maisan, paisan*) identical to those used in other areas of Java. The grave benefits from no distinctively Buda or Hindu decoration; indeed, once buried, even the directional orientation of the corpse cannot be determined. As other members of the funeral party watch from a distance, the priest finally takes his seat on a mat set atop the freshly covered grave. Facing south, he anoints the food trays placed before him, and recites a short prayer peculiar to Tengger funerals:

> Hong! Fire worship from the east; it is not a human fire but the fire of Hyang Betoro Suworo; let the fire become the fire of labor and turn back all sickness of the body; turn back all evil acts or utterances from parents, siblings, or holy spirits. You return now to the east, to your place in the east. Your place is the rice steamer, take with you all evil, as the water flows (here the priest anoints) float away float away to the sea that is your place. Hong! House and water given form, homage to Suwoho; Sri essence the fire worship all done.

Like many of the priest's prayers, this one is recited in a fashion that renders it virtually inaudible to all those assembled. Although it does not seem, therefore, to inform popular conceptions as to burial and the afterlife, it does provide several interesting parallels with detail of other rites and other moments in the funeral process. The prayer's imagery, first of all, seems directly related to the wood and fire parallelism mentioned above. The body is purified through the cleansing agency of a deific fire from the east, a fire that removes the illnesses of the body and the curses that are most polluting, those which come from kin one may have offended or from spirits. The notion of curses from spirits and relatives is a common one in Java and Bali, as a metaphor of sorts for all those against whom one may have sinned. A similar image of fire, curses, and purification reappears in the much more elaborate prayer references of the *entas-entas* purification (Chapter 8). In this burial prayer, however, the image of fire purification is linked to the flow of water: sins removed by fire flow to the sea. Viewed comparatively (which is, of course, not how Tengger might view it), this imagery is clearly that of Indic Southeast Asia. It is also the fire-and-water imagery seen in the Kasada prayers, where water flows from the fires of Mt. Bromo (Chapter 3). The reference to the rice-steaming basket (*kukusan*), curiously, will reappear in the *entas-entas* purification, again in a context related to the purification of spirits of the dead. Impurities drain through the basket like water, leaving the pure substance (here the body and soul) like rice in the rice steamer. This is the task of the priest, to purify the soul, and allow its passage to another world.

After the burial ceremony, there is a brief, Karolike invocation back at the house of the deceased, inviting the soul for one last encounter with its living relatives. As in the Karo invocation of the family dead, the priest first gives homage and offering to the higher guardian deities, only then inviting the soul of the dead person to descend to the *petra* flower figurine. The words and movements of the rite are almost identical to those used in the Karo *sesanding* invocation, and, as in that ceremony, the living are invited to pay their respects to the soul of the dead (here one soul, rather than a collectivity) through the performance of a simple obeisance (*sembah bati, bakti*) in front of the *petra*. The priest concludes the rite by singing a song in which he appeals to the soul to return to the east; with a wave of his *sampet* ritual scarf at the end of the song, the priest dispels the spirit presence. The passage is done; the soul has departed. There are no additional post-mortem ceremonies, with the exception of the *entas-entas* purification of the collective dead, which only mature families sponsor and only once or twice in their life. Tengger do not celebrate the various prayer meals held in the lowlands at intervals after an individual's death (C. Geertz 1960:72). As always in Tengger, it is the priest's liturgy that defines ritual passage, not *kenduren* prayer meals. The passage in death is not into obscurity and darkness, but, according to popular understanding, into a world of ancestors periodically drawn again into the world of the living.

The Fate of the Soul   Death is an event fraught with uncertainty and at least the possibility of terror and confusion, and it is a well-worn theme in the anthropology of religion that funerary ritual helps to impose order and meaning on a potentially traumatic social event. It is important to recognize, however, that the kind of order a funeral can impose is not determined solely by the rite itself, and thus no amount of symbolic analysis can reveal its meaning unless the rite is situated in relation to the knowledge and experience actors bring to it. Funerary ritual thus draws on knowledge larger than itself. In the case of the Tengger funeral, however, this means that the rite not only summarizes what is known, it also points to a number of unknowns, areas of uncertainty or dispute in culturally shared understanding.

Even superficial examination of the Tengger funeral reveals its unambiguous familiarity, at least in certain respects. Death inaugurates a cycle of ritual preparation similar to that seen in other ritual events. Things fall quickly into place: neighbors bring food and fuel for the fire, women go about the business of food preparation, male householders receive male guests. The Tengger response to death is not to seclude the grievers from the world, but to draw them immediately into it—indeed into what is for Tengger the most sociable of events, the *slametan* festival. Death itself holds few abstract terrors. The corpse is set in the front room, and it is washed and clothed in front of a crowd of onlookers. Despite prayer references to the impurity and pollution of death, villagers do not think that contact with the body is polluting; the danger lies not in the corpse, but with spirits attracted to it. These are especially capable of attacking people emotionally distraught by the loss of a loved one; hence the emphasis placed on calm and the ready return to everyday routine is of spiritual importance. As the funeral procession moves to the cemetery, men take turns shouldering the litter on which the deceased is carried, and there is much conversation. Laughter is not considered out of place. To express one's condolences to the family of the deceased, it is understood, would be ludicrous, drawing attention to personal pain rather than diverting one's attention away. There are no post-mortem taboos for spouse or children, no funerary exchanges or mandatory visits from kin to the family of the deceased. To live alone is, of course, a sadness, and both widows and widowers are expected to remarry as quicky as is possible. Many elderly women have no such opportunity, however, and they may live alone or move in with a married child; no widower is capable of cooking for himself, so older men either remarry quickly or move in with their children.

Priestly ritual imposes this same sense of routine familiarity on the passage of the deceased. The soul of the deceased is blessed, given offerings, and finally dispatched to the heavens in a ritual structurally identical to that used in all invocation of family spirits. The role played by householders in this rite is equally well known: in the final invocation of the soul, the priest pauses mid-course in the rite, inviting householders to pay their respects to the soul of a person who was, perhaps only hours earlier, a living loved one. Kin come and piously bow to the soul of their dead relative, temporarily resident in the *petra* flower figurine. The gesture they make (*sembah bati*) is the same as used in Karo, the *entas-entas*, and other invocation of the ancestral dead. Personal loss is thus quickly drawn into ritualized pattern. The spirit of the deceased is at once close, present in the *petra*, and irreversibly distant, having ascended into a spiritual world with which intercourse is possible only through ritual form. The soul joins the community of other family and village spirits, spirits invited again and again to one's home for the rest of one's life. The ritual reciprocity of elder to youth is reversed, as now it is the child who honors parent and insures his elders' spiritual welfare. It is this cycle of social and spiritual interdependence that underlies villagers' conceptions as to the nature of the afterlife. The souls of the dead, it is known, remain in contact with the living until time has erased their memory and their individual identity is lost. Distant ancestors then join the assembly of guardian spirits concerned with the welfare of the village as a whole. The individual tie gives way to a more anonymous and collective relationship.

This vision of the afterlife accords well with ritual practice. Where there is little ritual precedent for cultural ideas, however, concepts tend to be vaguer and subject to much more dispute. Some people, for example, say that there is judgment after death, a rendering of accounts performed by an agent of God that is critical in determining one's happiness in the afterlife. Other villagers, however, reject this idea of judgment after death, insisting that everyone receives a "place" (*panggon*) in heaven (*khayangan*) regardless of one's activities in this life. According to this, the most popular view of the afterlife, heaven is a kind of social community, in which those related in this life are linked in the next. A minority of villagers take this notion even further, suggesting that heaven has its own *desa* village organization, complete with *pamong* officials, village chiefs, and priests. This vision of heaven, a native Durkheimism, is rejected by virtually all Tengger priests.

In traditional Tengger villages, unlike those influenced by the Hindu reform movement, little effort is made to establish some kind of doctrinal orthodoxy on matters not specifically addressed by ritual practice; hence there are a variety of ideas as to the nature of the afterlife. Many villagers speak of karmic law (*hukum karma*), but the idea is rarely extended into any precise doctrinal formulation. As is the case for many other Javanese, *karma* suggests the rather general idea that behavior in this life somehow affects one's fate in the next. For most people, why this is the case has more to do with a moral sense of balance than it does a notion of agental judgment. Few people see *karma* as something regulated by a supreme being as such; it is more a matter of life's general equilibrium. A small minority of Tengger in traditional Buda communities link the concept of *karma* to reincarnation (*nitis*). However, as in Bali (Belo 1953:1), it is generally thought that one is reborn into one's family line rather than into any number of human or nonhuman conditions. Although the concept of reincarnation is now being promoted by Hindu reformists, however, it seems to have long been a rather uncommon view on what happens after death. Some earlier observers of Tengger society (cf. Jasper 1926) have stated that no Tengger believe in reincarnation, but this seems an overstatement, judging by contemporary opinion in Buda communities.

There is one final minority belief as to the nature of the afterlife that deserves mention. In several villages of southern Tengger, people told me that spirits of the dead go to one of two places: either Mt. Bromo or Mt. Semeru. All ordinary people go to Mt. Bromo. Priests and chiefs, however, can go to Mt. Semeru, at least if they have been blessed prior to death in a ceremony called the *pembaron* or rite of "renewal" (see Appendix). According to this view, the distinction between commoners and village notables is maintained in the afterlife in a fashion that is radical, at least from the perspective of popular village idioms. The differentiation of ritual awards according to social status may have contributed to the demise of the *pembaron* rite, since its blatant social hierarchy may have appeared too inconsistent with the themes of popular Tengger religion. The *pembaron* has not been performed in southern Tengger since the 1940s, and it has not been celebrated in the north even within living memory. The demise of the rite is symptomatic of other stresses in Tengger ritual tradition, but this example is of particular interest because all historical evidence links the *pembaron* to a popular cult of Sivaism once practiced in many areas of Old Java (see Appendix). The ethnographic example suggests once again that rituals that are noticeably out of step with the ancestral emphasis of popular Tengger religion have, at least in recent Tengger history, fared poorly.

None of these ideas of reincarnation, *karma*, or judgment after death is exclusively Tengger, and none is specifically communicated in the priest's funeral labors of purification and dispatch. Most of these ideas, instead, have their counterpart in popular Javanese belief, at least that of a *kejawen* or "Javanist" sort. Whereas the borders of Tengger as a

160

ritual community are discrete and easily defined, Tengger as a cultural community can be less easily distinguished from its neighbors. Tengger are Javanese, and whatever the precise detail of priestly liturgy, they are exposed to and influenced by cultural concepts also found in other parts of Java. There is thus a practical side to beliefs on the afterlife. Ritual praxis is what villagers know and respect first of all. The liturgy does not define an exhaustive belief system, however, as much as it helps to define what is core and what is periphery in those beliefs regarded as "Tengger." Core concepts are those related to the community of the living and that of the family dead. This is the relationship to which villagers almost always first refer when commenting on the importance of the ritual tradition. The same bottom-up view of ritual colors villagers' perception of the less familiar and more powerful guardian deities addressed by the priest in liturgy. Whatever their precise names and identities, it is thought that fundamentally these spirits are ancestral. The same vision of the spirit world informs what are the most widespread notions as to the nature of the afterlife. None of these beliefs is in any simple sense "generated" in priestly ritual. People do see and hear things in priestly ceremony, but when they do so most directly—as in the *sembah* obeisance before the *petra* figurine in which the soul of a loved one temporarily resides—what they see tends to confirm preexisting ideas. In ritual one meets one's ancestors. This is the central focus of ritual, and this is the issue on which people can agree when speaking of the nature of the afterlife. All other beliefs—as to karmic retribution, the precise location of the heavens, or whether there is judgment after death—are in some sense peripheral to what is regarded as "Tengger" belief. Ritual praxis does not exhaust the fundamental questions concerning transcendent reality, but it helps put them in proper perspective, a Tengger one.

The ancestral emphasis of religious commentary and belief in Tengger was repeatedly impressed on me during the first months of my field research. What confidence I had gained among Tengger priests only served to confirm this impression. Most priests, however, continued to regard me somewhat nervously, mindful (as I was later told) that Dutch officials had taken and never returned ritual paraphernalia, and also fearful that my research might be subtly intended to encourage Tengger conversion to either Christianity or Islam. It was thus with some surprise and real satisfaction that I began to have conversations about the liturgy with one young priest who was just beginning its study with his father. In speaking one afternoon about the Hindu reform movement in northern Tengger (which this man and his father opposed), the young priest summarized the difference between Balinese and Tengger belief by noting that "Balinese worship *dewa*, but Tengger worship family spirits (*roh leluhur*)." The *dewa* of Balinese belief—Siva, Brahma, Visnu, and others—are not part of Tengger worship, he added, although people have heard of their names and respect Balinese belief as kindred with that Tengger. Some eight months into my research, this comment was consistent with everything I had thus far learned. For a variety of reasons related to priests' fears as to my intentions, no priest had yet allowed me to tape or transcribe any but the most elementary ritual prayers. These prayers—mostly ritual announcements (*mekakat*) composed in an entirely modern dialect of Javanese and directed to human observers of rituals, not to the spirits—confirmed what I had been told by ordinary villagers as to the purpose of Tengger ritual. I was familiar with the Kasada and Karo myths, and the basic distinction between family and guardian spirits. At this point in my research, Tengger tradition appeared to resemble that found in other areas of Indonesia similarly preoccupied with ancestors and territorial spirits. There appeared, moreover, to be a kind of Durkheimian consonance between social organization and cosmological forms, the hierarchy of each paralleling the order of the other.

I was therefore genuinely surprised when, several days after our conversation, the young priest returned to my house one night to report what he thought was a rather startling discovery. In studying the prayers for a rite he was yet incapable of performing, he had repeatedly come across some of the spirit names of which we had spoken only several days earlier. The prayers he was studying were from the *entas-entas* purification of the dead, the most powerful and complex of all priestly liturgy. His father, this young man said, was still reluctant to speak of these things with me, and insisted that his son learn the depth of the liturgy from his own study, not our discussions. Only a month after this discussion, however, the elder priest consented to his son's request that I be allowed to examine the prayers he was studying. The prayers were written in Latin script, in a small notebook, and it was through their examination that I came to understand in a more substantive fashion what I had heard from other villagers: that the knowledge to which the Tengger priest is heir is a difficult, complex knowledge, containing mysteries far removed from the truths of the visible world.

· 8 ·

RITUAL FORM AND MEANING:
THE *ENTAS-ENTAS* PURIFICATION

As with so much of their ritual tradition, when asked by outsiders the purpose of the *entas-entas* ritual, Tengger almost invariably respond by identifying it with a lowland Javanese rite. An *entas-entas*, they comment, is a *nyewu*, which is to say, a commemorative *kenduren* prayer meal held one thousand days after an individual's death. Whatever the strategic intent of such a comment, the fact is that in all but the most general sense the parallels between a *nyewu* and an *entas-entas* are rather restricted. An *entas-entas* is, to be sure, a post-mortem ritual, but its form and meaning are very different from that of the *nyewu*. In Old Javanese and Tengger dialect, the word *entas* means to go upward or ascend.[1] The Tengger *entas-entas* serves not simply to commemorate the dead, but to aid in their passage to heaven. The rite remembers not a single individual, moreover, but the collective dead of a family. It is held, therefore, not one thousand days after an individual's death, but whenever an adult family has amassed the substantial capital required to sponsor this ritual and its extensive social festivities. The ceremony is organized, finally, not around a *kenduren* prayer meal, but around what are the most complex and powerful of the Tengger priest's liturgies. Its prayers are the longest, its offerings the most abundant, and its ritual the most powerful of any household ritual performed by a priest. No other ceremony so exhaustively reveals the emphases of Tengger tradition and its differences with lowland ritual tradition.

All of the interpretive tensions of Tengger ritual tradition are prominent here, as well. The ancestral bias of popular cosmology, the lack of integration between priestly liturgy and popular myth, and the widespread faith that the liturgy contains truths too powerful for commonsense understanding—all of these features of Tengger cultural interpretation acquire added depth in light of the *entas-entas*. From an outside analytic perspective as well, the rite provides insight into what the priestly tradition may once have been, and why it has become what it is today.

[1] The term *entas* has similar connotations in Balinese, and is similarly used to describe the ritual purification of souls for their ascent to the heavens (cf. Covarrubias 1937:298; Hooykaas 1973:10).

The Ritual Background

The date for an *entas-entas* has to be determined six or more months in advance of the rite's actual celebration. The priest is responsible for choosing the exact date, which he fixes according to numerological and calendrical information that he obtains from his *petungan* book. He also sets a date for the performance of a *semeninga* ritual announcement, which in effect opens preparations for the ceremony. The *semeninga* for an *entas-entas* usually occurs five or six months in advance of the rest of the purification rite. It is only after this preliminary incense announcement that the husband and wife who are sponsors of the upcoming *entas-entas* may visit their ritual exchange partners, politely requesting aid in meeting the expense of the festival, and thus securing the return of the hundreds or even thousands of dollars in loans and gifts earlier made to exchange partners (Chapter 10). To use the repayments for anything other than the ritual preparations, or to fail to perform the *entas-entas* after having announced it to the gods, is considered an extremely grievous sin.

General preparations for the *entas-entas* begin several weeks prior to the actual celebration. Gifts of cash and goods pour in from exchange partners, and there are several days of festive cooperative labor (*sayan*) to collect wood for the festival's kitchen fires, to build the veranda (*tarop*) under which guests will dine and dance, to whitewash house walls, to extend the kitchen and build additional stoves, to make rice and maize flour for sweets, and, in short, to prepare the hundreds of things necessary for the upcoming festivities. Technical preparation for the priestly liturgy begins only one day prior to the festival. The priest's ritual assistants help in the cooking and composition of *sajenan* offerings, and the fabrication of the flower figurines (*petra*) to which the souls of the ancestral dead will be invoked. The *petra* figurines are the responsibility of the *wong sepuh*, or the priest's "elder ritual assistant" (Chapter 9). Each *petra* stands about eighteen inches high, and is made from a long fibrous leaf known as *tlodok* or *klodok*, which is doubled over to form the doll's body, and ruffled at the base to make its feet. The face is made from a four-centimeter square of white palm leaf decorated with small incisions to make geometric eyes, a nose, and mouth. A small bouquet of edelweiss, sometimes mixed with marigold, creates the *petra*'s hair.

Petra are prepared for three categories of spirit guests: the family souls to be purified for ascent to heaven, an equal number of family souls who come as "witnesses" (*saksi*) to the ritual purification, but who are themselves not ritually purified, and a special guardian deity (not the soul of a deceased relative) whose duty it is to witness the purification and then lead the purified spirits in their passage to heaven. Only close lineal relatives are supposed to be included among the souls to be purified: parents, siblings, children, grandchildren, and, if not purified in a prior *entas-entas*, grandparents. Kin off the family line or from earlier generations are not supposed to be included in this group, but instead come as spirit "witnesses." The guardian deity invited to witness and lead the ritual purification is the most mysterious of the spirits invoked to *petra*. His figurine is clad in white cloth, and lacks the edelweiss hair. The spirit's role in ritual is relatively clear. When the human spirits are invoked to earth on the first day of an *entas-entas*, this deity leads the way. When the priest stands before the *tuwuhan* offering stand during the rite of great offering (*banten gede*), he addresses and invokes this same spirit. The same deity, finally, leads the souls of the dead through their final hour of purification during the *palukatan*, and afterwards leads them to heaven. Outside of this ritual format, however, the identity of this deity is vague. He bears no particular name, but is generally referred to as the "spirit of the region" (*roh kalurahan*), and is thus in some sense identified as one of the chief deities and a guardian of Tengger territory. Many people insist that this spirit is not one but two beings, a husband and wife. The white spirit is especially powerful among guardian spirits, but, when questioned, most villagers insist that only one trained in the mysteries of the liturgy can understand his, or their, precise identity.

The Ritual Work

An *entas-entas* is a three-day affair. The first two days consist largely of ritual invocations and offerings similar to those seen in most other Tengger rites. Family and guardian spirits are invoked the first night. Their arrival is greeted with communal meal taking, for which (in most villages) the village chief and other officials are supposed to be present, as dignitaries to greet the spirits. If there is to be *tayuban* dance entertainment, it is restricted this first night to village officials, the priest, dignitaries from neighboring communities and the lowlands, and close kin of the ritual sponsors.

From this first night on, the family spirits are accompanied by the white guardian spirit. After the dining and dancing, the spirits spend the remainder of the night in a specially constructed ritual attic (*pogo*) erected in that corner of the house that lies in the direction of Mt. Bromo.[2] The next day the spirits again descend from the attic and are

[2] Ritual attics are also used in some Balinese ritual, where they are associated with the

invited by the priest to occupy the specially prepared *petra* figurines. The *petra* will be possessed by the spirits for the next two days. They are first carried by their living relatives in a small procession from the house of a sibling of the festival sponsor to the sponsor's house itself. The white-clad *petra* is carried by the ritual elder at the front, followed by the *petra* of the family spirits, and finally a portable *gamelan* orchestra, some offering trays, and the stretched skin of a goat slaughtered the day before. The goat, decorated with marigold flowers, is referred to as the "prostrating goat" (*mendo kurepan*). The spirit of this animal will serve as the "vehicle" (*kendaraan*) for carrying the souls to heaven after their purification. The parade marchers carry the *petra* to the room prepared for the next day's ritual purification. The figurines are set out on a table known as the "holy water shrine" (*balai tirti*) and presented with more festival foods. Two thin palm-leaf strips hang to the right and the left of the offering table. On them are written the "titles" to be given to the human spirits by the white spirit at the completion of the ritual purification. The titles indicate clearly the purpose of this ritual labor:

Sang Hyang Sukma, Dewa Lanang	Holy Spirit, Male Deity
Sang Hyang Sukma, Dewa Wadon.	Holy Spirit, Female Deity.

The goal of the purification, clearly, is not simply to remove sin from the souls of the dead, but to bring about their deification.

Banten Invocation and Palukatan Purification   There is the usual presentation of offerings to family and guardian spirits at the beginning of the third day of the *entas-entas*, but ritual attention focuses on those events that take place at the end of the day: the "ritual of great offering" (*banten gede*) and the purification (*palukatan*) of the souls of the dead. The *banten gede* must take place first, since it is only through this rite's invocation and worship of the powerful world deity associated with the white-clad *petra* that the later labor of purification can take place. The *banten* ceremony serves, in effect, to mobilize spirits for an especially important ritual work.[3] Even to the casual observer, everything about

---

meru holy mountain, an image also seen in Tengger but not explicitly identified with the attic (for Bali, see Stutterheim 1956:72).

[3] The *banten* is used in most Tengger ceremonies where an especially powerful deity must be invoked. The *banten gede* ceremony in particular is used during Karo, the *unan-unan* (held every five years), and *walagara* weddings where *petra* ancestral figurines are prepared.

the *banten* ceremony suggests that it is a no-holds-barred event. An upright offering stand (*tuwuhan*), with two legs of palm leaf, sugar cane, maize, and other green stalks, and offerings of rice sweets and meat hanging from the vertical pole connecting the legs, is erected in a corner of the room lying in the direction of Mt. Bromo. All of the priest's sacred heirlooms (Chapter 9), displayed during only the most powerful of rites, are set on a mat beneath the *tuwuhan*, amidst *sajenan* offering trays and the priest's incense and holy water implements. One sees in Tengger none of the finely wrought works of art brought out in large Balinese rituals, but the idea here seems to be the same: old and sacred paraphernalia give added weight to the ritual labor in process.

The sponsors of the *entas-entas* (husband, wife, and children) join the priest and his assistants on the mat beneath the *tuwuhan*. The priest begins by standing, turning in the direction of the *tuwuhan* (which is to say toward Mt. Bromo), reciting a prayer and then taking his seat on the mat once again, beginning the appeal to world deity. Eyes closed in concentration, the priest takes a piece of incense into his right hand, moves it to his lips, and spits lightly on it three times as he begins the prayer of incense invocation. Finishing the prayer, he places the incense on the coals of the *prapen* brazier, and, as the smoke wafts up from it, touches its edges with the tip of his outstretched hands, palms up in supplication. Continuing his prayers, he takes his holy-water beaker, moves it through the smoke of the incense, and then anoints the offerings on the mat before him. Setting the beaker down, he then takes his incense brazier into hand, elevates it to just in front of his face, and rotates it counterclockwise three times in a horizontal plane. He continues to pray almost inaudibly as he sets the implement down again. At this point, one of his assistants stands, walks toward the *tuwuhan*, tears a leaf from its side, and makes an earth offering, using food from the *sajenan* moments earlier presented to, and presumably consumed by, the gods. (The offering will be placed at the kitchen fire at the end of the ceremony.) The assistant then passes out betel leaf and white strings (*gelang tebus* "purification string") to the family members observing the ceremony from just behind the priest. The strings, it is said, show the spirits that the family is now spiritually pure, and thus ready to proceed with the remainder of the *entas-entas* rite. The family members also consume a few grains of uncooked white rice removed from the purified *sajenan* offerings presented to the deities.

Still quietly reciting his prayers, the priest now stands, takes a branch of a banyan tree into his right hand, rolls it in a clay pot filled with coconut juice, and then anoints to the east, south, west, north, sky, and earth. With his assistant, he then walks back to the kitchen fireplace, where he anoints the earth offering earlier prepared by his assistant. He then walks to the front door of the house, anointing a similar earth offering, thus completing the *banten* ceremony.

After the *banten*, the priest and his assistants pause only long enough to disassemble the *tuwuhan* and set out the offerings for the *palukatan*. This is the longest and most technically elaborate of the priest's liturgies, lasting about thirty minutes. The most curious aspect of its performance is that the souls of the dead are invited to enter the bodies of their living relatives, who seat themselves at the center of the ritual floor. Through their role as "representatives" of their deceased relatives, the living thus play a direct role in the purification of the dead. Those chosen to play this role dress simply for the rite, women wearing a single batik cloth wrapped around their bodies, men shirtless and in trousers. No jewelry may be worn and one's hair must be uncovered and loose. The *petra* of those spirits to be purified are also stripped of the piece of clothing in which, up to this time, they had been wrapped. The white-clad *petra* and those figurines deemed "witnesses" to the ritual purification, however, remain clothed, and observe the ritual proceedings from a table at the side of the room.

As the time approaches for the rite to begin, adults and children gather round to watch. Of all liturgies, this one attracts the attention of the people, in part because of the role played by lay villagers in its performance, but also because of the event's theatrical qualities. As always, however, the priest makes no comment on the proceedings, or otherwise prefaces his performance of the complex liturgy. The offerings required for a *palukatan* are massive and complex. The priest's assistants work feverishly, placing unhusked rice stalks on a short legged bench (on which the representatives of the dead will sit), and covering them with a mat. They then set clay pots (*cepel, pengaron*) in front of the bench, one for each of the representatives of the dead who will sit on the bench. Into each pot go coins (said to be "provisions" for the spirits in their voyage), which the priest anoints with special holy water taken from a spring near Mt. Bromo. Once blessed, the pots receive their most important cargo, the *petra* figurines of the souls to be purified. Each pot receives just one, unless one of the *petra* is for a deceased child, who is thus grouped with an adult on whose "lap" the child will "be held" (*dipangku*).

The offerings for the purification ceremony are amassed on the floor between the bench and the mat on which the priest will sit. Standing about eighteen inches tall, bamboo containers (*kulak*) filled with uncooked rice sit before the clay pots, a coin and small string bracelet (to be worn by each spirit as its sign of purification) hidden in their interior.

Candles stand to the right and left of the line of bamboo containers. Next come the food offerings intended for the souls of the spirits to be purified, one setting for each spirit. There are freshly cooked cones of rice (tumpeng); palm leaf baskets filled with meat, rice sweets, and noodles; hot cups of sweet coffee; and casseroles of beef and gravy. In front of these foods for the ancestors, and closer to where the priest will sit, there is a veritable stack of food trays piled one atop the other, intended as sajenan offerings for the guardian deities. Each tray has its own distinctive assortment of meats, sweets, and rice cakes, and each is in theory designed to fulfill a different spiritual function. On the floor to the left of these offerings, there lies a leg of raw beef, known as the "spiritual earth offering" (tamping alus), and designed to attract the powerful demons whom the priest will, in the course of the purification ceremony, transform. The "prostrating goat" sits nearby, ready to bear its spirit passengers to heaven, once they have been purified.

When the ritual is ready to begin, at a sign from the priest, one of the ritual assistants goes to the front door and strikes a brass kenong seven times, and then returns to take his seat to the left of the priest. The priest's wife sits to the right of the priest, a portable clay oven set before her. The male and female "representatives" of the dead now enter the room, and take their seats on the short-legged bench. The priest covers them with a long white cloth (the sewek mulyo), then takes his seat and begins his prayers. He opens with a standard sequence of incense announcement, invocation, offering, and worship; only after this does the ritual proper to the palukatan begin. At a sign from the priest, a small gamelan orchestra in the corner begins to play a slow melody. The priest's assistants pour sugar over the hot coals of an incense brazier that they tend, sending up a thick cloud of sweet-smelling smoke. The priest begins his recitation of the prayer of world origins (purwabumi). He speaks slowly, punctuating his intonation with the occasional ringing of a bell, said to draw the attention of the spirits. At times he raises his voice in song, his eyes closed, his body swaying gently. To his right, his wife ignites castor-oil stalks placed beneath her clay oven, creating a low fire with which she proceeds to fry rice. She turns the sizzling rice slowly, periodically adding a few more grains from a rice-steaming basket (kukusan) to her right. When the priest completes his prayer, he nods to his wife, and the two of them stand and walk forward to the representatives of the dead seated on the ritual bench before them.

Here begins the actual purification of the souls of the dead. Beginning at the far left of the bench, the priest reaches down, takes the cloth covering the seated man's head, and pulls a needle through it three times. He repeats the same movement with the leaves of the petra

169

figurine sitting in the clay pot before the man. The priest continues down the line of the representatives of the dead in this fashion, sewing the cloth over the head of each, and repeating the same gesture with the *petra* figurine. Having finished, he then returns to the first man, this time taking a burning stalk of castor oil plant in hand and singeing the man's hair. He does the same to the flower hair of the *petra*, moving slowly down the line of representatives and flower figurines. Having finished this act, he returns again to the first man, this time with a small mandrake (*bebek*) in hand, its feet bound with a string to which is attached a cloth purse containing coins and betel leaf. The priest's wife stands next to him, placing a few grains of the rice she cooked moments earlier on the cloth cover over the head of each seated representative of the dead. The priest immediately steps in and moves the mandrake over the cloth in a scraping fashion, allowing the animal to peck at the rice. Once again the movement is repeated with all the representatives, and, at the end of the line, the priest hurls the bewildered bird across the room into the waiting arms of one of his assistants. The priest and his wife then repeat exactly the same action with every one of the representatives of the dead, this time, however, using a hen rather than a mandrake, once again finishing by hurling the startled animal through the air to his assistant. One more act of ritual purification remains. Returning to the top of the line, the priest recites a short prayer over the first man, anoints him with three quick movements, and then leans forward to do the same over the *petra* figurine in the clay pot before him. He then takes the *petra* in hand, rotates it in a counterclockwise circle three times in the interior of the clay pot, and then removes it and places it in a rice-steaming basket (*kukusan*) held by one of his ritual assistants. The priest continues in this fashion through the entire line of the representatives of the dead, finishing the labors of purification.

The priest at this point walks outside the house. There, by the front door, he anoints a green coconut sitting on a flat clay tray. He then enters the house once again, approaches the line of representatives of the dead, and, after reciting a short prayer, takes the white cloth covering them in hand and, with a sudden movement, pulls the cloth away while exclaiming, "All go!" The spirits are removed from the bodies of the living. The representatives of the dead run from the house and, as the first person reaches the doorway, they are greeted with the loud "whoosh" of the priest's assistant bringing a machete down on the previously anointed green coconut. The *palukatan* is done.

There are several more small ceremonies after the *palukatan*. Most importantly, the *petra* figurines are once again clothed, put alongside the *petra* of the spirit "witnesses" to the purification, and, with a song and a wave of the priest's scarf, enjoined to return to the heavens. (The goatskin, meanwhile, has remained lying on the floor.) The ritual work done, the priest, his staff, and the sponsors of the rite share a communion meal to mark the close of the purification. The rite is thus brought to a close, its transformation complete.

Reading Ritual Form

There is nothing quite like it, this third day of the *entas-entas* purification. No other rite rivals the complexity of its prayers, the scale of its offerings, or the drama of its performance. The billowing incense smoke, the priest's melodic incantation, the *gamelan* accompaniment, the density of offerings—all these things have their counterpart in other Tengger rites, but never with such an explosion of imagery and detail. The richness of that detail is alone sufficient to indicate that, whatever its precise meaning, something very important is occurring in the *entas-entas*. What that is, however, is not an issue on which all Tengger agree. As with so many of their core rites, this one is the subject of conflicting interpretations, the inconsistency of which suggests once again that the cultural meaning attributed to a rite is not determined in any simple way by the verbal and gestural symbolism embodied in ritual ceremony.

At the most general level of conception, there are two opposing views on the spiritual purpose of an *entas-entas*. The first, espoused in villages of southern and northeastern Tengger, suggests that the rite must be performed if a soul or group of souls is to achieve final peace in heaven (*khayangan*). Without the rite's performance, a soul is condemned to wander aimlessly forever, lacking a secure resting spot in the afterlife and thus bothering those of its living descendants who should have insured the spirit's purification and ascent into heaven. According to this view, in short, all of the dead must be purified in an *entas-entas*; hence if a family is too poor to sponsor the ceremony, it is supposed to make arrangements with relatives so that the souls of its relatives can be purified by incorporation in someone else's ceremony.

The second opinion as to the purpose of the *entas-entas*, espoused almost exclusively in villages of the Tengger northwest, insists that far from being a spiritual obligation incumbent upon all families, the rite need be, and should be, performed only by those villagers sufficiently affluent to shoulder its substantial expense. The whole point of the ritual, according to this view, is to pay homage to one's family elders, giving them the ritual attention that they gave their children and relatives when they were alive. Performance of the rite does not in any way affect the welfare of the dead in the afterlife, I was told; nor does nonperformance detract from the spiritual standing of those not honored with such an act of filial homage. The rite is a personal statement of respect from a family to its deceased elders; it does not seek to intercede with higher deities on behalf of those elders. Not surprisingly, given this view of the rite's purpose, poorer villagers in northwest Tengger are far less likely to sponsor an *entas-entas* than their counterparts in the Tengger south and northeast (Chapter 10).

What is curious about these conflicting views of the *entas-entas* is that they are formulated in the face of a ritual that in performance is remarkably consistent throughout the Tengger region. There is some small variation from village to village in the exact name of certain portions of the three-day rite, and some of its embellishments vary according to the training of different priests, but throughout Tengger, the *entas-entas* is a three-day ceremony that concludes with much the same *banten* invocation of world deity and *palukatan* purification of the dead. Even the detail of the *palukatan* finale—with its cooking, bell-ringing incantation, sewing, hair-burning, rice scraping, and bird throw-ing—is much the same from village to village. People from different regions of Tengger are often well aware of this fact, since they visit other villages during such large rituals, and they have an opportunity to observe different priests perform the same rites. If ritual symbolism is a "vehicle" of meaning, the performative vehicle here looks every-where the same, but for some reason it yields, at least at this general level of interpretation, divergent meanings.

The very generality of such exegeses, however, is part of the problem. Whatever people have to say as to the ultimate purpose of the *entas-entas*, their accounts differ much less seriously as soon as they turn their attention to the explication of specific details of the rite. Proponents of both views on the ultimate meaning of the rite agree, for example, that the *banten* ceremony is designed to secure the attention and blessing of a powerful world spirit without whom the later *palukatan* cannot occur. People from different areas of Tengger also agree on the themes of purification seen in the *palukatan* itself. The heavy incense, the bell ringing, the priest's singing, the gamelan melodies, and the abundant offerings are all intended to attract the attention of powerful spirits whose presence somehow—and just how is not something on which most people can comment—secures the blessing of the family dead, so that the latter may ascend into heaven. The rice and coins in the bamboo containers (*kulak*), villagers point out, are provisions for that journey. The string placed in the same container will be worn by the family spirits after their purification, as a symbol of their spiritual purity for the gods who will greet them as they come to heaven. Purification itself, villagers add, is product of the priest's labors. His acts of sewing, singeing hair, and scraping rice from the heads of the representatives of the dead are all designed to remove impurities from the souls of the dead, who are said to have "borrowed" the bodies of their living relatives so as to undergo the ritual purification. When the priest throws the mandrake into the air, he is urging the souls of the dead to prepare for their flight. When the priest's assistant severs a green coconut with a machete as the representatives of the dead run from the ritual house, he cuts all remaining bonds between the souls of the dead and their living relatives. The souls then ascend to heaven on the back of the "prostrating goat," led by the white-clad guardian deity who calls out to the other gods the new names, and spiritual status, of the now deified spirits of the dead.

Not all villagers, of course, are familiar with the details of this ritual interpretation, and even those who are are not always interested in making so discursive an outline of the purification ritual as I have constructed above. For a variety of reasons, however, more villagers seem capable of supplying bits and pieces of exegetical commentary on this rite than they can with some others in the priestly repertoire. In part this is due to the sheer detail of the purification ritual, much of which is performatively (rather than just verbally) elaborate, and at times even theatrical. Although there is no emphasis placed on lay villagers (outside the sponsoring family) observing the ritual performance, many do because of the drama of the rite, and because a neighbor or kinsperson may be among the semi-clothed representatives of the dead. In addition it is well known that this rite is the most powerful of household rites. The priest may sometimes celebrate lesser rituals off in a corner of the room while elsewhere people eat and dance, but this never occurs with the purification ceremonies during the third day of an *entas-entas*. All social festivity must come to a halt. In some villages, moreover, the priest's purification prayers are recited into a microphone and broadcast through loudspeakers into the larger village—which, by the performative standards of Tengger tradition, is nothing less than astounding.

The fact that there is this body of exegetical commentary on the rite, and that it takes much the same form in different areas of Tengger, makes all the more perplexing the inconsistency between different regions' accounts as to the ultimate purpose of the rite. Informants in northwest Tengger, after all, also note that the *palukatan* removes impurities from the souls of the dead; at least they say this when talking about specific details of the rite's performance. When confronted with what looks like an inconsistency between these latter explanations and the claim that the rite ultimately is not necessary for all of the dead, villagers simply deny any contradiction, retreating once again to bland generalities concerning the importance of respect to one's elders, and the role of the *entas-entas* in conveying such respect.

When, in the second year of my research, I moved from south Tengger to the northwest, however, I learned that there is a history to the northwest's revisionist interpretation of the *entas-entas*. In the course of a long discussion with a village chief, I pointed out the discrepancy between northwestern and southern Tengger perspectives. With a heavy sigh, the village chief conceded that northwestern Tengger had also once considered the *entas-entas* a ritual incumbent upon all families, until the present generation, when village officials promoted the new interpretation of the rite as a noncompulsory act of filial piety. The reasons for the change, the chief added, were primarily economic. Village officials felt it was important to lighten the burden of ritual expense on the poor, and to encourage investment in agriculture rather than ritual festivity.[4] At first resisting the change, priests in the region eventually went along, bowing to the authority of village chiefs.

The result of this revision has been that, once again, there is a serious lack of continuity between liturgical detail and officially sanctioned commentaries on the same liturgy. This example of ritual reinterpretation has the merit, however, of having occurred recently, hence it illustrates more clearly certain aspects of ritual interpretation in Tengger. First, it reveals once again that the formal symbolism embedded in a rite, even when seen and heard, need not dominate the public process of ritual exegesis. Unlike some other Tengger rites, the details of the *entas-entas* still communicate to some people, even in the face of an official commentary (promoted by the chiefs) that would deny the apparent truth of this communication. What allows the one discourse to neutralize the cultural significance of the other is not the symbolism of the liturgy, but the political authority of the official doctrine's spokesmen. Tengger chiefs have always acted as stewards of the tradition, and it is this authority that has supported the revision of the popular meaning of the *entas-entas* in the Tengger northwest. The formal symbolism of the liturgy is not the sole arbiter of its truth. No amount of formal analysis

---

[4] It is conceivable that officials could have reduced ritual expense in ways that would not have restricted the rite's sponsorship to the affluent. The largest portion of ritual expense, after all, is incurred in the social festivities that accompany *entas-entas*, not in the ritual celebration itself, and these could have been restricted. Officials could also have proposed that the poor sponsor collective purifications, as sometimes occurs with cremation in Bali. These innovations, however, would have altered the status implications of the ritual festival, and village leaders appear to have opted for a plan that altered the religious meaning of the rite instead.

of the liturgy's symbolism will uncover this revisionist ritual meaning. The liturgy's truth, like that of all ritual, can be understood only by situating the rite in a larger universe, subject to an authority and discourse always more complex than that of ritual alone.

The example highlights another peculiarity of Tengger tradition. The revisionist campaign in the northwest has not challenged or directly reworked the forms of priestly liturgy. These have been left more or less intact, despite the tension between the new doctrine and what they might reveal to observant witnesses to the rite. The example nicely illustrates a more general quality of Tengger ritual organization. Priestly liturgy and "official" doctrine are subject to different social pressures, and different tempos of change, because each medium is embedded in a social environment subject to different practical contingencies. In performing and transmitting the liturgy, Tengger priests are subject to a different sort of cultural accountability than are the accounts of popular ritual tradition. It is this critical nexus—the way in which different forms of cultural knowledge are subject to different social controls—that provides clues for understanding the uneven quality of Tengger ritual reproduction through time.

Work and Word: The Purification Viewed from Its Prayers

The division of ritual labor in Tengger effectively creates a parallel segregation of experience. Lay villagers cannot study the prayers of the liturgy in the ways that priests must. As the dispute over the meaning of the entas-entas indicates, however, the separation of roles and experiences is not absolute. Some people have regular opportunities to witness the liturgy from close up. Rituals like the palukatan have, in addition, unusually explicit gestural symbolism that lends itself to at least speculative interpretation. Finally, some priests recite their prayers more clearly than other priests, so that portions of many prayers are intelligible for people within hearing range who bother to pay attention. The segregation of lay villagers from the liturgy's rich language and gestural symbolism is, therefore, by no means absolute. As we shall see, moreover, there is considerable evidence that some villagers know a good deal more than they are willing or encouraged to say.

All of these considerations make more problematic the question of the cultural status of priestly prayer. Is it irrelevant to the rite's cultural meaning? Or indeed, should prayer be considered the very key to ritual's truth? Traditional philological approaches to literate liturgical religions have often not bothered to ask how social actors experience sacred texts.[5] Many scholars have provided us with fine translations of religious documents from other societies. But they have often been less capable of indicating to what degree such translations correspond to the actual experience of members of that religious community in which the religious texts are employed. The philological approach to sacred literature makes good sense when one is primarily concerned with tracing the historical diffusion of literate religious traditions over wide social territories. This, for example, has been one of the important concerns of Dutch philologists in Bali, where scholars have been rightfully curious to know how much of Balinese religious literature can be traced back to an Indian counterpart. If our concern is with the way in which actors make sense of religious texts, however, our analysis cannot be restricted to textual reconstruction or linear translation. This is particularly true in such a context as Tengger, where access to liturgical literature is socially restricted and the tradition is designed to be envehicled in oral performances subject to social pragmatics much more complex than an individual's reading of a text. All of this throws into doubt any assumption that the meaning of prayer texts is the same for all actors, and reducible to simple translation.

Having said this much, I want in what follows to violate the interpretive principles used throughout this work, and look at the *banten* and *palukatan* prayers as if one could reduce their meaning to finished linear translations. Needless to say, such translation should not be identified as the "meaning" prayers have for lay villagers; nor can it be identified as the ultimate meaning of the prayers for priests. As I discuss in greater detail in the next chapter, there is an interpretive tension even in the heart of the priestly liturgy. Nonetheless, there is good reason to believe that something of what is reconstructed below is communicated to many Tengger priests. Some priests study their prayers assiduously, others do not; some priests have inherited linguistically well-preserved prayers, others have not. My primary interest in reconstructing the following prayers is for the moment philological and comparative. The prayers speak directly to the larger question of where Tengger liturgy may have originated and the difficulties it has encountered in a changing cultural present.

Banten Invocation and Purwabumi Prayer of World Origins   When, on the third day of an *entas-entas* ritual, the priest stands before the

---

[5] Alton Becker (1979) has proposed a "new philology" that would, among other things, directly address the problem of how actors actually experience the texts philologists study.

stalk-and-flower *tuwuhan*, facing Mt. Bromo, and opening the *banten gede* ceremony, he recites a prayer composed in relatively modern Javanese, but usually inaudible to most persons present:

> Hong! my lord my place of orientation is Mt. Masmahameru. . . .
> I receive the authority to arrange the beautiful flowers (*kusuma sari*) of Lord Guru. Guru's seat is in the essence of these souls . . .
> and their power is that of Sunan Prabu Guru, the all powerful and all high. (I ask) that he may take his seat in the beautiful flowers.

> I am entered by the essence of the all powerful spirit, and I prostrate myself in ritual supplication. Is it not I who am given authority by the Holy Lord? I hear with my right ear hear with my left, beauty beautiful homage to Siva beauty beautiful homage to Siva (*nomo Siwoho*). From these offerings I present the beautiful essence, *hong pekulun*.

The tone and references of this prayer clearly distinguish it from popular commentaries, but the prayer shows profound affinities with others the priest recites. The priest begins his address by describing the ritual context as, in fact, a supernatural terrain: he stands, he says, atop Mt. Meru, spiritual center of the world and meeting place with the gods. The *meru* image is the same as seen in the ritual symbolism of the Kasada ceremony at Mt. Bromo, similar to that once used across Indic Southeast Asia (von Heine Geldern 1942; Hall 1981:245). The "place of orientation" to which the priest refers appears to be the *tuwuhan* offering stand, the "beautiful flowers" (*kusuma sari*) of which are the point to which Lord Guru will descend. Guru is Siva as World Teacher. Here he is invited not only to descend to the ritual site but, according to the prayer appeal, to enter and possess the priest. This, then, is the source of the priest's ritual power; he is a vehicle for Lord Guru, much as he was a vehicle for the world spirit who possessed the priest during the Kasada rite. Unlike the Kasada rite, however, the *banten* shows no reluctance to name this powerful world deity. It is through Siva's power, the priest proclaims, that the rite about to occur will take place.

The *banten gede* then moves through a variety of other prayers, in which, most importantly, the priest invites the gods of the wind directions—Iswara (east), Brahma (south), Mahadewa (west), Visnu (north), and Siva (center)—to come and consume the essence of the offerings given. The *banten* prayer is only preliminary, however, to the specific ritual labor at hand. It draws the world deities to the ritual offerings so that their power may be utilized in the rite about to occur, here the *palukatan* purification of the dead. The *palukatan*'s offerings are set out, the representatives of the dead take their places, and the priest and his assistants take their seats on the ritual mat facing the offerings. The priest begins with the recitation of the standard opening prayers of invocation, offering, and worship. Shortly after them, however, the gamelan orchestra begins to play, the thick smoke of sugar incense wafts into the air, and the priest begins the recitation of the most powerful of purification prayers, the *purwabumi* "prayer of world origins." It begins with the description of a time outside of time, when no universe existed, and the first deities emerged from nothingness:

Hong! purwobumi kamuliane	Om! at the beginning of the world
Betari Umo mijil saking limun-limunane	The goddess Umo emerged from nothingness
Betari mulane ono betari	The goddess of origins was a goddess
Pingongko semine betoro.	Who became the seed for the other gods.

In Indian cosmology Umo or Uma is the consort of Siva, and at the same time his female manifestation. Like the *banten* prayer, therefore, the world at its origins is centered on Sivaness, here in world birth appropriately expressed in the female form of Umo. From Umoness there emerge the other first gods:

Sira muah mijil kang ponco dewoto	Together they emerged the five gods
Kongsi Gargo Mentri Kuruso	Kongsi, Gargo, Mentri, Kuruso,
Kang Kalilan Wong Pritojolo.	Along with the Pritojolo person(s).

In some versions of this text, the names of the five gods are garbled almost beyond recognition. Part of the problem in priests' recognition of these names is that, outside of this prayer, these five deities do not figure in other Tengger beliefs or other priestly liturgies. Nonetheless, from a comparative perspective, reference to these five gods is important, for they are none other than the famous "five *resi*" or holy seers of both Indian and Balinese tradition (Hooykaas 1974:129-35).

These, then, are the gods present at the origin of the world. The prayer goes on through several passages to describe what is in effect the creation of cosmic order from primordial chaos. There was as yet no system of directions, the prayer says, nor a world to which such directions could apply. Hence the goddess Umo works to create both from nothing, and she works with such intensity that her sweat flows like a river, creating the Ganges River itself. Other deities are born at this time as well: the goddess of the sea, Ibu Pertiwi (goddess of land), gods for the sky, the sun, the stars, and the planets. Each of the four wind directions is assigned its respective color. Order has appeared. Creation is not without its dangers, however. In the midst of emerging order, there appears a powerful demon who is the very incarnation of disorder and evil:

Singo nodo gegere	The roar of a lion
Sang dewoto kabeh	And all the gods took flight
Wojo kasilat	It had teeth exposed like fangs
Wiyung tutup kadi pereng	Lips as wide as valleys
Rejeng irung kadi sumur bandung	A nose as deep as a well
Netro kadi suryo kembar	Eyes like twin suns
Kerananiro kadi layaran	Ears large like two sails
Rambut kuwel agimbal	Hair ragged and matted
Ogah uger luguriro kang giri-giri	So tall was he that he caused fright
Luhuriro tanpo toro	As without parallel was his height
Tutup kemadiane akoso.	Covering half the sky.

The demon, of course, is none other than Kala or—Siva-center still—Siva in his demonic manifestation. It is the exorcism and transformation of this demon that the *entas-entas* rite must accomplish.

Kala is not alone, moreover; he is accompanied, the prayer says, by Durga, his female consort in evil. Accompanying the two of them there is, in addition, a veritable army of evil creatures, *buta* and *kala* demons who, as the prayer points out, lurk in livestock sheds, rice fields, doorways, under beds, in guest rooms, the kitchen, and storage sheds. From the perspective of contemporary Tengger ritual practice, the list is fascinating, for these are the very places that must be given *tamping* earth offerings at the conclusion of ritual services. Some modern Tengger deny the very existence of such evil spirits (Chapter 4), but this prayer clearly recognizes their reality, and seeks to stress the importance of their neutralization through ritual offering. Curiously, this is not the only reference the *purwabumi* makes to Tengger ritual practice, for it speaks of the importance of other rites as well:

Podo tuture dewoto	And these were the words of the gods:
Pujo purnomo kelawan tilem	(Perform) the worship at full and no moon,
Galungan kelawan penawungan Kasodo kelawan pitu	As well as during Galungan and Kasada, and during the seventh month;
Nyambek tiyo maring betoro Kolo tan ketedah Hyang Durgo!	Give homage to Kala and Durga; lest you be devoured by them!

Here we have an account of Kasada, Galungan, and other Tengger rites like no explanation heard in popular tradition. The purpose of these ceremonies, the prayer points out, is to keep the dangerous Kala and Durga at a distance, to remove their destructive danger from the world. No mention is made in this prayer of maintaining filial ties to guardian ancestors; Dewa Kusuma and other first-founding ancestors here appear to play no role. The prayer lacks entirely the localist vision of popular tradition; it speaks not of territory, ancestry, and Tengger tradition, but of a far more encompassing metaphysic related to the origins of the world itself. Ancestry gives way to world cosmology.

Here the *purwabumi* prayer draws to a close. It does so, in effect, by linking this cosmic drama to the specific ritual labor at hand. The gods, the prayer explains, consume the invisible essence of the offerings set out on ritual mats, and they receive the *puja* worship of the priest. Through these acts the gods-as-demons are exorcised (*diruwat*) and transformed once again into their "true forms" as beneficent deities.[6] This transformation marks the end of the *purwabumi* drama, and it is at this point that the priest turns to his wife and nods, so that she begins to sizzle moist rice on the small clay stove that she has before her. With this act, the priest launches into another prayer, one which, unlike much of the *purwabumi*, is written in a relatively modern form of Javanese. The priest explains in prayer the larger significance of the ritual labor in process:

Hong! I describe the worship of the sacred cooking container. The clay pot cooks. In it there cooks a skeleton which is that of the evil

[6] There is an anomaly in the versions of the *purwabumi* that I was able to collect. As the gods are transformed back into their true forms, Kala is said to become Wisnu, Durga Guru, and Kongsi Iswara. In most Indonesian Indic texts, Kala is related to Siva, Durga to Uma, and Kongsi is simply one of the five *resi*. It is unclear whether the transformations posited in the Tengger texts are related to something of more general significance, or whether they represent simple degeneration of understanding of the Indic tradition.

spirit Dustodurjono. The firewood is that spirit's bones. The tinder is his hair. The fire is the evil of his desire. The water is his urine. The cooking pot is his body. The rice-steaming basket (*kukusan*) is his anus. The rice itself is his teeth.

Here again, as in the *purwabumi*, evil is personified in the form of yet another spirit, Dustodurjono, and the priest's labor is in effect to transform and push back the threat of that spirit's evil. Here the labor of transformation is not only described in prayer, it is symbolically represented in the cooking by the priest's wife. This symbolic mimesis will be the basis for the rite's purification. As his wife cooks, the priest announces his challenge to evil:

You have finished preparing your soup. Of what does your work consist? It has pushed Dustodurjono back to the east, and with him have gone all of the impurities of the body. Let them return to their places.

The priest repeats this prayer for each of the four wind directions.

Having made his challenge to the forces of evil, the priest in prayer becomes more defiant, addressing each of the wind directions with the same challenge: "Although you would (falsely) call yourself the god Suworo, or Brahma, or Mahadewa, or Visnu," you are not. The priest's power is awesome indeed; he turns back evil by denying the very name that evil would give itself. But the priest does not stop there. He continues his verbal assault, proclaiming that he is "at the center protected by an iron wall, the roof of which reaches the sky." He is, in effect, impregnable, and he now invokes the true gods of the four wind directions and center (Iswara, Brahma, etc.) to his side and his struggle. All have been purified of evil, he announces; all have achieved their true form.

This is an important point of ritual transition. The priest has exorcised evil from the world in two separate actions. He has invoked the world deities to his side, recounted world creation, and, in short, assembled a veritable army of deities to help in his ritual labor. It is only at this point that the priest finally mentions the spirits of the family dead presumably present in the bodies of the representatives of the dead seated on short benches before the priest and ritual offerings. Still seated, he addresses those family spirits directly:

The door of the heavens has now been opened. May you follow the path to it. Your vehicle is the spirit of the prostrating goat, the chicken, and the duck. Your support is the string present in the *kulak* containers. Your supplies consist of the twenty-five *satak*

181

coins. May you not divert from your path! Your destination is heaven, beautiful, clear, and bright. Pure souls, return now, free, *hong pekulun*.

This prayer too is composed in a relatively modern dialect of Javanese, but it is not uttered in a fashion that would be audible to any but the priest's assistants, immediately to his side. Its ritual logic is nonetheless clear, and no doubt cues the priest himself as to what his next ritual duties are. Having addressed the family spirits, the priest now stands, walks over to the line of seated representatives-of-the-dead, and proceeds to perform his various labors of sewing, hair singeing, rice-scraping (with the mandrake and then the hen), and so on. During these labors the priest recites prayers the language of which is an easily understood modern Javanese. But again he speaks under his breath. Ritual word is nonetheless clearly linked to ritual work. When the priest "sews" the souls of the dead, for example, he says the following:

Hong! There is a spiritual gold needle from the heavens. It descends, and from it emerges a hand with a fingernail. Let it remove the illnesses and impurities from the bodies of those who are to be raised to heaven, as well as from those spirits who have come as witnesses to the ceremony. Let no one be left behind. May this act be done for eternity. These, the family spirits, are male gods, these the family spirits are female gods, *hong pekulun*.

Similar prayers describe the purification of the souls of the dead when the priest singes their hair, and enjoin the spirits not to deviate from their path to the heavens. Through this process the spirits of the dead are purified—and made gods. Separated moments later from the bodies of the living, they are free to ascend to heaven. The miracle of the liturgy is done.

Conclusion: Form and Ritual Meaning

It was only after almost a year of village residence that I won the trust of a local priest and was given access to the *palukatan* prayer. I was allowed to record and transcribe the prayers, which I then later checked with the priest, who patiently corrected all errors. This act of kindness resulted in what was, from a comparative and historical perspective, the most important discovery of this research project. The liturgy's *purwabumi* prayer of world origins has a direct counterpart in modern Balinese tradition. As Hooykaas's (1974) excellent study reveals, each year in Bali a ritual specialist known as the *resi bujangga* recites a prayer known as the *purwabumi* during the islandwide exorcism of evil spirits known as the *nyepi*. Portions of the Balinese prayer are identical, word for word, to the prayer of the same name in Tengger. The prayer's celebrant, the *resi bujangga*, is a nonbrahmanic priest, recruited from a hereditary title group known as *sengguhu* (Hooykaas 1974:53). The presence of the prayer both in Bali and in the Mt. Bromo region clearly indicates that the Tengger priesthood preserves a liturgical tradition once part of a larger, Javo-Balinese religious heritage. The status of the prayer's celebrant in Tengger and Bali today raises important comparative questions on the historical development of popular religion in Bali and around Mt. Bromo, questions to which I return in the appendix of the present work.

The anomaly of Tengger ritual interpretation is clearer from the perspective of the *entas-entas* ceremony. The prayers and actions of the liturgy display all of the features of consistency, repetition, and "integration" that we anthropologists regard as a condition for the creation of shared cultural meanings. Ritual offerings are coordinated with ritual labor and ritual labor with prayer. The *meru* or holy mountain imagery evoked in the *banten* invocation of world spirit resembles similar symbolism seen in the Kasada liturgy. The *banten* ceremony is used, moreover, in several rites—Karo, the *unan-unan*, and liturgically elaborate weddings—whenever the presence of the most powerful deity is required. The *entas-entas* prayers, of course, speak more clearly as to who this powerful deity is who must be invoked prior to all other spirits. It is Guru, Lord Siva, and the purpose of the most important of liturgies is to insure the balance of spiritual forces in the world by perpetually transforming Kala, Siva in demonic form, back into his beneficent incarnation as Guru-Siva. From the perspective of the *entas-entas* prayers, in short, the religious themes of liturgy appear consistent, constructed around this basic plan of invocation, purification, and the maintenance of spiritual balance. The liturgy itself is the primary tool in this effort. Its importance is explained in a self-referential fashion that provides the finest testimony to the internal consistency of the liturgy. In particular, the *purwabumi* prayer talks not only about the origins of the world and the specific task to be performed in the *entas-entas* purification; it talks about the liturgy as a whole, reminding those who utter the prayer to perform the liturgy's work, so that Siva and Uma remain in their beneficent incarnations. Ritual word thus speaks to its own importance.

This, at least, is the view from within the liturgy itself. If the internal coherence of a symbolic medium is a necessary condition for the creation of shared experience, however, it is not a sufficient condition. Popular interpretation of the liturgy exploits little of the complex detail internal

183

to the priest's prayers and ritual acts. Whatever villagers may actually see and hear of these, they make little mention of them in public. In particular, one hears almost no public reference to the parade of deities described in the liturgy. If asked about the existence of *buta* and *kala* demons, or deities like Siva, Brahma, Mahadewa, Iswara, and Visnu, villagers almost invariably respond by disavowing knowledge of such mysteries, and directing inquiries to the village priest. People speak more readily of guardian spirits and spirits of the family dead, the spiritual beings mentioned in popular religious narrative. From this popular perspective, ritual is first and foremost ancestral veneration, writ large or small according to the social dimensions of the group giving worship. Hence Kasada involves the worship of regional guardian ancestors; village rites invoke village guardians; and household ritual is primarily concerned with reinforcing the bond between the living and their deceased relatives. Cultural notions of society and the spirit world draw upon the same vocabulary, a spiritual one of ancestors and descendants. This is part of the reason for the appeal of these spirit notions. The same spirit categories are attractive, however, because a similar dual classification is recognized in rural *kejawen* traditions, where ancestors and guardian spirits also often play an important role. At such high levels of conception, of course, the precise identity of the spirits included in these categories is vague. Their very vagueness, however, allows them to accommodate what is in fact a wide variety of beliefs at lower, or less ideological, levels of conception. Although many Javanese speak of guardian and family spirits, in practice they construe the identity of such spirits in quite different ways. A rural Muslim community, for example, might include several of the nine "apostles" of Javanese Islam among its list of guardian spirits. In a more *kejawen* community, meanwhile, the list of guardian spirits may include deities of the earth, sky, mountains, and water—beings who would be considered unacceptably un-Islamic in a more orthodox Muslim community. Here in Tengger, one suspects that at least some villagers recognize that the guardian spirits of the Mt. Bromo region include in their ranks deities unfamiliar to other Javanese.

Indeed, the more one talks with lay villagers, the more it seems that at least some people understand the liturgy in terms different from those provided in myth, popular comment, or cultural directives from village chiefs. Most people have a general awareness of the "logic of construction" (Tambiah 1968:178) implicit in ritual appeal, with its neatly patterned protocol of invocation, offering, and homage. Most also recognize that there is a "hierarchy of languages" (Tambiah 1968:177) in ritual performance that in some sense parallels the hierarchy of the spirit world. Some deities, after all, may be addressed only through priestly *japa-*

mantra; others understand colloquial Javanese spoken by ordinary villagers. A similar hierarchy is visible in ritual offering. Some spirits receive mounds of intricate offering trays (*sajenan*) whereas others are thrown bits and pieces of leftover ritual foods. Not all spirits, evidently, are created equal. Finally, it is noteworthy that some priests recite their prayers more slowly and deliberately than other priests, to such an extent that—even if few people acknowledge the fact—some villagers must at times be able to hear references to Siva, Brahma, Visnu, and other deities. (Even my non-Javanese ears could make out these names in some prayers.) Although no villager is likely to understand the comparative or philological significance of these spiritual references, as ordinary speakers of Javanese, some would understand that these in fact are the names of the gods of Java before Islam.

Ordinary villagers thus "know" more than is expressed in myth or folk commentary. In a certain sense, however, this knowledge must be put in brackets. Since it receives no public sanction, an individual's understanding of the liturgy remains an unspoken truth, an unshared meaning. There is a tension between public discourse and personal inference, at least for some people. This does not mean that the symbolism internal to the liturgy is "meaningless." It does indicate, however, that we cannot assume that the words and gestures embedded in cultural performance automatically communicate meanings "internalized" by actors placed in their presence, or that the same cultural symbolism is equally meaningful to everyone. In our eagerness to explore the meaning of things in another society, we sometimes forget that a material symbol (be it a ritual gesture or phonic sign) is never itself a "meaning." Between the cultural object and its "meaning," the signifier and the signified, there is always a human subject, who must engage in active reconstruction for the symbol to yield a "meaning." This interpretive work depends upon more than the words and actions present in the cultural event; it evokes knowledge and sentiments born of a wider and always ongoing socialization. This socialization itself has a history and social organization, which insures that, as Bourdieu has noted, no cultural tradition is in fact "the undivided property of the whole society" (Bourdieu 1973:73). One's biography and social position influence what one brings to cultural performance, and what one is likely to see. One such social organization of knowledge here in Tengger insured that certain aspects of the tradition were elevated to the status of public truths, whereas others became unspeakable sacred mysteries.

In what way, then, is the formal detail of Tengger liturgy "meaningful"? When first discussing the Kasada ritual (Chapter 3), it almost looked as if we could ignore the obscure language interior to the liturgy, and deny it any role in Tengger religious experience. The impulse to a homogeneous model of cultural meaning aside, we can now appreciate that this is not quite the case. Popular commentary has a guilty conscience. The reluctance to comment on doctrinal matters, the tendency to direct all inquiries concerning the liturgy to the priest, and the generalized faith that there is more to the liturgy than can be put into words—all these things suggest there is "seepage" from liturgical form to popular experience. The same attitudes insure that what an outside observer might regard as "inconsistency" between the liturgy and popular commentary is in fact rarely experienced as such by villagers, but as further evidence of the mystery, wonder, and power of the ritual tradition. As we shall see (Chapter 9), however, there are limits to such cultural faith, hints of which can be heard even at the heart of the liturgy.

For the most part, however, ritual social organization in Tengger buffers the liturgy from popular regard, helping to maintain two almost parallel bodies of ritual symbolism, each internally consistent and sustained in its own social field. One particularly interesting aspect of this arrangement is evident in ritual performance. It is the less "articulate" cultural media (gesture, offerings, ritual implements) that are most directly accessible to nonpriests during ritual performance. These media are in some sense "meaningful," inasmuch as they are consistently patterned and seem capable of evoking general notions on the nature of Tengger identity and tradition. Nonetheless, these media are less capable of precise semantic communication than is prayer. Prayer taps the enormously complex logical and semantic resources of language to formulate its messages, and it is thus capable of communicating information of unparalleled precision and semantic depth. This is true, of course, only as long as speakers or hearers or prayers have the linguistic competence to understand the language of prayer itself; in at least portions of some priests' prayers, where the language is archaic or degenerate, such a competence might be lacking. For the largest portion of the priest's prayer corpus, however, there is no such problem. Symbolic media such as liturgical offering or gesture, by contrast, may be capable of evoking powerful feeling or general attitudes, but they alone can say much less than prayer about the specific identity of the liturgy's gods. The semantic imprecision of these more accessible ritual media has allowed villagers to interpret the liturgy in different ways during different historical periods. The rich language of the liturgy, meanwhile, has remained largely unheard, or unmentioned if heard, its semantic potential unexploited in public religious discourse.

All of these considerations make it very difficult to speak about ritual meaning as if this were a fixed quality stored within invariant ritual symbols. An analyst can avoid this problem, of course, by speaking of meaning at such a formal level of conception that it becomes, in effect, an observer-based construct that pretends to make no necessary characterization of native experience. For certain philological tasks, such a formal approach may be necessary and useful. But since it tells us little about the understanding of real people living in a particular time and place, this is not the interpretive methodology I have found useful in the present work. Social analysts influenced by Max Weber's notion of "social action" or the related concept of "symbolic action" (C. Geertz 1973e:10) have usually sought to listen more carefully to native voices and "actual existing meaning" (Weber 1978:I:4). The Tengger example suggests, however, that the problems inherent in such a contextual approach to cultural meaning may be more complex than sometimes thought. We cannot assume here an easy correspondence between action-in-the-world and meaning-in-actors'-minds, as at least some interpretive approaches do. Such ideal typical characterization is at best only a heuristic approximation that can be refined only inasmuch as we recognize "meaning" as an experience that assumes an active work of interpretation by real human beings, who bring diverse personalities, biographies, and social interests to the effort.

What the heuristic approximation does is allow us to speak of a realm of more or less shared meaning applied to and molded in cultural events such as the Balinese cockfight, Nuer sacrifice, or Tengger invocation of ancestral spirits. Like the native who develops a competence in understanding his own society, the enthnographer gradually learns what he identifies as the meaning of the actions of the people he studies. He does not worry about "making untestable inferences to any ghostly processes occurring in streams of consciousness from which we are debarred from visiting" (Ryle 1949:51). Like the native, in other words, the ethnographer assumes that actions have meaning, and that one does not need a theory of the brain or cognitive processing to talk, like natives, about their significance. Indeed, the ethnographer is probably truer to common-sense notions when he or she speaks as if action had a singular, shared, cultural meaning.

To question this ideology, and the theory of symbolic action built up from it, is not to retreat into the privacy theories of meaning against which Gilbert Ryle in philosophy and Clifford Geertz in anthropology have so effectively inveighed. It is, however, to recognize that the problem of understanding social action is not resolved merely by insisting that action has cultural import. Rituals, myths, political events and their ideologies may in fact be subject to widely divergent interpretation by

187

different social actors. This is a truism of contemporary social analysis, but it is not trivial, least of all methodologically. It suggests in particular that the problem of meaning is not yet solved until we have also asked "whose meaning"? Meaning is not a quality of objects or things in the world. It "is" only inasmuch as it is for a subject, a human being with a biography and social interests. It "is," therefore, only inasmuch as it is reconstructed by this socialized individual. An interpretive approach to cultural meaning thus cannot restrict its inquiry to knowledge that is intersubjective or collectively shared. Much that is of relevance to society and history, not to mention the poignancy of life itself, is not.

Recognizing these contingencies requires us to bracket the identity posited in some interpretive approaches between action and meaning until we have specified for whom the action is meaningful, and why. The "why" portion of this question requires us to attend not only to that which is present in a social action or cultural performance, but to the knowledge and social history of those for whom such things become an object of attention. Although less visible, these too play a role in the work of interpretation, and insure that actors always adopt a particular perspective on a shared social world. The perspective, moreover, is never entirely discursive or self-conscious. Here too our blanket notion of cultural "meaning" risks obscuring the fact that there are different types of knowledge. Some can be rendered in discourse; other knowledge involves the practical mastery of "knowing how." Still other sensibilities are neither discursive nor practical, but involve attitudinal frames that insure, for example, that some objects are impartially assessed, others ignored, and still others regarded as truths too great for understanding or challenge.

In a cultural domain as central to people's self-definition as religion, it is not surprising that official dogmas often deny any element of interpretive heterogeneity. What is curious about both Tengger and *kejawen* traditions, however, is that both assume that religious knowledge will vary with social position, religious training, and spiritual pedigree. In courtly areas of Central Java, with their persistent preoccupation with status inequality, this is perhaps not surprising. It is more peculiar here in Tengger, given the populist themes of public tradition. This raises a basic question concerning priestly knowledge and its social transmission. In rural communities as small as these, with their ancestral idioms and folk ways, why would the Tengger priest have remained faithful to a liturgy so far removed from the everyday world of family spirits and faceless guardian deities? Wherein originates this faith in an unspeakable truth?

· 9 ·

PRIEST AND PRIESTLY FAITH

No one role so fundamentally expresses the distinctiveness of Tengger ritual tradition as does that of the *dukun* priest. Although he shares his title with that of "the general magical specialist in traditional society" (C. Geertz 1960:87), the Tengger *dukun* is heir to a role quite different from that of his lowland counterpart. The role in Tengger involves none of the spirit mediumship, sorcery, herbalism, massage, or medicine often associated with the lowland *dukun*. The Tengger *dukun* is a priest, one among a community of village priests preserving a non-Islamic liturgical tradition in the Mt. Bromo region of East Java.

The Tengger priest may not always have been referred to as a *dukun*. In the above-mentioned prayer of world origins (*purwabumi*), the priest is referred to in one passage as a *resi pujangga*, a title with which at least some elder Tengger are also familiar. The title is of extraordinary comparative interest because it is the same as is still used is modern Bali to refer to the non-Brahmanic *sengguhu* priest who recites a *purwabumi* prayer similar to that of the Tengger priest (see Hooykaas 1974). The fact that in modern Java the Tengger priest is popularly known as a *dukun* rather than a *resi pujangga* is consistent with the general tendency in Tengger to speak of local tradition in terms similar to those used in other areas of modern Java. The common title does not hide the fact, however, that the Tengger *dukun*'s role is quite different from that of the general Javanese *dukun*, is a way which underscores the non-Islamic character of this popular priestly tradition.

Ngelmu: Ambiguous Knowledge

In general Javanese identify a *dukun* as a person learned in any number of traditional lores, techniques, or forms of esoteric knowledge. The title is applied to specialists in a wide range of fields, including midwifery, massage, spirit mediumship, herbalism, numerology, sorcery, and black and white magic (see C. Geertz 1960:86). What all such specialists have in common is their mastery of some kind of *ngelmu* or *ilmu*, that is, esoteric knowledge *par excellence*, involving the ability to see beyond outward appearance into the hidden reality of things. Mystically inclined Javanese sometimes contrast this form of knowledge with *ilmiah*, or the knowledge of external, perceptible realities. Western science provides the finest example of this form of knowledge. With proper training, almost anyone can learn such exoteric science. *Ngelmu* or *ilmu*, by contrast, is too powerful for such straightforward transmission. Mastery of its occult force can be achieved only in the course of what is usually specialized and secret training. Without such guidance, an unqualified student exposed to *ngelmu* risks inducing mental disorder or physical harm.

In part because of the exclusive manner in which it is imparted, and in part because of the shady character of the spirit forces with which it is associated, many Javanese regard *ngelmu* and its *dukun* practitioners with deep suspicion and, at least in some instances, even contempt. Clifford Geertz has noted that there is a widespread belief that *dukuns* "inevitably die a violent death" (1960:95). Many *dukuns* refuse to be referred to as *dukuns* precisely because of the ambivalence surrounding the role. The degree of such ambivalence, however, varies significantly according to the specific skill a *dukun* is thought to have mastered. Masseurs and herbalists, for example, tend to be regarded as technical experts more than magical occultists. Some may chant a phrase or two as they go about their business, but in general their *ilmu* is largely practical, of the visible world rather than the occult. Hence these *dukuns* excite little antipathy. The Javanese midwife (*dukun bayi*, see Chapter 7) is also in a way a technical expert, performing vital services related to pre- and post-natal care; hence she too attracts relatively little suspicion. Traditionally, however, many Javanese midwives also recited spells and prayers during various phases of their work. This aspect of the midwife's role has thus come to be regarded by at least modernist Muslims with a good deal more ambivalence, since many of the most commonly recited midwife prayers address spirits of the body, earth, and sky not recognized in Islam. As a result of this same tension, modernist village leaders in several Muslim communities to the west of the Tengger highlands have in recent years sought to reeducate village midwives and purge their services of non-Islamic prayer.

Dukuns involved in magic, curing, spirit mediumship, and sorcery tend to be regarded most ambivalently. As Clifford Geertz has noted (1960:96), this tension is in part a product of the inevitable intimacy of the *dukun*-patient relationship. The patient is dependent upon the *dukun*, yet uncertain of the outcome of the interaction. Given the secrecy that surrounds the knowledge utilized by these *dukuns*, moreover, the status of the *dukun's* powers is itself a potential source of anxiety for the patient. The most powerful of *dukuns* are often thought to interact "both with God and with devils . . . engaging both in devout supplications to a high God and in dubious contracts with less elevated spirits"

(C. Geertz 1960:96). Javanese *dukuns* attempt to neutralize such tensions by insisting on their breadth of learning, the strictness of their discipline, and the fact that they cure only with the help of God. But an ambivalence remains, nonetheless. That ambivalence in part results from the fact that reform Islam tends to regard all spirits not explicitly recognized in Islam as devils. This reformist attitude has not been explicitly adopted by all or even the majority of Javanese, but it has helped to cast further doubt on the legitimacy of *dukuns* and the spirits to which they appeal.

A general lack of ambivalence distinguishes the role of Tengger priest from that of the similarly named lowland *dukun*. The Tengger *dukun* deals not with shady spirits peripheral to religion, but with spirit beings popularly regarded as the very progenitors of society. The priest is initiated into his role not behind closed doors, but in front of thousands of fellow Tengger during the Kasada ceremonies at Mt. Bromo. His ritual authority is, in turn, much less a personal matter, and more a product of his training in a ritual tradition identified not with any single individual but with Tengger society as a whole. There are other indices of the Tengger priest's ritual preeminence and of the lack of ambivalence surrounding his role. During the seventh month (*wulan kapitu*) of each calendar year, for example, the priest (sometimes accompanied by the *wong sepuh* ritual assistant and a few other villagers) withdraws from social interaction, refrains from sexual intercourse, and purifies his body, so as to renew his ability to recite *japa-mantra* prayers. He fasts during certain days of the month, and on the others eats only white foods such as rice or maize meal. Here again people explain the priest's role, and the necessity of this spiritual regimen, by pointing out that the priest "represents" the village before the gods. It is he who masters the language with which they can be addressed, and he who inherits the ritual paraphernalia with which they can be received. His, villagers insist, is not *ngelmu* esoteric knowledge, but a religious tradition inherited from a pre-Islamic Java.[1]

---

[1] Other things also attest to the priest's exclusive ritual authority. Where a villager wishes to own and recite a particular prayer, traditionally he had to secure the prayer "authorization" of the priest through the celebration of a *slametan* in which the priest officially announced the prayer to the gods. *Wayang* shadow puppetry is also an area in which the priest's authority comes into play. Traditionally *wayang* was, and still today is, taboo throughout Tengger. Villagers insist that the spirits of Mt. Bromo do not like the medium. It seems conceivable, however, that the taboo may have historically originated in the Tengger priest's exclusive ritual prerogatives throughout the Mt. Bromo region. *Dalang* puppeteers—as figures who at least traditionally were thought to interact with spirits in performance—may have represented an undesirable challenge to priestly authority, and been banned as a result.

The Priest's Ritual Estate

With the exception of one northwestern village (which, as a result of disputes over a generation ago, now has three priests), each community in the Tengger region has only one priest at any one time, and this man is heir to a variety of ritual implements more or less standardized throughout the Tengger region. These include: an incense brazier (*prapen*); a bronze holy water beaker (*prasen*); a ritual cord (*sampet*) made of batik or bright yellow cloth, wrapped around the waist and shoulders in important liturgies; a ritual shirt known as the *baju antakusuma*, now no longer worn but preserved as a ritual heirloom; a *petungan* calendar for determining auspicious dates; and palm-leaf books (*kropak*) of prayers and ritual lore. Many priests also own other ceremonial items, including mats, clay pots, other pieces of old priestly clothing, and old bronze bells, a few of which are decorated with a thunderbolt image associated with Hindu priests in Old Java. Some of these implements provide additional clues as to the relationship of Tengger to an earlier Javanese Hindu tradition. The decorations and dates stamped on the holy water beaker, for example, suggest that in the fourteenth century Tengger priests were linked to a popular Sivaite priesthood found in other areas of Java and Bali (Chapter 2, Appendix). The ritual cord of Tengger priests similarly resembles that which was used by Hindu priests in pre-Islamic Java (see van Lohuizen-de Leeuw 1972:160). The *petungan* calendar also shows parallels with the old Hindu-Balinese calendar (compare Meinsma 1879 with Goris 1960:113). The *baju antakusuma*, finally, is identical in name and form to a ritual shirt worn by *resi* priests in Old Java and Bali (Scholte 1921), although a shirt of the same name is found in Javanese *wayang* and Central Javanese court tradition (Jasper 1926:26). The historical associations of these ritual implements are not known by modern Tengger, of course, but they provide further confirmation of the Tengger belief that their tradition had its roots in the religion of Old Java.

The Tengger priest is helped in ritual services by three assistants, whose activities once again distinguish the priest from lowland *dukuns* and highlight the priest's exclusive ritual authority. The first and most important of the assistants is known as the *wong sepuh*, literally, "elder," but in this context appropriately translated as "ritual elder." One of the *wong sepuh's* most important responsibilities is the fabrication and eventual cremation of the *petra*, or flower figurines to which family spirits are invoked. His role as *petra* caretaker is indicative of the ritual elder's general responsibilities. It is he, in effect, who is charged with the care and attention of family spirits once they have been invoked to a ritual site by the priest. Indeed, in any ritual where family spirits arrive or depart—weddings, funerals, purification of the dead, and others—the ritual elder must be there at the side of the priest, and on occasion he enjoys the privilege of presenting food offerings to those same family spirits (but never to the higher guardian deities), and addressing them in prayer.

The *legen*, or young ritual assistant, plays a less authoritative role in ritual service. Except when directly wielding them in the liturgy, the priest is enjoined from carrying his own incense brazier or holy water beaker. Hence before and after ritual services, the *legen* is responsible for carrying these implements to and from the house of the priest. He never recites prayers as such, and benefits from no particular instruction in religious doctrines. He does take responsibility, however, for announcing upcoming village rites to members of the community, and he is witness to virtually all priestly liturgy.

The third ritual assistant is a woman known as the *wong dandan* or "preparer." As her title indicates, she is responsible for the preparation of *sajenan* offering trays presented in the liturgy to guardian deities. (She is, however, not responsible for the ordinary food plates presented to family spirits; these can be prepared by ordinary villagers.) Although she recites no prayers and receives no doctrinal instruction, the *wong dandan* must have a detailed knowledge of some fifteen to twenty different types of *sajenan*, each of which varies according to ingredients and mode of preparation. The *wong dandan* is usually the wife of the ritual elder or *legen*, although the priest's wife in some communities plays this role, as well.[2]

Each priest selects his own assistants. Each assistant then usually occupies the role for anywhere from several years to a lifetime, the exact period of service varying from village to village. According to informants in a number of Tengger communities, the *legen's* role used to rotate annually among the young men of the village, so that every young man was supposed to work as *legen* at some point in his life (usually shortly after marriage). The practice appears to have been discontinued because of the difficulty involved in training a new *legen* year after year. The earlier rotating scheme, however, probably helped to bring male villagers into closer contact with the priest's liturgy. Although the *legen's* training

---

[2] In several northwest communities there is a fourth ritual assistant, the "keeper of the *sanggar*" (*Pak Sanggar*). This man is responsible for maintenance of the village spirit shrine, and acts as host for such large ritual festivals as Karo, a role elsewhere played by the village chief. Although historical evidence is lacking, my own suspicion is that this role was introduced in the area as a result of Dutch influence and pressures to secularize the village chief's role.

is more practical than it is doctrinal, it does allow a person to observe the detail of the liturgy from up close. Hence at one time the *legen*'s role may have been an important point of "seepage" between the detail of the liturgy and popular understanding.

There is a subtle cultural message implicit in the division of ritual labor between priests and their assistants. Priests prepare no offerings, announce no ritual events, and do not even carry their ritual implements outside of the liturgy itself. They leave the care and feeding of family spirits, once invoked in liturgy, to the ritual elder. Ritual is thus organized in a way which suggests that the priest's job is to attend to guardian deities, while his assistants busy themselves with the technical trivia of ritual preparation and the entertainment of family spirits. As in other aspects of ritual tradition, the division of ritual labor places guardian deities above other spirits, and identifies the priest as the sole person qualified to act as their ritual mediator.

Compensation for Ritual Services   During ritual festivals, family spirits are offered plates of ordinary food (*suguhan*) similar to those given to living guests at a ritual festival. At the end of a ritual, this food is returned to the kitchen of ritual sponsors or given to neighbors to be eaten. *Sajenan* offering trays for guardian deities, by contrast, are never simply returned to the festival sponsors. Instead, they are redistributed up the social ladder to the priest, his assistants, and, for some rites, the village chief. Who gets which offerings varies from rite to rite, and is specified by tradition. In general, however, the priest receives the lion's share of the food trays. The bigger a festival, however, the larger the proportion of offerings that goes to the priest's assistants and the village chief. In such a large rite as the *entas-entas*, nearly one-half of all offerings may go to these men.

Based on the average cost of the raw food items from which they are prepared, most *sajenan* range in value from about Rp 600 to Rp 2,000 (U.S. $1-$3.30). This is a substantial investment by the standards of rural Java. Different rites, in turn, require different types of offerings, ranging from one tray to as many as fifteen or twenty. The expense involved in preparing offerings thus varies considerably according to the rite. Rites of birth, for example, require only one offering tray at an average cost of Rp 600-1000 ($1-$1.66). A ritual for house construction costs about three to four times that amount; a small wedding Rp 3,500; a large wedding (complete with *petra* figurines and *banten* invocation) Rp 6,000-12,000; and an *entas-entas* purification of the dead from Rp 18,000 to Rp 40,000 (about $30-$65). Although large, these expenses are usually dwarfed by the cost of food, drink, and entertainment for the festivities that accompany at least large ritual events, as I discuss in Chapter 10. The burden of ritual expense, however, has prompted some villagers to call for a reduction in the frequency and size of religious festivals, a suggestion that has been most ardently promoted by certain elements in the Hindu reform movement (Chapter 11).

One ritual payment—that given the priest after the *sesanding* invocation of family spirits during the Karo rites (Chapter 5)—stands above all others. The fee for this service is in most villages established by the village chief, acting in consultation with the priest, and varies (judging by amounts I recorded during 1979 and 1980) from about Rp 600 to Rp 1,000 (approximately $1-$1.66). Since the average Tengger community has well over two-hundred households, the total payment is by Javanese standards very large, considerably more than the average annual income of many households in the region.[3] Of this amount, the priest usually receives about one-half, and the remainder goes to the village chief and the priest's assistants. Ritual service in Tengger thus has very real economic rewards.

There is an interesting historical footnote to the system of Karo payment. Prior to the early 1950s, Tengger priests were never paid in cash for celebrating Karo, but were given the *sajenan* offerings presented to the gods in the liturgy. In all other rituals, of course, this is still the proper way to compensate a priest for his ritual labor. The social and economic implications of this old method of Karo payment are quite different from those of the new system. According to village tradition, first of all, it is forbidden to sell ritual offerings. Hence the priest in the old days could not transform the mountain of ritual offerings he received each Karo into cash. He and his family could dry and then store the cooked rice portion of *sajenan* offerings; some of the meat could be similarly dried or smoked. But many of the food items in *sajenan* perish if not quickly consumed, and the priest's family alone could not eat all of the perishable food items they received. Hence in former times the priest each year used to redistribute much of his Karo "harvest" (as it is called). This created a kind of secondary food redistribution, from the priest to his neighbors, relatives, and fellow village dignitaries (who, as always, received larger portions than anyone else). The new system of cash payment makes all this social activity inefficient and unnecessary. Unlike *sajenan* trays, there are no restrictions on what the priest can do with the money he receives each Karo. As a result, the Karo harvest

[3] Widows in most communities are exempted from the tax. In some communities in recent years, in addition, officials have developed a stratified system of payments, whereby villagers are ranked according to wealth and pay more if wealthy.

is now redistributed much less widely, since it can be enjoyed privately. By virtue of this private income, the priest almost automatically qualifies as one of the most affluent men in every Tengger community. In a postwar era in which socioeconomic differentiation has increased, the shift to a more privatized ritual economy is consistent with changes occurring elsewhere in the village economy (Chapter 10).

Prayer and Ritual Labor

Ritual is the core of priestly tradition, and prayer is the heart of ritual. "The offerings may be insufficient and people's understanding less than complete," a southern Tengger priest once explained to me, "but what is important is the correct recitation of prayer (*japa*)." It is the priest's prayer appeal that is communicated to the spirits through the medium of incense smoke, and prayer that invites them to descend, consume the essence of the offerings, and, through their presence, bless the living. There is little in this ritual routine that allows for improvization or innovation. Despite prayer imagery which seems to suggest that the priest is possessed by a deity, for example, the priest at no point in his performance looks possessed or is otherwise in a state of psychic dissociation. In general, in fact, one finds in Tengger almost no counterpart to the possession behavior so common in Bali (Belo 1953). Occasionally a villager may dream of a deceased relative, or, even more rarely, be possessed by a bothersome earth spirit, but no one is ever possessed by the high deities invoked in priestly liturgy. Interaction with those spirits is left to the priest, and he approaches them exclusively through the medium of the liturgy, which is itself precisely formalized. Improvization in its performance would be not simply out of place, but wrong—a deviation from the tried and true ways of religious tradition.

The main body of the priest's prayers are referred to as *japa* or *japa-mantra*.[4] *Japa* is a Sanskrit word, which refers to a kind of prayer recited in an incantational, repetitive fashion (Gonda 1975:287). The term has a more general meaning in Tengger and other areas of Java, where it refers to prayers thought to have originated in ancient times and to be capable of bringing about spiritual or material transformation. *Japa* are thus thought to have a constraining or coercive power, either by virtue of their own word magic or by virtue of the spirits to whom they appeal. Tengger *japa* have another characteristic: they are always performed in conjunction with a prescribed gesture or ritual movement, such as the

---

[4] Balinese refer to their priests' recitation of prayers as *maweda*, from the term *weda*, itself derived from the Sanskrit *vedas* (see Hooykaas 1964:231). The term *weda*, however, is not used in Tengger tradition, although Hindu reformists have begun to use it.

anointing of offerings, obeisance to the gods, or any number of other things. A *japa* is thus not just words, but a conjunction of spiritually efficacious words and actions. A liturgy is, in effect, a sequence of *japa*; the most familiar such sequence is that of incense announcement, invocation, purification, and obeisance, seen at the beginning of most rites.[5] The prayers used in such a ritual sequence remain more or less invariant from rite to rite, with the exception of one short passage in the incense announcement in which the priest mentions the date of the rite and the names of its sponsors. Only after completing this opening prayer sequence can a priest turn to the prayers for the particular ritual event at hand, such as blessing a newborn, marrying a couple, or purifying the dead. Each of these ritual labors, in turn, has its own sequence of *japa* prayers.

It is a testimony to the priestly tradition's resilience as a regional heritage that the basic pattern of prayer and action seen for any particular rite varies so little throughout the Tengger region. There are, of course, small differences in performance style between different priests. Some anoint with overhand enthusiasm, others with deft flicks of the wrist; some touch the incense brazier during the invocation prayer with one hand rather than two. Even to a casual observer, however, ritual looks much the same from village to village. But the verbal portion of *japa* is less easily observable than the gestures that accompany it, and verbal variation between priests' prayers tends to be greater. Prayers composed in more archaic forms of Javanese, in particular, are sometimes linguistically degenerate, although this varies widely from priest to priest. There is a more alarming element of variation in the Tengger *japa* tradition, however. In the case of at least a few priests, prayers similar in name and purpose to those used by other priests display a thematic syncretism which suggests that they were at one point deliberately revised. Even at the heart of the ritual heritage, in other words, there is evidence of an ongoing struggle over the meaning of Tengger religion and its relation to Islam.

Prayer and Spiritual Vision   One of the most interesting and consistent points of variation in priestly prayer is evident as one moves from the more public prayers, particularly those that can be recited by nonpriests, to those recited by the priest and only in the framework of

[5] Each of these prayers is given a different name: the incense announcement is the *pemenyanan* or *dupa-dupa* (lit. "incense"); the invocation is the *sun warah*; the *pasucen* is the prayer of purification; and the priest's ritualized obeisance is called the *nyandak kebaseng* prayer, named after the betel quid (*kebaseng*) the priest takes in hand during the ritual action.

the most powerful liturgies. In the former group is a prayer known as the *mekakat*, a simple prayer of announcement used to mark the beginning or conclusion of some important phase in a large ritual. A *mekakat* is technically not a *japa* (and it should not be confused with the "prayer of incense announcement" that opens most priestly worship). It cannot be used to invoke deity, since it is always recited without the benefit of incense or offering. The prayer statement that it makes is more this-worldly, being directed to guests at a ritual festival, who include, in theory, family spirits previously invoked to the festival site. The prayer may be recited by a priest, his assistants, or even an ordinary villager. It may be used in a variety of contexts, for example, to say grace prior to the meal that marks the end of a *slametan* and the departure of the spirits. Similarly, it can be used to say grace for the family spirits when they are presented with foods during the course of an ongoing ritual festival. The speaker of the prayer sits or stands, facing any direction he wishes, and makes no parallel gestures during the recitation.

What is particularly interesting about the *mekakat*, however, is the simple fact that many people can recite it and, when it is recited, it can be easily understood by those who hear it. Its language is a relatively modern form of Javanese. If any prayer is available for public inspection, in short, it is this one, and, perhaps not coincidentally, the spiritual vision of this prayer seems close to public models of what ritual involves:

> Oh yes and thus it is that I the *sepuh*-person and all elders of the village, the village chief, the village messenger, the secretary, the forestry agent, the assistant chief, and the constable, with the priest and the *legen* assistant, and with all my brothers and sisters old and young, with those sponsoring the ritual work, as well as with those who are servants to it (*wong batur*), along with the spirit servants (*dewoto batur*), the male and female helpers to the *slametan*, together with all these people I ask for the holy blessing of this place.

Here we have a strikingly sociological vision of ritual work which closely parallels other popular commentary on what is involved in ritual. The speaker begins by identifying himself as a "ritual elder" (*wong sepuh*) and then proceeds to describe those who have joined with him to perform the ritual work; in the course of the description, he provides what is in effect a brilliant thumbnail sketch of village social hierarchy. He speaks, first of all, of the village elders: the village chief, his fellow officials, and, only after them, the priest and his assistants. The priest is thus accorded little of the exclusive distinction granted him, for example, in the Kasada prayers at Mt. Bromo. After the priest and his assistants come all "brothers and sisters" of the village, old and young, as well as the people responsible for sponsoring the rite.

The social vision implicit in the prayer resembles that seen in other popular commentary. At once familial and hierarchical, it speaks as if social distinction were primarily a matter of generation; the village elite is "elder" to everyone else. In the context of ritual performance, however, the chief and his officials are also shoulder-to-shoulder as "servants" (*wong batur*) in the ritual service. More surprising perhaps, the gods themselves are described in a similar fashion. "Spirit servants" (*dewoto batur*)—terms that in modern Tengger most commonly refer to the collective guardian spirits of a village—the community's spirits stand together with the living in common worship. The living are thus joined with the community of the spirits, in an intimate manner consistent with popular understanding of guardian deities as elevated ancestors.

As soon as one moves from the *mekakat* to the priest's *japa* prayers, however, the whole problem of prayer and spiritual vision becomes much more complex. Even the most accessible of the priest's *japa*, the *pemenyanan* incense announcement, describes a spiritual terrain much less familiar than that of more general public commentaries. The *pemenyanan* opens almost every priestly rite, and its language is a modern and thus easily intelligible form of Javanese. And it is the most accessible of the priest's *japa* not only because of its language but because it is the only one that may on occasion be recited by nonpriests.[6] Even a cursory examination of its contents, however, reveals a spiritual vision different from the language of folk tales and popular comments:

Hong! my lord my intention is one I offer the ritual celebration of Mr. and Mrs. X. I come so as to pay homage to *Gusti Hyang Widi* (God the All-Determining) whose word is as deity priest king father mother grandfather grandmother Nyokrobuwono. Eleven times I give homage to the first founders of the village, as well as to the guardians of the four wind directions, and the guardians of the spirit shrine (*sanggar*), the spring, Banaspati, Tunggulpayung, foremost among the village elders. With grandfather and grandmother source of the beginning, grandfather and grandmother source of the roads, grandfather and grandmother source of the spring, grandfather and grandmother source of lightning; with Mother Cloud who becomes

---

[6] In recent years the Hindu reform movement has begun to train people of nonpriestly birth in the recitation of the liturgy, at least in two northwestern communities. In other communities of the northwest, however, even the most ardent enthusiasts of the reform movement have rejected this innovation.

rain and showers down upon the crops of the children of Adam in the community of the faithful (*ummat*) of Lord God All-Mighty. . . . With Father Sky and Mother Earth, Father Adam and Mother Eve, with the seven days of the week, the five *pasar* days, the thirty *wuku* weeks, the eight *paguron* days, the *maulu* days numbering six, and the *pedangon* numbering nine; with the day, the month, the year, the *windu* cycle of years, the sun, the moon, the stars, the planets. . . . With Mother Lorowati to the east, Mother Purbogini to the south, Mother Purboindah to the west, Mother Purbokawi to the north; with Holy Betoro Isworo to the east, Holy Betoro Bromo to the south, Holy Betoro Mohodewo to the west, and Holy Betoro Wisnu to the north, and with venerable Wulungjati above and venerable Omberlekan below. . . .[7]

And so on. The prayer continues in this fashion through several more verses, addressing a long litany of deities who, in everyday commentary, are simply referred to as "guardian spirits." Contrary to the impression one generally receives in hearing myth and popular comment, the spirits here have a particular identity; they bear names after all. What was cosmologically unelaborate in the *mekakat* here in the *pemenyanan* gives way to a truly dizzying degree of detail. The guardian spirits are thus informed of the upcoming ritual service (this, of course, is the general purpose of the prayer of incense announcement), and drawn into the pattern of its worship.

The vision of spiritual cosmology is here already quite different from that expressed in myth, public account, and the *mekakat*. The invocation and the spiritual order it describes begin with God the All-Determining (*Gusti Hyang Widi*). From him, through his word, or at his instruction (*sabda dewa pandita ratu*) all other deities exercise their influence. His word (*sabda*) is as deity, priest, king, parents, grandparents, and the entire spiritual pantheon which follows. Deific word is at the origins of the cosmos. The general intent of the prayer is thus signaled from the start. The prayer is a litany of origins, which define the relationship of the spiritual world to the phenomenal one. What is fundamental about all of these spirits, the prayer seems to say, is that they—whether they be God Almighty, guardians of the wind directions, first founding human ancestors of the village, or grandparents and parents—in some sense founded the world inhabited by humans. The relationship of humans to the spiritual cosmos is one of creation and recreation through descent. The theme of descent is, of course, the same as is elaborated in popular

[7] This version of the incense announcement prayer is used in most villages of the Tengger northwest. I discuss a southern variant of the same prayer later.

Tengger religious festivals like Kasada and Karo. This prayer makes unambiguously clear, however, that the descent relationship between the human world and the spiritual cosmos is not one defined by literal genealogy alone, but by spiritual creation, dependency, and the ongoing guardianship of spirits for the human world.

With world origin and descent its primary themes, it is not surprising that the prayer lists most of the spirits of the cosmos either in sexual pairs—creation imagery *par excellence*—or quadripartite groups of four, the guardian configuration at its best. Many of the spirits listed are, in turn, conferred a generational title (*kaki* "grandfather," *nini* "grandmother") similarly expressive of this relationship of spiritual dependency and descent. We acknowledge, the prayer says, the first founders of the village, the four guardians of the *sanggar* shrine, the spring, the forest (*Banaspati*), and the village as a whole (*Tunggulpayung*). We also give homage, the prayer continues, to the guardian spirits of the village's founding, and those at the source of its road, its spring, and the lightening above. The full sequence of spirits here in the prayer is organized according to three related principles: sexual dualism ("grandfather and grandmother"), quadripartite tetrads (there are four couples), and generation. Nothing in the arrangement of the names is mere coincidence; all of it expresses the key themes of guardianship and descent.

The prayer continues this theme of ancestry and origins, invoking Mother Cloud (*Mbok Mendung*) who is, of course, the source of the rain that gives life to the crops. The crops are those of the earth and thus of Father Adam. Viewed etymologically, of course, this Adam is the Biblical Adam, introduced to Java by way of Islam. In this prayer, however, Adam is presented in his Javanese form, as Father Earth who receives the rain and supports the crops. The sky-earth relationship is readily inverted, however, as is evident moments later when the sky is referred to as male and the earth as female (Father Sky and Mother Earth). What is important in all this is the relationship of male and female and the creation they sustain. When I once commented to a Tengger priest that the Adam referred to in this prayer was an Islamic figure, he responded that what was important was not Adam's name, but that he was part of a "holy couple." "We believe not in the Adam and Eve of Islam," he explained, "but in blessing all couples." This of course echoes the theme of Karo: the two become one in wonder of creation.

The prayer continues its litany, moving in time and space away from the village. The days of the week and other units of time are referred to as if they too were part of the witnessing spirit presence. Although the spiritual association is now no longer recognized among Tengger, in former times each of the major categories of time was associated with a particular Indic deity (see Meinsma 1879; Domis 1832:340). The reference has now been lost, but the spiritual importance of the units of time still remains. The prayer then acknowledges larger aspects of the universe and draws them into its ritual work. It speaks of the four female deities of the wind directions and their male counterparts (who bear Indic names), and the spirits of above and below. Such is the spiritual nature of the universe, and the location of the human world within.

Although in a certain sense the imagery of the *pemenyanan* prayer is rather folksy, it is thoroughly coherent and rigorously systematic. Its detail far exceeds anything suggested by the categories of "guardian" and "family" spirits mentioned in folk commentary. The simple ancestral themes of the latter discourse here give way to a cosmological vision organized in terms of a intricate spatial and temporal hierarchy, in which generational images sound more like figurative expressions for relations of world creation rather than literal genealogical truths. The order of the universe is described in terms of ancestry and sexual duality, but, judging by the prayer's spiritual vision, these cannot be reduced to simple human terms. They are animating principles of creation, guardianship, and dependency which, while taking a particular form in the visible human world, also underlie the order of the universe as a whole.

From a philological perspective, of course, this prayer might be judged hopelessly syncretic. What is one to make, after all, of a cosmos in which Indic, ancestral, and popular Javanese spirits float about with no particular attention to the fact that they originate in different cultural traditions? The *bricolage* of the prayer, however, is little concerned with philology; it uses what is available and interesting to describe a wonderfully coherent vision of world order. Whatever their etymology, the spirits here are players in the grand symphony which is the universe.

Do the spirits mentioned in the prayer figure in other religious discourse or popular belief? Most villagers have heard of Banaspati, spirit of the woods, and the various spirits of the spring, the shrine, the earth and sky. A few villagers, in addition, are familiar with the male deities of the world directions (who bear Indic names); their female counterparts, however, do not figure in any wider cultural discourse. Nor do the spirits identified as the grandfather and grandmother of the roads, source of the spring, source of the lightening, and so on. That these spirits do not figure in a more public religious discourse, however, does not necessarily impugn their cultural reality. The prayers, after all, have their own truth, a mystery and power beyond that of everyday comprehension. This is the faith of the liturgy. As one priest noted, what is important is not our understanding of who the spirits are, but that they are "named in the *japa*; if they are there, they must be worshiped."

From Popular to Priestly Word: The Priest's Japa-Mantra
Although some priests denounce the practice, nonpriests in certain Tengger villages are allowed on occasion to recite the *pemenyanan* prayer. However, they never recite any of the prayers that follow the incense announcement in the sequence of invocation, purification, offering, and homage. The priest alone may utter these *japa*, for these not simply announce ritual intent, they invoke the gods and give worship in their presence. The prayer that follows the incense announcement, for example, addresses the gods directly. It is recited just as the incense begins to burn, conveying the message of the incense announcement to the gods. The language of the prayer differs profoundly from that of the incense announcement recited moments earlier:

Hong! Vessel of Bromo, hong Siwoho, you are all one with the smoke of the incense. Betara Suwara is the smoke, Betara Bromo is the spark, Betara Ludra is the ember, Betara Mahadewa is the coal, Betara Wisnu is the ash, Betara Sambu is the smoke's essence. Lord Guru, holy Lord of Fire, beautiful souls without end, without smoke, understand those associated with the fire.

Continuing the ritual sequence, the priest anoints the offerings before him while reciting the *pasucen* prayer of purification:

Now changing, I take into hand the place of purification, the holy water beaker (*prasen*). My world (*jagad ingsung*) is that of the dewa and betara. My place is the *japa mantra*. I give homage to the holy betara of the happy world (*jagad pramudito*) eternal world.

And so on. The prayers that follow in the opening invocational sequence utilize imagery, and make similar references to deities who, from a philological perspective, are unambiguously Hindu Javanese. There are no concessions here to first-founding ancestors or *kejawen* Muslim saints. Like the prayers of the *entas-entas* purification, these here are consistently coordinated with ritual gestures and the presentation of offerings. Word and act are neatly consistent and ritually coherent, even if their spiritual message has little to do with that communicated in more popular prayer or folklore.

Comparison of the various prayers of the priest makes all the more difficult any generalization we might wish to make about the spiritual vision of the prayer corpus as a whole. Even at the heart of the priest's liturgy, in particular, there is, we see, a cultural tension similar to that seen in comparing the detail of Karo or Kasada liturgy with popular comments on the same rites. The *mekakat* makes a spiritual statement similar to these popular commentaries, emphasizing the collective nature of ritual performance, a simple social hierarchy, and the bond between the living and their spirit ancestors. We learn little more about the spiritual world than is already known in myth. Less easily accessible to villagers, the *pemenyanan* prayer of incense announcement already begins to speak in terms more complex than those heard in the *mekakat*. Its vision extends far in space and time, situating the village in a larger spatial universe to which the community is bound by bonds of guardianship and descent. The dominant image used in the prayer is, in fact, descent, but it is described in such a richly variegated fashion that it becomes clear that this is not the ordinary descent of human to human.

Finally, and most distinctively, there is the large and more secret corpus of priestly *japa-mantra*, a sample of which I have discussed here and in the last chapter. The meaning of these prayers for priests or other Tengger cannot be defined in terms of the comparative or philological data an outside analyst might bring to their reading. For Tengger priests, in particular, these prayers were not experienced as "Indic" or "Hindu" prior to the emergence of the Hindu reform movement in the Tengger region. What, then, is the significance of these prayers? The linguistic decay of small sections of certain prayers makes their status as objects of linguistic interpretation extremely problematic. The largest portions of the priest's prayers, however, are clearly written and linguistically intelligible. The priest's coordination of ritual gestures with directives given in the prayers, moreover, indicates that the priests do heed their contents when they can. Ultimately, however, the question of what sense an individual priest makes of his *japa-mantra* depends on the wider socialization he brings to their reading, including most importantly the education he undergoes in learning them from his father. The quality of cultural knowledge is here again influenced by the social processes involved in its transmission. Historical evidence in Tengger indicates that over the past century there have been important changes in the "intellectual technology" (Goody and Watt 1968) involved in the transmission of the priestly liturgy. These have complicated the priest's task of understanding the liturgy, and, in some instances, may have compromised its resilience in the face of an Islamizing countryside.

Prayer Transmission and Priestly Faith

Traditionally, the Tengger priest was not only a ritual celebrant but a literary specialist as well. A young priest learned the liturgy through the study of the archaic script of Javanese in which the prayers were written. This was a system of "restricted literacy" (Goody 1968:11), in the sense that only the priest was trained in the script, and writing was used only for the recording and transmission of the priest's prayers. This literary aspect of the liturgy distinguished it from popular religious commentary, which was for the most part oral and unwritten.

Prayers were written on palm-leaf sheaves (*lontar*) tied together with string and bound between two small wooden covers. Known as *kropak*, such palm-leaf books were common in Java right up until the introduction of inexpensive Dutch paper in the nineteenth century. In Bali and at least some regions of Java, specialists of traditional lore frequently still use *kropak* books to preserve and transmit their knowledge. In Tengger, however, the *kropak* tradition underwent radical transformation in the course of the nineteenth century, affecting both the medium of cultural transmission and, to some degree, its content.

Elder priests report that in earlier times all priests could read the archaic script in which the *kropak* were written, but many could not write. Writing was a technical skill distinct from reading, as indeed is the case in many traditional societies (see Goody 1968). Throughout the Mt. Bromo region, however, there were always a few men who specialized in writing or copying *kropak*. These were the men to whom priests would turn when, after several generations in the damp mountain climate, older *kropak* began to decay, requiring replacement. Fees for copying an old text were high. According to the report of an elder priest, the average cost for such a service in the final quarter of the nineteenth century was one cow, or, in today's prices, about $350. The expense of this service may have helped contribute to its demise.

Writing during the second decade of the nineteenth century, the English administrator Sir Thomas Raffles showed a keen perception in describing the responsibilities of Tengger priest with regard to the *kropak* texts. The sacred books, he wrote,

> were handed down to them by their fathers, to whose hereditary office of preserving them they have succeeded. The sole duty required of them is again to hand them down in safety to their children, and to perform the *puja* (praisegiving) according to the directions they contain.

Despite the brevity of his comment (1965:I:330), Raffles clearly sensed many of the distinctive qualities of the priestly tradition, with its emphasis on ancestral precedent and fidelity to received ritual ways. That a prayer like the *entas-entas purwabumi* still resembles its Balinese counterpart provides proof of the practical force of the priests' faith. The priest was a religious *pujangga* (man of letters) in an agrarian society. Like rural Islamic scholars in premodern Java, he used his literacy above all for religious matters, and hardly at all for secular affairs. Unlike his Muslim counterpart, however, the Tengger priest did not use his literate technology as a tool for training a wider populace in the language and lore of sacred scripture. Nor, unlike the courtly literati in Central Java, did he have access to a wider literary tradition through which to situate and understand the references of his prayer texts. Judging by modern-day accounts, the priest's training in the liturgy was largely a quiet, private matter, something between father and son. The exclusiveness of this cultural education may have helped to protect the liturgy in a Java becoming Islamic. Inevitably, however, it also affected both the priest's relation to nonpriests and even his own ability to make sense of the prayers.

Sometime early in the nineteenth century, this system of literate cultural transmission was shaken. For reasons that are not entirely clear, some manuscripts began to be transcribed in a more modern Javanese script similar to that seen in Central Java. Other manuscripts, however, remained in the more archaic mountain Javanese script. The shift in script styles may have been influenced by the ongoing immigration of Central Javanese to the Eastern Salient and the rise of Central Javanese literati to prominence in the region. Although precise information on the change in writing systems is lacking, its effects were profound. By the end of the nineteenth century, only a small handful of Tengger priests could still read the archaic *kropak* script. According to the testimony of elder priests, many *kropak* fell into disuse because their owners could no longer read them. The manuscripts were thus relegated to their modern role as sacred heirlooms (*pusaka*) displayed during the most important liturgies. Other priests were reported to have worked vigorously to transcribe the old prayers into new Javanese script. A few did so directly from the old manuscripts. Others worked in conjunction with scribes, reciting the prayers so that the scribe could then record them directly. The shift to the new script was completed as initiates to the priesthood began to be trained in the more standard Javanese script rather than in the old. Often they were trained by non priests rather than their fathers. They read their prayers, finally, from paperbound notebooks rather than the more expensive palm-leaf *kropak*.

The consequences of these changes in prayer transmission varied widely around the region. In one instance in which I was allowed to compare two priests' versions of the *purwabumi* prayer, the version transcribed directly (so I was told) by the grandfather of its present owner was less linguistically degenerate than was the version of the other priest, which had been transcribed for the priest's father by a nonpriestly scribe. The example is only suggestive, since it is impossible to say with certainty that the differences in prayer language did not already exist prior to retranscription. A break had occurred in the social transmission of the liturgy, however, and it seems likely that, occurring at the time that it did, it complicated the problem of the preservation of the liturgy and its interpretation by priests.

Since most of the priest's prayers are composed in a readily intelligible mixture of Middle and Modern Javanese (Smith-Hefner 1983), however, quality of prayer language is a less serious point of variation in the prayer corpus of different priests than is the sheer number of prayers each priest has record of, and the attention he gives to them. These factors vary significantly between different priests, and appear to have been partially influenced by the change in literate technology in the past century. Not all priests appear to have had the full corpus of their prayers retranscribed; in many cases attention was given only to those used in the liturgy. One priest whom I knew particularly well, Pak Wagiman (see Chapters 11 and 12), for example, inherited an unusually large corpus of prayers from his father. Literate in both the old and new scripts, his father, Pak Wagiman said, had worked diligently to insure that the full corpus of his old prayers were rewritten in modern script. An elder priest when I met him, Pak Wagiman himself had devoted much of his life to the study of all of these prayers, and was widely regarded by other priests in the northwest as the most learned among them. His knowledge of the full prayer corpus had allowed him to compare Tengger prayer with Balinese when a Balinese *pedanda* priest visited the Tengger region in the early 1960s. The experience led Pak Wagiman to the startling conclusion that Balinese and Tengger worship many of the same gods. As a result of this discovery, Pak Wagiman became an important priestly enthusiast of the Hindu reform movement (Chapter 11). A Buda priest from southern Tengger represented the other extreme in his attitude toward the prayers. Although his great-grandfather had painstakingly transcribed old prayers into modern script, the young priest showed little interest in any prayers other than those directly required in ritual work. While showing me a large book of prayers transcribed by his great-grandfather, the young man casually noted that he had never bothered to read most of them. He simply used the book as a ritual heirloom displayed in the most important liturgies.

The example shows clearly that the problems plaguing the priestly tradition over the past century cannot be reduced to changes in the technology of cultural transmission, complex as these were. Literacy helped to give a greater fixity to the prayers, but it could not preserve unchanged the larger social world in which they played a part. Nor could the technology of prayer transmission forever specify how any particular priest should interpret what he read, or what he should adjust or change. These considerations have always depended on an attitude of faith brought by the priest to his study. That faith was informed not only by the liturgy, but by the young priest's experience of a larger, and sometimes changing, social world.

Priests usually begin their study only after having married, established a household, and otherwise become active adults in the village community. Prior to his initiation at Mt. Bromo, an initiate is accorded no special privileges. He is given no title, and does not benefit from any special religious instruction. In fact, prior to his Mt. Bromo initiation, the young man is allowed to study only the Kasada prayer (Chapter 3). Only after his initiation does he begin to learn more complex prayers, invoking a more mysterious spiritual pantheon.

Even in this phase of his study, however, the young priest proceeds in a fashion that seems to ease his introduction to the liturgy and to mute any potential cognitive dissonance. He begins his memorization with the *pemenyanan* incense announcement. As we have seen, this prayer paints a much richer picture of the spirit world than does popular commentary, but it nonetheless elaborates on familiar themes of descent and spirit guardianship. Having mastered this prayer and several others, the young priest begins to celebrate small rituals such as those for birth, house building, or haircutting. The elder priest sits by his son throughout these trial performances. He listens intently, immediately correcting errors of pronunciation or word order with a verbal snap. Slowly the young priest masters the elementary prayers, and, usually by the end of his first year of study, begins study of more complex rites. This study culminates with the young man's introduction to the prayer and action of the *entas-entas* purification of the dead (Chapter 8). Here again the young priest is allowed several trial performances, with his father sitting next to him. Having mastered its forms, the young man is finally allowed to celebrate the *entas-entas* by himself. This marks the end of his trial period; he is ready to replace his father. The elder priest then retires from the village scene, devoting his time to his farm and grandchildren, and only rarely assisting or replacing his son in ritual service.

Priestly education thus involves more than prayer memorization; it is an introduction into a religious world far removed from that of folklore and popular commentary. From this perspective, the young priest's plight resembles that of literate intellectuals in many traditional and complex societies. He is heir to an intellectual scheme far removed from the more settled understandings of his cohorts. The young priest, however, is not left entirely to himself in this passage. If he has listened and heard, he has already learned in growing up more general attitudes that prepare him well for his strange journey. He knows, for example, that the liturgy contains truths too powerful for ordinary understanding. If he has been attentive, he has perhaps noticed that ritual practice is more complex than myth or popular commentary bothers to explain. From the perspective of his more general socialization, therefore, a young man's introduction to the liturgy need not be intellectually disorienting. The prayers, after all, have the authority of the ancestors behind them; interpretive comment is inevitably their inferior. In any ordinary sense, they are not supposed to be "meaningful." As one priest put it, "one cannot pretend to understand the truth of *japa-mantra*." They are significant and powerful, nonetheless.

It is these larger and often implicit assumptions as to the nature of the liturgy—rather than any literate technology alone—that have helped to give the liturgy greater cultural conservatism than folklore or popular religious commentary. The liturgy's resilience has always been dependent upon an ongoing socialization and the social reproduction of an institutional order that kept ritual festival at the center of Tengger community life. Whatever the depth of their faith, however, Tengger priests have for several centuries been unable to look to any larger ecclesiastical community outside of the highlands for exemplary confirmation of the liturgy's truth. The popular religious traditions to which priests were exposed were those not of Hindu courts, but of the Eastern Salient, with its amalgam of Buda, ancestral, and Islamic influences. To a dangerous degree, therefore, the Tengger liturgy came more and more to be its own point of reference, a mystery removed from the idioms and attitudes of everyday society.

From this perspective, it should come as no surprise that some of the priest's more public prayers (the *mekakat*, the *pemenyanan*) appear to have been influenced by popular religious notions. More seriously in light of the cultural crisis of the nineteenth century, it should also not be surprising that some priests appear to have violated the primary injunction of the priesthood—to transmit faithfully the ritual tradition to the next generation—by replacing portions of traditional prayer with prayer prose directly influenced by a syncretic Javanese Islam. Nowhere is the force of this deviation more clearly illustrated than in the incense prayer used in a southern Tengger village. Although the remainder of the priest's prayers in this village are virtually indistinguishable from those heard in other communities, the priest's incense prayer—again one of the most conspicuous of priestly utterances—differs startlingly from the incense announcement discussed above (and first recorded in the northwest):

> Hong! my lord descendant of Allah descendant of Adam. True soul is the name of the incense, white tassle is the name of its smoke, white column is the name of the ember. I change all your names so that you are now the All-Knowing Messenger (*Bayan Tasdik*). I order you to invite all the servant spirits (*dewoto batur*) to the place of the village. After you invite those spirits, may they come and sit all together, here at the site of the offering, all together for this *slametan*.

As with the incense announcement from the Tengger northwest, this incense prayer begins by locating the religious tradition in terms of its origin and descent. Unlike the northwest prayer, however, this one says that the priest's holy work originated with Allah and Adam. These names could be interpreted in a pan-Javanese rather than orthodox Islamic sense, but the identification is startling, nonetheless. The message here is like that of the Aji-Mohammad myth; Tengger tradition is a child of or sibling with Islam. The "seepage" between liturgy and public culture now appears to go both ways.

The vision of the spirit pantheon in this prayer is rather startling, as well. It resembles on one level that of the earlier *mekakat*. Both refer to the guardian deities generically and facelessly as *dewoto batur*, "spirit servants," and both put those spirits shoulder to shoulder with human beings. But gone entirely from this southern prayer is any reference to the complex spatial and temporal hierarchy of the northwest's incense prayer. There is, one should note, an expanded version of this southern prayer of incense announcement. It is expanded through the addition of twenty-eight short stanzas, each identical to the others except that in each stanza the name of a different spirit is uttered and its presence thus invoked. The spirits addressed in this fashion are those of the stable, the kitchen, the fireplace, the *sanggar*, the village spring, and so on, through a long list of of twenty-eight, each of whom is a spirit associated with a specific site in the village. There is no reference to spirits of the world directions, no appeal to deities with Indic names. World cosmology gives way in the southern prayer to a more peculiarly village-centric emphasis. Of interest also in the southern prayer is its treatment of the incense, fire, and smoke. As in the northwest prayer, the incense is addressed as if it were alive. Here, however, the Indic or Old Javanese deities of the northwest prayer—Bromo the spark, Suwara the smoke, Ludra the ember, and so on—have been replaced with a more faceless, depersonalized, magical imagery. "True soul" is the incense; "white column" is the ember; "white tassle" is the smoke. Invocation of deity here gives way to magical command. World deities are replaced with local territorial spirits.

It is impossible to say precisely when this compromised prayer was adopted by some Tengger priests. Today it is used only by some priests in the Tengger south and northeast, areas influenced more than the northwest by a massive influx of immigrants during the nineteenth century. According to the testimony of the eldest living priest in Tengger, this more syncretic prayer was adopted by Tengger priests only in the time of his grandfather, in the last decades of the nineteenth century. According to this man—a perhaps partial source, since he is today a staunch supporter of the Hindu reform movement—several priests (including his own father) sought to unite priests against this and other borrowings from Islam. Several priests from the Tengger south, however, took offense at this action, which they saw as an interference in their ritual authority. Relations chilled between several priests in the northwest and their counterparts in the south, a tension that is remembered still. All this took place, of course, in the late nineteenth century— the time of the Ajisaka and Mohammad myth. Several Tengger communities had converted *en masse* to Islam (Chapter 11). Tengger tradition had entered a period of intense self-doubt.

The developments in Tengger at the turn of the century no doubt pushed a long-existing tension between priestly and popular tradition to a new extreme. To some degree this tension was the product of a lack of integration between a largely oral, popular culture, and a restricted literary tradition. The "intellectual technology" (Goody 1968) that sustained the literate tradition of the priesthood, however, was never an autonomous social mechanism. Preservation of the liturgy always depended on more than the technical mastery of reading skills or the restricted nature of priestly literacy. Ultimately, the cultural reproduction of the liturgy depended upon its continuing role in community life and upon the faith of the priesthood in the inviolability of sacred word. "The soul duty required of them is to hand them down in safety to their children, and to perform the *puja* (praisegiving) according to the directions they contain. . . ." Religious faith is not generated, integral and whole, in ritual performance alone. It is always informed by a larger cultural dialogue. That dialogue in nineteenth- and twentieth-century Tengger included word of changing ways. Based on a field study conducted in Tengger in the 1860s, Meinsma's comments hint of changes that no doubt influenced this non-Islamic tradition's painful self-evaluation (1879:138):

Islam in recent years seems to have made considerable progress, for only the population . . . lying in the immediate vicinity of Mt. Bromo remains unconverted. However, most probably this will not remain the case much longer. Already there are two village chiefs in the remaining Tengger region who have converted to Islam.

Conclusion: The Power of Ritual Word

Despite the enormous historic and cultural gulf between India and Tengger Java, Gonda's description (1975:248) of the Indian *mantra* still accords well with the Tengger view of the *japa-mantra*:

> The spoken word is an act, an exercise of power, revealing an attitude of the speaker, and containing something creative. . . . The performance of ritual acts, the exertion of influence upon the Unseen, the utilization of power as a rule requires a vocal expression of the officiant's will, desire, or intentions; the verbal reference to a desired result becomes an instrument producing it.

Like the Indian *mantra*, the Tengger *japa* thus raises the question, wherein originates the "magical power of words" (Tambiah 1968)?

There is no reason to assume that the conditions sustaining faith in the efficacy of ritual language are necessarily the same in all societies. What is interesting about the Tengger example is that ritual words are accorded power by the faithful even when they are not, in any propositional sense, directly accessible or intelligible. How can this be? And what does it suggest for a more general understanding of ritual efficacy? The Tengger priest's role provides what are the most important clues for resolving this problem. His ritual paraphernalia, his assistants, and his exclusive ritual prerogatives all serve to reinforce the idea that the priest is the primary intermediary between the living and their gods. Other practices—the priest's seventh-month fast, his central position in the Mt. Bromo ceremonies, his ownership of the village's sacred heirlooms—in effect also institutionalize the priest's role in such a way that his authority is well established outside of or prior to any single instance of ritual performance. The example suggests that in our effort to determine why ritual language is often viewed as a vehicle of sacred power, it is not enough to look at the content of ritual speech alone. Ritual speech must always be situated within the larger setting of authority and social position. It is this larger context that helps to define whether the propositional value of ritual words is or is not important in sustaining belief in their sacred power. The power of ritual language, in other words, may at times be more directly dependent upon the *said* of ritual

212

speech, and other times not. To determine when and why this is so, we have to examine the social context in which ritual speech functions, and not content ourselves with the formal analysis of ritual texts.

The Tengger example can again serve as a case in point. Here the role attributes of the priest and generalized notions as to the importance of the ritual tradition to a large degree influence popular attitudes on the power of ritual language. The felicitous celebration of Tengger liturgy does not depend upon villagers' understanding what the priest says in prayer. Sometimes the priest performs rites in the name of the village without other villagers seeing or hearing what he does. This is an extreme example, but in general much of Tengger ritual performance seems organized in such a fashion as to neutralize the rites' dependence on nonpriests' understanding of the propositional meaning of prayer language. There is little effort to draw people into the words of the liturgy. Often the priest speaks inaudibly. Listening to liturgical prayer is not identified as an activity that brings blessing to ordinary villagers. In short, ritual speech seems practically organized in a fashion consistent with popular understanding of its role: its language is directed toward the deities, not toward people of this world. The efficacy of ritual speech depends in turn not on people's understanding of what is being said, but on the prayers being performed by the right person in the right fashion under the right circumstances. Here the role authority of the Tengger priest is subject to little of the dispute that plagues lowland *dukuns*. Everybody knows who the Tengger priests are; the role is systematically institutionalized. Tengger do not have a problem with freelance or illegitimate priests, because the social restrictions on access to the role are much more systematic and public than for lowland-style *dukuns*. It is this consensus on the authority of the Tengger priest that helps to sustain popular faith in the power of ritual speech often unheard or poorly understood.

Levi-Strauss's (1963) analysis of a Cuna shaman provides a notable contrast, where the efficacy of ritual speech depends to a large degree on what is said and heard.[8] The shaman aims to effect a cure, and he is able to do so only inasmuch as he is capable of "recreating a real experience" (Levi-Strauss 1963:194) in the mind of his patient through

---

[8] One of the merits of Levi-Strauss's discussion is that, unlike most structuralist studies, it is concerned not merely with formal *langue*, or the "underlying" system of language, but also the pragmatics of ritual speech (*parole*). Elsewhere structuralist studies sometimes do not even bother to inquire as to whether the "codes" in question are actually part of the competence of real social speakers or actors. It should be noted here, however, that Levi-Strauss's Cuna analysis is largely conjectural, based on his creative hypotheses as to how the Cuna shaman uses the prayer text, not on actual observation.

the recitation of a myth. The mythic narrative must be communicated, we are told, in a "very precise and intense way," so that the patient becomes "psychologically aware of its smallest details" (193). The rite's effectiveness thus depends on the shaman's ability to engage the patient in the images of the mythic prayer, provoking a transformation in his patient's psyche, "making it possible to undergo in an ordered and intelligible form a real experience that would otherwise be chaotic and inexpressible" (198). The efficacy or failure of the rite can be immediately assessed by observing whether the patient experiences the cure and is drawn from his or her physiological impasse. Ritual speech is here participatory because it must be if it is to achieve its end.

All of this is, of course, unthinkable and unnecessary in the ritual performance of the Tengger priest. The formal nature of the liturgy precludes repetition or clarification. It is the deities and not a specific human psyche that are here the most important object of prayer address. To deviate from ritual form so as to insure more effective communication with human observers would be absurd, a misperception of the real purpose of liturgical speech. The pragmatics of prayer here are premised on a model of speech interaction entirely different from that of the Cuna shaman, and it is these premises that serve, in effect, to elevate the priest's speech above the demand of immediate accountability.

One need only think of Evans-Pritchard's (1937) gyrating witch doctor to find another example in which the efficacy of ritual language depends in large part on the ability of the speaker to engage those present in the performance in what is said and done. Conversely, one need only think of the Balinese *pedanda* priest, piously mumbling his obscure Sanskrit texts, to think of another ritual tradition in which ritual effectiveness is not directly dependent on engaging observers in what is said and done. With the Balinese *pedanda* and the Tengger priest, the larger social context—the role of the priest, the glowing authority of his tradition, the preeminence of the gods, and so on—has already made the effectiveness of ritual prayer on the whole a foregone conclusion, at least in most ritual events. But the conclusion is never entirely certain. At times at least some people are listening, trying to render accountable what is said in ritual performance. If they are people of structural importance in the ritual system, their judgments may ultimately affect the cultural status of such prayers. Even in Tengger, as we have seen, some of the priest's prayers have been subject to self-conscious revision. The demand for propositional accountability has left its mark.

Obviously the larger speech context informs the performance of the South American shaman. As with the modern psychoanalyst to whom Levi-Strauss compares the shaman, a patient must have the faith to hear the word, and that faith is informed by life experiences and tradition. The shaman also must conform to certain cultural notions as to what his role involves. Nonethless, the overall effectiveness of his performance depends much more than that of the Tengger priest on the shaman's ability to communicate a myth; he must affect a human psyche, focusing and giving coherence to its experience. In an important sense, as Tambiah has noted, "all ritual, whatever the idiom, is addressed to the human participants" (Tambiah 1968:202). The engagement of ritual participants in the words and images of ritual language, however, is not everywhere of the same importance in sustaining a faith in the power of sacred words. Faith always has a larger history and social depth. At times it may place ritual language above the demand for discursive "meaning."

Something of this sort seems to have helped the young priest in his study of the Tengger liturgy. The youth brings to his learning well-formed sensibilities as to the importance of the ritual tradition. For many priests, this larger faith renders the "discontinuities" of ritual culture noncontradictory and whole. Like other villagers, the priest has heard echoes of a meaning not public, and seen glimpses of an inexpressible spirit world. It is this sensibility which insures that from the start the priest's voyage into the world of the liturgy is undertaken with an attitude of wonder and the certainty of faith.

· 10 ·

THE ECONOMICS OF RITUAL
REPRODUCTION

Since examining village organization in Chapter 4, our discussion has focused on the organization and meaning of Tengger ritual in a changing Java. The problem of how this or any other ritual system reproduces itself through time, however, involves more than these already complex questions as to how a people makes sense of their tradition and identity. Ritual is a mode of social practice. It is thus an activity that depends not only on ritual meaning and spiritual intent, but also on the mobilization of people and resources in patterned social process. This periodic mobilization may be constrained by political and economic considerations other than those of religion alone. This same activity may have social consequences quite apart from those religiously intended, consequences that nonetheless return to the social environment as constraints and "causal influences on human action" (Giddens 1979:7). Here in Tengger, as we shall see, ritual practice affects and is affected by village social and economic organization. The requirements and consequences of ritual practice extend across social fields. They link the cultural imperatives of the ritual tradition to the more mundane concerns of status, power, and economic morality. Through this arrangement, ritual acquires a peculiar social momentum, motivated by concerns other than ritual piety alone. At the same time, however, social and economic activities are affected by religious concerns. As a result of both inflections, ritual maintains its central role in Tengger social life.

This arrangement is important for understanding the larger themes of Tengger ritual culture. Many of them—the ancestral bias of popular commentary, the general lack of an exegetical tradition, the belief that all villagers are equal and alike (pada-pada)—have been reinforced by ritual's role in community life. Ritual is also linked, however, to social hierarchy. In communities otherwise known throughout Java for their lack of marked socioeconomic differentiation, ritual festivity has always been an arena in which the expression of status distinction is considered acceptable. People of social standing are, quite simply, big ritual sponsors. They are also supposed to be generous donors, since festival elaboration depends upon a complex system of gift giving between ritual sponsors. The practical linkages implicit in this arrangement are important for understanding why the ritual tradition has remained such a force in community organization. A household expresses its piety and social distinction through festivity. This duty is all the more incumbent upon wealthier villagers. A portion of their wealth is regularly consumed in elaborate ritual festivals that exhaust years of savings in several nights of festival glory. Private wealth is thus channeled into an acceptable public good, one that honors the gods, demonstrates a family's social excellence, and supports the maintenance of the ritual system as a whole.

All of this makes for what appears to be a well-integrated ritual, status, and economic system. This mode of integration has been one source of the ritual tradition's cultural resilience in an Islamizing Java. As with most social systems, however, the persistence of this one depends upon a network of contingencies far more complex than may be recognized by any single actor. Changes in one sphere of activity may unintentionally bring about changes in another. As we shall see, since Indonesian independence the continuing investment of wealthy villagers in traditional ritual consumption has set in motion a process of ritual inflation that threatens to diminish ritual sponsorship among the less affluent. Festival elaboration, combined with increasing socioeconomic differentiation, has in fact eroded the popular base of ritual social organization, and promises to promote fundamental adjustments in Tengger religion and self-perception.

Festival Scale and Labor

Whenever spirits are invited to a ritual site, some kind of communion ceremony must be celebrated afterwards by the priest and ritual sponsors. In small rites, this may involve no more than the priest's perfunctory consumption of a few handfuls of rice. In large ceremonies, however, the same function is served by several days of feasting and entertainment. It is the latter type of ritual festival with which I am concerned in this chapter, since it is the large festivals that are supported by ritual gift giving and that play a central role in the economic and status system of the village. The most important of these large ritual festivals are those associated with the wedding *walagara* and the *entas-entas* purification of the dead. No other rites rival these in the size and expense of their acompanying festivities. None plays as central a role in the expression of social distinction.

The social scale and expense of these rites vary significantly. When one of their children marries, all parents are obliged to sponsor a *walagara* accompanied by some kind of social festivity. Since this ritual obligation falls equally upon everyone, the expense of this rite varies widely. The *entas-entas*, by contrast, is more consistently expensive,

217

both because it is universally regarded as the most important of rites, and because it is sponsored only after years of careful planning and saving. In both kinds of rites, however, there is no exact norm as to how large and expensive festivities should be.[1] Like the conspicuous production seen in festive agricultural labor (Chapter 4), it is all a matter of the wealth, social standing, and strategic interests of the festival sponsors. Sponsors can skimp on food, invite few guests, and neglect to provide entertainment. Or they can slaughter several head of cattle, invite hundreds of guests, and truck in the finest theater troupes in all Java. The range of expense seen in the wedding *walagara* reflects these varied interests, and the differing degrees of festival elaboration they promote (Table 3).[2]

It is, of course, difficult to convey a proper sense of the magnitude of these expenditures for rural Javanese. At the time of research, the exchange rate for U.S. dollars in East Javanese banks fluctuated from Rp 600-630 per dollar, following a recent devaluation of the Indonesian rupiah. A kilogram of rice in the lowlands at this time cost Rp 150-180, or Rp 200-230 in these mountain communities. Field laborers' wages varied widely around Tengger, from a low of about Rp 150 in several southern Tengger communities, to Rp 350 in several of the more commercially oriented communities of the north. The average wage throughout the region was around Rp 250 per day (for six to seven hours of field labor), or approximately 40 cents. From this perspective, a typical wedding in the Tengger south cost almost 200 times a field laborer's

[1] There is no precise number as to how many guests must be invited. The smallest *entas-entas* festival I attended, however, had just fewer than one hundred guests.

[2] Tables 3-6 in this chapter are based on an economic survey of ritual festivals performed in the two communities in which I established field residence. The sample included forty ritual events, thirty of which took place in the southern field site (referred to in these tables as "southern village #1"), and ten of which were in the northern village of residence. The sample in the north is smaller because I lived there a briefer period of time, and because ritual festivals were less frequent than in the south, although the village itself was slightly larger. As a result of the small sample, figures for the northern village are probably biased toward more expensive ritual events. Each survey was conducted in the days immediately following completion of a festival. Sponsors were questioned on the number of guests invited, the number who actually came, the number of festival laborers and *sumbangan* exchange partners, volume of gift contributions, *bowo* payments, entertainment and food costs, and food gifts dispatched to neighbors, relatives, and village officials. Expenses were determined by aggregating figures on the volume of goods accumulated and consumed, and assigning each type of good a money value according to current market prices. Where possible, villagers were asked to consult their *sumbangan* books for details on expenses. It is a testimony to the patience of villagers—and their own keen interest in keeping track of ritual expense—that they without exception kindly provided this detailed information.

Table 3. *Wedding Expenses*

	Guests	Non-Household Workers	Total Cost
Least expensive wedding	20	10	Rp 11,000
Mean wedding, south	45	15	Rp 45,000
Mean wedding, north	125	15	Rp 100-150,000
Most expensive wedding, south	500	138	Rp 850,000
Most expensive wedding, north	533	250	Rp 2,582,000

Table 4. Entas-Entas *Expense*

	Guests	Non-Household Workers	Total Cost
Mean *entas-entas*, southern community	300	69	Rp 430,000
Mean *entas-entas*, northern community	540	175	Rp 1,750,000

average daily wage, while the same rite in the north was almost 500 times this figure for daily wage labor. Even the least expensive wedding I encountered cost 44 times the average field laborer's daily wage.

The mean expense involved in sponsoring an *entas-entas* is even greater than that involved in weddings, and shows greater disparity between the north and south (Table 4).

The dramatic difference in mean festival expense between the northern and southern village is in part related to the fact that, as discussed in Chapter 8, the purification rite in the northern village has in recent years been redefined as an optional ceremony incumbent only upon those sufficiently affluent to shoulder its expense.[3] For both weddings and purification ceremonies, figures on expenses from the southern village are more typical of ritual expenses throughout the region as a whole.

The greatest portion of the expense involved in a ritual festival goes

[3] The sample for ritual purifications in the northwest community included only five events, as opposed to ten in the south, and this smaller sample size may also have reinforced a bias for more expensive festivals. Nonetheless, the basic contrast in expense is, I believe, relatively accurate.

not toward ritual offerings as such, but toward food and entertainment. A Java bull cost an average of Rp 200,000 at the time of my research in 1979, or approximately $320. A bull is the minimum requirement for cuisine at large weddings and almost all *entas-entas*. In the northwest community cited in the figures above, Java bulls were no longer esteemed as festival food, having been replaced by the "Australian cows" recently introduced into the region, and selling for an average of about $500. The largest festival celebrations slaughter two or three of these animals, often in addition to chickens, ducks, and goats.[4] This shift to more expensive festival fare is typical of recent changes in ritual economy throughout many communities of the Tengger northwest and northeast. Although the total number of guests for the average wedding or *entas-entas* is greater than for corresponding festivals in the south, the average cost of a northern festival has nonetheless risen at a rate far disproportionate to that numerical increase. Part of this increase is product of the larger quantities of meat made available to guests in northern festivals. But other aspects of northern festivals have been made elaborate as well. Today no large festival can go without electrical generators (rented in lowland cities) for lighting and powering loudspeakers. Alcohol provided for festival dancers tends today to be expensive manufactured beer rather than cheap Javanese gin. Entertainment in the north is also more lavish. The local *ludruk* theater troupes, staffed by village youths, which were once considered appropriate for festival amusement have disbanded over the past fifteen years in villages of the northwest, because festival sponsors now prefer to go to lowland cities to hire Java's finest troupes for village performances. *Tayuban* dancers are also brought in from faraway towns at considerably greater expense than charged by their counterparts in southern Tengger communities.[5] These and other aspects of

[4] The largest ritual festival I attended involved the slaughter of thirty chickens, six goats, a water buffalo, and four bulls.

[5] In the southern community, most *tandak* dancers received Rp 15,000 (about $24) for three days of dancing. A single festival could include from two to eight such dancers. In the northwestern community, by contrast, *tandak* dancers were paid twice this amount, and were transported in from towns 120 kilometers to the west of the highlands. Festival sponsors must also pay for transportation and food costs, and sometimes pay to have the women escorted to and from the festival event. The district government discourages *tayuban* dancing by making sponsors pay a stiff entertainment tax of about $50 per performance. A smaller tax is imposed on other forms of entertainment: $10 for *ludruk* theater, $2 for *wayang kulit* puppetry. *Ludruk* troupes hired in the lowlands can also be very expensive. The mean cost of transporting, housing, feeding, and paying a full troupe brought up from Surabaya (based on a sample of three events) was $550. Local *ludruk* troupes cost about one-tenth that amount, but they have become unfashionable in recent years, as festival styles have become more elaborate and expensive.

ritual festivity have all served to inflate ritual expense over the past fifteen years in villages of the Tengger northwest, a period roughly corresponding to the switch to intensive commercial agriculture in the region (see below).

One of the greatest expenses incurred in ritual festivity throughout all regions of Tengger, however, is related to the "nonhousehold workers" cited in the figures of the two tables above. Known as *betek* (for women) and *sinoman* (for men), these festival workers are an important part of every elaborate ritual festivity. Festival laborers are chosen from among relatives, neighbors, and ritual exchange partners, and they come in numbers which—like the *sayan* festival labor employed in agriculture (Chapter 4)—far exceed the simple technical needs of ritual festivity. The excess in numbers is deliberate, of course, for it is these workers as much as the regular guests whom the host wishes to entertain and honor. To have too few festival workers is to be stingy and high-handed, as if they were important only for the performance of festival tasks. To have an abundance of workers, by contrast, is one of the most important indices of a successful festival, and a testimony to the wide-ranging support network only a prestigious individual can weave.

Working as *betek-sinoman* is thus usually considered an honored opportunity to participate in what are the most important social events in village life. Each worker, or husband and wife team, is invited personally to the festival by its sponsors, usually several weeks prior to the festival's actual occurrence. Workers may bring their children to the festival site, and enjoy the delicious festival fare without the polite reserve of more formal guests. Expanded to include several cooking fires, the kitchen for a ritual festival is in a certain sense the second of two social centers for the event. It is here that family and friends enjoy the intense bustle of the festival without the formality of front-room guests. In at least some communities, in addition, the sponsors of a festival are barred by tradition from entering the kitchen, and thus must delegate supervisory authority to someone else. For the hosts to busy themselves with direct supervision of food preparations would risk introducing an air of servility into the gay activity of the kitchen.

It is, in fact, these festival workers who put the greatest strain on food expenditures in large celebrations. They and often their children eat regular meals (rather than the single meal to which an ordinary guest is entitled) throughout the course of a *slametan*. They also receive food gifts (*ater-ater*) at the festival's completion, in recognition of their services. Hence, although their number tends to be less than that of the regular guests, their total consumption is far greater. The example here is very similar to that seen in festive agricultural labor (*sayan*), where laborers are also mobilized in numbers that exceed the simple utilitarian requirements of the task at hand. Deviation from utilitarian efficiency suggests the importance of nonutilitarian ends. Festival sponsors are not simply fulfilling ritual obligations in inviting large numbers of guests and workers, they are also making a statement about their social position, reaffirming social bonds, feasting the village, and setting standards for future festival events. Sponsors have, of course, the option to minimize expense by reducing the number of guests and workers. Indeed, many ritual sponsors do. Poorer villagers, for example, are not expected to sponsor lavish ritual events, and, as we shall see, there are good reasons besides those of limited financial resources why they cannot do so. For those people thought capable of sponsoring large ritual festivals, however, an economizing strategy violates the larger social consensus as to how festivals should be carried out, and ultimately wins nothing but contempt. The economic logic of the festival system, in other words, is constrained by the concern for prestige and social distinction. The practical force of such social constraint is no clearer than in the *sumbangan* exchange system that supplies the capital for large festivals and creates a social momentum for the ritual system as a whole.

The Sumbangan *Ritual Exchange System*

No Tengger institution so clearly expresses the curious mix of egalitarian idioms and practical hierarchy typical of Tengger communities as the ritual exchange system (*sumbangan, gentenan*). The system serves to reduce economic differentiation within the village while at the same time enhancing status inequality. In supplying the capital for ritual festivals, it also lubricates social relationships, drawing villagers into a cycle of giving and receiving at the heart of village social interaction and the ritual tradition alike.

The principles upon which the exchange system is based are consistent throughout the villages of the Tengger region. Just prior to marriage, young men and women begin to give gifts of money and goods to relatives and friends sponsoring *slametan* festivals. After marriage, a couple gradually expands its network of *sumbangan* partners, in preparation for the time that the couple too will sponsor ritual festivities. Gifts given are sometimes solicited by ritual sponsors, usually at the same time that the sponsors invite a man and a woman to work as laborers at the upcoming ritual festival. Other times, however, a couple takes the initiative in the exchange by sending unsolicited gifts of goods or money to the home of ritual sponsors prior to a major festival. Engaging in such *sumbangan* exchange is a basic social responsibility, one that marks an individual's passage into adult social life and the most esteemed of adult social activities, ritual festivity. Not to engage in such exchange is, in effect, to isolate oneself from village social life, and to risk remaining a social juvenile.

The relationship established between exchange partners is strictly dyadic. Each relationship has its own history, and each individual has his or her own list of exchange partners. Even spouses may keep separate records of their exchange partners, although this practice is less common among couples long married. Each instance of exchange is carefully recorded in the recipient's *sumbangan* book. In places where few people own books or magazines, the attention villagers give their record books is nothing less than amazing. Books are organized like an accountant's ledger, with columns for the name of each donor, his village of residence, the item given, and (in some cases) its equivalent cash value. Where money is received, the amount is recorded, and sometimes translated into an equivalent value in terms of kilograms of rice—an accounting practice intended to provide checks against inflation, which in much of modern Indonesia's history has rendered money a very unstable standard of value. At the completion of a festival, a host usually examines his records of gifts earlier given to exchange partners, then recalculates his new debt by subtracting the value of the earlier gift from that just received, leaving the amount now owed to the exchange partner. Illiterate villagers often have this accounting done by a relative, friend, or the village school teacher.

As described thus far, this ritual credit system is similar to that seen in other areas of Java where the *slametan* tradition is strong. Several additional features of the Tengger system, however, distinguish it from its lowland counterparts. First, the amount returned for an earlier gift is always supposed to exceed the value of that earlier contribution. If I, for example, were to give 50 kilograms of rice to an individual, he would later make return payment on that gift with 50 kilograms plus an additional 20 or 30, or some other item in excess of the original gift's value. This surplus return on the earlier payment is not interest on a loan, but a new gift, designed to keep the exchange relationship open. Villagers insist that the "siblingship of the exchange must not be broken." To make return payments in a tit-for-tat fashion is a serious affront to the good faith of exchange partners, since it suggests that one no longer wishes to maintain the social relationship that exchange partnership ideally entails. Only in old age is it proper to close exchange relationships, after one's children are married and one can thus retire from the bustling camaraderie of *slametan* festivity.

The second distinctive feature of festival exchange in Tengger is related to this first. Gifts given in festival exchange (or, more exactly, their equivalent value) can be recalled by their donor only for use in other ritual festivals. An individual may have given the equivalent of several hundred dollars of goods to exchange partners, but unless he plans to sponsor a festival with priestly ceremony, there is no way he can get back his investment. The system creates, in effect, an "exchange sphere"(Bohannan 1967; Barth 1967) from which goods (or, again, their equivalent value) are not allowed to move once invested. The sphere in Tengger is defined not by the type of goods that circulate within it, as is so often the case in special spheres of exchange, but by the use to which, once invested, they can be put. The rice exchanged in *sumbangan* networks, after all, is ordinary rice, capable at least in theory of all sorts of alternative uses. Social regulation of the *sumbangan* exchange, however, restricts the utility of rice to festival uses alone.

There is a third and final restriction on Tengger economic activity related to these first two, although for a variety of reasons its practical force has diminished in modern Tengger. As mentioned in an earlier chapter, maize, the traditional staple in Tengger, cannot be sold in the marketplace, even though prior to the recent shift to commercial agriculture maize was by far the most extensive cultigen. Since it could not be sold for money, surplus maize was available to be channeled into two social spheres where its use was deemed proper: harvest parties (*sayan*) and ritual festivals. The practical force of this restriction has diminished considerably in recent years, since in many parts of Tengger maize is no longer the primary cultigen, and rice is the preferred staple for festival events. In an earlier era, however, restrictions on maize sale helped to insure that surplus production of the most important cultigen was channeled into two distinctively Tengger social domains.

Indeed, the overall effect of these economic restrictions is, or at least traditionally was, to harness economic and social activity to the carriage of ritual festivity. All villagers of social standing must engage in exchange partnerships, thereby committing a good portion of their wealth to ritual festivals. Once two people enter into an exchange relationship, pressures against closure insure their continuing commitment of economic resources, just as restrictions on the use of exchange goods outside of ritual festival insure that goods given can be used only for additional ritual festivals. The interests of social standing are thus linked to economic exchange and ritual piety, supporting the reproduction of the festival system as a whole. In the process, surplus wealth is drawn into a form of economic consumption that benefits from widespread public approval, unlike more exclusive, privatized consumption goods. Economic investment and consumption are thus given a distinct social focus

(Hefner 1983b), one related to the social rhythms and values of the village rather than the interests of foreign manufacturers or international consumption styles. This is an important point, because all evidence indicates that the festival system plays, or played, an important role in maintaining the appearance of economic homogeneity within Tengger communities. It did so, however, not by equalizing ownership of the means of production or directly redistributing wealth in a system of "shared poverty" (C. Geertz 1963). The motor of the exchange system is consumption, not production or distribution as such, and through its operation a significant portion of the wealth of affluent villagers is removed from the circuit of productive investment (where it would enhance economic differentiation) and channeled into less "productive" consumer goods—ritual festivals—benefiting from widespread moral approval.

There are practical limits to the exchange system, however. The social benefits of *sumbangan* exchange, first, are clearly biased toward more affluent villagers, which is to say toward those who can build extensive exchange networks and sponsor lavish ritual festivals. The poor are less capable of responding to the intermittent demands for money or goods required by the system, hence are less likely to maintain large exchange networks or sponsor flashy festival events. Where poverty is generalized—or generalizing—ritual piety is itself potentially jeopardized. The second point is related to this. Where socioeconomic differentiation increases, differences in festival lavishness could become so great that the bottom end of village social strata finds few rewards in committing its limited resources to prestige events in which it is, in effect, doomed to failure. Such a possibility is no small matter in a region as densely populated as modern Tengger. The festival exchange system works better, in other words, where the village is relatively unstratified (in economic terms) and where all players in the festival field find sufficient possibility for status reward.

Finally, and perhaps most fundamentally, the whole system of ritual investment continues to operate effectively only as long as there exists a widespread consensus among villagers that such investment is worthwhile. Most Tengger are aware that their ritual tradition is more expensive than its counterpart in neighboring non-Tengger villages. Since the beginning of this century, in addition, they have heard of neighboring Islamic communities where modernist-minded leaders have banned *tayuban* dancing and *ludruk* theater. The urge to economize, however, has been constrained by the general identification of festivity with Tengger religion itself, as well as by the exchange system's built-in bias toward those who support it. There are some villagers who refuse to abide by this consensus, but, at least until very recently, they have been penalized for their views and viewed as socially marginal. In a modern Tengger exposed to ever greater numbers of imported consumer goods, more directly involved with the surrounding society, and increasingly committed to commercial agriculture, however, the conditions are ripe for an assault on this social consensus. There are, as we shall see, signs that such an assault is now occurring.

From a historical perspective, however, one additional virtue of the festival exchange system is worth noting. With its practical embeddedness in village social exchange and networks, the system seems peculiarly well adapted to accommodate immigrants from outside the village, at least as long as they respect local ways. Once inside the village, immigrants are obliged to do what everybody else does—give goods and money to festival sponsors and build an investment that can later be used for one's own ritual festival. An individual need not concern himself with the complex detail of priestly liturgy. The priest takes full responsibility for the ritual service and performs much of his ritual work off in a corner during quiet moments of the larger festival. Moreover, most Javanese understand the concern for family and guardian spirits which, according to popular notions, is at the heart of priestly rite. Even in a modern Tengger affected by decades of Islamic reform in neighboring non-Tengger communities, it is not uncommon to see immigrant men in Tengger villages sponsoring ritual festivals, complete with priestly liturgy. One such event I witnessed began with a lowland-style post-mortem prayer meal (nyewu), with Arabic prayer recited by the sponsor's lowland relatives. After the tweny-minute rite was over, there then began a three-day entas-entas festival, with all the usual feasting, dancing, and ritual invocation of the family dead. During such events, of course, doctrinal issues take back seat to a more social-minded driver. Inevitably, however, the doctrinal accommodation can go both ways. The largest festival I witnessed in Tengger was a five-day celebration held in a Tengger community with a large resident Muslim community. Some 2,000 guests and 500 laborers enjoyed dancing horsemen, pole-climbing contests, tayuban dancing, lavish meals, and first-rate wayang wong and ludruk troupes brought up to the isolated community from Surabaya. The total cost of the event was almost 4,000 dollars. The elderly husband and wife who sponsored the festival explained to me that their religion was "both Buda and Islam." Their syncretism was ritually evident. Besides the Tengger priest's liturgies, there was at one point in the five-day event a kenduren prayer meal celebrated by an Islamic modin. The rite was intended to bless the several dozen village children (including the grandsons and granddaughters of the festival sponsors) who, that very same week, had just begun formal instruction in Islamic prayer at the village's recently erected mosque.

Other Types of Festival Exchange

The *sumbangan* exchange is the largest and most deliberate of several exchanges that help to provide the capital for ritual festivals. It provides the largest single portion of the capital mobilized in large events (see Table 5). Several points stand out in this table. The first is that the role of *sumbangan* as a source of capital for ritual festivals is statistically almost identical between the village of the northwest and that of the south, despite the fact that festivals in the northwest are on average more expensive than their counterparts in the south. Hence while the *sumbangan* as a proportion of total festival expense remains the same in the two areas, its actual cash value in the northwest is much greater than in the south. A second point of interest can be seen in comparing the figures from the *entas-entas* with those from weddings. The larger and more expensive *entas-entas* festival draws a greater proportion of its total capital from *sumbangan* exchange than do weddings. This statistic is consistent with a savings strategy about which villagers themselves speak readily. It is better to save *sumbangan* credit until one is ready to sponsor a single, very large festival, villagers say, than to disperse it into several smaller festival events.

Other exchanges of goods and money take place in the course of a ritual festival besides the *sumbangan*. Several have been noted elsewhere in the present work, such as the *sajenan* offerings given to the priest at the completion of a liturgy and the food gifts (*ater-ater*) sent by the sponsors of large festivals to village officials, the priest, and festival laborers. There are two other types of exchange, however, that play a more substantial role in the capital accumulation required for any large

Table 5. Sumbangan *as Percentage of Total Festival Expense*

All festivals, north and south	44%
All festivals, north	45%
All festivals, south	43%
Entas-entas festivals	53%
Wedding festivals	32%

Note: These figures are again based on a survey of forty festival events. It should be noted that several of the wedding festivals surveyed involved the collection of no *sumbangan*, since the events were small and the hosts did not want to incur any additional exchange debts.

festival. The first is also known as *sumbangan*, although it is recognized as an entirely different type of exchange than the *sumbangan* discussed above. *Betek* and *sinoman* festival laborers claim that they are "embarrassed" (*isin*) to come "empty-handed" to a festival, even if they have already made a formal *sumbangan* contribution to the sponsors. Hence women workers always arrive bearing a few additional kilograms of sugar or rice, whereas men bring a carton or two of good quality cigarettes. Although the total value of such goods can be substantial (averaging anywhere from one to three dollars per person), they are not recorded in a notebook. They are considered free gifts, given "voluntarily" (*sukarila*) rather than with an eye to ritual investment.

There is, however, another form of exchange which, like the formal *sumbangan* discussed earlier, is recorded in a notebook, although the social restrictions on it are less complex than those surrounding the *sumbangan*. This exchange, known as the *bowo*, always takes the form of a cash payment made by the guest to the host during the course of a festival. Variants of the *bowo* are found throughout rural Java (see C. Geertz 1960:66; Jay 1969:218), although the exact terms of reciprocity vary widely. In the most common pattern, a male guest at the end of a *slametan* meal discreetly hands an envelope containing money to the host. This is intended to help defray the costs of the *slametan*, and will be repaid with a similar amount of money whenever the guest hosts a *slametan* festival. The Tengger *bowo* differs from this pattern in several key respects. First, it is given by both male and female guests. More importantly, it is made in full view of other guests, usually at a table where friends of the festival host sit recording the name of the donor, his or her village of residence, and the amount given.

Bowo relationships are not really recognized social alliances like the formal *sumbangan* exchange. No surplus need be returned when the *bowo* is repaid, since the relationship need not be perpetuated. *Bowo* partners are not identified as "siblings" in the same fashion that *sumbangan* partners are. *Bowo*-ing, in other words, is more a basic social responsibility than it is a formal mechanism of social alliance. No guest to a festival with *bowo* would dare think of leaving without paying it. A host may, however, refuse *bowo* payments, particularly where he considers his meal festivities too simple to merit *bowo* (which, in theory, is supposed to help defray the costs of the meal), or if he does not want to incur additional *bowo* debts himself. The exact amount an individual gives varies according to one's social status, relationship to the festival sponsors, and elaborateness of the event itself. Guests always pay a larger *bowo* if a bull has been slaughtered to provide meat, and larger yet if there is some form of entertainment such as dancing or theater.

Bowo payments in the south tended to average about Rp 500 for women and Rp 750-1,000 for men; payments were about twice that in the northwest. A high-status individual such as the village chief usually makes a *bowo* payment about twice that of the average amount. All in all, the amount of capital accumulated from the *bowo* payments is substantial, although it represents a smaller proportion of total festival expense than was the case for *sumbangan* (see Table 6).

As a proportion of total festival expense, *bowo* contributions amount to about one-half the total volume of *sumbangan* contributions. Both forms of festival exchange represent in effect socially regulated systems of ritual capital formation. But their social organization is quite different, and their role in ritual capital formation appears to have been reversed in the years since the Great Depression of the 1930s. Prior to that time, villagers say, *bowo* payments tended to be more evenly distributed than they are today. With the occasional exception of the village chief or priest, all guests to a festival contributed the same amount of *bowo* money, and they did so without anyone bothering to record just who paid what amount. *Sumbangan* contributions were also made in earlier times, although amounts given were not as large as they are today. The *bowo* was the single most important source of capital for festivals. The economic chaos of world depression, Japanese occupation, and Indonesian independence all contributed to the eventual demise of this less rigidly stratified system of ritual exchange. Cash was alternately a scarce resource for villagers, and then a worthless one made meaningless by the ravages of inflation. It was during the depression, villagers say, that some people became unable to make *bowo* gifts at festivals, and the amount paid by any one person came to vary according to one's means. Indeed, the festival system as a whole suffered throughout this period. Few villagers sponsored elaborate festivities. When, after almost thirty years of neglect, the festival system revived in the late 1950s, it re-emerged in a more stratified form. Wealthy villagers, in particular, came to rely more heavily upon *sumbangan* contributions than *bowo* payments in accumulating the capital required for large festivals. The recording of *bowo* and *sumbangan* payments—an innovation introduced into the region in the late 1930s—became the norm.

Table 6. Bowo as Proportion of Total Festival Expense

All festivals, north and south	18%
All *entas-entas*	26%
All weddings	12%

The shift to greater reliance upon *sumbangan* gifts in ritual capital formation represented a practical recognition that the burden of ritual savings could no longer be evenly divided among members of the village community. Whereas the *bowo's* demand for contribution is, or was, generalized (all guests pay, and most people used to pay the same amount), the *sumbangan* system in effect segregates villagers into stratified networks of exchange partners. The wealthy tend to exchange with the wealthy, and the poor with the poor, since people of similar economic standing are likely to have similar capital needs and similar capabilities to respond to those needs. Tengger still point to the importance of *bowo* and *sumbangan* as evidence that the village is one community of kin, but this egalitarian idiom overlooks the fact that the ritual festival system has changed profoundly over the years, largely in reaction to larger developments in the socioeconomic organization of the community as a whole. Moreover, these changes in the economic organization of ritual festivals continue in a manner that may ultimately help to redefine public attitudes on ritual performance itself.

Recent Changes in Ritual Economy

Viewed from the perspective of its socioeconomic organization, Tengger ritual shows once again how much it is a total social fact touching all facets of economic, political, and cultural life. There is no independent church to sponsor ritual festivity in these communities. Households linked in complex networks of giving and receiving here assume primary responsibility for the task of accumulating the social and capital resources required for household festivals. And this of course is the critical strength and weakness of the ritual festival system. Where ritual exchange is strong, the festival cycle is likely to be strong; where it is weak, ritual performance itself may be imperiled. Comparison of *sumbangan* organization in three villages (see Table 7) reveals how profound can be differences in the size of *sumbangan* networks.

Examining the figures first from the perspective of differences of land wealth within the village, it is clear that in all three communities the land wealthy have an average number of exchange partners twice as large as that of the land poor. This only confirms a general impression evident in village social activity. The land poor tend to be less active in festival events, either as sponsors or workers, than are the more affluent. In a social system stressing the substantiation of relationships through the exchange of resources, the poor have less to give, and a good deal less to gain socially. One hears this in conversation with the village poor. They tend to restrict their *sumbangan* exchange to immediate kin.

Table 7. Number of Exchange Partners per Household,
according to Wealth and Village

	Southern Village #1	Southern Village #2	Northern Village
Mean no. exchange partners,			
All households	32	3	17
Households owning > 2 ha. land	48	8	22
Households owning < 1 ha. land	24	2	10
Percentage of households with:			
No exchange partners	11%	57%	11%
1-5 exchange partners	16%	78%	35%
20 or more exchange partners	59%	2%	25%
Mean landholding, households with:			
5 or fewer partners	.61 ha.	1.2 ha.	1.1 ha.
20 or more partners	2.49 ha.	3.0 ha.	2.3 ha.

Note: Figures in Tables 7-9 are taken from a larger survey of household economy performed in 342 households in three Tengger communities. "Number of exchange partners" refers to persons with whom either a husband or wife has a recognized *sumbangan* relationship at the same time of the interview. Figures in Tables 8 and 9, as well as the first three rows of figures in Table 7, include only households married ten years or more. Younger households were excluded so as to control for newlyweds still engaged in building their exchange partnerships, or too young to have sponsored a major ritual festival.

The demand on resources that active participation in *sumbangan* exchange involves is a luxury they can ill afford. Since they have few exchange partners, they are less often invited to come to work as *beteksinoman* festival laborers. The overall effect of the poor's restricted exchange networks is, as we shall see, a restricted ability to participate in and sponsor ritual festivals.

The most remarkable variation in the figures, however, is seen in comparisons between villages. Although the wealthy in all villages have larger exchange networks than the land poor, network size varies profoundly between villages. The middle village, "southern village #2," deserves special mention here, since in this community exchange activity is almost nonexistent. The average family maintains only three exchange ties; the poor two, the wealthy eight. The village mean as a whole is just one-tenth that of the neighboring "southern village #1," which lies only four kilometers away, and one-sixth that of the northern village. This middle village displays a pattern of festival exchange organization similar to that of neighboring Islamic communities, and I include it here in part as an example of that organization. The restricted scope of *sum-*

bangan exchange is consistent, in fact, with the cultural history of the community. Founded in the late nineteenth century by Buda immigrants from the lowlands and a handful of local Tengger, this community is today only marginally Tengger. The local dialect is lowland-style *ngoko*, without the distinctive Tengger markers. Islamic *kenduren* prayer meals are celebrated as often as Tengger priestly rites, and a number of villagers have gone off to the lowlands to engage in Islamic study. The ritual cycle and the exchange network that supports it are here weak not because of poverty but because this community only weakly identifies itself as Tengger.

If this middle village is characteristic of the Tengger periphery, the other two communities neatly exemplify two variant patterns found in the heart of Tengger itself. As noted in an earlier chapter, the southern village (#1) was only opened to vehicle transport and commerical agriculture at the end of my period of residence there in 1979-1980. It was in many ways typical of the less economically stratified communities of the Tengger highlands now being drawn into important economic and social development. At the time of my research, house styles were still relatively uniform. Women's dress still consisted largely of traditional *kain* cloth, not the western-style *rok* common in the northwest. The village chief owned the only television. No village youth had ever graduated from junior high school (which would have required schooling outside the village). The only Muslim residing in the village was the local elementary school teacher.

The northern village was, by contrast, one of the most affluent in all Tengger. Villagers had been experimenting with commercial crops and chemical fertilizers for almost twenty years. The Dutch had earlier operated commercial agricultural enterprises in the community. In the central hamlet of 2,000 people, there were twenty trucks, thirty-five motorcycles, and twenty-nine televisions. Large brick-and-plaster homes, built by lowland carpenters, had been built by the wealthy farmers of the village. A number of youths had graduated from high school, and a handful had even gone on to college. This village was, in addition, one of the two centers for the Hindu reform movement in the northwest, although its leaders rejected the policy of reducing festival expenses adopted by reformists in a neighboring community (Chapter 11).

The southern and northwestern community are thus two different poles in a changing Tengger, the one an example of a more traditional subsistence-oriented Buda community, the other a more highly differentiated, moderninzing Hindu community. The differences in *sumbangan* organization between the two villages are indicative of larger changes affecting ritual economy throughout Tengger. In the southern village, the size of a household's *sumbangan* network is on average twice that of the northwest village, for all economic strata. Approximately the same percentage (11 percent) of all households in each village have no exchange partners, but only 16 percent of all households in the south have one to five, as opposed to 35 percent in the northwest. Those who have small exchange networks in the south tend to be land poor, owning on average .61 hectare of land, but this is less clearly the case in the northwest, where those with small exchange networks have an average of 1.1 hectare of land per household (and practice a more productive agricultural regimen). The pattern suggests a movement away from extensive exchange bonds in the more economically differentiated northwest village. This restriction is also seen at the other end of the *sumbangan* scale: 59 percent of all households in the south have more than twenty *sumbangan* partners, as opposed to just 25 percent in the northwest. The difference is not directly related to variation in landholding, since mean landholding for households with extensive exchange networks is roughly equivalent in both villages (2.49 compared with 2.3 hectares). It is the *sumbangan* exchange system itself which is in general less extensive in the northwest. For all economic strata, the mean number of exchange partners in the northwest is almost one-half that in the south.

The figures on exchange partnership have to be compared, however, with the earlier figures (Table 5) on *sumbangan* capital as a proportion of total festival expense. The figures in the north (45 percent) and the south (43 percent) are almost the same. Since there are fewer *sumbangan* partners on average in the north, and since the mean cost for ritual festivals is 2½ to 4 times that in the south, all evidence indicates that *sumbangan* partners in the north on average make far larger contributions of capital and goods than those in the south. The expense involved in exchange partnership in the south is less, and it is spread over a much larger number of partners (a mean of thirty-two per household in the south as against seventeen in the north). Even the land poor in the southern village maintain a wider exchange network (twenty-four partners) on average than do the land wealthy in the northwest (twenty-two partners).

What is one to make of such statistical comparisons? It should be noted first that the southern pattern of exchange organization is more characteristic of most other Tengger communities than is the more restricted pattern of the northwest village. In addition, although statistical evidence is lacking, the more restricted pattern of exchange in the northwest community appears to be a recent development, judging by the comments of older villagers. Villagers in the northwest sometimes complained of this constriction in *sumbangan* networks, insisting that it was a recent development, and attributing its occurrence to the increased costliness of ritual festivals and to the reluctance of wealthier villagers to extend their exchange networks beyond those households capable of making substantial gifts. If this development is indeed a recent one, it is consistent with a general pattern of decommunalization occurring in the economic organization of the northwest community. The wealthy in that village have expanded the reference range of their consumption tastes, eagerly emulating lowland preferences for new consumer goods. Although they continue to invest substantial amounts of capital in ritual festivals, their introduction of new consumer goods into the village arena has put pressures on middle-income villagers to diversify their consumption investments, too. It is perhaps this larger context of a diversifying range of consumer preferences, as the economist would put it, which must be kept in mind when we compare figures from northern and southern Tengger on sponsorship of the most esteemed and expensive of Tengger ritual festivals, the *entas-entas* (see Table 8).

Performance of the *entas-entas* cannot be directly correlated with size of *sumbangan* networks or landholding alone, since, as noted earlier, the *entas-entas* in the northwest community has been redefined as an optional ceremony incumbent only upon the wealthy. Nonetheless, the information in Table 8 gives some sense of a different balance of ritual piety, economic investment, and social stratification in the three Tengger communities. Not surprisingly, in the marginally Tengger community (southern village #2), sponsorship of the rite is lowest: fewer than one-fifth of all adult households have fulfilled the duty. The more affluent in the same community, however, tend to be more diligent in ritual performance. Over one-half of the land wealthy have performed the rite. The status implications of ritual performance, one suspects, are showing.

The more remarkable comparison, however, lies between the southern village (#1) and that in the northwest. Almost three-fourths of the adult population in the southern community has performed the *entas-entas*,

Table 8. Percentage of Households Sponsoring the Entas-Entas *Festival*

	Southern Village #1	Southern Village #2	Northern Village
All households	72%	19%	39%
Households owning < 1 ha.	57%	9%	14%
Households owning > 2 ha.	84%	56%	63%

Note: See note to Table 7.

compared to only two-fifths in the northwest. The northwest community, one must remember, is by all objective measures far more affluent than that in the south, hence differences between the two villages cannot be reduced to simple economic measures. Within each community sponsorship of the rite does increase as one moves from the land poor to the land wealthy. In the southern community, however, the pattern is much less stratified, with a large proportion of land poor (57 percent) sponsoring the rite. This compares with only 14 percent of the land poor in the northwest community. The difference in sponsorship by the land poor in the two communities is, of course, consistent with the stricture in the northwest that the wealthy alone are required to perform an *entas-entas*. Poverty and affluence are relative matters, however, and here they are relative not only to the incomes of fellow villagers, but relative to the expense involved in sponsoring an *entas-entas* festival. The recent inflation in the festival's cost in the northwest (Table 4) has pushed the average cost of an *entas-entas* to over $2,500, as opposed to less than $700 in the southern community. Northwest villagers complain that they would not "dare" sponsor an *entas-entas* today without at least slaughtering an Australian bull, while at least some of their southern counterparts continue to sponsor the same festival with no more than a goat and a few chickens. The lavishness of ritual festivities in the north has thus kept pace with recent gains in income (themselves product of the shift to intensive commercial agriculture), but for villagers unable to keep up with this inflation in ritual expense, it has occurred at the expense of ritual performance itself. The controversial efforts of leaders in a neighboring northwest community to put a cap on ritual costs by restricting the size of festivities (Chapter 11) is in part a response to this same inflationary spiral.

Variation in sponsorship of the *entas-entas* is paralleled by another—sponsorship of *tayuban* dancing and *ludruk* theater. Here, as in many other areas of the Eastern Salient, these are the most popular art forms in rural areas, and their sponsorship in Tengger reveals once again the varied pattern of festivity and status in different villages (Table 9). The figures from the marginally Tengger village (southern village #2) are again consistently low, except for the land wealthy. The more interesting contrast again lies between the northwest and southern village (#1). Almost twice as many households in the latter village sponsor these art forms as in the north (57 as against 29 percent). Sponsorship remains high even among the land poor in the south, 34 percent as opposed to just 8 percent in the north. Figures are generally comparable between the two communities only for the land affluent (75 as against 57 percent).

Just what does this variation indicate? Different frequencies of festival

Table 9. Percentage of Households Sponsoring Ritual Arts
(Tayuban or Ludruk)

	Southern Village #1	Southern Village #2	Northern Village
All households	57%	12%	29%
Households owning < 1 ha.	34%	0%	8%
Households owning > 2 ha.	74%	40%	57%

Note: See note to Table 7.

sponsorship are related in part to differences in the expense of entertainment in the two villages. The dancers, the drink, the food, and the theater troupes are all more expensive in the north—on average, three to four times more expensive than in the south. The search for excellence has prompted affluent northwesterners to travel hundreds of kilometers to hire the best female *tayuban* dancers in East Java, and to Surabaya to find the finest *ludruk* troupes in all Indonesia. Such elaborate festivities have been promoted by the affluent at least in part so as to raise the status of Tengger tradition in the eyes of its neighbors. In the process of elevating the standards of excellence, however, affluent villagers have pushed people of more modest means out of the festival arena. In the southern community, by contrast, even poor villagers have an opportunity to sponsor modest ritual festivals, with smaller feasts and perhaps a local *ludruk* troupe for entertainment. The opportunity to be the proud host of the village and its guardian ancestors remains a goal affordable to middle and even lower-income families, because the standards of consumption have not been inflated to unattainable heights.

The differences in festivity between the two communities are all part of far-reaching changes now shaking Tengger ritual economy. Ritual performance has always been linked to the effort to achieve social recognition and to set standards of cultural excellence. Villagers would exhaust years of savings in three nights of festivity rather than in the purchase of more private consumer goods, which by no means benefited from the widespread moral approval of ritual festivals. The system has not yet entirely changed. The inflation in ritual expense seen in the northwest is evidence that ritual festivity is still very much a mark of status. As incomes have increased, therefore, so too has the cost of ritual festivity. But not everyone's income has increased proportionately. Income disparities within the northwest community are greater than those typical of other areas of the highlands. Given the present pace of agricultural commercialization other communities are likely to experience a similar measure of stratification in the years to come.

All this is occurring at roughly the same time that villagers are moving more regularly into the surrounding society and becoming acquainted with the consumer goods that have flooded the Indonesian market since the early 1970s. Differences of clothing, household goods, house styles, education, and investment once considered indices of "lowland" life are now becoming very much "Tengger." The rapidity with which this is now occurring throughout the region—always following, it seems, in the footsteps of roadbuilding and the switch to full-blown commercial agriculture—is nothing less than astounding. Villagers have become well aware of the alternative uses to which capital once expended in ritual festivity can be put. Children are leaving villages of the northwest to continue their education in the lowlands. Motorcycles are a passion. One is not supposed to "dress like a farmer" now when visiting the city. But to speak of an awareness of "alternative uses" makes far too individualistic what is also a social process. People have long recognized that Tengger spend a greater proportion of their income on ritual festivity than do their Muslim neighbors. At least until recently, however, many Tengger have insisted that certain kinds of economic goods consumed in lowland communities were, for some reason, not appropriate for Tengger village life. There was a moral economy at work here, channeling wealth into a form of consumption that benefited from high public regard because of its identification with Tengger religion and identity. This moral system was itself dependent on the continuing reproduction of a larger institutional order and the social consensus that went with it. The complexity of the system was no doubt never entirely apparent to village actors. But its continuing existence was vital if the social and religious interests of actors were to remain compelling and real.[6]

This larger social environment is now in the process of change, however. Villagers are increasingly active in the surrounding society, and

[6] It is from this perspective of the unintended consequences and constraints of practical activity that the interpretive methodology used in the present work differs from that of some other interpretive approaches. In particular, I take issue with the argument that "the integration of an institutional order can be understood only in terms of the 'knowledge' that its members have of it" (Berger and Luckmann 1966:65). As seen here in Tengger, the knowledge, intentions, and preferences of actors are all influenced by social and historical conditions about which actors may have little knowledge. Actions have unintended consequences that escape from "the scope of the purposes of the actor" (Giddens 1979:59) but nonetheless influence the reproduction and change of a social order. Max Weber himself noted as much, insisting that a science of social action must attend to "processes and phenomena which are devoid of subjective meaning" but nonetheless influence meaningful action (see Weber 1947:93). To understand social action and cultural ideas, in short, we have to attend to more than ideas. There can be no detour around activity and history.

"interested" in sharing some of its styles and rewards. Economic differentiation is on the rise. With capital increasingly diverted into non-festival spheres, the social focus of consumption is changing in a manner likely to enhance economic differences rather than mute them. From this perspective, the southern village is merely at the tail end of a regional transformation that began in the late 1960s. The northern community is in the vanguard of the same change, although other villages, poorer and more densely populated, may be unable to emulate its success. In both economic and cultural affairs, Tengger have been irreversibly drawn into modern Indonesia and, beyond that, a larger world system.

What do these changes in ritual economy mean for a tradition long buoyed by this people's populist sensibilities and ancestral ideas? Traditionally renowned for their aggressively egalitarian speech, down-to-earth etiquette, and rustic mountain ways, Tengger have entered a new phase of sociocultural development. With it will come new challenges to their identity, and a new balance of local and national allegiances.

The Hindu reform movement—our final chapter in this story of identity and cultural reproduction in a changing Java—takes these same developments as its point of departure. At a time when Tengger seek to affirm a less parochial religious identity, the Hindu reform movement proposes to identify Tengger religion with Hindu tradition elsewhere. At a time when Tengger communities are experiencing greater socio-economic differentiation, and the social bases of ritual festivity are eroding, the Hindu reform movement proposes to elevate religion above the local social terrain and develop a commitment to ritual forms less directly dependent upon the rhythms of social life. Tengger as a moral community is changing. The Hindu reform movement seeks to provide a vocabulary for expressing, and shaping, that change.

ISLAMIZATION AND HINDU REFORM

In the interval between my first visit in mid-1977 and my return in late 1978, the number of Tengger communities officially identifying themselves as "Hindu" increased from eight to sixteen (of a total of twenty-eight villages). Equally importantly, the region's head priest (*lurah dukun*) had, after almost fifteen years of acrimonious dispute, finally embraced the Hindu designation and come to support the introduction of Hindu religious instruction into Tengger elementary schools. In 1979, the first of several Balinese-trained (and ethnically non-Tengger) teachers arrived in the region. Following a model first used a decade earlier in the Tengger northwest, classes were established to train school children and elders alike in the recitation of Sanskrit prayer, an innovation that was greeted enthusiastically by many villagers. A religious administration, the *parisada*, was organized in villages throughout northern Tengger to supervise religious instruction, register all Hindu marriages and deaths, and to implement policies developed by higher-level (and non-Tengger) *parisada* operating out of Surabaya and Bali. For the first time in modern times, Tengger religion was formally affiliated with a religious organization headquartered outside of the Tengger region itself.

Although it was born in controversy, the Hindu reform movement in Tengger had by 1980 begun a new and more aggressive phase of expansion. The movement's success continued to provoke argument, however. Nearly half of all Tengger priests still oppose the movement, identifying it explicitly as a betrayal of Tengger tradition, and it is unclear whether they can be brought into the organization's fold. Even within the Hindu reform leadership, moreover, serious differences of opinion exist, and in several instances these have resulted in radically different policies with regard to the preservation of priestly liturgy. Contemporary Tengger, in short, is in the midst of yet another phase of an ongoing debate on tradition, religion, and identity. In a general sense, this controversy is but the most recent expression of a cultural crisis dating back to the fall of Hindu Majapahit. The terms of the present dispute, however, are quite modern, showing the influence of political and religious developments in the modern Indonesian nation state.

Independence

The collapse of the occupying Japanese administration and the declaration of Indonesian independence in August of 1945 marked the beginning of a new era in Tengger and other areas of Indonesia. Located in the mountains above the republican strongholds of Surabaya, Pasuruan, and Probolinggo, the Tengger mountains served as a temporary place of refuge for thousands of urban lowlanders who fled the invading colonial forces in late 1945. Most of these refugees eventually returned to the lowlands, but the guerrilla forces opposed to the reimposition of colonial rule stayed, using the highlands as a staging ground for attacks. Tengger communities provided food and refuge for the resistance forces, and a good number of local men joined directly in the nationalist struggle. Several military engagements took place in the region (including one two-day bombardment by Dutch artillery around Mt. Bromo), and the presence of guerrilla fighters set the tone for development in Tengger over the next generation. Many of the republican soldiers were men from orthodox Islamic communities on East Java's north coast, and in this region of Java, Muslim leaders played a dominant role in resistance organization. Soldiers in several lower-lying Tengger communities organized classes in Islamic religion. Village chiefs in several communities were replaced with local Muslim men. Tengger heard rumors that the newly established Indonesian nation was ultimately to become an Islamic republic.

After the signing of a peace treaty in December of 1949, Tengger joined with other nearby communities in building grade schools, meeting halls, and roads. Old-fashioned homes of wood and thatch were replaced in the early 1950s with new structures with cement floors, tile roofs, and glass windows, most of the materials being transported by horse and human labor from lowland markets. In the rich wetlands below the Tengger highlands, however, the populist groundswell of early independence soon gave way to a bitter contest between Islamic and communist organizations. The large sugar and rice estates between the highlands and the north-coast cities of Pasuruan and Probolinggo provided fertile ground for a fast-growing Indonesian Communist Party (PKI). Towns in the same region were for the most part strongholds of Muslim parties. As throughout much of rural Java during this period (Jay 1963; Ricklefs 1981), political competition shattered the delicate balance between Javanist and orthodox Muslim communities, as urban-based political parties sought to expand their role in national politics by mobilizing followers in the countryside.

Village leaders in Tengger attempted to keep their communities free of such party rivalry. Most villages continued to vote as a bloc for the ruling Indonesian Nationalist Party (PNI), just as today most vote in a similarly uniform fashion for the ruling government party (Golkar). The Communist Party had only a handful of followers in two of the twenty-eight Tengger villages, and Muslim parties attracted votes only in those communities with a Muslim population. In the mid-1950s, however, several events shook the calm of the Tengger region. Several weeks before the general elections of 1955, Muslim fundamentalists in a village just below the Tengger northwest destroyed a well-known Hindu shrine regarded as spiritually powerful by local and Tengger villagers alike. During the same period, a loosely organized coalition of non-Muslim lowlanders had begun to operate in several non-Tengger villages just to the west of Tengger settlement. The movement's leaders sought (unsuccessfully) to woo Tengger leadership with a political alliance dedicated to a "return to the religion of Majapahit." The Tengger community, however, was heatedly preoccupied with its own internal debate. Leaders in the northwest had begun to explore the possibility of establishing organizational ties with Balinese Hindus. At roughly the same time, leaders in several northeastern communities were publicly flirting with the possibility of converting to Islam. The stimulus to action in both areas had been the sudden and shocking collapse of Buda tradition in several communities to the southeast and southwest of Tengger, areas where the cult of Ajisaka had once been strong, but where Islamization was· now in full swing.

The End of Buda: The Besuki Example

Besuki (a pseudonym) is a community of 3,000 people located in rolling foothills 30 kilometers to the east of the city of Malang, and about 12 kilometers from the nearest, higher-lying Tengger community. Besuki has been an important drop-off point for Tengger produce since the end of the last century, and until the 1950s it had a substantial Buda community with strong ties to Tengger. Indeed, up through the first decades of the twentieth century, many Besuki residents referred to themselves as Tengger. Since the early nineteenth century, however, there had also been a large number of Madurese and Javanese Muslims residing in the community, who were more reluctant to identify themselves fully with the customs of the region. Temperate climate, an altitude (900 meters) well suited for cultivation of commercial crops, and proximity to major urban markets all combined to make Besuki an attractive frontier area for immigrants from Central and East Java. According to village legend, the first founders of the village were a man from Central Java and a woman from Tengger, both of whom arrived in the village at the end of the eighteenth century. The man brought a water buffalo and the woman Tengger potatoes. From its beginning, therefore, Besuki was identified as a mixture of uplands and lowlands, the Tengger element

241

identified in some sense as "female." Although little else is known of the lives of these early pioneers, they are said to have been of Buda faith. A priest living in the village performed village and household rites of the same name and ritual form as those used elsewhere in the Tengger mountain region.

Folk histories recount that the Dutch-Java war (1825-1830) brought the next wave of immigrants to the area, as large numbers of Central Javanese fled the conflict. The immigrants brought with them, it is said, a new commercial crop—coffee. First introduced in the Priangan highlands of West Java, coffee cultivation spread rapidly to other sparsely populated hillside areas of Java in the years prior to mid-century (C. Geertz 1963:66). It was a crop well suited to make good commercial use of mountain terrains—many of them, as here in Besuki, the fallow lands of swidden cultivators—regarded by the Dutch as "waste lands."

Intensive cultivation of the coffee crop in Besuki, however, would begin only several years later, with the arrival of yet another wave of immigrants. These newcomers were Madurese, and their entrance in the area was directly encouraged by the Dutch administration. The Madurese formed two distinct social classes: entrepreneurs awarded large tracts of land by the government (land often regarded by villagers as part of their swidden holdings), and landless laborers brought by the entrepreneurs to work the land. Folk histories report that these landless laborers were known as *santri*, the same term as used throughout Java to refer to people trained in orthodox Islam. Contemporary villagers deny, however, that the term in this region originally had anything to do with religious orientation. A *santri* was simply a landless laborer who worked other people's holdings, and to work in this fashion was known as to *nyantri*. This new social relation of production had never before been seen in the area. The term's religious connotation may not have been entirely inappropriate, however. Folk commentaries today indicate that these Madurese immigrants were also the first in the village to perform daily Muslim prayer. And they were the first to gather for public prayer each Friday, in Muslim fashion.

Most other villagers at this time were Buda. A Tengger-style *dukun* resided in the community and maintained active ties with priests in higher-lying villages of the Mt. Bromo region. Villagers celebrated the Karo all-souls festival each year, and most also made the annual pilgrimage to Mt. Bromo during Kasada. The local dialect, however, was mixed. Some people spoke a standard dialect of Javanese; others spoke the variant common throughout the Mt. Bromo region; and still others used both. Early Central Javanese immigrants to the village, it is said, had respected the priestly tradition, and consistently identified themselves as Buda. The Madurese immigration, however, introduced an element of religious tension into the community. Around 1860, for example, a religious dispute (the details of which no one knows today) culminated with the departure of the long-time village leader (a man of Central Javanese birth). This man eventually took up residence in a higher-lying, exclusively Buda Tengger community, where he is still venerated in a *punden* burial shrine. The next Besuki village chief was also Buda, and was also of immigrant background (from Singosari). He presided over a community increasingly divided between a predominantly Buda population, residing in the village's upper hamlet, and an assortment of orthodox and syncretic Muslims living in a lower hamlet, more actively engaged in the coffee industry than subsistence agriculture. The new chief attempted to mediate between the two religious communities. Although he was Buda, he lived in the lower Muslim hamlet. He encouraged Muslims to participate in the annual village *slametans*. Most Muslims did participate in the Karo and *pujan* festivities, but they insisted that Muslim rites of life passage (marriage, birth, burial, and post mortem ceremonies) replace Buda-style priestly rites. Religious tensions surfaced again at the death of the Buda village chief. According to folk histories, the chief instructed that he was not to be buried in an Islamic fashion but cremated in the *sanggar* shrine above the village. The chief's instructions provoked a bitter debate, but were eventually overruled. The chief was buried, and his clothes were given to Buda residents for cremation in the *sanggar*.

This event was but one index of the slow decline of the Buda population. The upper, or Buda hamlet had none of the traders, coffee merchants, or large landowners of the lower-lying Muslim community. Most of the Buda population engaged in subsistence cultivation of maize and vegetable cash crops, with some peripheral cultivation of coffee. Some of the poorer Buda residents, in addition, worked the coffee lands of the Muslim merchants. The economic subordination of the upper hamlet continues today in Besuki.

Coffee merchants resided in the lower hamlet. At first most were Madurese, but their numbers eventually included Javanese of local and immigrant background. The merchants managed large tracts of coffee land for the colonial government, in exchange for a share of their product wealth. Actual cultivation of the coffee was carried out by the *santri* sharecroppers, who at first moved from village to village throughout this mountain region, but eventually were awarded small tracts of land and thus took up residence in communities throughout the area. The coffee merchants devoted their energies to commerce, monopolizing not only the coffee harvest but the growing trade in vegetable produce for nearby urban markets. It was from among this wealthy trading class that the next village chief was chosen in the early 1870s. He was a man by the name of Haji Mohammad Saleh, the grandson of a Tengger priest, and the first person in Besuki to have made the pilgrimage to Mecca. Mohammad Saleh was the son of one of the first Buda men in the community to break into the coffee trade previously monopolized by Muslim immigrants; in the course of his career, Mohammad Saleh's father converted to Islam. Although a Muslim, Mohammad Saleh himself was reputed to have dabbled in Javanese mysticism, and he abided by the injunction of the Ajisaka tale, popular throughout the region at this time. As village chief, Mohammad Saleh continued to support Buda-style village festivals, although he did not use a Tengger priest to perform household rites of passage.

In neighboring communities at this time, however, the process of decline of Buda was also gaining momentum. It appears that almost all communities in the area had been Buda at the beginning of the century. Movement of immigrants into the area throughout the century, however, left the indigenous Buda population increasingly isolated in small hamlets surrounded by larger communities of immigrant Javanese and Madurese. The acceleration of the coffee industry in the region, moreover, not only drew large numbers of Muslims to the region, it also effectively stripped indigenous swidden farmers of the land resources they required to maintain their mode of swidden production. The swidden economy was thus irreversibly destroyed, and its agents disadvantaged relative to the immigrant coffee cultivators. The immigrant Muslims brought with them a new mode of production, characterized by far more hierarchical social organization, and they preserved extraregional ties that gave them a distinct advantage in commerce. Their Muslim faith, moreover, provided them with the terms for a social identity less narrowly defined in terms of parochial social allegiances. Economic and religious changes thus went hand in hand, as new relations of production and exchange facilitated, and were facilitated by, the spread of Muslim faith.

The declining status of the Buda community was sometimes signaled in curious ways. In the first decade of the twentieth century, for example, village leaders in Besuki and neighboring communities led a campaign against first-person pronouns used in Tengger dialect (*eyang, isun*), insisting that villagers use standard Javanese pronouns (*aku, kulo*). Elder Besuki villagers report that the chiefs exhorted them by saying, "You are not Tengger, so why should you speak like them?" Some older villagers continued to use the Tengger dialect into the 1950s, but its use became rare thereafter. A world was changing, as cultural traits once common to a region were stigmatized as non-Javanese and backward.

Despite the long presence of Islam in the area, and despite the role of Islam in protest movements in many areas of rural nineteenth-century Java (Kartodirdjo 1972), it was only in 1910 that the first Islamic prayer house (*langgar*) was erected in any of the region's communities. The site was Kembar, seven kilometers from Besuki, at an important market to which urban traders regularly came. It was, in fact, the merchant community in that village which promoted the construction. The same group of men sponsored the construction of the region's first mosque ten years later. Besuki was not far behind, erecting its first mosque in 1922, on the site of a former ancestral shrine. In the mid-1930s, moreover, Besuki was the focus of a campaign for reformist Islamic education, sponsored by Muhammadiyah modernists operating out of the city of Malang. Muhammadiyah teachers gave nightly courses in Arabic prayer and Islamic religious doctrines, and spoke regularly in the village mosque.

All of these developments were part of far-reaching changes affecting the countryside. Already around 1900, the last remaining pocket of Buda population in Kembar had, under pressure from village leaders, voted to replace the annual Karo festival with a more acceptably Javanese *bersih desa*, a rite of village purification similar to that found in other areas of Java (see C. Geertz 1960:79). Village leaders promoted the change by citing what they argued were the excessive expenses of Karo and the need to perfrom religious services in a "Javanese fashion." The Buda hamlets in neighboring communities continued to celebrate Tengger-style village festivals (Karo, the four *pujan*, *barian*, and so on) well into the 1950s. But almost everywhere these rites were publicly identified as "village custom" (*adat desa*) and denied any association with "Buda religion." For household rites of passage, meanwhile, restrictions on priestly activity were more severe. In a number of communities (including Besuki), the priest was barred from performing rites of death and burial beginning in the 1930s, a policy that may have been related to the activities of Muhammadiyah teachers. During the same period, all marriages were required to have an Islamic *kenduren* prayer meal. A Tengger-style *walagara* could still be celebrated, but only after the Muslim rite.

During the Indonesian independence struggle, finally, Besuki's Buda population was dealt a further blow. The village was a hub for guerrilla activity, in large part because its chief was active in an armed Islamic militia. Dutch forces eventually attacked the village with an armored vehicle, killing thirty village men, and replaced the chief with a puppet administrator. The guerrilla village leader would return triumphantly, however, at the end of the independence struggle. A devoted, modernist Muslim, and an enlightened, progressive administrator, this chief initiated programs for extending village roads, building a school and hiring a teacher, pumping drinking water into the community, and reconstructing village homes using cooperative labor. He also furthered religious reform. In the year prior to the 1955 elections, he banned *tayuban* dancing and alchohol consumption, integral parts of the annual Karo festivities. He withdrew his support for village sponsorship of *pujan*, *galungan*, and other Tengger-style village rituals, with the exception of Karo. He forbade the public reading of the Ajisaka and Mohammad tale. The core of Buda ritual activity was thus removed from the public sphere, to be celebrated quietly in the home of the village priest, supported by contributions from those villagers who wished to support Buda festivity.

In the aftermath of the destruction of the Indonesian Communist Party and widespread bloodletting in the countryside, Besuki's Buda population suffered its final reversal. Unlike some other areas of rural Java (see C. Geertz 1972; Ricklefs 1979), the political turmoil of 1965-1966 did not lead to a revival of non-Muslim organization in this region. There had been no communist organization in Besuki, and the village experienced no loss of life. But the bloodshed in communities just below this village was sometimes severe, and in its aftermath word spread throughout the region that those not professing a recognized world faith—understood by most people at this time to mean either Islam or Christianity, although Buddhism and Hinduism were now formally recognized by the government—could be accused of being communist. It was in these circumstances that Besuki's village chief struck a deal with the Buda portion of his community: he would continue to support the celebration of Karo and protect the Buda villagers if they ceased referring to themselves as Buda and began identifying themselves as Muslim. They would not be required to pray or attend mosque services, but they were expected to tolerate the few minutes of Islamic religious instruction their children would receive each day in elementary school.

The proposal met with strong opposition at first, but eventually it was accepted by the leaders of the Buda community. Buda villagers thus began to refer to themselves as Muslim, usually qualifying the reference by adding that they are "Javanese Muslims" or "Buda Muslims." These terms were still widely used by villagers when I visited Besuki in 1979. In the fourteen years since the decision, however, the number of people still supporting Karo festivities by preparing offerings for ancestral spirits has dropped precipitously, from about 150 households to 80. Islamic programs in the community during the same period have grown dramatically. A new village chief who came to power in 1968 has overseen a massive program of construction and Islamic education. Eight *langgar* prayer houses have been built or entirely reconstructed; the mosque had been refurbished. Three adult prayer groups meet twice weekly to study Islamic texts. Four youth groups engage in the same Islamic study, their chanting broadcast each night into the village over a battery-run loud-speaker. Each month, in addition, there is a gathering of men at the village chief's house to pray for village welfare. In 1978, having completed his program of religious building, the village chief led a group of eight villagers on pilgrimage to Mecca.

Now an elderly man in his seventies, the village priest still performs the full array of Tengger-style village rites each year, although he does so privately in his own home, in the presence of his assistants. He also celebrates household rites for those villagers requesting them. When I asked him what will become of his religious tradition, he responded that Buda was "finished" (*entek*), and said that he would not transmit his prayer tradition to his sons (who identified themselves as Muslims). He still makes the annual pilgrimage to Kasada, he pointed out, and still speaks regularly with Tengger priests, but when he dies Besuki's priestly heritage will, too.

Priests and leaders in Tengger communities during the 1950s and 1960s were well aware of developments in Besuki and other non-Buda communities in transition to Islam. These events more than any others shook the resolve of many leaders, and raised doubts for many concerning the viability of Tengger tradition in a modernizing Indonesia.

The Rise of the Tengger Reform Movement

Just prior to the tumultuous national elections of 1955, a Tengger elementary school teacher from the northwest village of Ngadiwono made a ten-day trip to Bali, an event that marked the first official contact between Tengger and Balinese in modern times. Village chiefs in the Tengger northwest had instructed the teacher to contact Balinese religious officials and discuss their efforts to achieve official recognition as a national religion (which, at that time, the Balinese had not yet succeeded in achieving). Balinese officials told the teacher that they knew of the Tengger region, and recognized its Mt. Bromo and Mt. Semeru as lands sacred for all Indonesian Hindus. These officials then invited Tengger to send four students to Bali to study as high school students. Although the program would last only several years, the contact was a significant one. One of the four high school students to go to Bali would eventually become village chief of Ngadiwono, and would play an important role in the movement for affiliation with Balinese Hinduism.

It was not until 1959 that village officials in the northwest assembled to discuss affiliation. The meeting followed a series of discussions village leaders had had concerning religious matters. With the encouragement of govenment officials in Pasuruan sympathetic to the Tengger plight, Tengger had earlier explored the possibility of allying themselves with urban Buddhists (most of whom are Chinese). Tengger had ultimately rejected this proposal, in part because the Buddhist organizations were dominated by Chinese, and because, after observing the ritual traditions of the urban Buddhists, Tengger officials concluded the two groups had little in common. Contacts between Tengger and Balinese had been more encouraging, and the reports of Tengger returning from visits to Bali led many leaders to conclude that affiliation with the Balinese was a more promising policy. Local Tengger tradition, in addition, had long identified Balinese religion as kindred with that in Tengger, "Buda Bali" or "Buda Hindu" rather than "Buda Jawa" (Javanese Buda). Lowland government officials and leaders from the Tengger northwest both agreed, however, that Tengger could not afford simply to identify their religion as a local faith, unaffiliated with any larger religious organization. Hence at the end of a month of often stormy debate, village leaders voted— with two village chiefs in particular bitterly protesting—to proceed with the plan for formal affiliation with Balinese Hinduism.

It was unclear, however, just what the meeting had accomplished, and what to do next. Only leaders from the Tengger northwest (eight of twenty-eight Tengger communities) had been in attendance, and, once the decision for affiliation was made, there was no formal institution throughout Tengger with which to implement any kind of program. Indeed, Balinese religion was not yet officially recognized as a legitimate world faith by officials in Jakarta, so the conference's decision had no formal effect on the status of Tengger religion in Indonesia's Department of Religion. All of this quickly changed, however, in 1962, when the Balinese finally succeeded in having Balinese Hinduism recognized as a legitimate national religion. This development reopened the affiliation issue in the Tengger northwest, and officials moved quickly to contact the Office of Religion in Surabaya and to file papers indicating that northwest Tengger was to be officially identified as Hindu. In late 1962, officials from the Surabaya Department of Religion, with the help of Balinese religious officials, sponsored month-long courses in Hindu re- ligion for village officials from the Tengger northwest. At the end of 1962, a formal ceremony was held in which village officials and lowlands administrators gathered to declare the Pasuruan Tengger territory a Hindu domain. Not all officials from the Tengger northwest attended the ceremony, however, and no leaders came from the twenty Tengger communities outside the Pasuruan region. This schism was reinforced throughout the 1960s and early 1970s. The northwest launched more educational programs and developed a regional religious administration (the *parisada*) to supervise religious policy. In 1968, the community of Wonokitri invited Balinese craftsmen to come to the village and supervise the construction of a Balinese-style temple at the site of the village *sanggar* shrine.

Beginning in the 1960s, village officials from the northwest sought to persuade leaders from the northeast to join them in the Hindu movement. Officials in several communities in the northeast, however, had been severely shaken by the conversion of Besuki and neighboring Buda communities to Islam. Higher-level officials from the *kabupaten* of Probolinggo—most of whom were Madurese—were also much less sympathetic to Tengger tradition than were the largely Javanese officials in Pasuruan who had encouraged Tengger in their efforts. In the early 1960s, finally, an event took place in one northeastern community that shaped the course of religious developments for years to come. The priest and village chief in this northeastern community announced to their fellow villagers prior to the Karo season that Karo would no longer be celebrated. The community was to convert to Islam; Buda religion was a thing of the past. This announcement sent the whole village into confusion. After several days of informal meetings, villagers met with the village chief and priest and announced that they could not abide by their leaders' decision. There was no precedent for such a move, but eventually both the village chief and priest resigned their posts, and were replaced by villagers committed to Karo and Buda ways.

Throughout the 1960s and 1970s, most village leaders in the northeast continued to keep their distance from the Hindu movement in the northwest. As leaders in the northwest had done a decade earlier, leaders in the northeast sought to establish contacts with Buddhist organizations in the urban lowlands. Just as in the northwest, all of these alliances proved unsuccessful, because the Tengger "Buda" found little in common with Indonesian "Buddhists" (also referred to as *agama Buda*). The quiet efforts of village leaders in the northwest, however, slowly began to bear fruit. In the mid-1970s, the first village in the Tengger northeast officially joined northwest Tengger in identifying itself as "Hindu" and accepting Hindu educational programs. In 1977, the head priest (*lurah dukun*) of the entire Tengger region, a priest from the northeast, made a visit with several northwestern officials to Bali, and, as a result of this trip, finally announced his adherence to the Hindu movement. In the course of his visit, he recounts today, he "came to understand things I did not understand before" in his own ritual tradition. His visit to Bali allowed him not only to learn about the culture of that island, but to begin to develop a new perspective on the liturgical tradition to which he as priest had been heir.

The Interpretive Tensions of Hindu Affiliation

The weaknesses of the Tengger reform movement were related in part to the religious social organization on which the movement was built. At each step of its way, for example, the movement was handicapped by the absence of any truly regional political or ecclesiastical structure. An informal consortium of northwest village officials sponsored the school teacher's trip to Bali in the 1950s, but those officials had no formal authority to draw other village leaders into the effort or the affiliation plan that eventually resulted from it. Efforts to establish lines of communication with leaders in other areas of Tengger were limited to informal arenas of interaction such as visitation during household ritual festivals or discussion at Mt. Bromo during Kasada. Programs initiated after 1962 in the Tengger northwest were interesting in this regard, for they were organized not through existing Tengger organizations but through the one administrative structure readily available to leaders in the region—the national administration. A handful of village leaders invited their administrative superiors up to Tengger to witness a formal declaration identifying northwest Tengger as a Hindu region. The announcement was formally written up and filed with the Department of Religion in Surabaya, and enabled village officials to request the services of the Hindu bureau in the Department of Religion. In organizational terms, in other words, the reform movement launched its initiative by plugging into an already existing administrative structure located outside and above the Tengger region.

The reform movement displayed other shortcomings of Tengger ritual organization, as well. Priests played almost no role in its leadership, which was dominated by village chiefs and other officials. Only a handful of priests even attended the 1959 convocation, and arguments concerning affiliation with Balinese Hinduism were posed almost exclusively in practical political terms, not doctrinal ones. A lowland administrator present at the 1959 meeting and sympathetic to Tengger religion expressed surprise in my discussion with him in 1980 when I pointed out to him that there were many similarities between Tengger and Balinese ritual practice and prayer. Although he expressed pleasure at hearing this, he told me that this issue was not at all discussed during the 1959 meeting. Debate had focused on the need to develop an organization capable of representing Tengger religious interests in a modernizing

Indonesian nation. Matters of doctrine and spiritual cosmology were not addressed.

The official's comments were interesting, for they revealed how little the movement for Hindu affiliation was motivated by internal intellectual preoccupations or a Weberian "disenchantment" of a once magical world. The driving force for Hindu affiliation was not the collapse of traditional beliefs as to the nature of the supernatural, but the problems of self-definition and legitimation posed by increased involvement in an Indonesian society in which Islam is the dominant religious idiom. Once initiated, however, Tengger contacts with reformist Hindu Balinese did help to promote changes in at least some people's perceptions of this regional ritual tradition. The high school youths who first went to Bali, and their relatives who eventually visited them on the island, were pleasantly surprised to learn that Balinese, like Tengger, use *sajenan* offerings in worship, as well as incense, holy water, and *japa-mantra*. Gradually other parallels between the two traditions were noticed. Villagers who had been to Bali pointed out to me that Balinese have *prasen* holy water beakers similar to those seen in Tengger. Their prayers, like those of the Tengger priest, are often composed in Kawi Javanese. They believe in the importance of calendrical cycles similar to those known in Tengger. The parallels noted by villagers tended to be general and practical, rather than doctrinal, but they appear to have made a deep impression on many people. What these people were experiencing was the development of a wider frame of reference through which to evaluate their tradition. The implements, rites, and purposes of Tengger tradition began for some villagers to evoke the recognition of a wider Indonesian Hindu heritage rather than a simple sense of ancestral ways. A similar reconceptualization of tradition, with an increased awareness of the roots of that tradition in a large religious heritage, has of course been experienced by many Javanese Muslims over the past century. Here in Tengger, the example indicates once again how the meanings Tengger attribute to their ritual tradition are not somehow "stored" in its symbolic interior, but are informed by the larger, and changing, historical experience people bring to its interpretation.

The ability of those who favored affiliation to revitalize popular perception of the ritual tradition, however, was restricted by both the social organization that had long protected the liturgy and the new religious organization that developed to coordinate Tengger religion with the larger Indonesian Hindu community. The division of ritual labor involved in the transmission and performance of priestly liturgy to a large degree remained in place even as the Hindu reform movement developed. Those who favored affiliation made no real effort to examine the priest's liturgy, to probe its interior for hints of its historic origins, or to demonstrate that there was indeed profound cultural parallel between the Tengger liturgy and much Balinese belief. Given the attitude of villagers (including most of those who favored affiliation) toward priestly prayer, to do so would have been to subject the liturgy to an exercise utterly inconsistent with its sacred authority. Perhaps even more importantly, none of them was even vaguely qualified for the enormously complex task of sifting through the priest's liturgy and comparing its difficult language with Balinese traditions, which were, for the most part, equally inaccessible. The Department of Religion in Surabaya, of course, similarly lacked the scholarly tools to perform this task; it is part of an administrative bureaucracy, not a cultural research team. Finally, for anyone to have proposed such an investigation of the contents of the liturgy would have amounted to a direct challenge to the status and religious authority of the priest, for an end that would have been from the very start unclear. Hence those who favored affiliation concentrated their organizational efforts in enterprises apart from those of the Tengger priest, whom they left for the most part to play his traditional ritual role.

The organizational backbone of the affiliationist movement is known as the *parisada,* an administrative structure directly linked to organizations developed by Balinese in the 1950s to achieve national recognition of their religion. Boon has discussed the Balinese *parisada,* noting that they sought to rationalize traditional Balinese religion primarily through reduction of ritual expense, popular religious education, emphasis on the concept of a monotheistic God above the teaming pantheon of other deities, and the development of a rationally organized religious administration with a sophistication comparable to that of Muslim Indonesians (1977:240). Anyone familiar with the dramaturgical, ritualistic emphases of traditional Balinese religion can immediately appreciate the profundity of these proposed changes (see C. Geertz 1973d). One can also recognize the degree to which the organization and religious emphases of the *parisada* movement were shaped in a nation state dominated by Indonesian Islam.

The first contact of Tengger with *parisada* organization came not in Bali, however, but through the Surabaya-based Department of Religion. This is an important point of detail because, unlike Balinese villagers, for example, Tengger villagers were not familiar with the larger religious milieu in which the *parisada* originated. The Hinduism of which Tengger learned was thus a very streamlined, modernist version, which was so removed from the flesh and blood of popular Balinese religion that it made difficult Tengger recognition of parallels between their religion and that of the Balinese. The *parisada* and elementary school religious teachers who come to Tengger, for example, tell villagers that Balinese cremate their dead, do not circumcise, pray in Sanskrit, have sacred scripture known as the *Weda*, and perform prayer thrice daily. All of these characterizations are true enough of some modern Balinese Hindus. But the Indian Vedas have never been found in traditional Balinese literature (Hooykaas 1964:231); many Balinese do not cremate their dead; and most ritual prayer in Bali is composed both in Kawi-Javanese and Sanskrit. The thrice-daily prayer of which the teachers speak is also a reformist innovation, not a traditional Balinese practice.

None of this detracts from the sincerity or importance of the *parisada* effort. But it has tended to make the movement's appeals remote from the practical emphases of Tengger tradition, and thus has obscured some important parallels between Tengger and Balinese religion. Despite this fact, the *parisada* organization has achieved some genuine organizational successes in Tengger. Villagers have responded eagerly to the *parisada's* instruction that ordinary villagers learn to pray. The prayer they learn, known as the *sembahyang Hindu*, is a Sanskrit chant composed in Bali to serve as a ritual counterpart to the *salat* prayer of Muslims. Coming from south Tengger (where I was still living at the time), I could scarcely believe my eyes the first time I witnessed some 150 school children praying in the Wonokitri *sanggar*. Kneeling devoutly behind the village priest and chief, eyes lowered, ritual flower in hand, and reciting slowly and clearly the Sanskrit prayer they had studied in school, the children displayed a piety in prayer I had never seen any nonpriest adopt. They and their parents took an obvious pride in their ritual role. A new quality of ritual responsibility has been added to the traditional role of lay people in ceremony, and villagers seem genuinely pleased.

The most significant of the reform movement's innovations, however, has been the development of the *parisada* itself. When a village formally declares itself Hindu, one of the first things its leaders must do is appoint two or three men to act as local *parisada*. These men then undergo religious instruction under the supervision of the Hindu bureau in the Department of Religion in Surabaya. A *parisada's* duties include registration of births, marriages, and deaths, the dissemination of religious materials in the schools, and, most conspicuously, educational commentary on religious matters at village rites such as Karo and the *pujan*. This last duty is among the most interesting. It insures that priestly ritual is in at least some instances accompanied by an exegetical commentary that explains the meaning of the rite and its relation to Hindu spiritual belief elsewhere. In the instances that I observed, priests never played this role as *parisada* spokesman. The latter are instead recruited from the ranks of village officials, school teachers, and others from among the educated elite of the community. In a certain sense, therefore, the *parisada's* role is an extension of the traditional ritual role of the Tengger village chief. In the past, it was always the chief rather than the priest who would speak about religious matters during large village rites. The Tengger priest, in other words, continues to act as a ritual specialist and not as a religious educator. The continuing segregation of the priest's role from that of religious spokesman, however, inevitably preserves the distance between the liturgy and popular religious commentary. Moreover, Tengger priests have not for the most part benefited from the religious instruction that *parisada* receive. They remain peripheral to the reform organization, marginal contributors to the religious revitalization.

Perhaps unlike their Balinese counterparts, however, most Tengger *parisada* tend to see themselves as defenders of priestly ritual tradition rather than its reformers. Here again their role is consistent with that of the traditional village chief. With one important exception that I discuss below, Tengger *parisada* have been cautious and discriminating in their interaction with higher level Balinese and Javanese religious officials. They have responded enthusiastically to some innovations—popular prayer, religious education in the elementary schools, and the *parisada* organization itself—but resisted most policies that might tamper with the form of priestly rite itself.

The Hindu religious teachers who began entering Tengger elementary schools in the late 1970s, however, have a more ambivalent attitude toward Tengger tradition, and this attitude has affected some religious policies. At the time of my research (1978-1980), there were no Tengger in the ranks of these teachers. Most were Javanese men from the Blitar region of East Java who had undergone religious instruction at one of the two Hindu teachers' colleges in Indonesia: in Denpasar, Bali, and Blitar, East Java. These youths were first-generation descendants of the Hindu movement that began around Blitar in the 1950s and 1960s, in response to political tensions between syncretic Javanese and orthodox Muslims. What distinguishes these teachers from the Tengger whom they instruct is that they come from areas where, prior to the Hindu Javanese movement itself, there was no priestly or liturgical tradition comparable to that in Tengger. Their understanding of the Tengger situation is thus very limited, usually formulated in terms that reflect the categories they learn in their formal schooling. Hence Tengger priestly rite is a kind of *adat* or local custom, these teachers say, which must be respected as custom but distinguished from true religion (*agama*). The teachers told me that they had been instructed to "go slowly" in

254

"teaching religion" to Tengger. They knew virtually nothing of the content of the Tengger priests' prayers, and lacked both the technical competence and practical opportunity to learn otherwise. The religious teachers' views on Tengger tradition are thus at odds with those of most village *parisada*.

They are not at odds with the *parisada* in all communities, however. In one northwestern village, the local *parisada* were influenced by Balinese *parisada* and the religious teachers to adopt a radically new policy with regard to priestly liturgy. The *parisada* convinced the village chief that religious growth in Tengger was moving too slowly, and it was time to substitute genuine religious prayers and rites for the *adat* ceremonies conducted by the Tengger priest. Hence a new policy was adopted: for those rites deemed truly "religious" (*agama*), the Tengger priest's traditional prayers were to be discarded and replaced with prayers brought by the *parisada* from Bali. The religious ceremonies in which this substitution would occur were weddings, the *entas-entas*, the four village *pujan*, and *galungan*. Other rites traditionally performed by the Tengger priest (including, astonishingly, both Karo and Kasada) were said to be *adat* or customary ritual. Hence the Tengger priest could continue to perform them as before, using the old prayers. One purpose of this policy was to reduce ritual costs. The rites brought from Bali were smaller and less expensive than those traditionally used in Tengger, and the village chief saw this reduction in expense as a necessary step for the economic development of the village. The larger purpose of the ritual revision, however, was doctrinal. *Adat* custom is not religion; and the Tengger priest's liturgy was deemed *adat*. The *parisada* in this village explained to me that there was also another problem. People did not "sufficiently understand" the old prayers; not even the priest could explain what they were about.

The ironies of the revisionists' argument are of course enormous. The distinction between "custom" and "religion" which they used in downgrading the importance of the traditional liturgy was the very same distinction that Javanese Muslims had long sought to impose on Tengger, and that most Tengger had resisted. In developing organizational and doctrinal principles to advance their struggle, the Balinese *parisada* had, in effect, incorporated this distinction into their religious policies and then sought to introduce it into Tengger. Islamic doctrinal categories finally entered Tengger religion through a cultural back door. There was another irony to the revisionists' effort. Although they claimed to have discarded the old prayers in part because no one really understood what they meant, the new prayers brought by the *parisada* only replicated this problem, as my conversation with the priest in the village concerned indicated.

I asked Pak Legari about the new, Balinese prayers he uses now in the *entas-entas*. Had he had an opportunity to study them with *parisada* officials? No, he explained with some embarrassment. He had only received instruction on which offerings to use in the rite, what gestures to make, and when to recite different prayers. He and his assistants (whom he referred to as *nayaka*, a Balinese term) memorized the prayers, but they were very difficult to understand, because the prayer language contained much Sanskrit and Old Javanese. Pak Legari showed me a sample of the prayer book, and I could see that its language was more difficult than that used in most prayers in the liturgy.

It is hard to describe the bitterness that the ritual revision has provoked in other villages of the Tengger northwest. Even the most ardent enthusiasts of the Hindu reform movement have denounced the policy. The senior priest in the Tengger northwest, one of the earliest priestly supporters of the affiliation movement, tried to call a meeting of priests to forbid the change in the liturgy. His effort failed, however, in part because there was no institutional precedent for priests from different villages interfering in the religious policy of one another. The elder priest's reaction to the ritual revision was interesting, however, for it revealed how one man's involvement in the affiliation movement had led to his reinterpretation of the ritual tradition.

This elder priest, whom I will call Pak Wagiman, was an intense, intelligent figure whose life spanned most of this century's cultural turmoil in Tengger. Pak Wagiman had never been circumcised, because his father (also a priest) had been one among a handful of priests in the northwest who rejected the practice as Islamic. That same man had been in the forefront of the opposition to the Ajisaka and Mohammad tale, viewing the account as tainted with Islamic beliefs. Pak Wagiman's grandfather was among the last Tengger priests well versed in the reading of old *kropak* books. Pak Wagiman's father had learned the skill much less fluently, but he had endeavored to transcribe the old prayers into modern Javanese script. As a consequence of his efforts, Pak Wagiman today had what was perhaps the richest corpus of priestly prayer and literature in all Tengger. He had several thick notebooks of writings— prayers for rites no longer performed, old myths recited by his father and grandfather, variant forms of the liturgy, and bits and pieces of prayers he had learned from Central Javanese visitors to his village or mystic *dalang* puppeteers from the nearby lowlands. Pak Wagiman was, in every sense of the word, an intellectual, in a village world that accorded little public role to intellectuals. As a youth, he was among the first generation of villagers to receive Dutch education. He was the only villager from his generation to have gone on to middle school, where he received extensive instruction in Christian theology. In speaking with me about Tengger religion, he would often make polite digressions, making sure that he had made his point by drawing a parallel or pointing out a contrast between his religious tradition and mine.

When the family of a priest in a nearby village converted to Islam, leaving no son to assume the elder priest's role, it was Pak Wagiman who was called in to train a replacement. When village chiefs in the northwest began to discuss the possibility of affiliation with Balinese Hinduism, priests from villages in the region quietly came to him, trying to decide what their attitude should be. Pak Wagiman responded cautiously. He had never been to Bali, never witnessed Balinese ritual, and, as he put it, considered himself "Javanese, not Balinese." Yet village leaders seemed prepared to move ahead on the affiliation policy without bothering to win the approval of local priests. Pak Wagiman remained quiet, biding his time. A visit by a Balinese priest to the Tengger northwest finally provided him with the opportunity he had hoped for. He asked to meet with the priest one afternoon, to speak with him privately. During the encounter, Pak Wagiman did what he often did with religious visitors to the region: he asked the man to recite his prayers, and then listen to those of a Tengger priest. The result of this chance meeting, Pak Wagiman explained, changed his life:

"I realized that the *dewa* Balinese worship are those that we in our prayers address." He then proceded to show me what he meant, reciting a long portion of a Balinese prayer he had memorized during his meeting with the Balinese visitor, and then reciting a Tengger prayer which contained the names of many of the same deities. "These were the words of our ancestors," he exclaimed. "And they are Hindu. Today, even if I go to the lowlands, I say out loud that I am Hindu. Even in Pasuruan, I will tell people that I am Hindu." Pak Wagiman explained that there had always been things in his prayers that he did not understand. He had bought books on mysticism in the lowlands, listened to *wayang* puppetry on the radio, and talked with religious visitors to mountain Tengger, all in an effort to understand the meaning of his prayers. But their meaning became clear only after his meeting with the Balinese. "How would you expect us to understand all that we learn as priests," he said, "after centuries of not knowing other Hindus?"

Even among priests, of course, Pak Wagiman's experience is distinctive. He is one of the brightest and best educated of priests. He has probably the richest assortment of prayers owned by any Tengger priest. And he has always had an intellectual passion for resolving the unanswered questions posed by the liturgy to which he is heir. In a profound way, however, Pak Wagiman's experience was indicative of more general changes of interpretation experienced by at least some of the participants in the Hindu reform movement. Their social universe had expanded. The range of ideas they brought to bear on Tengger tradition now included more than knowledge of shared ways or traditional public commentaries. Their growing knowledge of Balinese tradition and Javanese history was adding new depth to the traditional notion that Buda Tengger and Buda Bali were, in some unfathomable way, brethren.

Pak Wagiman's example also indicates, however, the limitations of the reform movement in revitalizing Tengger tradition. Although he had perhaps the most sophisticated awareness of Tengger and Balinese religion of any priest or villager, he had no forum through which to communicate his knowledge, and no authority to intervene in the programs of the *parisada*. Pak Wagiman was simply a retired and respected priestly elder; *parisada* officials could not possibly know why what he knew was important for Tengger Hinduism. The reform movement had preserved the long-standing segregation of priestly and secular authority in the formulation of religious policy. Priests are responsible for the recitation of the liturgy, not for its explanation. Pak Wagiman's authority was even limited in relation to other priests. His attempts to stop the replacement of the traditional Tengger liturgy with Balinese ritual forms met with failure:

> Pak Wagiman looked visibly distressed when I asked him about the neighboring village's revision of traditional liturgy. "Do they not understand that Tengger prayers invoke Hindu dewa?" he exclaimed. "Do we not refer to Iswara, Brahma, Mahadewa, Visnu, and Siva? These people do not understand what they are doing because they do not understand the prayers." Many priests, he said, were too young and inexperienced with the liturgy to understand the gravity of the change. "To understand the prayers may take many years." Why had the priest in the neighboring village gone along with the ritual revisions, I asked? "The priest is just a villager," Pak Wagiman explained, "so when village leaders make a decision, he must obey like a villager."

Conclusion: Social Change and Religious Reform

They make peculiar bedfellows, this alliance of Balinese reformists and Tengger mountain folk. The dispute over prayer reform illustrates the tensions between the policies of the two groups. The Balinese *parisada* had intended that the prayer reform initiated in the one Tengger community would be carried out in all Hindu villages of the region. Tengger *adat* had to be "perfected" (*disempurnakan*) by introducing true religion (*agama*) into its ritual forms. The great majority of Tengger *parisada*, however, have balked at the proposal, effectively preventing its application to other villages now for almost ten years. They have reacted enthusiastically to *parisada* programs that expand religious activity to include education and popular prayer. But they have consistently hesitated to rework existing priestly rite. It is for them already religious.

The changes introduced by the Tengger *parisada* are genuine nonetheless, and promise to guide religious development in much of the region over the next generation. The problems confronting the movement are great. It is unclear, for example, whether the remaining Buda priests will join forces with their Hindu brethren. Hence, as the programs for education and religious reform gather momentum, the cultural distance between Hindu and Buda Tengger may become dangerously large. One senses, moreover, that the resistance of some Buda priests may not be entirely ideological. At least some of the hold-outs are located in communities more radically affected by nineteenth-century immigration than was the Tengger northwest. These are communities in which the tale of Ajisaka and Mohammad is still popularly regarded as the only definitive charter on the relation of Tengger to Islam. Were the priest or village chief to go ahead with Hindu affiliation, some villagers might defect, rejecting Tengger religion entirely. One senses this may be a fear among some Buda priests.

Overpopulation, landlessness, and increasing economic differentiation within communities may also erode the sense of common ways and ancestral solidarity upon which Tengger religion traditionally relied. In this light, some of the *parisada*'s more radical reforms may begin to have greater appeal. Even Buda Tengger spoke to me at times of the need to reduce ritual expense so that more villagers could afford to sponsor rites. As new and more expensive forms of nonritual consumption compete for the limited resources of households (Hefner 1983b), and as social prestige comes to be expressed in ways other than ritual lavishness alone, less economically demanding forms of religious devotion—like the prayer gatherings already popular in Wonokitri—may

be greeted with enthusiasm. In communities increasingly internally differentiated, emphasis on religious education and explicit doctrine may
take precedence over the diffuse and less discursive imperatives of shared
ancestral ways.

From the perspective of these recent developments, it is not surprising
that the reform movement arose in the Tengger northwest, and that its
proponents were village chiefs and more cosmopolitan members of the
village elite. The northwest was the first portion of Tengger territory
to be linked by road to the lowlands (around 1910), well over one-half
century before road construction elsewhere in the region. It was in the
northwest that Dutch enterprises (hotels, a dairy farm, sanitariums) were
most active, and where agricultural innovations have almost always
begun. The northwest's interaction with the surrounding society has at
the same time been more bounded and controlled than that experienced
elsewhere in Tengger. The northwest was never overwhelmed by lowland immigrants, largely because by the time the immigration process
gathered steam in the nineteenth century, this region was already the
most densely populated in Tengger. Fewer communities in this region
experienced the bitterly divisive conflicts between Buda and Islam seen
in communities like Besuki. Finally, and not insignificantly, *kabupaten*
regency officials in the Pasuruan region here seem since independence
to have adopted a more sympathetic attitude toward Tengger religion
than has sometimes been the case in other regions of Tengger. They
have encouraged Tengger contacts with non-Muslim organizations, and
supported Tengger efforts to attain recognition as a legitimate religious
community. The consequences of this social history are evident today
not only in the Hindu reform movement but in the fact that people from
the northwest tend to be more self-confidently "Tengger" than their
counterparts in other areas of the highlands. At the same time, they are
more comfortable in speaking Indonesian and *kromo* Javanese, pursuing
higher education in the lowlands, and discussing aspects of their religious
tradition.

What does the Tengger example say about social change and religious
reform? Leaders in the northwest took the lead in promoting the affiliation movement in large part because they, as village representatives
before the national administration, were keenly aware of the political
and cultural ambiguities of locally based religion in modern Indonesia.
In certain respects there is a parallel between their position and that of
the African traders discussed by Horton, who choose to convert to Islam
or Christianity so as to move more easily from the village into the larger
society. In keeping with his neo-intellectualist perspective on religion,
Horton suggests that the advantage of conversion in such circumstances

is that the doctrines of world religions provide ready-made cosmological tools with which to handle the intellectual challenges posed by a person's involvement in a vastly expanded and unfamiliar social terrain. The religious thought of small-scale societies, Horton suggests, also provides a "theoretical" framework for the "explanation, prediction, and control of space time events" (1971:94). Since most people in such societies live their lives in the familiar world of small communities, however, the spirits invoked as theoretical entities to explain the intellectual challenges of the world tend to be conceptualized in rather parochial, localistic, terms—ancestral spirits, territorial guardians, nature deities. The traditional religions of tribal or small-scale societies may have the concept of an all-embracing supreme being, Horton notes, but such a deity becomes the object of real intellectual attention only when people move out of small villages into a larger social macrocosm of unfamiliar peoples, territories, and customs. At that point, Horton suggests, the local spirits of traditional cosmology cease to have a sufficiently encompassing explanatory range. Hence deities defined in more global, overarching terms are called into intellectual service, since they alone are sufficiently general to be applicable to the widened social horizon.

The intellectualist perspective on cosmological change is interesting because it draws our attention to something that often does seem to accompany the incorporation of small communities into larger social, political, and cultural orders: the development of (or greater emphasis on) more generally phrased doctrines, explicit statements of belief, and expansive spiritual cosmologies. The question is whether this development is, as the intellectualist argument would have it, primarily motivated by the need to develop "theoretical" tools to explain and control events in a now larger world. What such a view risks neglecting is the way in which cultural beliefs and habits themselves become politicized as symbols of identity and difference with a people's increasing involvement in a larger social "macrocosm." Even in the smallest and most isolated societies, of course, customs play a political role as indices of political and ethnic distinction. Political incorporation exacerbates this problem tremendously, however, and presents a kind of moral and political challenge quite different from the "explanation and control" described in intellectualist accounts of religion. Cultural legitimation becomes a central preoccupation, and a good deal of the "intellectual" attention of the standard bearers of a minority religious tradition may be devoted to responding to the challenge of the dominant religious community.

This process is clearly illustrated here in Tengger. From the perspective of its intellectual concerns, the movement for Hindu affiliation was at first a largely defensive initiative. It sought to develop the vocabulary whereby an already existing religious tradition could be rendered legitimate in the eyes of the cultural managers of the surrounding society. It was only after its inception that the reform movement began to promote fundamental changes in existing religious belief. The crisis that promoted the movement's appearance, in other words, was primarily one of legitmacy and survival, not intellectual coherence as such. The doctrinal reforms it helped introduce were stipulated not by internal intellectual criteria, but by the standards of the dominant religious community in a nation of which Tengger were, willy nilly, very much part. Explanation and control—at least the sort of which intellectualist theoreticians speak—were here less important than a political economy of religious culture.

This is not to minimize the real changes that may have occurred in Tengger religious belief over the past century. The Hindu reform movement was but the latest in a series of developments that had shaken the tradition over the past few decades, and many of these earlier adjustments showed signs of genuine intellectual adjustment or rationalization. There is an important theoretical lesson here. The example suggests that we need to exercise caution in making too rigid a distinction between "traditional" and so-called "rationalized" or "world" religions, as brilliantly but all too expansively conceived in Weber's (1956) religious sociology. In discussing the differences between small-scale and "world" religion, it is more helpful to begin by examining the differing constraints of social scale and cultural diversity to which the two traditions respond, rather than beginning with a distinction that from the start identifies rationalization as the distinctive characteristic of world religion. The latter approach, a Weberian one, lends itself all too easily to modern ideological bias, and risks obscuring the fact that religious rationalization—the reordering of beliefs in a fashion consistent with new social experiences—occurs at different times in the religions of all societies. Surely there has been no lack of assessment and doctrinal adjustment here in Tengger over the past century. If we are to employ an ideal-type dichotomy to discuss different religions, a more useful distinction is not rationalization per se, but social scale, cultural diversity, and the constraints each of these impose on the formulation of religious appeals.

By definition, world religions span a variety of ethnic, political, and linguistic communities. This almost trivially apparent aspect of their social organization imposes communicative and ideological constraints quite different from those characteristic of small-scale societies. Religion in the former instance cannot assume a simple isomorphism between the community of faithful and the social world of everyday life. A world religion, in other words, must to some degree create a kind of secondary identity, capable at least in theory of linking people otherwise distinguished by more primordial allegiances of speech, custom, and interaction. Many of the distinctive cultural features of world religions seem shaped by this social contingency. They proclaim the truth of holy scripture, pronounce universal commandments, and elevate prophets and divinities for all humanity. People from diverse territories and polities are enjoined to recognize a single holy land. By elevating religion above local social terrains, world religions attempt to articulate a more generalized, elaborated code capable of shaping a religious allegiance above the clamoring diversity of restricted social groupings and local ways of speech. In practice, of course, this universal imperative is in tension with the social reality of world religions. Whatever their appeal to a unitary truth, the fact remains that they are professed by men and women educated to truths more diverse than the doctrines of religion alone. Whatever the claim of world religions to a single community of faithful, the fact remains that they are institutionalized in political worlds animated by needs and imperatives other than those of the faith alone. To whatever degree it is a cultural reality, however, the unitary appeal of world religious doctrines is not trivial. It distinguishes these religions from those of most tribal societies, and is a structuring force in their historical development.

Throughout most of its recent history, Tengger religion did not have to build a community across an enormous social expanse, but was able to ground its appeals on the more general, and largely unspoken sensibilities born of common life ways in a restricted social terrain. It was the depth and breadth of religion's weave here, as in many local traditions, which in some sense placed the tradition above the need for explicitly formulated statements of doctrine. Religious truth lay in *ngaluri*, all that is preserved in the present by virtue of its origin in the ancestral past. *Ngaluri* did not define a neatly prescribed religious domain, but evoked the ideas and emotions of a diffuse but shared social existence. Common socialization here bore the burden of doctrinal elaboration. It is important to note, however, that there was little about this tradition which was unchanging or "irrational," as the "traditional religion" label sometimes suggests. In the Kasada myth, the Ajisaka tale, and other cultural documents, there was evidence of an ongoing effort to reorder shared beliefs in the face of changing social realities. On this point, the ideal-type dichotomy of "traditional" and "world" religions is too crude. We must remind ourselves that the utility of such characterizations lies in the social and historical processes to which they point, not in the delineation of two empirically tidy dichotomous types.

Tengger, for example, may never have been a politically autonomous "traditional" society, and its religion was never merely "local." Originating in a dialogue with Java's earlier Indic community, and later molded by the challenge of Islam, Tengger religion, like so many in modern world history, fits neither of the two ideal types. Like other religious traditions nurtured at the margins of larger societies, it is something else, and can only be understood by recognizing the formative importance of its interaction with the surrounding society. Tengger has always been very much part of Java.

The development of Tengger religious culture thus illustrates many of the dynamics of religious change in Java as a whole. The collapse of the island's Hindu-Buddhist states destroyed the political foundation for what had once been an islandwide Hindu religious community. Tengger had been part of that community, and its priestly tradition quite clearly shows that at least the Sivaite-Hindu community had sunk its roots into the countryside (see Appendix). In the centuries following Majapahit's collapse, however, Java's Hindu-Buddhist ecclesiastical communities slowly disappeared. Their sources of court patronage were eliminated, and no doubt so too were many of the literary and aesthetic traditions upon which the cultural intelligibility of their appeals depended. Elements of the Indic heritage survived, of course, and, particularly in isolated areas of the Eastern Salient, some Buda priests appear to have continued operating right up to the present century. Moreover, throughout even Islamic Java, village traditions preserved cults of founding ancestors and territorial spirits, a religious cosmology consonant with the political realities of a loosely integrated rural society and with the practical preoccupations of peasantry. The exemplary influence of Java's courts, regional and insular commerce, and the growth of the Islamic community itself, however, all created the social foundation for a less parochial religious tradition, and thus nurtured the continuing growth of Islam. These developments climaxed in the nineteenth century, when colonial penetration, the demise of the traditional aristocracy, and improved communications with the rest of the Islamic world (Kartodirdjo 1972; Ricklefs 1981) created the conditions for the construction of a new national identity, in which a revitalized Islam would, for many people, be a key term. From the perspective of the Tengger mountains, there can be no doubt but that one of the most important processes of the past century has been the uneven but powerfully continuous Islamization of vast areas of Java's countryside.

Although its social organization was primarily anchored in the village, it is important to remember that the cultural appeal of Tengger religion was never purely local. It too sought to identify with a religious community beyond its own borders. Even when they spoke of ancestors and territory, Tengger continued to refer to their religion as *agama Buda*, the religion of Old Java, the religion, so they thought, of non-Muslim Javanese. This appeal to a larger religious community was still heard in the Ajisaka myth. There Tengger tradition was presented as kindred with all that established by Ajisaka, the Javanese culture hero. Or so it was hoped—the formula for an alliance between Tengger and other non- or nominally Islamic Javanese foundered in the face of modern realities and Java's continuing Islamization.

The Hindu reform movement in Tengger, therefore, is not the first effort to link Tengger to a larger religious community, and it will not bring about cultural rationalization where previously there was none. The movement is only the most recent expression of tendencies implicit in this Javanese people's entire history. Today's appeal, of course, addresses the complex realities of contemporary Indonesia, where cultural accountability is demanded in national rather than regional terms. The reform movement is a response to this demand. A religious vocabulary and social identity are being constructed simultaneously. The new religious dialect is less directly dependent upon the density of local interaction and the unspoken assumptions of customary ways. A sense of religious solidarity with Balinese, Central Javanese Hindus, or, for that matter, Indian Hinduism cannot be built up from the intimate realities of greetings exchanged Tengger style, conversation shared around kitchen fires, or drinking and dancing with the ancestors. Although still vital, such sensibilities will now be supplemented with instruction in a more general religious vocabulary, richer perhaps in discursive injunctions, because necessarily poorer in the shared life ways and unspoken sensibilities upon which more restricted religious communities can, and do, build their faith.

· 12 ·

CONCLUSION

Tengger tradition provides a curious variation on the themes of Indic influence in Southeast Asia. Much of the most characteristic Indic symbolism is visible, but always reworked in a fashion consistent with the popular history of the region. Cultural space is focused, for example, on a *meru* sacred mountain, a meeting place between gods and humans (von Heine Geldern 1942; Hall 1981:245; C. Geertz 1980:114). But no royalty has superimposed itself on this *meru*. The mountain is home instead to a deified ancestor from whom all Tengger are said to have descended. The same folk variation on Indic themes occurs, as we have seen, in village and household ceremony. The annual all-souls festival (Karo) shows parallels with Prapanca's fourteenth-century description of the ritual invocation of Majapahit's queen mother to a *puspa* flower figurine; the queen's spirit descends to the earth for several days, and is honored throughout with food, drink, and dance (Pigeaud 1962:IV:183). In her presence, Pigeaud has commented, "all humans were considered equals" (1962:IV:193). Karo involves similar ritual patterns, but the ancestry it invokes is always collective, and the celebration is communally sponsored. Household ritual shows a similar concern with village and ancestral spirits. Their invocation in priestly rite, it is thought, insures the welfare of the living, the abundance of the earth, and the flow of life-giving water upon which all things depend.

It is impossible to say with absolute certainty how popular religion in modern Tengger differs from its Old Javanese progenitor. The fall of Majapahit marked a turning point in Javanese civilization, and created the conditions that led eventually to the dilemmas of modern Tengger. Java's Eastern Salient was Balkanized into small pockets of folk tradition, lacking the regional integration to some degree afforded by earlier Hindu-Buddhist courts. In the north coast and Central Java, Islam—albeit a local variety—became the religion of state. The Hindu-Buddhist ecclesiastical communities once dispersed throughout Java's countryside gradually disappeared. Tengger remained to provide testimony to earlier priestly ways, but its isolation in an Islamizing Java made it destined to increasing doubt and problems of self-definition. The region lacked the courts, castes, and religious scholars of neighboring Bali. It had few dramatic arts that might familiarize villagers with a spiritual cosmology similar to that encoded in priestly liturgy. The maintenance of the

tradition was thus characterized less by popular fidelity to formal doctrines than by commitment to that which stood above explicit doctrine:
a sense of shared social ways, symbolized in religious appeal to collective
ancestors. The specialized liturgy of the priest was drawn into a more
general religious process, and identified as the spiritual foundation for
society's natural and social continuity.

It was not the force of cultural meanings alone, however, that focused
this people on their ritual tradition. The ritual tradition was embedded
in a larger system of social practice. The roles of priest and chief, ritual
savings and exchange, restrictions on agricultural production and consumption, the role of religious festivals in the expression of social status—these and other things combined to create a system in which ritual
performance was but the culmination of general social rhythms. There
was an ongoing and reflexive interaction between social activity in these
upland farming communities and cultural ideas as to the populist nature
of Tengger identity and the role of the priesthood in it. The interaction
helped to recreate a social environment in which received cultural truths
as to the ancestral nature of the tradition appeared consonant with the
communitarian contours of social reality. Social practice and cultural
ideas seemed marvelously well integrated one with the other; or so it
seemed in those communities where the tradition was preserved. In a
changing Java, however, the processes sustaining ritual reproduction
could be undermined with small shifts in consumption, a change of
village leadership, or the erosion of popular faith. "Change, or its po-
tentiality, is thus inherent in all moments of social reproduction" (Giddens 1979:114), because society is animated by forces more complex
than the intentions of its actors, and cultural meaning is dependent upon
more than received symbolism.

To understand Tengger tradition has therefore required that we move
beyond simple hermeneutic appreciation of its meanings to an investigation of the social and historical conditions that made certain shared
meanings possible and others mysteries better left unsaid. Central among
those historical conditions was, of course, the ongoing Islamization of
Java, especially the growth of a revitalized rural Islam in the nineteenth
and twentieth centuries. Within Tengger society itself, however, the
ritual tradition was socially organized in such a way that the cultural
impact of these developments was uneven. Popular notions as to the
nature of the tradition were constructed in the course of an ongoing
dialogue with the surrounding society. The liturgy itself, however, was
sustained in a very different social field, in which literacy, restricted
social access, and a socialized faith helped to give the formal terms of
the liturgy a fixity that popular religious culture lacked. This dual econ-

omy of cultural knowledge allowed the tradition to shape and accommodate the challenge of an Islamizing Java. By cloistering the liturgy, however, it also made the tradition's popular significance problematic.

The reproductive logic of this arrangement helped to explain problems of meaning which, viewed from a symbolic perspective alone, might have appeared anomalous. Had we assumed, for example, that ritual culture was uniformly integrated, its symbolism equally accessible to all actors, the (now very much qualified) discontinuity between priestly liturgy and popular commentary would have remained an anomaly. In the face of such a dilemma, one might invoke the principle of symbolic "plurivocality," insisting that the different meanings attributed to the same rites formed one more example of how cultural symbols can mean different things to different people. Such a response substitutes a theoretical generality for real explanation, however, and would have severed an important line of inquiry into the way in which the social channels through which knowledge is transmitted affect who is likely to have what kind of experience. The Tengger example requires us to recognize, in other words, that there is a distributional aspect to cultural knowledge, one which insures that not everyone in the same society need have the same understanding of public symbols and actions.

As soon as one moves away from a "resolutely separatist approach" (Eickelman 1978:512) which assumes that cultural knowledge is something flawlessly coherent and equally accessible to all, and instead examines cultural knowledge as something subject to differing modes of distribution and control, the lack of integration seen between priestly liturgy and popular experience seems not only less anomalous but, in an entirely unintentional sense, adaptive. Tengger could claim no cultural autonomy from larger Java. Although their social organization allowed the priest to continue to perform his liturgies, their position in larger Java insured they could not ignore the island's far-reaching changes. As Sperber (1975) has noted, explicit and expressly imparted knowledge, like that of the priest's liturgy or the Ajisaka myth, makes sense only inasmuch as it is the object of an underlying tacit knowledge. It is this fact which insures that cultural meaning is never simply "internalized," and cultural symbolism is never just a vehicle conveying prefigured truths. The actor must add something, must construct an understanding by engaging in an interpretive work that depends not only upon explicit public symbolism, but upon intuitions and tacit knowledge informed by a much wider and ongoing experience. The visible part of a rite, the audible part of a myth, make sense only in light of something invisible or unheard in the cultural artifact. In modern Tengger, these tacit intuitions were shaped in a social environment quite different from that of fourteenth-century Majapahit. Hence in a Java that no longer spoke of *resi pujangga*, the Tengger priest came to be known as a *dukun*. In a Java no longer awed by a *meru* scared mountain, the Kasada myth identified Mt. Bromo as a *punden* shrine to a first-founding ancestor. Public references to Brahma, Visnu, and Siva were by the end of the nineteenth century silenced in favor of a myth that spoke of a pact between Ajisaka and Mohammad. The Java in which the *resi pujangga's* liturgy originated no longer existed. The institutional arrangements that supported the ritual tradition could better insure the transmission of priestly liturgy than they could its unchanging interpretation by a wider public. The very institutions insuring the liturgy's preservation also insured its limited role in a changing popular culture. The priest was thus left quietly to experience a more complex spiritual vision.

The priest's experience is surely "cultural" in the sense that the liturgy's forms are socially transmitted, and the priest comes to their encounter with culturally informed sensibilities as to how he should understand what he will see and hear. But an individual's experience of any cultural medium, any rite or proverb, any political event, is never a finished social fact. To speak then, as I have done in this work, of social or meaningful action is not to posit an automatic identity between action-in-the-world, the public idioms that describe it, and the actual experience of actors who see and hear both. At times in ethnographic reporting it may be convenient or necessary to speak as if social experience were unambiguously homogeneous. But even the most public and conventionalized of cultural media—myths, liturgies, ideological charters—are never conveyed as finished meanings, their significance specified from within. A symbol, a rite, or an utterance alone is not yet a "meaning"; a signifier becomes a signified only inasmuch as there is a human being, with a biography and socialization, to make sense of it. The interpretation of cultures can thus never hope for the closure of a Hegelian mind, for meaning originates not in the immutable essence of significant objects, but in the efforts of real people disposing of diverse competences to make sense of their world. To recognize the complexity of cultural interpretation need not lead to a pessimistic resignation in the face of other minds the experience of which is inexhaustible. Our claim is not to absolute knowledge but to intelligibility. The analysis of society and meaning thus moves in two directions. The one is toward the examination of everyday practical reasoning, and the cognitive mechanisms it assumes. The other, the approach I have found useful in the present work, is outward from the individual and collectivities toward history and society, which is to say, toward the conditions that socialize actors and thus shape the intuitions they bring to bear on received

269

cultural forms. Such analysis can never exhaust human experience, but it can help bring it within range of intelligibility.

In all human experience there is this confrontation between public cultural forms and socially informed but individually reconstructed knowledge and intuition. What is fascinating about this process in Tengger is that the social organization of the ritual tradition insured that much of the priest's interpretive work would not, and in a certain sense could not, be tapped as a source of public truth. Tengger has long been all too much part of Java. In most of recent history, therefore, the Tengger priest has been in the awkward position of directly experiencing a complex cultural object, the truth of which he has been enjoined not to reveal.

I sensed somethings of the priest's dilemma, the burden of his solitary knowledge, in my conversations with Pak Wagiman (Chapter 11), and in particular in a prayer that he kindly gave to me as a parting gift my last week in his village. I had spent long hours around kitchen fires with Pak Wagiman, engaging in the gently unfocused discussion considered polite between guest and host. Like most other priests, Pak Wagiman was generally reluctant to discuss the contents of prayers directly, since he regarded their utterance as a holy act. Yet he was always sensitive to my inquiries, and, so I thought at times, eager to discuss matters for which he had no other forum. He was the rare sort of individual who stands out in any society—nowhere to go with his uneasy brilliance, driven by an exhausting interior monologue; out of step, in short, with the casual good nature of his Tengger cohorts. As always, he gave me the prayer with only the briefest comment. It was clear, however, that the prayer was intended as a parting gift, one which, I suspected, said something about his vision of a world about which he could say little further:

> Hong! *pekulun* I watch the *wayang* puppetry of Lord Guru. It is he who guides the puppet shadows, and heavenly spirits who play the *gamelan*. Holy shadows on the screen, hey! The audience is drawn tense with the movement. Yet there are no people at that moment, invisible are those who watch invisible. The movement is exciting and the handwork deft. The audience is drawn into the play, but what they see is invisible an illusion those who watch invisible those who watch invisible.

APPENDIX

Resi *Priesthood in Tengger and Bali, a Comparative Note*

I have not attempted in the present work to make a systematic comparison of Tengger and Balinese ritual tradition. Since the analysis has raised questions on the history and origins of the Tengger priesthood, however, it may be worthwhile to add a brief and somewhat speculative comment on parallels between the Tengger priest and a similar Balinese celebrant, the *resi bujangga*. The comparison suggests that there are indeed important and direct relationships between Tengger and Bali, and summarizes rather neatly the contrast between popular Indic tradition in Bali and that in a Java becoming Islamic.

In the *purwabumi* prayer (Chapter 8), the Tengger priest is referred to as a *resi pujangga*. A simiar title (*resi bujangga*) is still today used in modern Bali to refer to a popular ritual celebrant who bears strong resemblance to the Tengger priest. The Balinese *resi* is a low-caste (that is, non-Brahman and non-*triwangsa*) or commoner priest. He performs no courtly ritual, but serves the 93 percent of the Balinese population of commoner caste (Hooykaas 1964:243). The *resi* role is restricted to people of *sengguhu* birth, a commoner title group, but only those *sengguhu* actually ordained as priests are said to be *resi bujangga*. Like high-caste *pedanda* priests, the *resi bujangga* is privileged to prepare holy water—mainstay of Balinese ritual—and is also entitled to wear a priestly robe and mitre (Hooykaas 1973:15).The specialty for which the *resi* is most famous, however, is his role as exorcist of demons in the annual ritual day of silence (*nyepi*). In the course of these ceremonies, high-caste priests give worship to the Indic gods of the heavens while, just to the side of them, *resi bujangga* priests present offerings to the demons of the lower world. The *resi's* services are said to banish these demons from villages around the island for another year (Hooykaas 1974:53; Covarrubias 1937:281).

What makes the *resi's* role of such comparative interest is that it is here that he recites the "prayer of world origins" (*purwabumi*) also found, in a somewhat shorter form, in the Tengger purification of the dead (*entas-entas*, Chapter 9). Comparision of the two prayers reveals line-by-line parallels that are nothing less than astounding, given the fact that Balinese and Tengger tradition have probably not had direct cultural contacts for several hundred years. The prayer provides com-

271

pelling evidence of a direct link in earlier times between the two ritual traditions.

In the present discussion, however, I am primarily interested in the more general identity attributed to the Balinese *resi*. As in Tengger, there is in Bali a ritual divison of labor related to the type of spirits different specialists are qualified to address. The *pedanda* or high-caste priest addresses higher and more consistently "Indic" world deities. At least in the presence of *pedanda*, by contract, the *resi bujangga* is identified as a specialist for "dedicating the offerings to the evil spirits" (Covarrubias 1937:281), or more precisely, spirits of the lower world. Given the paucity of literature on the Balinese *resi*, it is difficult to determine if this characterization is that of high-status priests, ethnographic observers, or the *resi* himself. There is some evidence to suggest that the *resi* is at times involved with the worship of upper-world deities as well. The *resi* prepares holy water, after all, an activity that presumes the ability to invoke beneficent upper-world deities. Hooykaas offhandedly comments, in addition, that when the *resi bujangga* is not in the presence of *pedanda* "one should not be astonished" (which is to say that it is astonishing, given the *resi*'s identification as a lower-world specialist) to see him perform ceremonies elsewhere associated with high-status *pedanda* (Hooykaas 1973:16).

The best evidence that the Balinese *resi* is not exclusively concerned with the spiritual netherworld is the *purwabumi* prayer itself. As in the Tengger priest's version of this prayer, the *resi*'s work is here clearly identified with the transmutation of the demon gods Kala and Durga back into their beneficent form as Siva and Uma. This goal is accomplished in the course of a long account that links the transformation to the very origins of the world and its ever-present balance of spirit forces. "Exorcism" occurs, but it is not a simple act of exorcism, as one might expect after having heard that the *resi* is a specialist of netherworld spirits. The *resi*'s rite is as much concerned with elevated Indic spirits as any *pedanda*'s ceremony, at least to judge by the evidence of the *resi*'s prayers.

So why is the Balinese *resi* identified with the lower world? And what does his identity say about Tengger and Bali? It is impossible to say with absolute certainty exactly how the Tengger and Balinese *resi* may have once been related. Equally importantly, whatever identity each priest may have had five centuries ago would have depended on the relationship of each to other categories of priests in the countryside and courts. On this point precise ethnohistorical data is lacking.

There is an additional clue, however, as to the earlier identity of the

Tengger priest. Besides the title of *resi pujangga*, Tengger priests could, until quite recently, receive another ritual title, the *baru* or *tiyang baru* ("*baru* person"). This title was restricted to those men who underwent an initiation ceremony late in life, the purpose of which was to allow one to "die and be reborn," purified of all sin. Priests who knew of the ceremony compared its purfication to an *entas-entas*, saying it was like being purified in an *entas-entas* before death. The *baru* ceremony is no longer practiced, and I came across it in field work only in the course of tracking down some related historical information in discussions with elderly villagers. The eldest priest in the Tengger south said that the rite was last performed in the 1930s; he lost his father's prayer notes for the rite in 1946, when Dutch forces swept through the village and burned a field hut in which an assortment of holy texts had been stored. His own efforts to obtain copies of the prayer ended in failure. Northern priests (as my own inquiries confirmed) told him they had never heard of the ceremony; one southern priest had, but he had lost the prayers for the rite several decades back, during a crisis related to the village chief's conversion to Islam. According to both priests' accounts, priests and—the ritual alliance theme again—village chiefs could undergo the *baru* ceremony. If this is true, it makes less clear just what the relation is between the *baru* and *resi* roles; clearly one is not exclusively a priestly role. What is clear about the *baru* role in Tengger however, is that it entailed specific spiritual privileges. *Baru* people were the only ones whose souls were allowed to ascend to Mt. Semeru at death; ordinary priests and villagers went to Mt. Bromo. This identification of social and spiritual hierarchy is, of course, consistent with Indic tradition elsewhere in Southeast Asia. In Bali, for example, royalty (unlike commoners) are supposed to ascend directly to heaven at death. It may very well have been the radically undemocratic overtones of the rite in Tengger that contributed to its demise in modern times.

The historic interest of the *baru* role, however, is that a similar title is identified in Old Javanese literature as "one of the groups of men officiating in popular (Shiwaite) ceremonies" (Pigeaud 1962:IV:105). Although Pigeaud himself does not link the *baru* priests to what were known as *mandala* communities, one is tempted to suggest that in Tengger there may have been such a relationship. The tone of the Tengger priest's old prayers, their lack of reference to non-Indic deities, and their appeals to Siva and Uma (or Kala and Durga) suggest that here in Tengger a cult of Siva and Uma may have been superimposed on a preexisting mountain tradition. The *mandala* image, moreover, appears frequently in the Tengger priest's prayers, and it is easy to speculate

that Old Tengger communities may have resembled the *mandala* villages
described by Pigeaud (ibid.:486):

> a popular cult of Shiwa and Uma. The probability of a substratum
> of ancient Javanese worship of mountain deities and chthonic powers
> is great. . . . Probably the *mandala* people . . . men, women, and
> children, as a rule living in remote districts in the wooded hills of
> the interior of the country, engaged in agriculture. . . . Their being
> mentioned together with *janggans* . . . is suggestive of a close
> connection with the common agriculturalists.

Whether the priests and people of the Mt. Bromo region lived in *mandala*
communities or not, a similar integration of religious specialists into
rural communities may very well have existed in Old Tengger.

This historical speculation can be used to raise some general questions
concerning the changing historical roles of the Tengger and Balinese
resi. Viewed from the perspective of their prayers, both are celebrants
of some popular form of Sivaite worship. They differ not so much in
the contents of their liturgy as in popular conception of their roles. The
Balinese *resi*, quite simply, is low in the priestly hierarchy, whereas the
Tengger priest has come to be identified as the preeminent celebrant of
a whole people's ritual tradition. The status contrast summarizes a larger
world of differences related to the social development of Indic tradition
in popular Java and Bali. The Balinese *resi*'s status is product of developments in larger Bali. His and all other popular priestly roles have been
defined by the push and pull of court hegemony. The courts set the
standards by which ritual is assessed, and noncourtly ritual is defined
as inferior to that of courtly "exemplary centers." The courts have their
own special priests, as well, the *pedanda*, through whom they celebrate
"stupendous cremations, toothfilings, temple dedications, pilgrimages,
and blood sacrifices, mobilizing hundreds and even thousands of people
and great quantities of wealth" (C. Geertz 1980:13). The process, as
Geertz has noted, sustains a political hierarchy and reproduces the standards of its own preeminence. The *pedanda* sits to the side of the king,
and his ritual role in court ceremony sets standards of exemplariness
for all the realm. *Pedanda* not only officiate at the island's most prestigious ceremonies, they also trace their descent back to Javanese Majapahit, spend years studying obscure Sanskrit texts, and, in short, out-
celebrate all other types of ritual celebrants on this little island. This,
of course, is the key to the *resi bujangga*'s lowly ritual status. It is the
brilliance of high-caste *pedanda*, not the contents of the *resi*'s prayers,
which insures that in the presence of *pedanda* the *resi bujangga* is
identified as a netherworld specialist. But "one should not be astonished"

if on occasion the *resi* turns around and performs rites that the more exalted *pedanda* may not think appropriate.

In Java, the destruction of Majapahit insured that, if he survived, the Tengger priest would not suffer the same problems of status as commoner priests in Bali. The collapse of the Hindu-Javanese state replaced the dynamic of the exemplary center state with that of religious antagonism. Central Java, of course, had it exemplary centers, and these may have had limited influence at times on the Eastern Salient, but the Tengger priesthood could look to no courtly counterpart in an Islamizing Java. In the eyes of their neighbors, the Tengger priesthood was not one more rural variation on a ritual theme elaborated all the more gloriously at the court, but a relic of past and heathen ways.

There is no clearer evidence of this tension than the Kasada myth. The center to which this myth directs a people's attention is not an Indic court but a mountain people's spiritual ancestor. This origin myth seeks to shield Tengger from the outside rather than proclaim the common glories of a shared tradition. This is not to suggest, of course, that even in classical Java the people of the Mt. Bromo region did not identify themselves as descendants of the spirit of the mountain. The priesthood spoke, however, of another truth, one consistent with the Sivaite concerns of larger Java. The destruction of Majapahit insured, in effect, that the ancestral myth would be more compelling than that of Sivaite mystery.

Even at that, however, the Kasada myth may retain a trace of other truths. The ancestral guardian of the mountains, Dewa Kusuma, may at one time have been a compromise figure between priestly and popular culture. A *dewa* is, after all, a rather curious title for a mere human ancestor. In Indic tradition elsewhere, *Kusuma Dewa* ("god of the flowers") is Kama, the god of love, desire, and flowers. The name is also used in Bali as a subtitle for the *pamangku* priest's manual (Hooykaas 1973:12). In Tengger tradition, however, the *kusuma* or flower reference may have been drawn from closer to home. In *banten* ceremonies, as we have seen, the *tuwuhan* offering stand is composed of stalks, flowers, and leaves. The *tuwuhan* acts, moreover, as a kind of Siva-stand, since it is Guru-Siva whom the priest invites to it. In the *banten* prayers, in addition, the priest speaks of "receiving the authority of the flowers" in practically the same breath that he asks Siva to enter him and give him spiritual power. It is thus temptingly easy to suggest that at one time Siva, diety of the flower stand, may have also been known as Dewa Kusuma, "god of the flowers."

The destruction of Java's Hindu-Buddhist courts and ecclesiastical communities indirectly insured that the Tengger priest would escape the status dilemmas of his popular Balinese counterpart. His liturgy would become that of a region and people, not merely the stuff of netherworld worship. Cultural hierarchy in both regions was much affected by history and society, and illustrates well the larger differences of development in the Balinese *negara* (C. Geertz 1980) and a Java becoming Islamic.

BIBLIOGRAPHY

Barnes, R. H.
1974 *Kedang: A Study of the Collective Thought of an Eastern In-donesian People*. Oxford: Clarendon Press.

Barth, Fredrik
1967 "Economic Spheres in Darfur." In Raymond Firth (ed.), *Themes in Economic Anthropology*, pp. 149-74. London: Tavistock Publications.
1969 "Introduction." In Fredrik Barth (ed.), *Ethnic Groups and Boundaries*, pp. 9-38. Boston: Little, Brown and Co.

Becker, A. L.
1979 "Text-Building, Epistemology, and Aesthetics in Javanese Shadow Theatre." In A. L. Becker and Aram A. Yengoyan (eds.), *The Imagination of Reality*, pp. 211-43. Norwood (New Jersey): Ablex Publishing.

Belo, Jane
1949 *Bali: Rangda and Barong*. Monographs of the American Ethnological Society XVI. New York: J. J. Augustin.
1953 *Bali: Temple Festival*. Monographs of the American Ethnological Society XXII. New York: J. J. Augustin.

Berger, Peter, and Thomas Luckmann
1966 *The Social Construction of Reality*. Garden City: Doubleday and Co.

Bodemeijer, C. E.
1901 "Rapport naar aanleiding van de Nota betreffende het Tenggergebied van den heer H.M. La Chapelle." In *Tijdschrift voor Indische Taal-, Land-, en Volkenkunde uitgegeven door het (Koninklijk) Bataviaasch Genootschap van Kunsten en Wetenschappen* 43:311-30.

Bohannan, Paul
1967 "The Impact of Money on an African Subsistence Economy." In George Dalton (ed.), *Tribal and Peasant Economies*, pp. 122-35. New York: Natural History Press.

Boon, James A.
1977 *The Anthropological Romance of Bali: 1597-1972*. Cambridge: Cambridge University Press.

Bourdieu, Pierre

1973 "Cultural Reproduction and Social Reproduction." In Richard Brown (ed.), *Knowledge, Education, and Cultural Change*, pp. 71-112. London: Tavistock Publications.

1977 *Outline of a Theory of Practice*. Cambridge: Cambridge University Press.

Brandes, J.L.A.

1913 "Oud-Javaansch Oorkonden." In *Tijdschrift voor Indische Taal-, Land-, en Volkenkunde uitgegeven door het (Koninklijk) Bataviaasch Genootschap van Kunsten en Wetenschappen* 60.

Carey, P.B.R.

1979 "Aspects of Javanese History in the Nineteenth Century." In Harry Aveling (ed.), *The Development of Indonesian Society*, pp. 45-105. Queensland (Australia): University of Queensland Press.

Collier, William L., Gunawan Wiradi, and Soentoro

1973 "Recent Changes in Rice Harvesting Methods." In *Bulletin of Indonesian Economic Studies* 9:2:36-45.

Collier, William L., Soentoro, and Irna Soetomo Basuki

1979 "Pengamatan tentang Pemilikan Tanah serta Land Reform di Jawa."In *Prisma* 8:9:17-31.

Covarrubias, Miguel

1937 *Island of Bali*. New York: Alfred A. Knopf.

Dhofier, Zamakhsyari

1978 "Santri-Abangan dalam Kehidupan Orang Jawa: Teropong dari Pesantren." In *Prisma* 7:5:48-63.

Domis, H. J.

1832 "Aanteekeningen over Het Gebergte Tinger." In *Verhandelingen van het Bataviaasch Genootschap van Kunsten en Wetenschappen* 13:325-56.

Douglas, Mary

1982 "Passive Voice Theories in Religious Sociology." In M. Douglas, *In the Active Voice*, pp. 1-15. London: Routledge and Kegan Paul.

Eickelman, Dale F.

1978 "The Art of Memory: Islamic Education and Its Social Reproduction." In *Comparative Studies in Society and History* 20:485-516.

1979 "The Political Economy of Meaning." In *American Ethnologist* 6:386-93.

Ensink, Jacob

1978 "Siva-Buddhism in Java and Bali." In Heinze Bechert (ed.), *Buddhism in Ceylon and Studies on Religious Syncretism in Buddhist Countries*, pp. 178-98. Göttingen: Vandenhoeck and Ruprecht.

Evans-Pritchard, E. E.
1937 *Witchcraft, Oracles, and Magic among the Azande.* Oxford: Clarendon Press.

von Freijburg, G.G.L.
1901 "Rapport." In *Tijdschrift voor Indische Taal-, Land-, en Volkenkunde uitgegeven door het (Koninklijk) Bataviaasch Genootschap van Kunsten en Wetenschappen* 43:331-48.

Gearing, Frederick O.
1973 "Anthropology and Education." In J. J. Honigmann (ed.), *Handbook of Social and Cultural Anthropology*, pp. 1223-49. Chicago: Rand McNally.

Geertz, Clifford
1960 *The Religion of Java.* New York: Free Press.
1963 *Agricultural Involution.* Berkeley and Los Angeles: University of California Press.
1965 "Modernization in a Muslim Society: The Indonesian Case." In Robert N. Bellah (ed.), *Religion and Progress in Modern Asia*, pp. 93-108. New York: Free Press.
1968 *Islam Observed.* Chicago: University of Chicago Press.
1972 "Religious Change and Social Order in Soeharto's Indonesia." In *Asia* 27:62-84.
1973a "Religion as a Cultural System." In C. Geertz 1973g, pp. 87-125.
1973b "Ethos, World View, and the Analysis of Sacred Symbols." In C. Geertz 1973g, pp. 126-41.
1973c "Ritual and Social Change: A Javanese Example." In C. Geertz 1973g, pp. 142-69.
1973d " 'Internal Conversion' in Contemporary Bali." In C. Geertz 1973g, pp. 170-89.
1973e "Thick Description: Toward an Interpretive Theory of Culture." In C. Geertz 1973g, pp. 3-30.
1973f "The Integrative Revolution: Primordial Sentiments and Civil Politics in the New States." In C. Geertz 1973g, pp. 255-310.
1973g *The Interpretation of Cultures.* New York: Basic Books.
1980 *Negara: The Theatre State in Nineteenth-Century Bali.* Princeton: Princeton University Press.

Geertz, Hildred
1959 "The Balinese Village." In G. W. Skinner (ed.), *Local, Ethnic, and National Loyalties in Village Indonesia: A Symposium*, pp. 24-33. Cultural Report Series No. 8. Program in Southeast Asian Studies. New Haven: Yale University.

1961 *The Javanese Family*. Glencoe: Free Press.

1963 "Indonesian Cultures and Communities." In Ruth. T. McVey (ed.), *Indonesia*, pp. 24-96. New Haven: Human Relations Area Files.

Giddens, Anthony

1979 *Central Problems in Social Theory*. Berkeley and Los Angeles: University of California Press.

Gonda, J.

1952 *Sanskrit in Indonesia*. Nagpur (India): International Academy of Indian Culture.

1975 "The Indian Mantra." In J. Gonda, *Selected Studies*, IV:248-301. Leiden: E. J. Brill.

Goody, Jack

1968 "Introduction." In Jack Goody (ed.), *Literacy in Traditional Societies*, pp. 1-26. Cambridge: Cambridge University Press.

Goody, Jack, and Ian Watt

1968 "The Consequences of Literacy." In Jack Goody (ed.), *Literacy in Traditional Societies*, pp. 27-68. Cambridge: Cambridge University Press.

Goris, R.

1960 "Holidays and Holy Days." In J. L. Swellengrebel (ed.), 1960, pp. 113-29.

Hall, D.G.E.

1981 *A History of South-East Asia* (4th ed.). New York: St. Martin's Press.

Harris, Paul and Paul Heelas

1979 "Cognitive Processes and Collective Representations." *Archives Européennes de Sociologie* 20:2:211-41.

Hefner, Robert W.

1982 "Identity and Cultural Reproduction among Tengger Javanese." Ph.D. dissertation, Department of Anthropology, University of Michigan.

1983a "Ritual and Cultural Reproduction in Non-Islamic Java." *American Ethnologist* 10:4:665-83.

1983b "The Problem of Preference: Ritual and Economic Change in Highland Java." *Man* (n.s.) 18:669-89.

von Heine Geldern, R.

1942 "Conceptions of State and Kingship in Southeast Asia." *Far Eastern Quarterly* 2:15-30.

Holt, Claire

1967 *Art in Indonesia*. Ithaca: Cornell University Press.

Hooykaas, C.

1964 "Weda and Sisya, Rsi and Bhujangga in Present-Day Bali." In

Bijdragen Tot de Taal-, Land-, en Volkenkunde 120:231-44.
1973 *Religion in Bali.* Leiden: E. J. Brill.
1974 *Cosmogony and Creation in Balinese Tradition.* The Hague: Martinus Nijhoff.
1977 *A Balinese Temple Festival.* The Hague: Martinus Nijhoff.

Horton, R.
1971 "African Conversion." *Africa* 61:2:91-112.

Hull, Terence H., and Valerie J. Hull
1976 "The Relation of Economic Class and Fertility." Report Series No. 6. Yogyakarta: Gajah Mada University Population Institute.

Irvine, Judith T.
1979 "Formality and Informality in Communicative Events." *American Anthropologist* 81:4:773-90.

Jasper, J. E.
1926 *Tengger en de Tenggereezen.* Batavia: Druk van G. Kolff.

Jay, Robert T.
1963 *Religion and Politics in Rural Central Java.* Cultural Report Series No. 12. Program in Southeast Asian Studies. New Haven: Yale University.
1969 *Javanese Villagers: Social Relations in Rural Modjokuto.* Cambridge: MIT Press.

Juynbull, H. H.
1921 "Zodiakbekers." In *Encyclopaedie van Nederlandsch-Indie,* pp. 838-40. Leiden: E. J. Brill.

Kartodirdjo, Sartono
1966 *The Peasants Revolt in Banten in 1888: Its Conditions, Course, and Sequel. A Case Study of Social Movements in Indonesia.* The Hague: Martinus Nijhoff.
1972 "Agrarian Radicalism in Java: Its Setting and Development." In Claire Holt (ed.), *Culture and Politics in Indonesia,* pp. 70-125. Ithaca: Cornell University Press.
1973 *Protest Movements in Rural Java: A Study of Agrarian Unrest in the Nineteenth and Twentieth Centuries.* Singapore: Oxford University Press.

Keeler, Ward W.
1982 "Father Puppeteer." Ph.D. dissertation, Committee on Social Thought, University of Chicago.

Koentjaraningrat, R. M.
1960 "The Javanese of South Central Java." In G. P. Murdock (ed.), *Social Structure in Southeast Asia,* pp. 88-115. Chicago: Quadrangle Books.
1961 *Some Social-Anthropological Observations on Gotong Royong*

Practices in Two Villages of Central Java. Modern Indonesia Project. Ithaca: Southeast Asia Program, Cornell University.
1963 "Review of *The Religion of Java.*" *Majalah Ilmu-Ilmu Sastra Indonesia* 1:2:188-91.
1967 "Tjelapar: A Village in South Central Java." In R. M. Koentjaraningrat (ed.), *Villages in Indonesia,* pp. 244-80. Ithaca: Cornell University Press.

Kohlbrugge, J.H.F.
1897 "De Legende van Kyahi Koesomo." In *Tijdschrift voor Indische Taal-, Land, en Volkenkunde uitgegeven door het (Koninklijk) Bataviaasch Genootschap van Kunsten en Wetenschappen* 39:428-29.

Kumar, Ann
1976 *Surapati: Man and Legend.* Leiden: E. J. Brill.

La Chapelle, H. M.
1899 "Nota Betreffende Het Tengger-Gebied." *Tijdschrift voor Indische Taal-, Land-, en Volkenkunde uitgegeven door het (Koninklijk) Bataviaasch Genootschap van Kunsten en Wetenschappen* 41:32-54.

Leach, E. R.
1954 *Political Systems of Highlands Burma.* Boston: Beacon Press.

Leclerq, Jules
1897 *Un Sejour dans l'Ile de Java.* Paris: Librarie Plon.

van Lerwerden, J. D.
1844 "Aanteekeningen Nopens de Zeden en Gebruiken der Bevolking van het Tenggers Gebergte." In *Verhandelingen van het Bataviaasch Genootschap van Kunsten en Wetenschappen* 20:60-93.

Levi-Strauss, Claude
1963 "The Effectiveness of Symbols." In C. Levi-Strauss, *Structural Anthropology,* pp. 186-205. New York: Basic Books.

van Lohuizen-de Leeuw, Johanna Engelberta
1972 "An Indo-Javanese Representation of a *Bhujangga.*" In J. Ensink and P. Gaeffke (eds.), *India Maior,* pp. 157-60. Leiden: E. J. Brill.

Meinsma, J. J.
1879 "Over de Tijdrekening Bij de Tenggereezen." *Bijdragen Tot de Taal-, Land-, en Volkenkunde* 27:131-49.

Nadel, S. F.
1951 *The Foundations of Social Anthropology.* London: Cohen and West.

Nakamura, Mitsuo
1976 "The Crescent Rises over the Banyan Tree." Ph.D. dissertation, Department of Anthropology, Cornell University.

van Niel, Robert
1979 "From Netherlands East Indies to Republic of Indonesia: 1900-

1945." In Harry Aveling (ed.), *The Development of Indonesian Society*, pp. 106-65. Queensland (Australia): University of Queensland Press.

Noorduyn, J.
1978 "Majapahit in the Fifteenth Century." *Bijdragen tot de Taal-, Land-, en Volkenkunde* 134:2-3:207-74.

Ortner, Sherry B.
1978 *Sherpas through Their Rituals.* Cambridge: Cambridge University Press.

van Ossenbruggen, F.D.E.
1977 (1916) "Java's Monco-Pat: Origins of a Primitive Classification System." In P. E. de Josselin de Jong (ed.), *Structural Anthropology in the Netherlands*, pp. 32-59. The Hague: Martinus Nijhoff.

Peper, B.
1970 "Population Growth in Java in the 19th Century: A New Interpretation." *Population Studies* 24:71-84.

Piaget, Jean
1970 *Structuralism.* New York: Harper & Row.

Pigeaud, Th. G. Th.
1960-1963 *Java in the 14th Century* (5 vols.). The Hague: Martinus Nijhoff.
1967 *Literature of Java* (3 vols.). The Hague: Martinus Nijhoff.
1977 (1928) "Javanese Divination and Classification." In P. E. de Josselin de Jong, *Structural Anthropology in the Netherlands*, pp. 61-82. The Hague: Martinus Nijhoff.

Poerwadhie-Atmohihardjo
1957 "Adjisaka Sanes Babad Utawi Sedjarah." *Djaja Baja* 11:20:13-20.

Rabinow, Paul, and William M. Sullivan
1979 *Interpretive Social Science: A Reader.* Berkeley and Los Angeles: University of California Press.

Raffles, Thomas Stamford
1965 (1830) *The History of Java* (2 vols.). Kuala Lumpur: Oxford University Press.

Ramseyer, Urs
1977 *The Art and Culture of Bali.* London: Oxford University Press.

Rassers, W. H.
1959 "Siva and Buddha in the East Indian Archipelago." In W. H. Rassers, *Panji, The Culture Hero*, pp. 63-91. The Hague: Martinus Nijhoff.

Ricklefs, M. C.
1979 "Six Centuries of Islamization in Java." In N. Levtzion (ed.),

Conversion to Islam, pp. 100-128. New York: Holmes and Meier.
1981 *A History of Modern Indonesia*. Bloomington: Indiana University Press.

Ricoeur, Paul
1979 "The Model of the Text: Meaningful Action Considered as a Text." In Rabinow and Sullivan (eds.), 1979, pp. 73-101.

Robson, S. O.
1981 "Java at the Crossroads." In *Bijdragen tot de Taal-, Land-, en Volkenkunde* 137:259-92.

Rouffaer, G. P.
1921 "Tenggereezen." In *Encyclopaedie van Nederlandsch-Indie*, pp. 298-308. Leiden: E. J. Brill.

Ryle, Gilbert
1949 *The Concept of Mind*. New York: Barnes and Noble.

Schneider, David M.
1976 "Notes toward a Theory of Culture." In Keith H. Basso and Henry A. Selby (eds.), *Meaning in Anthropology*, pp. 197-220. Albuquerque: University of New Mexico Press.

Scholte, Joh.
1921 *De Slametan Entas-Entas der Tenggereezen en de Memukur Ceremonie op Bali*. Weltvreden: Albrecht and Co.

Schrieke, B.
1955 *Indonesian Sociological Studies* (2 vols.). The Hague: W. van Hoeve.

Scott, James C.
1976 *The Moral Economy of the Peasant*. New Haven: Yale University Press.

Siegel, James
1969 *The Rope of God*. Berkeley and Los Angeles: University of California Press.

Slametmuljana, Benoit Raden
1976 *A Story of Majapahit*. Singapore: Singapore University Press.

Smith-Hefner, Nancy J.
1983 "Language and Social Identity: Speaking Javanese in Tengger." Ph.D. dissertation, Department of Linguistics, University of Michigan.

Soepanto
1962 "Ceritera Rakyat Tengger." Unpublished manuscript. Yogyakarta: Lembaga Sejarah dan Antropologi.

Sperber, Dan
1975 *Rethinking Symbolism*. Cambridge: Cambridge University Press.

Stoler, Ann
1977 "Rice Harvesting in Kali Loro." *American Ethnologist* 4:678-98.

Stutterheim, W. F.
1956 "Some Remarks on Pre-Hinduistic Burial Customs on Java." In W. F. Stutterheim, *Studies in Indonesian Archaeology*, pp. 63-90. The Hague: Martinus Nijhoff.

Swellengrebel, J. L.
1960 *Bali: Life, Thought, and Ritual*. The Hague: W. van Hoeve.

Tambiah, S. J.
1968 "The Magical Power of Words." *Man* (n.s.) 3:175-208.
1970 *Buddhism and the Spirit Cults in Northeast Thailand*. Cambridge: Cambridge University Press.

Taylor, Charles
1979 "Interpretation and the Sciences of Man." In Rabinow and Sullivan (eds.), 1979, pp. 25-71.

Tindall, B. Allan
1976 "Theory in the Study of Cultural Transmission." *Annual Review of Anthropology* 5:195-208.

Turner, Victor W.
1969 *The Ritual Process*. Chicago: Aldine Publishing.

Weber, Max
1947 *The Theory of Social and Economic Organization*. Talcott Parsons (ed.). New York: Free Press.
1956 *The Sociology of Religion*. Boston: Beacon Press.
1978 *Economy and Society* (2 vols.) Berkeley and Los Angeles: University of California Press.

Wessing, Robert
1978 "The Position of the Baduj in the Larger West Javanese Society." *Man* (n.s.) 12:293-303.

White, B.
1976 "Population, Involution, and Employment in Rural Java." *Development and Change* 13:587-610.

Wibisono, Singgih
1956 "Tengger." *Bahasa dan Budaya* 4:6:1-48.

Wolf, Eric
1967 (1957) "Closed Corporate Peasant Communities in Mesoamerica and Central Java." In Jack M. Potter, M. N. Diaz, and G. M. Foster (eds.), *Peasant Society*, pp. 230-46. Boston: Little, Brown and Co.

INDEX

Abangan Muslim, *see* Javanese Islam

Abu Bakar, Usman, Umar, and Ali, 127, 130. *See also* Ajisaka

Adat, concepts of religion and, 37, 111-12; in Javanese Islam, 104-10; in relation to wedding ceremony, 152; in Tengger Hindu reform, 254-59. *See also Ngaluri; Cara* Tengger

Afterlife, notions of, 158-62, 273

Agama, see Adat

Ajisaka, 16, 127-41, 241, 246, 259

Alphabet, mythic origins of, 128, 132, 137

Antaboga serpent, 126, 130. *See also* Ajisaka

Ater-ater, see Ritual exchange

Badui, 7n

Baju Antakusuma, 192

Banten Gede offering, 120-21, 166-68, 176-77, 183; in relation to earlier Sivaite worship, 275

Barth, Fredrik, 10

Bawon harvest shares, 101

Betek-sinoman ritual workers, 221-22, 228, 231. *See also* Ritual exchange

Boon, James A., 252

Bourdieu, Pierre, 185

Bowo payments, *see* Ritual exchange

Bromo, Mt., 24; in early Javanese religious literature, 24n, 25; in Kasada tale, 56-58; as a *punden* ancestral shrine, 59, 75, 266; prayer to the spirit of, 60-61; as anchor for directional symbolism, 67-69; in belief concerning the afterlife, 160, 273

Buda religion, 4, 6, 39-41, 265; and Hindu reform, 239, 259; collapse of, 241-47. *See also Adat*; Hinduism

Burial: directional symbolism and, 67, 132, 156; and afterlife, 153-62

Cara Tengger, 38-39. *See also Adat; Ngaluri*

Circumcision, 34, 144-45, 147, 256. *See also* Ritual specialists

Coffee cultivation, role of, in influencing immigration and religious change, 31-33, 91, 242-44

Colonialism, entry of, into Tengger region, 33-35

Conversion, religious, 7n, 106; from Buda to Islam, 241-47; theories of, 260-65

Culture: in anthropological theory, 10-12; as socially transmitted, 12-14, 175, 205-208; oral and literate, 12-13, 205-11 *passim*; as socially distributed, 14-15, 268. *See also* Interpretive theory; Social action; Symbolism

Culture System, Netherlands, 32, 91

Danyang village shrines, 5, 58, 108

Death, attitudes toward, 154-55, 158-62

Desa, 76. *See also* Settlement organization

Dewa Kusuma, 54-56, 62, 70-71, 180, 275. *See also* Kasada festival

Dewoto batur, 199, 210. *See also* Spirits

Dewotocengkar, 129, 133. *See also* Ajisaka

Dhofier, Zamakhsyari, 107n

Dukun: Javanese and Tengger notions of, 8, 189-91; *lurah*, 50, 239; midwife, 143-44, 190; circumcision, 144-45; *juru kunci*, 51n, 108-109. *See also Ilmu* esoteric knowledge; Priests, Tengger; *Resi pujangga*

Dulor mpat birth spirits, 143. *See also* Spirits

Dustodurjono, 181

Dutch-Java War, 242

Eastern Salient, 7n, 23, 28-30, 31n

Economy: Tengger agriculture and land use patterns, 91-92; land distribution, 93-95; moral economy, 96, 101, 237; division of labor, 96-102; festive cooperative labor (*sayan*), 98-102, 164, 221;

Library of Congress Cataloging in Publication Data

Hefner, Robert W., 1952-
Hindu Javanese.

Bibliography: p.   Includes index.
1. Hinduism—Indonesia—Java.   2. Tenggerese—
Religion.   I. Title.

BL1163.8.J38H43   1985   306'.6'095982   85-3426
ISBN 0-691-09413-6 (alk. paper)

Printed in the United States
104369LV00003B/271-276/A